"They Know I Know Everything"

My life in the eye of relationship between France and Africa

Robert Bourgi
Interviews with Frédéric Lejeal

"They Know
I Know Everything"

My life in the eye of relationship
between France and Africa

Max Milo

© Max Milo, Paris, 2024

www.maxmilo.com

ISBN : 978-2-31502-250-2

To my parents, who showed me the way.
R.B.

To Cassie, Malou and Max, the only reason.
to Flo, Angelo, Joelma, Katy, Caro, Marie-France, Manu, Dounia and all
the others without whom this book would not be possible.
F.L.

Libreville, Palace by the Sea, Presidency of the Gabonese Republic, January 1988

I only met Roland Dumas once, during the 1988 presidential campaign in France. We met in the anteroom of Omar Bongo's office. Chirac had sent me there to remind him that a campaign is expensive, especially a presidential one. I was waiting to be received, chatting with the aide-de-camp, when François Mitterrand's friend and man of secret missions, future president of the French Constitutional Council, arrived.

"Hello, Bourgi, how are you? I think we've come for the same thing..."

The red light came on. Respectfully, I put him in front of me. He rushed into the office, much to the dismay of the aide-de-camp, who glared at me and told me I'd been wrong. Roland Dumas came out a little heavier than when he went in, then made this comment, with a mocking air:

"Don't worry Bourgi, I've left some for you!"

Once in Omar Bongo's office, I received quite a beating:

"Idiot! Why didn't you come home first?"
"Dad, I couldn't do it, it's still protocol."
"You're an idiot! We had to get home before he did. As a result, he took Jacques' share. Now, what I'm going to give Chirac is cut in half!"
"Forgive me, Dad, but could you please warn Monsieur Chirac?"

He called him to tell him not to worry and that all he had to do was get me back to Libreville within the same week.

9

Foreword

In the autumn of my life, at the end of a career that has seen me serve some exceptional characters and rub shoulders with many insipid ones, I decided to gather my memories, archives and personal notes in this book, *Memoirs* of a Life Spent Wandering the Franco-African Arcane.

Having long welcomed them into the incense-filled atmosphere of my office on Avenue Pierre Ier de Serbie in Paris, journalists and media alike are familiar with my prodigality for confidences and first-hand information. Whether they took place in France, Africa or the Middle East, my missions, just like my role for my political family or with African heads of state, were known to all and commented on with regularity according to current events in Françafrique or French politics.

For the first time, however, I've decided to go a lot further, by summoning up my whole life without exception, from my childhood with my parents and my fascinating father, Mahmoud, to my actions as an influential lobbyist, via my dealings with very high dignitaries or the organization of transports of funds from Africa to France.

"Extorted" during fifty hours of interviews with finesse and intelligence by journalist Frédéric Lejeal, a cutting-edge Africanist and former editor-in-chief of *La Lettre du Continent,* these confessions paint a picture of what I was given to do, hear and see. With a wealth of details, anecdotes and revelations, he recounts scenes which, because of their explosive, even breathtaking aspect, may leave the reader totally stunned. But that's the truth, the only truth that matters.

In spite of these unpublished testimonials and documents, contemptuous critics calling me "sulphurous", "intriguing", "an occult messenger" will no doubt continue to work to discredit me, as they have done for so many years, constantly stumbling over the hard pips of my reality.

To bring their investigations to a screeching halt, all they have to do is replay the debate that *Mediapart* organized on January 28, 2023 between Eva Joly, the judge who investigated the Elf affair, and myself, to understand that Robert Bourgi's name remains the source of every fantasy, of a false image, of a falsified legend fabricated by rumor, ignorance and even slander[1].

In fact, my name does not appear at any time in this resounding affair, any more than it does in the many scandals in Franco-African relations, from Angolagate to BMA (Biens Mal Acquis) to Carrefour du Développement. What were my real missions? Fund transfers, mainly at a time when they were authorized, "services", high-intensity influence, strategic connections, eminently sensitive missions for which official diplomacy was showing its limits. The 2010 release of the young Frenchwoman Clotilde Reiss, imprisoned in Iranian jails, is just one of many examples. For me, it was a source of great pride.

Does this mean I can use these *memoirs* as a screen for criticism of my behavior, my ethics, my associations or my perfectly assumed lifestyle choices? Obviously not. Although I decried the Franco-African system, I don't deny having benefited from it and served it *ad nauseam*, to the point of denouncing its turpitudes, excesses and shortcomings in 2011, in the *JDD*. By providing readers with a sincere and even more lucid look at this entire facet of French diplomacy and political life, this book is simply the logical continuation of that interview.

Robert Bourgi

1. Debate between Eva Joly and Robert Bourgi, "Mediapart's Total Day", Cité Fertile. https://www.youtube.com/watch?v=oXOcFrkBrXk

Chapter 1: In the Shadow of Mahmoud Bourgi

We are all more or less the product of the environment in which we grew up. Your father, Mahmoud Bourgi, is a veritable guardian figure. What role did he play in shaping your personality?

Dad was born in 1893. As his passport indicates, he was blond and blue-eyed. He came from a family of peasants from the village of Ramadié, in southern Lebanon, a few kilometers from what is now the State of Israel.

His father, my paternal grandfather, was a modest camel driver. He traded the produce of the land, which he sold throughout the region, sometimes even as far away as Syria. My father accompanied him on these journeys, which they both made on foot.

Goods from the family orchard—oranges, mandarins...—were transported by camel. A particularly poor and deprived region, southern Lebanon was already predominantly populated by Shiite Muslims.

From the beginning of the 20th century, this context led many Lebanese to emigrate around the world, to Australia, the United States and Latin America, as well as to Europe and Africa.

All Lebanese families were involved in this first great wave of migration. For example, my uncle, my father's elder brother, landed in New York at the end of the 19th century, before settling in Chicago, Detroit and Michigan City, Indiana. Once an American citizen, he met his future wife, an American, with whom he had several children, including William, nicknamed "Bill", and David.

My uncle's name was Mohamed Ali. He changed his name to "Allie" to sound more English. David would later become a pilot and senior officer in the US Air Force, and William an American diplomat. He was stationed in Beirut. He ended his career as a U.S. Secret Service agent in Tripoli and Benghazi, Libya.

For the record, my uncle from Chicago had been a member of the Incorruptibles, the police officers charged with enforcing the laws prohibiting the consumption, sale and trade of alcohol. Hence the ease with which he got his sons into the army and the intelligence service. I first met William in 1981, in San Francisco.

Didn't your uncle suggest that your father join him across the Atlantic?

He wrote to my father in the years 1918-1919, at the end of the war and with the decomposition of the Ottoman Empire, asking him to join him. Let's face it: my father was a simple peasant, a poor wretch.

The year was 1923. He took a boat from Beirut, traveling fourth class, as it were. Taking advantage of a long stopover in Marseille, he met a number of Lebanese living in the city, who convinced him to stay and settle there. Father Bourgi was not in the United States, but in this already cosmopolitan city! He stayed from August 13, 1923 to August 9, 1924.

What was he doing?

He worked as a porter, which is the same as a docker. He was short and stocky, but phenomenally strong. He was an imposing figure. At the port, he carried loads and luggage. He lived on rue Bernard Dubois, a very working-class neighborhood not far from the Gare Saint-Charles.

A year later, he took a boat back to New York, but for reasons I don't know—he himself will never know—the ship stopped in Dakar.

The capital of French West Africa (AOF), where the Lebanese presence is already marked.

The year was 1924. He met up with the local Lebanese community. Although influential, it numbered no more than a hundred.

A self-taught adventurer, my father had learned to read in Koranic school and write Arabic. He landed on his own and found work with a Lebanese man married to a Senegalese woman who had been living in Ouakam for 10 years.

14

Still carrying loads?

Yes, he was employed as a porter. He loaded sacks of foodstuffs, cloth, a heap of goods. He slept on a mattress on the floor of his boss's house. He confided to us that for years he'd had nothing but bread and peanuts to eat, in order to save money.

He then left Ouakam to settle in Dakar, where he opened a fabric trading store. A combination of interpersonal skills and luck enabled him to grow steadily richer. His business grew. He bought from the big French colonial trading posts such as SCOA (Société commerciale de l'Ouest africain) and CFAO (Compagnie française d'Afrique occidentale).

He sold his fabrics to the locals. He was easily trusted. His honesty was his main quality. What's great is that he later hired the Lebanese man who had employed him as a porter when he first arrived in the country.

Where was this store located?

In the Sandaga district. As his business flourished, he quickly came to the attention of the Lebanese community. At the same time, he decided to bring in relatives from Lebanon, cousins and acquaintances from neighboring villages.

At first, they worked for him, then prospered in their own right. Today, the Bourgis represent one of Senegal's wealthiest families. Whenever I visit Dakar, I never fail to meet some of my generation. Like me, they are in their 80s.

With his success, your father started a family.

In Senegal at that time, the Lebanese community was mainly made up of single men who were trying their luck in Africa, in search of a better future. My father was alone for a long time. He returned to Lebanon as soon as he could afford it, this time in second class! He returned to Ramadié, distributing gifts, offerings and money.

It was there that he met Mohamed Assaad Abou Khalil, the mayor of Tyre[2], the country's fourth-largest Shiite-majority city, of which he would remain the emblematic mayor for over a quarter of a century. My father proposed to his eldest daughter, Nazar. She gave him his first child—Ali—the eldest in our family. Ali still lives in Dakar.

---

2. Today Sour or Sûr.

15

Sadly, Nazar died as a result of childbirth. She is buried in the Soumbédioune cemetery in the Senegalese capital. Finding himself a widower with a young child to look after, my father decided to return to Lebanon to entrust him to his in-laws. It was then that he befriended Manar ("lighthouse" in Arabic), the youngest daughter of the same mayor of Tyre.

My mother-to-be was only 18. Sandrine Rousseau didn't yet exist! They were married in 1934 and sailed for Dakar on March 9 of the same year aboard the Giulio Cesare. They arrived in Senegal on June 4.

What happens to the first child?

Ali stayed with his grandparents in Tyre until 1951. I don't know why my father entrusted him to his in-laws.

My mother, on the other hand, bore him thirteen children, including twins, of which I am the survivor. Although he didn't speak or write French, my father, who tended to use sabir, prospered. In the 1940s, he was one of the wealthiest Lebanese in Senegal, a country where he knew most of the dignitaries and political leaders.

What's your position in this imposing family?

After Ali's birth came René, Suzanne, Simone, Lili and Maye, all of whom have since passed away. Albert, my brother and future professor of public law, was born in 1942. Then there was Liliane, who has just celebrated her 80th birthday. My twin brother Hassan and I were born in 1945. He died of dysentery at 18 months. Then came Mohamed Hassan and Rassika, who also disappeared, then Rassek, also a future lawyer[3], Nouad and, finally, a last sister also named Maye. She is a sinologist, with a doctorate in Chinese literature, having defended her thesis in Mandarin at the Sorbonne.

---

3. Defender, among others, of the Senegalese state.

Chapter 2: Sweet Dakar

What kind of family environment did you grow up in?

In the 1930s, my father's innate sense of commerce made him increasingly comfortable financially. He owned several cars, which was not a common sight in Dakar. This affluence enabled him to open other stores. He was well known, appreciated and close to the French colonists, with whom he had established many contacts. This situation prompted him to leave Sandaga and move, with my mother, to rue de Thiès, in the beautiful city center. This street is now called Galandou Diouf[4].

Along with my brothers and sisters, we were all born in this house, with the exception of Maye, who was born in 1953 at the Bouchard clinic in Marseille. I remember that the midwife, assisted by a nurse, came regularly to the house. Her name was Madame Casahous. Her son now runs the eponymous clinic on rue de Thiong in Dakar.

The house still exists. It's a one-storey house with ten bedrooms. We lived happily together. We'd go to the beach, on excursions to Gorée. Albert[5] and I would play soccer with the neighbors. Mostly French and Lebanese. The Senegalese didn't live in the neighborhood, only the adjacent streets. But we shared all our leisure activities with them. We'd meet in the street. We spoke Wolof. From this came many "brothers" in friendship.

---

4. A teacher and journalist, Galandou Diouf (1875-1944) was a French deputy from 1934 to 1940, the second African parliamentarian elected to the Chamber since the beginning of colonization, after Blaise Diagne. He was mayor of the commune of Rufisque from 1919 to 1923.

5. Born in 1942. A constitutionalist close to left-wing circles in Africa, Albert Bourgi taught public law at the University of Reims and directed the Center for International Relations Studies at the same university. He was also a columnist for the weekly *Jeune Afrique*. The author of numerous books, including *Le Printemps de l'Afrique*, co-written with journalist Christian Casteran, Hachette, 1991.

17

What were the family customs like?

We never ate at our parents' table. Served by the household staff, the children ate lunch and dinner on their own. The youngest were naturally looked after by the nannies. The only one who lunched with my parents was René, the eldest. There was also my uncle Abdallah, whom my father had brought over from Lebanon in the 1920s.

Dad maintained a great distance from us, who were always impressed. He had a look that was hard to bear. A look of steel. He didn't trade with us. I don't remember ever being kissed or hugged. He imposed himself with authority. We lived in an Arab-Muslim world.

My mother was more urbane and literate. She had studied at a Christian school in Tyre. She had her school-leaving certificate, which was rare for a Shiite girl in those days. She could therefore read and write French. She was very sophisticated and elegant compared to the rough peasant my father was.

In fact, she contributed a great deal to his rise by dressing him up and socializing him. He was also very elegant. He had his suits made to measure in Marseille, by the couturier Charles Georges. His ties came from Charvet et Sulka in Paris.

Your mother pushes the whole family to study.

We all attended the Notre-Dame institution in the Plateau district, run by the nuns. My sisters continued their education at this school. The boys were enrolled in private French schools before attending the Lycée Van Vollenhoven, better known by its diminutive name "Van Vo"[6].

It was at this time that our first names were Frenchized, as Muslim names were refused. The eldest, René, was called Rouda. I was Riad Jaffar before becoming Robert.

Was it important to your father that you study?

No. We all agree that without our mother we'd all have ended up as shopkeepers. On the other hand, thanks to my father, I was able to learn Arabic, which opened many doors for me later on.

---

6. Today Lycée Lamine Gueye.

"Van Vo" was a benchmark in the French West Indies.

Dakar was the capital of this historic bloc. All the elite of the sub-region sent their children there.

What was your relationship with the French?

There's no point hiding it: they were racist towards Africans. From primary school teachers to high school professors, many of them abused and bullied blacks. In primary school, when I attended the Franco-Senegalese school on the Plateau, avenue Franklin Roosevelt[7], I remember that at the start of each school year, the French, the "little whites" as we called them, were systematically placed at the front of the class, with the Lebanese and Africans at the back. I've never forgotten it.

Did they talk politics at home?

I'd hear about African politics, but mostly I'd see lots of visitors. My father had forged close ties and a personal relationship with MP Galandou Diouf. There was also a close relationship with Lamine Gueye, a member of parliament from the Section française de l'Internationale ouvrière (SFIO), mayor of Dakar and minister in the Fourth Republic.

These political figures regularly visited him at home. I vividly remember Lamine Gueye's Cadillac, donated by the American administration. As soon as he arrived at our house, a huge crowd would gather. It was the 1950s. I was 6 or 7 years old. He had a majestic bearing. We called him "Papa Lamine" and his wife, a West Indian, "Maman Lamine". We were close to his son Ibrahima, known as "Iba", now deceased.

My father also knew the great Senegalese religious leaders. Mourides, Tidjanes, Lebous. He frequented El Hadj Ibrahima Diop, El Hadj Seydou Nourou Tall and El Hadj Omar Ndir.

Paradoxically, you're not raised in a godly environment.

As much as my father prayed his five daily prayers, my mother did not. True, there was no pork or alcohol in the house, but my mother's tastes clearly leaned towards France, with a real desire to assimilate. She would buy books in French and read them to us.

---

7. Today the Diap-Diop Franco-Senegalese school.

19

Aside from visits from notables and your father's connections, how did you perceive Senegalese political life?

We were totally unaware of this. However, we were aware of the dissensions between Lamine Gueye's SFIO and Léopold Sédar Senghor's Bloc Démocratique Sénégalais (BDS). My father was a "Laminist" until Senghor's death in 1968.

His wealth had made him one of the main financial backers of his political party. He helped his electoral campaigns in his capacity as president of the Lebanese community. He asked his compatriots to make often colossal contributions. For each campaign, there were also lanterns, ancient traditions and torch-lit retreats. My father financed them in Dakar, but also in Saint-Louis. When the lanterns were paraded, they regularly passed in front of our store and our home.

Your father traveled a lot for supplies.

Thanks to his prosperity, he regularly travelled to the Lyon region of France, the silk region, England and Germany to source quality products.

And in Lebanon?

He made his last trip there in 1933. Ditto for my mother. He brought his first child, Ali, back to Dakar in 1951. That was the year we met him. My mother adopted him immediately.

Chapter 3: A Loyal Gaullist

What did Mahmoud Bourgi do on the eve of and during the Second World War?

As Lamine Gueye and the religious leaders sided with De Gaulle, my father followed them from day one, without really understanding the context. It was pure followership in the great Senegalese tradition. The fact that leading figures such as El Hadj Nourou Tall and El Hadj Ibrahima Diop had sided with De Gaulle convinced him.

Although he wasn't Martin Heidegger, he had a feel for situations. He was instinctive, which got him into trouble. After the failed Free French landing attempt in Dakar, from September 23 to 25, 1940[8], he was arrested on the orders of the Provichist High Commissioner for AOF and AEF, Pierre François Boisson[9], and taken to the Thiès reform camp. He spent a month there before being released.

This was not activism against the Petain administration.

My father had no political thoughts or intentions. He followed in Lamine Gueye's footsteps out of affection for and devotion to de Gaulle. Apart from the episode at the Thiès camp, he was left to get on with his business.

---

8. Known as the "Battle of Dakar" or "Operation Menace", this landing pitted the pro-Gaullist Free French Forces (FFL), aided by British and Australian forces, against forces loyal to the Vichy regimes in an attempt to rally Senegal to Free France. The former lost out. Some 200 soldiers were killed, more than 500 wounded and the capital was badly damaged.

9. A senior French civil servant, High Commissioner for French Africa and colonial administrator appointed Governor of French West Africa (AOF) in August 1940, Pierre François Boisson (1894-1948) was condemned by the High Court of Justice, in the aftermath of the Second World War, for the crime of national indignity for his support of the Vichy regime.

However, he crossed paths with Claude Hettier de Boislambert, a key figure in the Resistance and a close collaborator of De Gaulle in London. In August 1940, along with René Pleven and Colonel Philippe Leclerc, he was tasked with rallying the African colonies to the Free French movement[10].

Rallying began with Cameroon. Squadron leader Claude Hettier de Boislambert took command of Douala and then Pointe-Noire. However, his landing in Dakar on September 23, 1940 was unsuccessful. He was arrested and interrogated by the Vichy authorities.

My father met him then, but he knew nothing of the historical dimension of the character. When Free France took hold in Africa from 1943-1944, my father began to rub shoulders with many French supporters of Charles de Gaulle. Civilians, soldiers, government officials.

Did he meet de Gaulle when he came to Dakar on January 25, 1944[11]?
We introduced her to him. His Gaullist streak was above all dictated by affect, but it would have many implications, notably in the mobilization of funds to support the future Rassemblement du peuple français (RPF)[12].

Co-founder of the RPF in April 1947 and member of the National Council, Jacques Foccart is a leading figure in the Gaullist party. Delegate for the French overseas departments and territories, he was appointed advisor to the Union française in 1951. In this capacity, he was responsible for developing and consolidating networks of support for General de Gaulle. He relies on your father.
My father was one of the very first members of the Senegalese section of the RPF and one of its first major contributors. Financing political parties was far from prohibited. His ability to mobilize the Lebanese Shiite community throughout the AOF was real. In Paris, they knew it. He

---

10. Resistance fighter and companion of the Liberation, Claude Hettier de Boislambert (1906-1986) was squadron leader during the "Battle of Dakar". A member of the Consultative Assembly in 1944, he headed the Extra-Metropolitan Resistance group, and was a member of the Colonies, Finance and Information commissions, as well as rapporteur for the Colonies budget. He was a Member of Parliament from 1951 to 1955.
11. Touring the French West Indies, General de Gaulle delivers the first major speech of his tour in the Senegalese capital, at the Lycée Von Volhenhoven.
12. Based at 5, rue de Solférino, Paris, the Rassemblement du peuple français (RPF) was founded on April 14, 1947. It folded in 1955.

first met Jacques Foccart on his very first trip to Africa, in 1949. He stayed at the Hôtel du Globe on rue Vincent.

The meeting had been organized by the RPF's heralds in the country, both in political and business circles. Despite their twenty-year age gap, the two men hit it off immediately. Thereafter, whenever Jacques Foccart visited Dakar on his African tours, he would meet and chat at length with Mahmoud Bourgi. He would come to lunch at the house. Sometimes, he would even be dressed in a saroual, which was quite unlikely.

In his *memoirs*[13], Jacques Foccart describes Mahmoud Bourgi as *"extremely kind, very loyal, informed and influential"*. Do you find him in this description?

Absolutely, the reason is simple: he was powerful within the unstructured Lebanese community. He knew everything and was informed of all rumors and plans.

As I've already mentioned, he had brought over many Lebanese and dignitaries from southern Lebanon who were, in a way, indebted to him. Members of his family, but also of the Abou Khalil family from which my mother descended. This community grew.

From 1947 onwards, his contacts in the colonial administration convinced him to create an organization capable of representing the interests of these Lebanese nationals. This he did with the Comité libano-syrien du Sénégal, of which he was the first president. He remained at its head until 1960. This structure quickly became indispensable.

Jacques Foccart introduced him to other personalities, including Georges Pompidou, in the early 1950s. By virtue of his status, my father literally obliged the Lebanese to pay money into the RPF. Not just those from the Senegalese section, but from all the sections in Africa. The Gaullist party earned part of its subsidies in this way. This money was repatriated to Dakar and sent back to Paris, where it contributed to the life of the party.

---

13. *Foccart parle. Entretiens avec Philippe Gaillard*, Fayard/Jeune Afrique, Paris, February 1995, pp. 112 and 113.

Georges Pompidou, then director of the Rothschild bank.

It was rare, not to say impossible, that my father, as chairman of the Lebanese-Syrian committee, didn't meet or talk with the high-profile personalities visiting Senegal. In the 1950s, Pompidou was head of the Rothschild bank. He was visiting the country after a detour in Mauritania. The ties would endure. In his *Journal de l'Élysée* covering the Pompidolian period[14], Jacques Foccart regularly mentions Bourgi's name. He evokes "mon brave Bourgi"[15] when talking about his visits to Senegal, but also "mon vieil ami Bourgi"[16] when reporting on his tours to Georges Pompidou, now President. He says: "I saw 'Bourgi', without a first name, without a title, without anything". He said "Bourgi", and that was enough. In the same *Memoirs*, my father confided to Foccart that, without France, Léopold Sédar Senghor would not have stayed in place for 24 hours in the face of the social and student unrest the country was experiencing in the early 1970s[17].

This financing already benefited from the CFA franc.

The colonial currency was strong, and the volume of money transferred was substantial. The many branches of the RPF in Africa enabled funds to be mobilized throughout the Empire. Jacques Foccart orchestrated the whole system, and General de Gaulle was well aware of this. In fact, part of Foccart's influence was due to this work and these actions.

Still referring to your father, Jacques Foccart describes him as one of Africa's greatest connoisseurs, and one of the best-informed personalities in the French West Indies. Thanks to him, he explains, *"I knew not only what was going on in Senegal, but also in Sudan and Upper Volta"*[18].

Sensitive information was passed on to him by religious leaders like El Hadj Nourou Tall and key civil figures in the Empire. He took part in all events. He supported them financially, while maintaining exemplary

---

14. Jacques Foccart, *Journal de l'Élysée: la fin du Gaullisme,* tome V, 1973-1974, Fayard/Jeune Afrique, Paris, 2001.
15. *Ibid,* p. 533.
16. *Ibid.* p. 397.
17. *Ibid,* p. 401.
18. *Op. cit.* p. 113.

loyalty. As proof of this, he always distanced himself from Léopold Sédar Senghor, who would make him pay for it once he was president.

Jacques Foccart uses the verb *"tramer"* deliberately. Does this mean that your father was up to no good in Senegal or, more broadly, in French-speaking Africa?

He wasn't an "Honorable Correspondent", but he trusted him with everything. And my father was a formidably well-informed man.

However, he was not an intelligence agent.

No, that didn't stop all the officials from the Service de documentation extérieure et de contre-espionnage (SDECE)[19] from meeting him, starting with Maurice Robert, then a captain stationed in Dakar[20]. He, too, was familiar with our company.

Loyalty was second nature to my father. I've kept that quality. So, for example, why am I so close to Michel Aurillac?[21] Because my father was very close to his father, Jean Aurillac, an outstanding French overseas administrator in Senegal in the 1940s and early 1950s[22].

Beyond his loyalty to de Gaulle, did he know why he supported the RPF?

Of course, the ultimate goal was to return De Gaulle to power.

---

19. France's foreign intelligence service, created in 1945 and replaced on April 2, 1982 by the Direction Générale de la Sécurité Extérieure (DGSE).
20. A member of SDECE and responsible for Africa, Maurice Robert (1919-2005) was post commander in Mauritania in 1947, then in Senegal from 1955 to 1959. A close associate of Jacques Foccart, he was also ambassador to Gabon (1979-1981) and head of the African branch of the Elf group (later TotalEnergies).
21. Énarque, State Councillor, former Prefect, Member of Parliament and Vice-President of the Indre General Council, Michel Aurillac (1928-2017) was Minister for Cooperation from March 16, 1986 to April 2, 1988.
22. A graduate of the École coloniale, Jean Aurillac (1903-1967) began his career in 1928 as administrator of civil services in Indochina. He was then chief of staff to Admiral Decoux (1942-1945), the last Governor General of Indochina, and then Director of the Interior for the General Government of the French West Indies. (1948-1949). He returned to Indochina as chief of staff to General de Lattre de Tassigny, then served successively as High Commissioner (1950-1952), Governor of Overseas France (1953), Head of the Political Affairs Department of the Ministry of Foreign Affairs, in charge of relations with the Associated States (1955-1958), Consul General of France in Singapore (May 1958) and Minister of France in Albania (1961-1963).

25

Why the rift with Senghor?

Léopold Sédar Senghor was especially popular in Thiès and the bush. He tried to approach my father as soon as Lamine Gueye was defeated at the deputation[23] via an emissary: Joseph Mbaye. But my father renewed his loyalty to Gueye. He didn't betray him. Senghor did not win his support. Even colonial officials, including Senegalese governor Don Jean Colombani[24], failed to persuade him to help this rising star.

I remember that when Lamine Gueye died in June 1968, my father paid his respects at his home on Avenue de la République, before Senghor, who was still President of the Republic. My father was devastated.

What were the consequences of this mistrust?

Senghor *blacklisted* Papa from all presidential protocol. The doors closed. He was no longer invited anywhere. He complained to Claude Hettier de Boislambert, High Representative of the French Republic in Senegal, who resolved the dispute. My father and Senghor never met. Fortunately, from Bernard Cornut-Gentille to Pierre Messmer[25], Mahmoud Bourgi knew all the senior representatives of the colonial administration.

For the record, when Jacques Chirac visited the Congo on October 8, 1980, to attend the centenary of the founding of Brazzaville, he introduced me to Georges Pompidou's former Prime Minister. We were staying at the Olympic Hotel run by Robert Felicciaggi, a member of the Corsican Assembly who was murdered in 2006 in the parking lot of Ajaccio airport. I'd like to take this opportunity to pay tribute to this lifelong Gaullist and absolute loyalist of Jacques Chirac and Charles Pasqua.

---

23. A Senegalese politician, Amadou Lamine Gueye (1891-1968) was Under-Secretary of State at the Léon Blum Council Presidency from 1946 to 1947, and leader of the Senegalese Socialist Action Party. A French deputy and then senator from 1945 to 1959, he was also the emblematic mayor of Dakar from 1945 to 1961 and the first president of the Senegalese National Assembly from 1960 to 1968.
24. Diplomat Don Jean Colombani (1903-1977) was a colonial administrator, commander of the Dakar and Cape Verde circles, then Governor of Senegal from 1955. A close associate of Jacques Foccart, he became governor of Niger in 1958, then France's first ambassador to the country after its independence in 1960.
25. A member of the FFL, Pierre Messmer (1916-2007) was a colonial administrator. General de Gaulle's Minister of the Armed Forces from 1960 to 1969, he was appointed Minister of State for Overseas Departments and Territories in 1971, before becoming Prime Minister from 1971 to 1974. A member of the Académie française, he is the author of *Les Blancs s'en vont. Récits de décolonisation*, Albin Michel, 1998.

26

At the Olympic Hotel, where the French from Brazzaville had met up with Chirac and his delegation, I took the liberty of apostrophizing Pierre Messmer, asking him if the name Bourgi reminded him of the time when he was High Commissioner General in Dakar. He immediately made the connection with my father, telling Chirac:

"You know Jacques, Mr. Bourgi was a considerable figure in Senegal, a committed patriot."

In front of an astonished Jacques Chirac, I evoked Messmer's former great collaborators in Dakar: the Risterucci and other Jean Sicurani[26]. It was an emotional moment.

So many times, when I was 12 or 13, these personalities came to the house. Jacques Chirac would often talk to me about this discussion, which, in my opinion, gave him a better grasp of the importance and permanence of Franco-African networks. This meeting sealed a strong relationship between us, even if, later on, figures such as the hilarious Jacques Godfrain would challenge this closeness[27].

In the 1950s, François Mitterrand fought de Gaulle for influence in French-speaking Africa. He succeeded in swaying Félix Houphouët-Boigny within the Union démocratique et socialiste de la Résistance (UDSR), a center-left formation co-directed with René Pleven[28]. Leader of the African Farmers' Union (SAA) and of the Ivorian branch of the Rassemblement démocratique africain (RDA), "Houphouët" was considered a pro-communist. Why didn't your father's socialist affinities via Lamine Gueye and the SFIO lead him to join forces with Mitterrand, Minister for Overseas France from 1951?

Because de Gaulle was a true Oriental. He quickly became a cult figure in our family. We were into the tales and legends of the Orient. He followed de Gaulle through his speeches. Admittedly, he was related

---

26. A soldier, diplomat and senior civil servant, Jean Sicurani (1915-1977) was a colonial adminis-trator, notably in French West Africa.
27. Born in 1943, a Gaullist and member of the Service d'Action Civique (SAC), Jacques Godfrain was Minister for Cooperation from 1995 to 1997. He was a Member of Parliament from 1997 to 2007 and Mayor of Millau from 1995 to 2008.
28. Founded in June 1945, the UDSR was led by personalities such as Jacques Soustelle, François Mitterrand, René Pléven, Eugène Claudius-Petit and Jacques Kosciusko-Morizet. Classified as center-left, it disappeared in June 1964. Jacques Foccart was briefly one of its members, before taking part in the creation of the RPF.

to Lamine Gueye, but the latter, though a SFIO member, admired the General. This loyalty earned my father French nationality in 1947. With my brother Albert, we accompanied him on many meetings, as we often had to translate his sabir.

Jacques Foccart did business in the West Indies via his company—Safiex—founded with Henri Tournet and Georges Flicourt, a former member of the Bureau central de renseignements et d'action (BCRA). Was he in contact with your father in this respect?

Yes, they quickly got into the import-export business, trading goods and commodities. Whenever my father came to France, he would meet Jacques Foccart at the company's headquarters at 3 rue Scribe, in Paris, opposite the Grand Hôtel where he stayed[29].

During all this time, your mother refused to return to Lebanon. What was the reason?

His father came to Dakar in 1954. For the record, he wore a tarbouch. However, my mother always complained that he had pulled her out of school and married a much older man. She suffered greatly from this. She followed our schooling assiduously.

Then came the tragedy of his untimely death.

She died of a heart attack on July 29, 1960. Multiple pregnancies weakened her heart. She is buried next to her older sister, Nazar, in the Soumbédioune cemetery in Dakar, where two of her children, Maye and my twin brother Hassan, are also buried.

---

29. Today Intercontinental Opéra.

Chapter 4: Corsican Loves

How did your father feel about Senegal's independence?

To be honest, he wasn't in favor. Senghor was in ambush. He wanted France to hold on at all costs.

As a child and teenager, who did you feel closest to?

Definitely Albert. We were very close until the late 1990s. Our quarrel was sparked by François-Xavier Verschave's book[30], *Noir silence. Qui arrêtera la Françafrique?*[31] which particularly scratched me in certain passages, making me out to be a schemer, a toxic character. I blamed my brother for concealing from me his collaboration with this author. I blamed him terribly. This led to a twenty-year break with my much-loved and admired brother. I suffered a great deal. Twenty years is a long time.

Did you already have an interest in law?

No. In high school, I followed the normal curriculum and I'll put you at ease on one point: I was a passable student. I was only good in Latin, history-geography and French. Once I'd passed my baccalaureate, I enrolled, like many of my fellow students, at the Faculty of Law in Dakar.

Did your father remarry after your mother's death?

He remarried seven years later, in July 1967. A marriage we all rejected out of love for our mother. His new wife was a distant cousin living in Dakar. She gave him seven children, whom I never saw. He died in 1979

---

30. Founder of the Survie association, François-Xavier Verschave (1945-2005) was one of the leading critics of Françafrique. He has published several works on the subject, including *La Françafrique, Le plus long scandale de la République*, Stock, 1998.
31. *Noir silence. Qui arrêtera la Françafrique*, Les Arènes, Paris, May 2000.

and is buried in the Yoff cemetery. He had stopped his business in 1965. My mother's death had affected him greatly. Jacques Foccart made him an Officer of the National Order of Merit.

He was also a Freemason.

Yes, even if he didn't know much about it. He felt the need to be like his African friends. He was in the Grand Orient at a very high rank.

Later, you'll borrow this posture from him: loyalty to men while remaining informal.

That will be my guiding principle. Jacques Foccart gave me my foot in the door. Admittedly, I joined the Union pour la nouvelle République (UNR)[32] very early on, then the Rassemblement pour la République (RPR), but I was always careful to approach people, starting of course with Foccart. I always visited him. I regularly went to say hello to him on the rue de l'Élysée, at the Safiex or in his apartments at 95 rue de Prony when Valéry Giscard d'Estaing dismissed him as Secretary General for African and Malagasy Affairs[33].

He was a great help to me and gave me many contacts for my thesis. Thanks to his contributions, I was able to meet Michel Debré and De Gaulle's aides-de-camp, including colonels Gaston de Bonneval[34] and Jean Martin d'Escrienne[35].

What profession were you destined for?

I spent two years in Dakar, and the rest at the Faculty of Nice, until I obtained my Diplôme d'Etudes Supérieures (DES) in Political Science. I had the idea of continuing my studies with a state thesis, but I had to earn a living. I had already met my wife, Catherine. She was expecting our first child, Olivier. I wanted to continue my studies while working in a cooperative.

---

32. Gaullist party founded in October 1958. It succeeded the RPF and disappeared in 1967.

33. From 1960 to 1974, Jacques Foccart orchestrated France's African policy from the Élysée Palace, as Secretary General for African and Malagasy Affairs. Valéry Giscard d'Estaing put an end to his functions as soon as he came to power.

34. A former student at Saint-Cyr-Coëtquidan, Gaston de Bonneval (1911-1998) was aide-de-camp and one of General de Gaulle's closest collaborators from 1945 to 1964.

35. An officer in the 1st Free French Division, Jean Martin d'Escrienne (1922-2014) was aide-de-camp to General de Gaulle from 1966 to 1970.

Why Nice?

With the events of May 1968 in France, the Dakar faculty was blocked. I was part of a group of students sent to Nice to complete their studies. I already knew France, as every summer we went to Marseille, where my father had owned an apartment since 1949.

Why Marseille? Firstly, because he had lived there in the 1920s. Secondly, because he used to associate with Gaston Deferre's father, who was a leading Dakar lawyer in the 1930s, and whom he had approached several times in the course of his business dealings. He often spoke to us of this man and of a certain Jacques Mouradian, whom he met regularly on rue Edmond Rostand in Marseille. Mouradian was Jacques Foccart's correspondent and SDECE's man in the city. He was later appointed High Commissioner to the New Hebrides and then Ambassador to Madagascar.

When did you meet your wife and under what circumstances?

At the Faculty of Law in Nice, in 1969. Catherine was in her first year, I was in my fourth. She was Corsican and a brilliant student at the Lycée Laetitia Bonaparte in Ajaccio. A friend of mine invited me to a party where she was.

Hence two other loves: for her and for the Emperor.

He already fascinated me. What's more, my future wife's family apartment happened to be across the street from her birthplace, more precisely in front of the bedroom. It took me a while to get to know my future in-laws. And with good reason: I was in Corsican territory! Catherine kept repeating:

> "You can still come, but you won't be received and you won't be seen".

His father was a math teacher and his uncle, Paul Vittori, an early Gaullist Resistance fighter. He even has his own plaque in Ajaccio. It was unveiled in September 1993 by Philippe Mestre, Edouard Balladur's Minister for Veterans and Victims of War, during François Mitterrand's visit to mark the 50th anniversary of the liberation of Corsica. Paul Vittori was a member of SDECE's Service Action (SA).

31

In Nice, you can see that Dakar is not so far away.

My father didn't help me anymore. I had cut all ties. When I arrived in the city, I was housed in room 3305D of the Jean Médecin housing estate in La Lanterne.

I was tired of being poor. I only earned 300 francs a month. In other words, nothing. So much so that, every evening, a blackfoot woman who worked at the Resto U, and with whom I'd befriended, would bring me up some bread, jam and butter. I'll never forget her.

I then decided to contact Michel Alliot, Edgar Faure's chief of staff and Minister of Education, who taught at the Dakar Law School from 1957. He owned a villa in Ngor. I knew him because he was also in business with my father. They both traded tomatoes with the utmost discretion.

After receiving my letter, he immediately made an appointment for me with the rector of the faculty, Robert Davril. His secretary, Mademoiselle de Chicourt, welcomed me on a red carpet. He gave me what I wanted: a position as a pawn in the lycée hôtelier, 100 meters from the university.

The principal, a certain Mr. Armisen, was waiting for me. I opted for the position of boarding master. My salary suddenly shot up to 1,300 francs. It's such a small world. I learned that the young lady from Chicourt was from Dakar. I knew her family from the colonial administration. I was friends with one of her nieces.

When do you meet your in-laws?

Seven months after meeting Catherine, on April 1, 1970. She had received the green light from her father. I celebrated my 25th birthday with my in-laws. Why did I wait so long? Because my future father-in-law had made inquiries about me, even going so far as to ask the French ambassador in Dakar for information about my family. Once reassured, he welcomed me with open arms. Paul Vittori, the man behind the investigation, became "Tonton Paulo" to me.

Marriage followed.

December 7, 1972 at the 13th arrondissement town hall. Paul Vittori, a member of Amicale Action, was my wife's best man. It was all the more impressive given that he had invited his friend, the great resistance fighter Hubert Germain, then deputy of the 13th arrondissement.

For my part, I brought along a number of VIPs, including Jacques Foccart, who attended the after-ceremony drinks reception. My best man was my childhood friend Patrick Danon. We went to school together at Van Vo. His father was a lawyer in Dakar.

Once you've completed your studies in Nice, you'll embark on a state thesis.

As soon as I had obtained my DES, I went up to Paris to begin it. The subject was thoroughly discussed with Foccart: "Le général de Gaulle et l'Afrique noire 1940-1969" ("General de Gaulle and Black Africa 1940-1969"). At the same time, I had to support myself and my family.

After my experience as a pawn, I worked at Lira Films, the company of film producer Raymond Danon, Patrick's uncle, but it wasn't enough. My wife had given birth to our first child in August 1973. At the same time, she graduated from the Certificat d'aptitude à la profession d'avocat (Capa) in Paris. The idea of touring Africa through a teaching partnership was taking shape.

Why didn't you become a lawyer like your wife?

I wanted to go all the way, as far as possible.

A thesis on de Gaulle and Africa is a commonplace. Why this subject? As a tribute to your father or out of genuine interest?

De Gaulle remained engraved in my mind, in my imagination. There was an adoration for him at home, where his portraits were everywhere. This subject combined both my African roots and the life of the man I admired most. I wanted to show how Africa had historically shaped de Gaulle, and the continent's considerable weight in his politics.

Taking advantage of my desire to work on the continent, Jacques Foccart pushed me. He recommended me to the head of the Political Science department at the Sorbonne, the Resistance fighter, hard-line Gaullist and member of the Special Air Service (SAS), Pierre Dabezies, who was also a Free French Cadet[36]. I met him at his home on rue de la

---

36. Born in Casablanca, Pierre Dabezies (1925-2022) belonged to the Free French Forces. A native of Saint-Cyrien, he pursued his military career in a number of theaters and as aide-de-camp to Pierre Messmer, Minister of the Armed Forces, before embarking on an academic career. With a doctorate in public law and political science, and an agrégation in law, he taught throughout his career at Sorbonne University, as well as at IEP and ENA.

Cerisaie. He immediately agreed to supervise my work, even though he didn't know I was going abroad.

How do you end up in Benin?

Through my brother Albert, another doctoral student in the family. In Paris, he introduced me to Nathanael Germain Mensah, head of the Department of Legal and Economic Sciences at Cotonou's Faculty of Law. He was looking for a teacher of public law. I met him near the Ministry of Cooperation, rue Monsieur[37]. I dedicated my thesis to him. He died in 1979, before I could defend it. This period in Benin was a turning point in my life. You could say that this mission gave birth to my African identity.

What happens next?

Nathanaël Germain Mensah presented my file and my diplomas to a certain Mr Haïkine, in charge of recruiting cooperant staff at Rue Monsieur. The deal was done. He came back to me and said he'd be expecting me in Cotonou in a month.

Haïkine confirmed the news to me by phone, asking what channel I had used to get Mensah to insist on recruiting me. It has to be said that he wasn't exactly thrilled, as my application had forced him to reject a candidate, a Frenchwoman with a double-particle name.

As the name Haïkine was ringing in my ears, I asked him if there was a link with a Yvan Haïkine, a person I knew. He was, no more and no less, her son, a former student at Van Vo. His father was at the cooperation mission in Dakar at the time. My life has been a succession of timely encounters.

Why didn't you apply for a position in France?

I absolutely had to go to Africa, it was my calling. But I didn't know any other country than Senegal.

---

37. Located at 20, rue Monsieur, Paris, the Hôtel de Montesquiou, built by architect Alexandre-Théodore Brongniart, was the historic headquarters of the French Secretariat of State for Relations with the States of the European Community, then the Ministry of Overseas France and the Ministry of Cooperation. Put up for sale by the French government in 2009, it was bought by the People's Republic of China, which set up its embassy in France.

Chapter 5: Jacques Foccart, the Mentor

In 1973, you found yourself working in Cotonou for the French government.

In November to be precise. I was living in a villa in the chic Haie vive district. I was an assistant lecturer at the Faculty of Law. Cathy had just graduated. She was working at Boulogne town hall, thanks to Georges Gorse and Paul Graziani. Like me, she had never been to Africa, apart from Dakar, where she spent two summers in a row in the early 1970s.

I set out as a precursor with the feeling of immediate integration. I bought a Diane 6. As Catherine was to join me, she had to register with the Cotonou bar, which was not easy for a Frenchwoman. Nathanael Germain Mensah suggested I talk to the Minister of Justice and Keeper of the Seals, Barthélémy Ohouens, a military officer, who in turn referred me to the Ministry's Director of Civil and Penal Affairs, Béatrice Kérékou.

The latter was none other than the wife of the Head of State. When we saw each other, we looked at each other for a long time before recognizing each other. She had been a student at the Faculty of Law in Dakar! We had been students the same year.

Your first meeting with Mathieu Kérékou?

In power since 1972, her husband was quickly introduced to me. I was the little teacher-co-operator propelled into the presidency, at the Marina Palace. In those days, when you uttered the name Mathieu Kérékou, many people were stunned. And it didn't get any better with the attempted coup d'état in January 1977. We were in the midst of a Marxist revolution. I met him at a university reopening. For her part, Béatrice Kérékou had found my wife an internship with Jean-Florentin Féliho, one of the country's most prominent lawyers.

35

I spent years of absolute happiness in the former Dahomey. At the end of a speech to mark the start of the university year, the dean of the faculty introduced me to "Comrade President". I kept in touch with him afterwards, even after he left office[38].

How do you reconcile your research work in France with your teaching mission in Africa?

I regularly went back and forth between France and the continent. In Paris, I would visit the Gaullist archives at 5 rue de Solférino, the Documentation française and the Chancellery of the Order of the Liberation.

As I've already mentioned, Jacques Foccart facilitated many of my contacts. Claude Hettier de Boislambert, Grand Chancelier, gave me many details. At Documentation française, Foccart introduced me to Professor Robert Cornevin, who opened even more doors for me.

Pierre Dabezies was also extraordinary with me. I met dozens of personalities. I mentioned Michel Debré, but there were many others, including Georges Gorse, Jean-Marcel Jeanneney, Maurice Couve de Murville and Jean Foyer.

To what extent does Jacques Foccart contribute to your thesis? Does he provide you with any revelations or personal insights on certain points?

He had his own opinion on the subject and shared with me his analysis and reading of events. I was in constant contact with him. He would send his letters, not to my personal address, but to the Mission d'Aide et de Coopération headed by André Guéna, the brother of Minister Yves Guéna, one of his close collaborators[39].

On January 16, 1977, the attempted coup d'état by Robert "Bob" Denard, better known as Opération Crevette, plunges you into a whole new context.

---

38. Born in 1933, Mathieu Kérékou died on October 14, 2015.
39. Politician, Resistance fighter, Gaullist and writer, Yves Guéna (1922-2016) was a minister under President Pompidou, President of the Constitutional Council and Mayor of Périgueux from 1971 to 1997.

You could say that! After three wonderful years, we celebrated the end-of-year festivities of 1976 in Corsica, before I returned to Benin alone at the beginning of January. My wife was due to join me on the 16th of the same month. Her UTA flight was diverted to Abidjan. As for me, I had a front-row seat. We were staying not far from the beach where the mercenaries landed in the early hours of the morning. I could hear "Aim well and walk!" From my balcony, I saw a column of white soldiers marching up the avenue. There was shooting everywhere. I took refuge in my bathtub. I'd never seen mercenaries before. I didn't know what they were.

The radio announced that they had been repulsed, but that didn't stop me from being taken away manu militari when, outside, I tried to go to the home of my friend Guy Dupeyron, the director of SITEC, another local resident who died from a fall from his horse. Considered a mercenary, I was taken to Camp Guézo with other Yovos[40]. Vincent Guézodjé, the Minister of National Education, another military man, visited us. He was amazed to see me. We'd been placed in the middle of the courtyard in full sunlight. He had me released. Two soldiers took me home in a jeep. That was enough to give me a good scare. I later related this story to Mathieu Kérékou. The bathtub joke would come up at each of our subsequent meetings.

As a connoisseur of Gaullist policy in Africa and the role of Jacques Foccart, did the idea that he might have been behind the coup attempt ever occur to you?

Of course you can.

Have you spoken to him about it?

Well afterwards. He confirmed that Bob Denard never did anything without being informed. He was aware of the affair alongside Félix Houphouët-Boigny and Omar Bongo, President of Gabon, where there was a very large Beninese community. The operation was a total fiasco, with the mercenaries withdrawing.

Why the shadow of Foccart behind this attempt at destabilization when he was no longer attached to the presidency?

---

40. "White" in *Fon.*

37

Don't try to understand. With Jacques Foccart, you had to know when to stop asking questions as soon as you felt embarrassed or uncomfortable by your excessive curiosity.

He did, however, vaguely confide in me that he had been "involved" in the operation. In addition to the presidents of Gabon and Côte d'Ivoire, he mentioned the role of King Hassan II. The revolutionary power of Benin bothered all these dignitaries. The mercenaries, some sixty in all, had stayed in the Cherifian kingdom before launching their operation.

You say that in Benin, you live a truly African life. What do you mean by that?

Surprisingly, I hadn't traveled anywhere else on the continent. I'd stayed in Senegal. In Benin, I discovered the authenticity of African nature and culture. So much so, in fact, that Senghor's Senegal finally seemed to me too Frenchified.

I was observing the Beninese revolution, which interested me. I was literally adopted by the Beninese. I became interested in their history and rituals, starting with voodoo.

What do you do in your spare time?

I played tennis at the Yacht Club and, occasionally, at the French Embassy with Ambassador Michel Van Grevenynghe or his First Counsellor, Georges Rochiccioli, a true friend with his wife Annie. I looked after my son. Free time was scarce. I was preparing my thesis. I worked every morning from 5 to 8. We'd take Olivier to school, and I'd drop Cathy off at her practice. I'd join my classes, then come home to work again.

Do you frequent Benin's elite?

By my functions, necessarily. But not a single Beninese frequented the Yacht Club. We spent many Sundays and evenings with our friends, lawyers, magistrates and university professors. We were close to people like Robert Dossou[41], who had not yet married Christine Desouches[42].

---

41. Born in 1939, Robert Dossou is a politician, lawyer and professor. He chaired Benin's Constitutional Court from 2008 to 2013.
42. Born in 1946, Christine Desouches holds a doctorate in political science and is the daughter of Maurice Ulrich, chief of staff to Jacques Chirac, Mayor of Paris. A lecturer at Paris 1 University, she has long worked for the Organisation internationale de la Francophonie (OIF).

Did you visit other countries?

I went to Togo without meeting Gnassingbé Eyadema, for lack of contact.

How often did you spend time with Béatrice Kérékou?

Every week until her downfall, in 1976, after a scandal involving her sexual habits. Her husband repudiated her. He even disbarred her from the judiciary. As I'm no Tarzan, I distanced myself. I stayed in Benin from 1973 to July 1977, after which I was appointed to Nouakchott.

Chapter 6: A French-African Network: Club 89

Mauritania is a very different Africa from the one you've known until now.

That's what I was looking for. I arrived in Nouakchott after applying for a transfer. Four years in Benin seemed long enough. My thesis was progressing well. I wanted to see something else. Jacques Foccart telephoned President Moktar Ould Daddah to obtain a position for me[43]. I was appointed to the École nationale d'administration (Ena), where I taught political science and geopolitics. My course was entitled "Major contemporary political issues".

Where did you live in Nouakchott?

In an apartment facing the central market. I was happy, because this country brought me closer to Dakar. I bought a Volkswagen Polo and drove from Dakar to Nouakchott once a month, passing through Rosso.

Does your wife follow you wholeheartedly?

She arrived in February 1978 with Olivier, our first child. She immediately found a practice: that of Ogo Kane Diallo, a Moorish-Senegalese and friend of Moktar Ould Daddah. I left Mauritania in 1979 and went straight to Abidjan.

In the meantime, a major event is taking place: the defense of your thesis.

---

43. Moktar Ould Daddah (1924-2003) presided over the Islamic Republic of Mauritania from November 28, 1960 to July 10, 1978.

In June 1978 to be precise. In addition to Pierre Dabezies, the jury was made up of Edmond Jouve and Gérard Conac, leading constitutionalists specializing in Africa. We owe them many African state constitutions.

I was awarded a mention Très bien with congratulations from the jury and *imprimatur*. My work, published by the Librairie générale de droit et de jurisprudence (LGDJ), is kept at the Bibliothèque nationale. Finally, I was awarded a doctorate in public law and political science.

This thesis also marks your entry into the holy of holies of the French right.

It introduced me to all its top officials. When Jacques Foccart takes your appointments himself, people don't hesitate to welcome you. And they remember you, believe me.

Jacques Foccart, who once again intervened on your behalf in Côte d'Ivoire.

And he didn't beat around the bush: he phoned "Houphouët". It's in this country that I'm really going to change politically.

How important was the "Old Man", the nickname given to Félix Houphouët-Boigny, to him?

He was the pillar of the Franco-African networks, the figurehead. He preferred him to all the others, including Omar Bongo. He liked his presence, his charisma, his quick wit. There's no need to hide it: referring to Omar Bongo, de Gaulle often told him that he needed to "educate this boy".

And he adds:

> "It's all very well to replace Léon Mba as you did, and to have mobilized your legal experts to tailor-make a constitution for him, but he needs to be roughened up and strengthened."

Félix Houphouët-Boigny, the only African president praised by de Gaulle in his *Mémoires*, is of a different dimension. He was a political mastermind of the highest order. An admirer, Foccart called him every Wednesday, if not every day.

Founded in 1981, Club 89 is the think tank of the Rassemblement pour la République (Rally for the Republic)[44]. It was in Abidjan, where you launched its first African branch, that your personality took shape: that of an intermediary between France and Africa. First on behalf of your *mentor*, then on behalf of your political family.

With the personal blessing of Jacques Chirac, who had just failed in the presidential election. It was he who asked Alain Juppé and Michel Aurillac to sign me up to the club, and in 1981 I became its national delegate for developing countries. It was said that I had a special interest in Africa.

This appointment marked the beginning of my rise in the field of French African policy. Incidentally, we all wanted to reflect on major national and international issues while preparing our candidate for the 1988 presidential election. Michel Aurillac was its first president. Alain Juppé, its co-founder, was General Secretary. All the leading Chirac members frequented the club.

Do you follow the Mayor of Paris out of political affinity or because he's Foccart's favorite?

I had already followed Jacques Foccart in his support for Jacques Chaban-Delmas in 1974, before switching, like him, to Jacques Chirac following the creation of the RPR. The most decisive event was my first meeting with him, at the end of 1976. It undoubtedly won me over.

Under what circumstances?

In Benin, I was very close to the French ambassador Michel Van Grevenynghe, whom Foccart had asked to look after me, as it were. I had become a friend of the head of the Mission d'Aide et de Coopération, André Guéna, who was, as I mentioned earlier, Yves Guéna's brother. Networks" flourished in Africa. If you met one person, you could reach twenty others. That's why I was able to move so easily and quickly in this galaxy.

Everyone knew that I was close to the outgoing Secretary General for African and Malagasy Affairs. It was in 1976, during one of my visits to France, that Jacques Foccart asked me to address a note to Jacques

---

44. Party founded by Jacques Chirac in 1976. It disappeared in 2002, to be replaced by the Union pour un mouvement populaire (UMP).

Chirac at the Château de Bity in Corrèze, to introduce myself and congratulate him on his resignation from Matignon. I then joined the RPR without question.

Where did you first meet him?
At his office in the Palais Bourbon. I waited a few minutes at the Café Le Bourbon before being received in the company of Foccart. I stayed for a quarter of an hour. We talked about Africa. He was already interested. We promised to keep in touch, but I didn't see him for a while.

Why?
Objectively, none. My studies, life, constraints. On the other hand, I corresponded with him regularly. We talked about politics. I told him what Africans thought and said about him.

When do you see him again?
In 1980, on the occasion of an interview for the magazine *48 États africains*, whose Guinean editor, Edge Ndiaye, was a friend of my father and our family. A former student of the Lycée Van Vo with my brother René, he wanted an interview with the Mayor of Paris about Africa. He had previously asked me to interview François Mitterrand on the same subject. Jacques Foccart had talked me out of it, saying I wasn't intellectually trained enough for the exercise.

It's true that I had little culture on the left. My heart beat irremediably to the right. I hadn't even read books like *Le coup d'État permanent* or *L'abeille et l'architecte*. Before the interview, the communications director for the Mayor of Paris, Bernard Niquet, a future prefect, warned me that I had fifteen minutes. I left an hour later. Niquet regularly poked his head through the door, and Chirac scolded him:

"Niquet, we'll let you know!"

At the end of the interview, he invited me to the famous Brazzaville centenary in October 1980.

Africa is becoming an increasingly important part of our thinking.
He knew all the stakes of this continent, which was already courting him. I remember the sumptuous reception given in his honor by Denis

Sassou Nguesso, another Marxist-Leninist president at the time, for this anniversary in the Congolese capital. The relationship between the mayor of Paris and Sassou, a dashing revolutionary soldier, was extraordinary. They were like brothers. This closeness drove the Soviet ambassador to the Congo mad.

At that time, before the creation of Club 89, I was already chairing the Côte d'Ivoire committee supporting Chirac's candidacy for the 1981 presidential election. I would like to point out that on that occasion, he personally appointed me as his representative for this election, as is shown by several documents in the appendices to this book. I therefore signed in his own name, which didn't prevent malicious people from claiming throughout my "career" that I didn't know him...

Côte d'Ivoire had a considerable influence on France's African policy. Thanks to "Houphouët", of course, but also to the presence of a very large French community and thousands of aid workers.

Are you interested in Valéry Giscard d'Estaing's "Messieurs Afrique", such as René Journiac or Martin Kirsch?

Absolutely not. They did, however, know of my existence.

Who managed Africa in the nascent RPR?

Faced with Jacques Foccart, there wasn't much room to exist. He was crushing everyone. Maurice Robert worked in his field, the secret services. But Foccart compartmentalized enormously. Each person had their own perimeter and area of intervention, with a thick hermetic cordon around them. Few people managed to penetrate his inner circle. Even collaborators like Fernand Wibaux[45] were rarely invited to his famous house in Luzarches, Val-d'Oise, apart from the large reception he organized there every year.

---

45. A diplomat, senior civil servant and member of the French Resistance, Fernand Wibaux (1921-2013) was diplomatic advisor to the Chirac government from 1986 to 1988 and a close political advisor to Jacques Foccart. Several times ambassador to the continent (Mali, Chad, Senegal), he held other senior positions such as managing director of the Office du Niger (1956-1960) and chief of staff to Cooperation Minister Jean de Lipkowski (1976). He also served as French High Commissioner in New Caledonia from 1985 to 1986.

And Michel Dupuch?

Nor was he an intimate[46]. The "Doyen" would see him when he visited Abidjan each year to celebrate the June 18, 1940 call to arms. The reception took place at the French embassy, where Foccart had an office even though the Socialists were in power. The two men would later fall out when called upon to work together after Jacques Chirac's victory in the 1995 presidential election.

Why?

As soon as the election results were announced, Omar Bongo was in Paris. As soon as Jacques Chirac's victory was known, he organized a reception in honor of Foccart, who sincerely thought he would return to work at the Cellule[47]. In theory, he was to work with Fernand Wibaux, Colonel Pierre Voïta and yours truly.

But that was without the intervention of Dominique Galouzeau de Villepin, who set about torpedoing the scheme. I didn't even get a folding seat! Michel Dupuch was finally appointed to 2, rue de l'Élysée. Jacques Foccart, Fernand Wibaux and Pierre Voïta will have an office at 14, the headquarters of the private staff. Foccart never went there, until his death on March 19, 1997.

The 89 Club is run by Maurice Robert, a key figure in the French secret service in Africa. What is your relationship with him?

He never managed the club, at least never on African issues. And at no time did he interfere in my affairs as an official representative of the RPR or as the club's national delegate.

I often had lunch with him when I was in Paris. We had an excellent relationship. However, he knew better than to interfere with what I was doing. Michel Aurillac would talk to him about me, which was perfectly understandable. That was the end of it.

---

46. A diplomat born in 1931, Michel Dupuch was French ambassador to Côte d'Ivoire from 1979 to 1993, before being appointed Africa advisor to Jacques Chirac from 1995 to 2002.
47. A garden-level office at 2 rue de l'Élysée, headquarters of the French presidency's diplomatic advisors, "La Cellule africaine" or "La Cellule" is the historic headquarters of the advisors responsible for covering this continent.

How are you perceived by the Ivorian section of the RPR?

I can't say that I felt a great deal of affection for this branch. Nor at national level, for that matter. Nobody was ever really kind to me. It always took Foccart and Chirac's arbitration for me to advance and climb the ladder.

Because of your origins?

Essentially. I was considered "the token Arab". The looks, the contemptuous remarks, the detestation, even the hatred towards me were legion. Racism was in full swing. The jealousy came from bitter, envious people, as I would meet so many of them throughout my life.

It's true that I wasn't just another development worker. I had established relations with "Houphouët", Governor Guy Nairay[48] and Alain Belkiri, the irremovable Secretary General of the Ivorian government[49]. I received the most senior right-wing figures visiting the country. I met with Ambassador Michel Dupuch at least once a month, which only served to accentuate the resentments.

Jacques-Noël Giacomoni, the local RPR delegate and representative of the Union des Français de l'Etranger (UFE) in Abidjan, who combined this role with that of head of Compagnie Générale d'Electricité (CGE), had a tenacious dislike of me. The same was true of Philippe Delmon, a development worker seconded by the French Ministry of Economy and Finance to the Central Bank of Côte d'Ivoire, and Michel Bujon, another banker. The entire French development aid elite in this country abhorred me. As for Marie-Antoinette Isnard, the RPR delegate for the French abroad, she vomited me.

You became Jacques Foccart's correspondent.

Yes. What my father had been unable to do because of his inability to write French, I was able to do at a higher level and with the utmost discretion.

---

48. Born in Saint-Anne, Guadeloupe, and deceased in Abidjan in August 1999, Guy Nairay was President Houphouët-Boigny's chief of staff from 1960 to 1963, then his main collaborator on the most sensitive issues. From 1993 until his death, he was special advisor to President Henri Konan Bédié.
49. Secretary General of the Government of the Republic of Côte d'Ivoire from May 1958 to November 1990, then Secretary General of the Ivorian Presidency until the death of Houphouët-Boigny on December 7, 1993.

47

Your emerging trademark.

All the official bodies, whether advisors or cabinet members, have never put up with informality. And from the informal to the sulphurous, many took the plunge, attributing all the dirty tricks to me. The fantasy box was opened.

Who are your contacts at the RPR?

I frequented Jacques Chirac's entourage. Cabinet directors like Jean-Paul Bolufer or his director of international affairs, Jacques-Henri Richard.

Are you in charge of the Club 89's other African branches?

I helped set up the Dakar, Bamako and Libreville branches. But the Abidjan branch, founded by myself, was by far the most important and financially impressive.

Is the RPR already financed through these channels?

My father had taken the initiative. I took over in 1981 with the feeling that I had to carry out extremely sensitive missions.

While you're in Abidjan, you take the opportunity to visit Guinea, a country whose regime interests you.

In 1981, during an interview with Félix Houphouët-Boigny, I asked him about Ahmed Sékou Touré. It's true that he didn't leave me indifferent. A few days later, Governor Guy Nairay asked me to come to his office where the Côte d'Ivoire ambassador to Guinea, Lazeni Namogo Poto Coulibaly, was staying. I owe it to him to have organized my first trip to Conakry and my meeting with Ahmed Sékou Touré. In the Guinean capital, I stayed with my friend Guy Lafont, the local manager of UTA[50].

The day after my arrival, I had lunch with the Guinean president, to whom I presented my thesis. He fascinated me. He was a handsome man with a melodious voice, piercing eyes and perfect elocution. I immediately felt at ease, despite the violent nature of his regime. At his home, I met and befriended key figures such as his Prime Minister Louis Lansana Béavogui[51], his formidable brother Ismaël Touré and ministers such as

---

50. Union de transports aériens.
51. Louis Lansana Béavogui was Minister of Foreign Affairs before becoming head of government from 1972 to 1984.

the Minister of Justice. We always had lunch together around the Head of State. I sat on his right.

On a second trip in 1982, I had a real tête-à-tête with him at the Sekhoutouréya[52]. I plucked up my courage and asked him some rather suicidal questions about his relationship with Jacques Foccart. He had been at loggerheads for many years with Foccart, whom he regarded as the devil, not least because of the operations launched the day after the country gained independence on October 2, 1958, in an attempt to destabilize it and make its president pay for his refusal to join the Franco-African Community[53].

I was frank about it:

> "What's the latest on your relations with Monsieur Foccart?"
> "Bourgi, I know you're close to him. You told me about your work on de Gaulle and Africa. I read it and appreciated it. One day, he and I may meet again. What's more, here in Conakry. But I'd like to say that if he had successors, none of them replaced him, even if they were carrying out de Gaulle's orders."

They did meet again. First in France, on the occasion of Ahmed Sékou Touré's famous visit in September 1982, at the invitation of François Mitterrand and the new Socialist government. He took advantage of this official visit, from September 16 to 20, to pay his respects to Jacques Chirac, Mayor of Paris. Jacques Foccart took part in the meeting. It was a reunion.

"I had a great time," Chirac tells me.

He would meet Jacques Foccart again in Conakry. This meeting was facilitated by Félix Houphouët-Boigny, the French businessman and entrepreneur Jean Lefebvre and the influential French ambassador to Guinea, André Lewin, who became close to Béchir Ben Yahmed, the founder and owner of *Jeune Afrique*. He even became a columnist for this weekly. As for me, I saw him one last time, in Libreville, shortly before his death. He was no longer a rock.

---

52. Name given to the presidential palace in Conakry.
53. One of these operations, Operation Persil, supervised by Jacques Foccart, involved the injection of counterfeit Guinean franc bills via the SDECE, with the aim of bringing about a collapse of the national economy through hyperinflation. This operation, mounted in 1960, was coupled with an attempt to destabilize the country by sending arms and mercenaries to the regime's opponents.

Chapter 7: Secret Money for the RPR

Was Jacques Foccart making you understand that it would be a good idea to raise funds in Africa on behalf of the RPR?

He never asked me. I took the initiative myself during a meeting with Jacques Chirac at Paris Town Hall. Foccart had already enlightened him at length about my father's financing of the RPF from 1947 to 1957.

In turn, I made it clear to the Mayor of Paris that, as he was very well introduced to the Lebanese community in Africa, it could support his political action. He was delighted, but asked me how the generous contributions would be channelled to France. I already had my ideas on the matter and on how to organize...

When do you start mobilizing these funds?

Immediately after his defeat in 1981. He asked me to "continue the fight".

The club's Ivorian branch is the most powerful in French-speaking Africa.

The richest, unquestionably. I acted as an intermediary for a community of almost 100,000 people, occupying all the lucrative and strategic sectors of the country.

How did you go about it? Were the donors all from the same community?

Under my authority, my function and my status, there was no contribution of any importance whatsoever outside the Lebanese community. I didn't concern myself with other donors, supporters or admirers of Jacques Chirac, particularly French, nor with other communities.

51

Who managed donations from French contributors?
I was unaware of this and had no mandate to deal with it.

How often did the Lebanese donate?
The notion of periodicity didn't exist. It was up to me when we met.

The sums climbed according to the political agenda and ambitions of your "colt" in the run-up to the 1986 legislative elections and the 1988 presidential election.
The Lebanese in Côte d'Ivoire deeply admired de Gaulle, an admiration that was transposed to Jacques Chirac, who was, needless to say, de Gaulle's Secretary of State for Employment Problems, then for the Economy and Finance.

In fact, thanks to me, he already knew many of the country's Lebanese nationals. He met them individually or collectively at Paris City Hall or during his trips to the land of Akwaba. The meetings always took place at the Hotel Ivoire.

On the other hand, I must point out that I never had access to the "Houphouët" channel. This was the exclusive domain of the Chirac/Foccart duo. I never transported a single penny from Félix Houphouët-Boigny on behalf of the Mayor of Paris. This must be heard, read and understood.

How much money was collected?
Each mission never totaled less than 30 to 35 million CFA francs (convertible currency at the time).

How many years have these missions been organized?
From 1981 to 1986, during the five years I spent in Abidjan, just before joining the cabinet of Michel Aurillac, appointed Minister for Cooperation by Jacques Chirac during the first cohabitation and successor to Christian Nucci in this post. I left Côte d'Ivoire in March 1986.

How many missions were there?
Five or six were organized during my stay in Côte d'Ivoire.

During this short period, more than 200 million CFA francs, or almost 5 million French francs—a considerable sum at the time—were channeled into the RPR's operations.

In fact, twice as much, since the CFA franc was worth twice as much as the French franc.

How were deliveries made? Who did you give the *cash* to?

I had relays at the departure and arrival points of each mission. As soon as I needed to travel to France with cash, I informed President Houphouët-Boigny's chief of staff, Governor Guy Nairay. He always accompanied me to the plane at Abidjan international airport. The money was contained in travel bags carried by an Ivorian emissary. Of course, nobody searched them. That was the whole point. When Governor Nairay arrived at the airport, I can tell you that everyone stood at attention.

In Paris, the emissary handed over the bags as soon as they left the plane to Jean-Claude Laumond, Jacques Chirac's personal chauffeur, who was waiting in the Paris mayor's car. I got out like all the other passengers. To be on the safe side, I never came into contact with that money. I must insist on this point: I never carried any bag myself. Once the "gift" was in the car, the emissary left and I joined Laumond.

From there, we'd either head for Paris City Hall, or stop off at Jacques Foccart's house on rue de Prony or at Villa Charlotte. Each time, we were given instructions as to where to stop. When we went to Luzarches, Foccart systematically offered us coffee in his salon. By the time we drank it, the Mayor of Paris had already called to see if we'd arrived. I have to say that, even without these missions, I met him whenever I was in France.

What interest did the Lebanese of Côte d'Ivoire and Africa have in giving?

You can't see any complex logic in this. This is very much part of Arab and African culture. First of all, as I said, there was a certain attachment to Gaullism. But for many, giving money was an outward sign of wealth and prosperity.

Incidentally, it opened up contacts and appointments. I had several of them come to Paris City Hall to meet Jacques Chirac and pose for a photo with him. That was enough for them. They were delighted and felt they were playing in the big league. Then they advertised it to the world. You don't have to look any further.

Jacques Foccart was one of the most influential figures of the Fifth Republic. He knew everyone, and was well-connected. How do you explain the trust placed in you for such sensitive missions?

Through my father's spiritual heritage. He saw in me a kind of continuum of loyalty and admiration for de Gaulle. What's more, we never stopped corresponding. In Africa, whether in Benin, Mauritania or Côte d'Ivoire, I had proven myself. I showed him what I was capable of. People talked to him about me, starting with the ambassadors on the spot. I was considered particularly reliable.

You become the official emissary of "Chiraquie" in Africa.

I was working for my political family. Only Jacques Chirac knew what was going on between me and Jacques Foccart. Dominique de Villepin was not yet privy to this secret. No doubt he had heard rumors and rumors in the corridors, but without any certainty as to their veracity. Jean-Claude Laumond was one of the very few people who knew the exact nature of what we were carrying.

Dominique de Villepin is not yet part of your circle.

No. However, he was seen more and more often in Jacques Chirac's office from the moment he was appointed chief of staff to Alain Juppé, Édouard Balladur's Minister of Foreign Affairs, from 1993 to 1995, during the second cohabitation. What was new was that I was asked to wait much longer in Jean-Claude Laumond's office, in the private parking lot of Paris City Hall. I had to wait for Villepin, who was passing through, to leave before going upstairs and handing over the funds.

Could this money be used to purchase real estate, for example?

It was used to run the RPR in the broadest sense of the term, but don't ask me what it was used for. I knew nothing about its destination or use. The donors, and later the African heads of state, gave it to me "for Jacques", as they liked to say. What happened to it was none of my business.

Were you taking a commission?

The question is hurtful. During one of Omar Bongo's visits to France, I was received at the Élysée Palace by Jacques Chirac, now President of the Republic, and his Gabonese counterpart. Dominique de Villepin always let me in once the photographers and officials had left. During the interview, Chirac asked me, with a look of bewilderment on his face:

> "Omar, how is it that for so many years all your emissaries have been accompanied by your 'Fiston', who is the only one to know the combination of the bags and their exact value?"

Bongo's response:

> "Because I've never missed a penny. We have total confidence in him. We are certain that there will be no evaporation."

I might as well tell you that I didn't take anything for personal use. For the record, the President of Gabon, who used to call me "Fiston", had a lucky number.

Steeped in ancient and mystical practices, he worshipped the number 3. The code on the travel bags therefore always bore only three numbers, known to him, to me and to Chirac, the final recipient. The code was 5.5.5.

For the record, in September 2005, during one of my many visits to the Élysée Palace for a fund-raising event, I was accompanied by the Gabonese ambassador to France, Jean-Marie Adzé. He had brought two bags full of money. We were in Villepin's office. The luggage was there on the floor, but Jacques Chirac had forgotten the combination. A little embarrassed, the diplomat said he didn't know it before turning to me. I handed Chirac an envelope containing the opening code in Omar Bongo's handwriting.

You're never the only one moving these funds.

Never. They have always passed through the hands of VIPs, cabinet directors, ministers, senior civil servants or diplomats. They had to be able to pass through customs unhindered.

55

You're a married, well-established teacher and family man. Your wife is a lawyer. Don't these convoys pose a problem of conscience, a problem of ethics?

I carried out these missions as normally as possible, although I was well aware of the danger involved in transporting the money. That's why there was always a henchman to carry them out.

At no time did I touch any of the money during its transfer, right up to the end of my "magisterium", if I can put it that way. The emissaries, such as Guy Nairay, knew the "transporters", as did I, but I didn't touch anything.

Did you have a diplomatic passport?

None.

Financing political parties in this way was legal. However, these cash sums were not declared.

I don't think so. There was no accounting, but that didn't concern me.

Were there ever any customs or Air and Border Police searches?

Not a single one.

In Abidjan, who were the most generous Lebanese donors or donors of Lebanese origin?

For the most part, they belonged to the Shiite community. There were about twenty of them, whom I saw whenever Jacques Chirac made me understand the need to raise funds. They were people like the businessman Nagib Zaher and many others, whose names I won't mention. They were very, very big contributors.

You managed the Ivorian branch of Club 89. What about the branches in other African countries?

Under my authority, only the Lebanese community in Côte d'Ivoire remitted money. I didn't deal with other countries. Not even Senegal. I can say, with full knowledge of the facts, that the Shiite Lebanese community in Côte d'Ivoire contributed significantly to Jacques Chirac's financial support. He'll remember that.

Subsequently, I became the appointed missus dominicus of all the African heads of state I worked for, with the emissaries they were willing to propose to me. They all gave Chirac a code name. Omar Bongo's, for example, was "Davin", as Jacques Chirac was still mayor of Paris[54].

Whenever a transfer was being prepared, Omar Bongo would call me and say two coded words: "Ifoura"[55] and "Davin". He would ask me to make an appointment with this or that minister or political leader "for Davin". I knew then with whom I was going to "work".

In Abidjan, on the other hand, I never dealt with these issues directly with Félix Houphouët-Boigny. As I've already said, this was the sole responsibility of Jacques Foccart and Jacques Chirac. Not a single penny from the "Old Man" passed through me during my stay in Côte d'Ivoire.

As a doctor d'État, a brilliant career as a teacher and researcher opens up to you, with the possibility of teaching at universities and grandes écoles. Do these sensitive missions convince you that a more gilded life is possible?

In Abidjan, I was busy collecting and transporting large sums of money on behalf of the Gaullist party. This was one of my activities, but not the only one. Later on, my activities became much more diversified. It's true that at the time, rubbing shoulders with such high-profile figures as Governor Guy Nairay and Georges Ouégnin[56] already gave me an idea of my growing influence.

As you build your character as a "lobbyist" between Paris and the African capitals, the enmities increase.

Mistrust came from the entire local RPR nomenklatura. But I wasn't obliged to anyone, it was a question of temperament. I've always preferred to work on my own. My direct contacts with Jacques Chirac, Jacques Foccart and the highest Ivorian dignitaries gave rise to an incalculable amount of pettiness. Everyone envied me. Even more so after the visits I organized to the Ivorian economic capital, first by Michel Aurillac as President of Club 89, then by Alain Juppé, General Secretary of the same club and Director of Economic and Financial Affairs for the City of Paris.

---

54. Jean Aveno Davin, mayor of Libreville from April 11, 1983 to April 13, 1989.
55. "Money" in the *Batéké* language.
56. Born in 1934, George Ouegnin was a senior civil servant and diplomat in Côte d'Ivoire, where he served as Chief of Protocol from 1962 to 2001.

I invited them in their official capacity. "Houphouët" welcomed them personally, even going so far as to charter his personal plane for a round trip from Abidjan to Yamoussoukro, where he kept them for lunch. The RPR caciques in Abidjan were furious. What's more, they knew full well I was collecting funds, to the point of complaining to Marie-Antoinette Isnard. Poor things. What they didn't know was that Chirac himself was the principal (laughs).

The Lebanese community in Abidjan is dominated by the Shiite movement. Do you take advantage of this to build your networks with Hezbollah?

I had no contact with Hezbollah other than with Sheikh Adnan Zalghout, the religious leader of the local community who interfered in the case of the French hostages in Lebanon. This fundamentalist was a true supporter of the movement. I used to meet him at dinner parties and sometimes visited him. His social life was abundant.

Did he help you penetrate Hezbollah's local networks?

I never penetrated these networks. I used several channels to try and secure the release of hostages Jean-Paul Kauffmann, Marcel Carton and Marcel Fontaine, as well as the later release of academic Clotilde Reiss in Iran in 2010.

What is your relationship with Lebanon?

I went there for the first time in 1982. Since then, I've returned once a year.

A pilgrimage.

At first, I wanted to meet my father's family and especially my mother's family. Her younger brother was Secretary General of the Lebanese Parliament. He introduced me to all the political authorities of the time, including the President of the Council and the President of the Republic. Every time I travel to this country, I meet some of its leading figures. Every trip brings me back to my origins.

Photo Album n°1

My father's identity card in 1924, a "blue-eyed" Lebanese.

RÉPUBLIQUE FRANÇAISE

PASSEPORT A L'ÉTRANGER VALABLE POUR UN AN

Mahmoud Bourgi on his arrival
in Dakar.

*My father's visa when he arrived
in Dakar from Marseille on the Guilio
Cesare, in June 1934.*

My mother's passport when she arrived in Senegal in 1934.

With my monozygotic twin brother, at 6 months. Where am I?

The beautiful family home in Dakar, rue de Thiès, where my brothers, sisters and I were all born. So many memories! This 1st floor was our home from 1937 to 1959, with my father's store on the first floor.

63

Our family home, avenue William-Ponty. We lived there from 1959 to 1961, on the top two floors.

A new family home, 10 rue Kleber, where we moved in 1961, on the 5th and 6th floors. My family still lives there.

Mom and Dad. I'm on the left.

With my brothers and sisters. I'm right up front in the middle.

65

In 1954, my parents, always extremely elegant, aboard the liner l'Île-de-France taking them to the United States.

At the age of 11, in 1956.

My father (2nd from left) surrounded by his loyal friends.
I'm in front of him, with my brother Albert.

67

The former Lycée Van Vollenhoven, also known as "Van Vo", will be my school from the 6th to the 12th grades. It was the largest French lycée outside mainland France. It was open to all the elites of the colonial Empire.

My parents and my brother René at the palace
of the Governor General of AOF, in 1959.

69

1962-1963. My best memories and my unforgettable classmates from the 2nd AB at "Van Vo" high school. I'm on the far left.

In 1963-1964, in 1st AB with my dear comrades. I'm at the very top.

Visiting Dakar in 1967, Imam Moussa el Sadr, the supreme leader of the Shiite community in Lebanon, is flanked by my father, on his right, and the French ambassador to Senegal, Jean Vyau de Lagarde.

In 1972, my father Mahmoud Bourgi received the insignia of Officer of the Order of Merit from the French ambassador in Dakar.

My wife, Catherine, on the day she was sworn in as a lawyer, in Cotonou, in 1974. To her left, her "boss", Me Florentin Féliho.

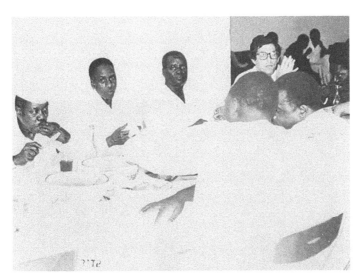

With the Guinean Prime Minister, Lansana Béavogui,
during my trip to Conakry in 1981.

Jacques Chirac, during a visit to Abidjan in 1983,
with my wife Catherine.

73

My first pilgrimage to Mecca, in 1989,
with my beloved brother, Hussein Yassine.

Chapter 8: An Advisor like No Other

In 1986, you left the Ivory Coast to join the cabinet of Michel Aurillac, Minister for Cooperation in Jacques Chirac's cohabitation government after the March legislative elections[57].

As a reminder, because it's important: Michel Aurillac's father, Jean Aurillac, Governor of France overseas, and my father were friends. Michel and I met in 1981, when Club 89 was formed.

You want to go further in your commitment.

I wanted to campaign, to test myself.

Did you have a personal diary?

Naturally. My relations with Jacques Foccart, Jacques Chirac and Michel Aurillac were very strong, and my position at the Club 89 enabled me to make the acquaintance of other major figures on the Republican Right, such as Alain Juppé and Jacques Toubon, a member of the RPR political bureau.

What was your state of mind?

I was reluctant to pursue a career in teaching. I felt I'd come to the end of a cycle as a cooperant. Four years in Benin, two in Mauritania and five in Côte d'Ivoire: I'd come full circle, even if Pierre Dabezies was urging me to take the agrégation.

Let's not forget that I never received a single franc from my activities on behalf of the RPR. My lifestyle remained the same. Nevertheless, I began

---

57. Appointed on April 2, 1986, Michel Aurillac held this portfolio until April 2, 1988.

to work on my influence. I knew what I represented and the quality of my relationships. I felt I could use my address book.

In insider circles, you're known as "Bob". Was it Jacques Foccart who gave you that nickname?

Yes, in fact, when Jacques Chirac or Dominique de Villepin pronounced the name "Bob" in front of African presidents, they immediately knew who we were talking about.

Michel Aurillac was the first president of Club 89.

And I'm the literal tenant! When the *think tank* was founded in 1981, it was based on the Rue de l'Université in the 7th arrondissement of Paris. But Michel Aurillac had his sights set on a bigger place, and approached me, as the RPR had identified a superb 200 m² premises in the building at 45, avenue Montaigne.

While I was still in Abidjan, Michel Aurillac asked me if I would agree to have the lease drawn up in my name. Quite a surprising request. I didn't understand it. And here I was, the club's official tenant on this prestigious avenue, right opposite Chanel!

Why this request?

I never knew. For Jacques Foccart, I must have seen this as "a mark of confidence" in me. I was based in Abidjan, but the French directories listed Robert Bourgi, 45 avenue Montaigne. The gas and electricity contracts were also in my name. It was all quite incredible.

How much was the rent?

It was around 50,000 francs, about €7,500 today. I have to say that, although the lease was in my name, it was Omar Bongo who, at my request, paid from the outset to support the RPR. He gave cash. Jacques Chirac knew all about it. There were a certain number of meetings, colloquia, lunches and dinners. They had to be paid for.

All the RPR meetings were held there.

It was a very influential circle. Jacques Chirac was a regular visitor. All the RPR deputies and senators attended. What a great bunch. It was there that Michel Aurillac quickly asked me to set up the African branches, which I did, although I didn't control all of them. During a meeting of the club's board of directors, the same Aurillac insisted on the need to appoint a national delegate for developing countries. I was unanimously appointed.

With this new role added to my relationships, I've put all my energy into it. Jacques Chirac himself let Félix Houphouët-Boigny, Guy Nairay and Alain Belkiri[58] know that he had confidence in me personally. In other words, I was speaking on his behalf, unlike the local RPR delegates who were after me.

You're helping it strengthen its African networks.

During a meeting at the Hôtel de Ville, in the presence of Michel Aurillac, he asked me to organize a visit for him to Abidjan and then Libreville[59]. There was no problem, even though I made him understand that, as an employee of the Ministry of Cooperation under Socialist leadership, I should not be prejudiced by this kind of mission.

Jacques Chirac retorted that, in the event of a problem, "Houphouët" would not hesitate to intervene with François Mitterrand, his friend. So I organized this mission for Michel Aurillac and his wife, Martine, who also holds high political office[60].

You already feel the need to make yourself indispensable.

I'd like to stress one point: no RPR representatives or staff were ever involved in these missions. The Club 89 was a powerful parallel network of this party.

Marie-Antoinette Isnard represented the French abroad. When she came to Abidjan, I attended all her meetings and dinners, which irritated her to no end.

However, I got on extremely well with the local RPR delegate, Jacques-Noël Giacomoni, a Corsican like my wife. He was very sympathetic. Unfortunately, his entourage formed a security cordon to prevent me from seeing too much of him.

---

58. Alain Belkiri, a French politician born in 1921, was Secretary General of the Ivorian government under Félix Houphouët-Boigny from 1958 to 1990.
59. This will take place in 1985.
60. Born in 1939, Martine Aurillac, a member of the RPR and then the UMP, was mayor of the 7th arrondissement of Paris from 1995 to 2002 and member of parliament from 1993 to 2012.

Did Marie-Antoinette Isnard soap you up?

She didn't show me much affection. Jacques Chirac would neverthe-less ask me to pay her a courtesy call on rue de Lille[61] whenever I was in Paris. We'd have lunch at Le Dauphiné, a restaurant on boulevard Saint-Germain near the Assemblée Nationale.

Michel Aurillac's trip reinforces your growing influence.

That trip, in 1982, showered me with praise. Enthusiasm was wides-pread. Chirac thanked me warmly and asked me to repeat the operation with Alain Juppé, whom he felt should be "opened up" to Africa.

A real challenge.

That was another story. As usual, I replied "no problem" before meeting him at the Economic and Financial Affairs Department of Paris City Hall. He had a bit more hair than today. I'm 6 months older than him. He was born on August 15, 1945, and I on April 4.

I said:

> "Alain, you were born on Emperor's Day and I'm married to a Corsican woman. Top là, I'm organizing this trip for you!"

We were in 1984, and he seemed delighted, except for one detail: he wanted his wife and children to come with him, and he was worried about how the trip would be paid for. On this last point, I put him at ease: first-class travel with the whole family. And, as with Michel Aurillac, everything was organized to perfection: interviews with Guy Nairay; lunch with "Houphouët"; a conference on Club 89 at Hôtel Ivoire; articles in *Fraternité Matin*, etc. In short, the whole package!

I was in the middle of preparations when he informed me that he wanted to take advantage of this trip to spend three days in Mali, in Dogon country. I almost choked. I made him understand the disres-pectful nature of such a request, especially in Africa. You're invited by the highest authorities of a country and you take the opportunity to go somewhere else? Unthinkable.

---

61. For a long time, the address of the RPR headquarters, at no. 123.

Has he gone back on his decision?

Worse still, he made it a condition sine qua non, even threatening to come alone if he failed to satisfy. Classic Juppé. I rushed off to see Governor Nairay and Georges Ouégnin, who had the same reaction as me. If there's one thing you shouldn't do in Africa, it's this.

The "Old Man" was very irritated by this attitude. Especially as Côte d'Ivoire was not lacking in tourist attractions. I informed Chirac and Foccart of these demands. Three days later, Alain Juppé curtly announced that he would be coming alone after all. At the same time, he had sent me a letter asking me to meet local RPR leaders and French citizens abroad.

So on the big day, I flew to Abidjan airport to meet him on his UTA flight. And then, to my amazement, who did I see? Juppé walking down the gangway with a member of the RPR staff in Côte d'Ivoire, greeted on the tarmac by all the members of the local section, smiling from ear to ear. In short, all those who hated me, starting with Michel Bujon[62]. It made sense. They wanted to get round me by proving that they could manage without me.

The aim was to give the visit an official flavour.

Above all, Juppé wanted to get in my face, as he was well aware of my dissensions with the RPR people in Abidjan. Marie-Antoinette Isnard had set it up. Suffice it to say that the visit was chilly. We put him up on the 10th floor of the Hotel Ivoire in suite 1052, at Club 89's expense, which was normal. I remember the number all the better as it was the suite Jacques Foccart systematically occupied during his stays in Abidjan.

All the appointments for the visit and the interviews were set. During lunch with the President, the latter spoke at length about North-South dialogue and the deterioration in the terms of trade, his favorite subjects. The meeting lasted over two hours. At the invitation of the "Old Man", we then went to Yamoussoukro and Daoukro to greet Henri Konan Bédié[63], before returning to Abidjan. I remember Alain Juppé describing him as "lazy".

---

62. Member of the Côte d'Ivoire RPR section from July 13, 1982 to July 13, 1988.

63. A central figure in Ivorian politics, Henri Konan Bédié (1934-2023) was Félix Houphouët-Boigny's Minister of Economy and Finance (1966-1977), before presiding over the National Assembly (1980-1993) and becoming Head of State from 1993 until his overthrow in December 1999. He headed the Parti démocratique de Côte d'Ivoire (PDCI), a Houphouët party.

The following day, a conference was held for around 100 guests. Alain Juppé, it has to be said, was remarkable. At the end of the stay, I had planned a cocktail party at the Hotel Ivoire in the presence of Guy Nairay and senior government figures. He turned up as if for a funeral, which won't improve his image. This was not the Juppé I saw at Hôtel de Ville. No doubt he missed his family. As for Dogon country, it remained a postcard.

Alain Juppé is not known for his love of Africa.
But that didn't stop "Houphouët" and Guy Nairay from making complimentary comments once the visit was over.

> "Bourgi, this man has the dimension of a future president of the French Republic," said the "Old Man".

He was delighted that I'd been able to introduce him to him.

Was Alain Juppé aware of the movements of funds you were organizing?
I never told him about it, and I don't know if he knew.

Not even through Chirac?
It was none of my business. I didn't interfere in his conversations with his close collaborators and lieutenants. Only Foccart, Nairay and the Lebanese in Côte d'Ivoire knew.

Houphouët, Nairay, Belkiri, Bédié... you quickly became known to the most senior figures in the Ivorian state.
I'd been living in this country for several years, so it didn't take long.

What about Laurent Gbagbo?
I saw him all the time. He was already very close to my brother Albert. The first time we met was at a conference on "General de Gaulle, the man from Brazzaville" at the Abidjan Law School, in front of a thousand students. He was teaching history.

For him, this was an unexpected opportunity. He was an opponent of Félix Houphouët-Boigny, and students are protesters by nature. At the end of our talks, he congratulated me on my "understanding of Africa" and came over to my place. We talked until 4 a.m. with champagne and vodka.

How do you relate to each other?

I think I can describe it as a "sincere friendship". He often invited me to his house afterwards, as he lived at La Riviera, a stone's throw from my home. That's where I met Simone. We became close friends.

What did the Ivorian presidency know about your meetings?

I warned Guy Nairay and Georges Ouégnin, who was always exquisite to me. He facilitated countless meetings for me. Jacques Chirac had a fraternal affection for him. As for Jacques Foccart, godfather to one of his children, he had boundless admiration for him, a rare feat on his part. Georges Ouégnin was undoubtedly an essential cog in the French-Ivorian relationship.

With him, you will be the first to visit Jacques Foccart's remains at his home on March 19, 1997.

We were alerted in the early hours of the morning by Odette Leguerney, his unfailing secretary. Catherine and I rushed to rue de Prony, where we saw him in his room, lying on his bed. Georges Ouégnin approached him, kissed his forehead and knelt down, singing an Our Father. That striking image has never left me.

Your brother Albert is a law professor, the opposite of your background. In Africa, you defend the Gaullist right, while he develops left-wing ideas. How do you live together?

He laughed at me and taunted me all the time. We met once at Omar Bongo's house in Libreville. He with his lifelong friend, the opponent Alpha Condé[64], and I alone. Bongo spent his time heckling and teasing him.

You teach law, a subject that symbolizes probity and respect for the law. At the same time, you're on the edge of legality, orchestrating the transport of millions of undeclared CFA francs. Was this always a problem for you?

Why was this? These movements towards political parties were not forbidden by law. François Mitterrand's Socialist Party took advantage

---

64. He was a political opponent who led, among others, the Rassemblement du Peuple de Guinée (RPG) before becoming President of Guinea from 2010 to 2021.

of these practices, as did other political parties, including the French Communist Party. One need only refer to the writings of François Mitterrand's advisor and collaborator, Laurence Soudet, or those of his cabinet director, André Rousselet, to understand that these movements were in full swing. There was nothing illegal about my interventions.

They were not declared to the tax authorities.

I didn't even care. I was a fund-raiser. What happened to them was of no concern to me. I was a perfect executor, using my influence with the wealthy Lebanese in Côte d'Ivoire.

I didn't ask myself whether I was breaking any moral or ethical rules. I saw it above all as support for my political family. In fact, I never did much to convince these wealthy businessmen and industrialists of the legitimacy of my approach.

Were you aware of any emissaries from other political parties coming to Africa in search of money?

The financing of the Socialist Party by certain African heads of state was an open secret. Félix Houphouët-Boigny, who had known François Mitterrand since the 1940s, was a major contributor. Omar Bongo also fed the PS. He had close ties with Roland Dumas[65].

François Mitterrand was a very loyal friend and, of course, an unusual character. Putting de Gaulle in a run-off at the age of 49 and remaining in opposition for 23 years before becoming president in his turn is impressive.

Roland Dumas was your counterpart in the Socialist Party.

I only met him once, during the 1988 presidential campaign in France. We met in the anteroom of Omar Bongo's office. Chirac had sent me there to remind him that a campaign is expensive, especially a presidential one. I was waiting to be received, chatting with the aide-de-camp when François Mitterrand's friend and man of secret missions, future president of the French Constitutional Council, arrived.

"Hello, Bourgi, how are you? I think we've come for the same thing..."

---

65. Roland Dumas (1922-2024) was head of French diplomacy from December 7 1984 to March 20 1986 and from May 10 1988 to March 28 1993. He was President of the Constitutional Council from March 8, 1995 to February 29, 2000.

The red light came on. Respectfully, I put him in front of me. He rushed into the office, much to the dismay of the aide-de-camp, who glared at me and told me I'd been wrong. Roland Dumas came out a little heavier than when he went in, then made this comment, with a mocking air:

"Don't worry Bourgi, I've left some for you!"

Once in Omar Bongo's office, I received quite a beating:

"Idiot! Why didn't you come home first?"
"Dad, I couldn't do it, it's still protocol."
"You're an idiot! We had to get home before he did. As a result, he took Jacques' share. Now, what I'm going to give Chirac is cut in half!"
"Forgive me, Dad, but could you please warn Monsieur Chirac?"

He called him to tell him not to worry and that all he had to do was get me back to Libreville within the same week.

Hadn't he had enough of being solicited from all sides, or was this part of a well-honed strategy?
I once asked him the same question:

"But Dad, why so much money handed out to everyone, all the time?"
"Son, I play just like at the races, except I bet on all the horses to be sure of a winner."

This was his philosophy, and he was able to convert all his counterparts to it. But his real and sincere love was for Jacques Chirac.

There is talk of "bridges" between Club 89 and Michel Rocard.
That would be a little later, in the early 1990s. One man always played an obscure and discreet role with him: his friend, his confidant, his éminence grise, Michel Dubois. It was he who toured Africa for his "boss". We sometimes found ourselves in Brazzaville on the same mission. He for Rocard, I for Chirac. His office was on rue de Varenne, opposite the Palais de Matignon. It was through him that, for the first time, I shook hands with François Mitterrand's former Prime Minister, who was fully briefed on my activities.

When I met him, I suggested he get in touch with right-wing personalities such as Jacques Toubon, then Minister of Justice and Keeper of the Seals,

83

whom he seemed to particularly like. So I organized a three-way lunch at the Bristol: Toubon, Rocard and myself. I called him Mr. Prime Minister. He immediately demanded that I be on first-name terms with him. I didn't see him again after that, but I kept very good relations with Michel Dubois. He was a close friend of Fidel Castro and a passionate Latin American.

You're a national delegate for Club 89 and a member of the RPR. Why didn't you opt for a political career as a member of parliament for the French abroad, for example?

Noting that I was succeeding in my activities on behalf of his party, Jacques Chirac suggested I run for parliament. Knowing my attachment to the island, he even considered Corsica. But that didn't interest me at all. I don't have the kind of character that can get me permanently involved in party politics and broad thinking. I like to work one-on-one in the hushed atmosphere of unofficial missions.

What were your official duties as political advisor to Michel Aurillac?

I put all my contacts with African presidents at his disposal. He was a tenant of the "rue Monsieur" of the highest quality, but before that, as part of the Club 89, I had already brought many ministers from the continent to him in Paris.

With his African pedigree, he was well known, esteemed and respected. Let's not forget that he was chief of staff to President Léopold Sédar Senghor and president of the litigation section of the Senegalese Supreme Court. He was also close to Abdou Diouf in the late 1950s.

On the other hand, some people did not hesitate to put obstacles in my way, starting with François de Grossouvre[66]. He had warned Aurillac, describing me as "the Iranian and the Shiite on duty". Quite deplorable.

What more specific files were you managing?

Instead, I was already acting as missus dominicus, dealing exclusively with political relations. I was in direct contact with him. I have to say that one day my secretary, Nathalie Ronce, whom I remember fondly, made

---

66. Resistance fighter, industrialist and influential senior civil servant, François de Grossouvre (1918-1994) was a close collaborator of François Mitterrand, in charge of sensitive missions from 1981 to 1985. The guardian of Mitterrand's secrets, he took his own life on April 7, 1994, in his office at the Élysée Palace.

me aware of some dissatisfaction within the cabinet regarding my attitude. It was not part of ministerial customs for an advisor to address heads of state or deal with the minister without respecting a certain protocol.

At his first cabinet meeting, however, Michel Aurillac reaffirmed my role as a natural and spontaneous contact for African presidents. We were later joined by Christine Desouches, who also had very high-ranking and close relationships.

This did not go down well with the other members of the cabinet.

One day, Bernard de Montferrand, the Director of Cabinet, asked to see me, to remind me of the etiquette of a ministerial team. Somewhat offended, he was astonished that I could speak unfiltered to African presidents.

I'm a pretty strong character, so I stormed into the minister's office. Michel Aurillac, whom I called by his first name, was in audience. I told him I had to speak to him urgently about this "skirmish". He immediately reminded Bernard de Montferrand that I had already been talking to African heads of state even before his appointment, and that he saw nothing but advantages in my approaching them outside the generally accepted rules.

From that day on, I enjoyed the best possible relationship with Bernard de Montferrand. After his appointment as diplomatic adviser to Édouard Balladur at Matignon, I saw him once or twice a week in his office. We became great friends.

Sometimes you deal with more ordinary matters, such as the inauguration of the last section of the Transgabonais railway. A ceremony that gives you reason to fulminate against official diplomacy.

That was on December 30, 1986. This section ran from Lastoursville to Franceville, the Bongo stronghold and terminus of the line. It was a very important and highly political project. Omar Bongo, whom I had known for a long time, was very keen on this project, which had been launched in the 1970s. Unable to make the trip, Michel Aurillac asked me to represent him alongside Bernard de Montferrand.

In Gabon, I felt right at home. But this trip brought me face to face with the total contempt shown by French diplomacy and the French state for advisors and personalities wrongly considered to be of second rank.

85

What do you mean by that?

The trip was all set. My driver dropped me off at Roissy airport, where we were to board a DC-8. It was the first time I'd flown on one of the official French fleet. Once on the plane, the protocol officer accompanied me to my seat. We went through the first row, then the second, then the third... I found myself at the end of the aircraft with the bodyguards and journalists. One more row and I was in the toilet!

Michel Aurillac had instructed me to be in the front row with his directeur de cabinet. But the guy from the Quai d'Orsay took great pleasure in making me understand that I was merely an advisor. I was on the picket line. My blood ran cold. I grabbed my little suitcase to get off the plane. Montferrand harangued me as I passed:

> "But Robert, what are you doing? I can't go off on my own, I don't know Bongo".

Once on the tarmac, I passed the Prime Minister's convoy. Jacques Chirac and Jacques Foccart got out of their car and spotted me. Chirac asked me what was going on. And Foccart, who must have experienced a similar mishap as an unofficial personality, commented:

> "Jacques, I'm guessing".

The problem was solved in two minutes. The protocol guy got a lecture. I was at the head of the aircraft on both the outward and return trips.

For the record, during the flight I spotted a room where Chirac, Foccart and architect Olivier Clément Cacoub, also on the trip, had retired. They all came out in jogging suits. I can assure you that seeing Foccart in a tracksuit was worth the detour! During the trip, however, I dined at the back of the plane with Antoine Vélutini, one of the Prime Minister's bodyguards, a Corsican, friend of my wife and a Chirac loyalist.

Chapter 9: A Hostage Crisis

As the 1986 legislative elections approached, you were still living in Côte d'Ivoire. Are you being asked to intervene more with the Lebanese in support of the RPR and its founding president?

Obviously from 1985 onwards. Jacques Chirac asked me to mobilize more of my Lebanese "friends". Several missions were organized by me to bring businessmen to Paris City Hall, with individual meetings at the end. A contribution was left at the end of each meeting.

In May 1985, the first French citizens were kidnapped in Beirut by the Islamic Jihad, a "subsidiary" of Hezbollah. Was this an electoral issue for the RPR? Is it expected to reap political dividends in the run-up to the elections?[67]

I hadn't really got to grips with the issue yet, but when Jacques Chirac received me at the Paris Town Hall, he spoke at length about it. He knew I was a Shiite and was well aware of my origins.

It should be pointed out that, in his mind, he had no intention of short-circuiting the action of the Executive and François Mitterrand on this issue. He did not want to reap any dividends. He joined the negotiating channels already activated by the President of the Republic, the ultimate goal being the release of the hostages.

---

67. Diplomats and Foreign Ministry officials stationed in Lebanon, Marcel Fontaine and Marcel Carton, along with journalist Jean-Paul Kauffmann and academic Michel Seurat, were kidnapped in March and May 1985 by the Islamic Jihad organization, close to the Lebanese Hezbollah. Further kidnappings followed in protest, among other things, against French aid to Iraq, which was at war with Iran.

He was attentive to this area.

He was passionate about the Middle East. His friendships with digni-taries like Saddam Hussein were well known. When he received me as an individual, we talked about Lebanon, Israeli politics, the Iran-Iraq war and so on. He knew all about my relations with the Arab world. He himself had an oriental streak that was easy to detect. I felt it as an Arab.

Are you offering to intervene?

Since 1982, I had initiated several audiences between him and Nagib Zaher, a wealthy industrialist and leader of the Lebanese Shiite commu-nity in Abidjan, in his capacity as president of the Lebanese World Cultural Union (ULCM), Ibrahim Baroud and Fouad Gandhour, vice-pre-sident of the ULCM with a strong presence in Guinea. Nagib Zaher was a regular contributor to the RPR in Côte d'Ivoire. All these personalities had already met Jacques Chirac at the Paris City Hall or in Abidjan, on the occasion of Chirac's various trips to the Ivorian economic capital.

With the hostage affair, I made it clear to the Mayor of Paris and his chief of staff, Maurice Ulrich, that the Shiite community in Africa had strong ramifications in Beirut that could be decisive in moving this issue forward positively. My relations with Nagib Zaher had long been excellent. He even thought he was in a position, along with other Lebanese persona-lities such as Ibrahim Baroud, to establish contacts with the kidnappers.

In 1985, I organized two visits, in May and December. Apart from Nagib Zaher, who only took part in the first visit, the delegation included Fouad Gandhour, Ibrahim Baroud and myself. I automatically informed Chirac and/or Maurice Ulrich, Michel Aurillac and Jacques Foccart of all my interventions on this issue. It was only later that Charles Pasqua entered the loop as Minister of the Interior and a party to the negotiations.

Nagib Zaher, owner of the Africof building and civil engineering company, is a personal friend of Félix Houphouët-Boigny. Why did he ask you to touch the Mayor of Paris?

Despite his closeness to the "Old Man", I was the driving force behind the Chirac/Foccart relationship. I invited all the Lebanese businessmen. I set up and prepared their audiences. As I said, Jacques Chirac had already received Nagib Zaher thanks to my interventions. Nothing could be done without me. I'd also like to pay tribute to Jacques-Henri Richard, who worked for the Mayor of Paris and was essential to the organization of these meetings. A discreet and very efficient man.

Based on the sub-Saharan model, were Middle Eastern networks a source of funding for the RPR?

I had no idea. Jacques Chirac compartmentalized a lot. As much as I was competent in West and Central Africa, I knew I couldn't go beyond that geographical boundary. He clearly told me not to get involved in the Middle East, let alone North Africa.

How do Nagib Zaher, Fouad Gandhour and Ibrahim Baroud convince you that their contacts in Lebanon are solid?

Personally, I didn't have a negotiating channel. I relied on my maternal uncle Ihsan Abou Khalil, Secretary General of the Lebanese Parliament, who is extraordinarily respected and who will try to intervene in this matter.

Conversely, Nagib Zaher, Ibrahim Baroud and Fouad Gandhour had excellent connections. When I began to grow up in the Chirac orbit, I could see that Zaher was gaining influence in Beirut, where he had leading businesses and contacts. He was moving his pawns forward. He introduced me to Shiite religious leaders like Sheikh Adnan Zalghout.

Once Jacques Chirac was appointed cohabitation Prime Minister in April 1986, the issue became one of his priorities.

From there, I made it clear that I had my own ideas on the subject. I wrote a memo setting out the elements that would enable me to claim to be helping him through Adnan Zalghout and the Lebanese networks in Côte d'Ivoire.

Jacques Chirac received the letter via Jean-Claude Laumond, who was shuttling between us. Maurice Ulrich asked to see me. I went to Matignon, making a detour to see Foccart, whose office was opposite the Prime Minister's office.

I told Maurice Ulrich what I thought I could do. He gave me the go-ahead. I then called Zaher, Baroud and Gandhour and told them I was waiting for them in Paris.

Maurice Ulrich asked us to go to Beirut, pointing out that I had an official role in this mission with a diplomatic passport. He urged us to be as discreet as possible, but gave me a telephone number to keep him

89

informed. No authority, not even the French ambassador, was informed of this visit. Present at the meeting, Sheikh Adnan Zalghout returned to Abidjan after the meeting with Ulrich.

In Beirut at the beginning of April, we met all the Shiite religious dignitaries as well as the President of the Lebanese Parliament, Nabih Berri, and other personalities such as Lebanon's pro-Iranian spiritual leader, Sheikh Mohammad Hussein Fadlallah, as well as the aging Ayatollah Mohamed Chamseddine and Abdel Amir Kabalan.

They gave us assurances. At my uncle's request, Nabih Berri received us. Secretary General of the Lebanese Parliament for 25 years, that's no mean feat.

Contacts established, Jacques Chirac travels to Côte d'Ivoire for his very first trip abroad as the new head of government. This was no accident.

It was April 12, 1986. I wasn't on the trip. As I said earlier, relations with Houphouët were exclusively between him and Jacques Foccart. However, I had prepared some language for the Prime Minister, who was welcomed by a head of state, and not just any head of state, at Yamoussoukro airport.

Jacques Chirac took advantage of his presence to meet Nagib Zaher and Fouad Gandhour.

Nagib Zaher confirmed that he was still able to establish contact with the French kidnappers.

Also in April 1986, the same delegation visited Paris again.

Maurice Ulrich received us. Nagib Zaher made it clear that Adnan could make "offers of service". The French authorities had high expectations of him. All these elements were passed on to Charles Pasqua, who became involved in the case.

Minister of the Interior, he took the initiative again.

Not at this stage, as I was still making progress with my team. Let's just say that, no doubt pushed by Jacques Chirac, he was becoming more and more interested in this affair. This complicated my position. Mandated by Chirac, I acted for him and him alone, while continuing to keep Jacques Foccart informed. But, obviously, this did not preclude other interventions such as that of the Minister of the Interior, whose relations with Foccart, it must be admitted, were not the most harmonious.

At this point, Paris asserts that there are no unofficial intermediaries involved in these negotiations. Only official channels are used.

This is obviously untrue. Even the local French ambassador was unaware of our movements.

How far did you think you could go with Nagib Zaher?

Until the liberation, since, during a trip to Beirut, we had received assurances from the Shiite religious leaders of Lebanon that they would do their utmost to help. To give you an idea of our level of contact, it was I who, in 1986, sadly informed Maurice Ulrich of the death of university researcher Michel Seurat.

Prior to yet another mission to Beirut, Jacques Chirac and his chief of staff had asked me to enquire about the situation, as there were worrying rumors of a deterioration in his health. I clearly remember telling Maurice Ulrich that one of the hostages had left. "One less" was our code word. He understood it.

From whom do you have this information?

From Sheikh Mohammad Hussein Fadlallah.

Do these dignitaries have any conditions?

None whatsoever. In retrospect, I think they were very willing. Without any mandate, I spoke in my official capacity, but they knew perfectly well who I represented and who I worked for. They assured us that they were making arrangements. That was enough to reassure us.

Will your intermediation finally lead to contact with the kidnappers?

We never made contact with them, nor did we know the substance of their dealings with religious leaders. It was completely out of our hands. We didn't get involved.

How do you get on with Michel Roussin?

In this case, I only spotted Michel Roussin, whom I obviously knew as Chirac's chief of staff at Paris City Hall, in the corridor leading from

Ulrich's office to his own. Given his background, he was necessarily involved. At what level? A mystery. No doubt a certain number of the protagonists were testing me without my knowledge. It's the law of the underworld.

As for my trips to Beirut, the one in May 1986—a week—was the only one I made with "my team" dominated by Lebanese Shiites from Abidjan. We came back to Paris to report on the trip, after which we all headed back to Côte d'Ivoire. After that, Nagib Zaher and Fouad Gandhour had nothing more to do with the affair. They had gone as far as they could in these difficult negotiations.

What's become of Nagib Zaher?

He's out of the picture. His contacts and channels with the Lebanese in Côte d'Ivoire have failed.

You decide to rely on Sheikh Abdel Monem El-Zein.

I launched the second phase of the negotiations by asking only His Eminence Sheikh Abdel Monem El-Zein, Khalife General of the Ahlul-Bayt, i.e. the Shiites, and head of the Lebanese community in Senegal, whom I had already spoken to Jacques Chirac about. He's the one who prays over my parents' graves and buried mine. That's no mean feat.

He assured me that he could help me, stressing that he was better introduced in Lebanon than Sheikh Adnan, who was considered too young. He also made his support conditional on the green light from my "big brother", Abdou Diouf. Abdou Diouf. Which I got. The Senegalese president was all the more inclined to help Chirac as the latter was the godfather of his daughter, Yacine, which not many people know.

Charles Pasqua takes a closer look at this new intermediary...

Initially, there was talk of organizing a meeting between the two of them in Paris. El-Zein had already established numerous contacts in Beirut. I didn't even know that Jean-Charles Marchiani was involved. It so happened that Charles Pasqua, who was due to pay a visit to Dakar, asked me to set up a meeting with El-Zein on the spot. At the end of the discussion, we drank his traditional "petit whisky".

You prepare the meeting carefully.

It took place in Dakar in 1987, during an official visit by Pasqua. Sheikh El-Zein didn't speak French, so I recruited an interpreter. Everyone was informed, including Abdou Diouf and his Director of Protocol, the extraordinary and late Bruno Diatta[68].

The Senegalese president had put the Minister of the Interior up in the "Queen's Room" of the presidential palace. This was the suite in which Queen Elizabeth and other prestigious guests had slept during their stay in Senegal.

I can still hear Pasqua, who was exceptionally well received, addressing me in a very Pagnolesque way in front of Daniel Leandri:

> "Do you realize, Robert, that I'm going to put my butt where Queen Elizabeth slept!"

Where was the meeting held?

At the Islamic center presided over by El-Zein. There were 200 people in the prayer room. Pasqua greeted everyone before retiring in private. The interpreter was a Christian childhood friend, Mr. Salim Taraf, who had an even better command of Arabic than I did. I had therefore taken all the usual precautions. The hearing took place between the four of us.

Sheikh El-Zein unfolded his program and expressed his desire to visit Beirut, initially on his own. I was designated as his sole interlocutor. Pasqua punctuated this first interview by saying:

> "France will be grateful to you. That's all there is to it."

He reported to Abdou Diouf, before heading back to Paris.

What is his attitude towards you? Does he see you when you ask?

Even though he'd already put his bloodhounds on the trail, he would receive me whenever I asked. Sheikh El-Zein was also welcomed as soon as he thought he had new information. He came to Paris either from Beirut or Dakar, and held a Senegalese diplomatic passport.

---

68. The Senegalese counterpart of George Ouégnin in Côte d'Ivoire, Bruno Diatta was the emblematic chief of protocol of the Senegalese presidency from 1979 until his death on September 21, 2018. He served under the presidencies of Léopold Sédar Senghor, Abdou Diouf, Abdoulaye Wade and Macky Sall.

Sheikh El-Zein calls you every day when he's in Beirut.

On each of his visits to Lebanon, he kept me informed on a daily basis. During a mission in 1987, he told me that things were moving forward and that he wanted to meet Pasqua. I went to meet him at Roissy airport in an unmarked car, with Daniel Leandri. It was the very first time he had met the Minister, in France, at Place Beauvau. He told him he was "very confident". Charles Pasqua, however, felt the whole thing was dragging on.

El-Zein went back to Lebanon on a mission, at the end of which he again asked to see Pasqua in Paris. It was midnight. I still remember that the Minister, annoyed, came down from his private apartments in his robe. El-Zein assured him that the hostages would be freed during his third trip to the Lebanese capital.

Pasqua looked at him, increasingly doubtful. After the interview, he said:

"My friend, your good man is taking us for a ride!"

Hence the entry of Jean-Charles Marchiani.

Nobody told me, for one simple reason: he had told me himself at a meeting in the office of the Minister of the Interior. He even asked me to accompany him to Beirut, while promising to get me a revolver. I rejected both proposals outright.

I was never a member of the Marchiani team and never once traveled with him on this affair. But I knew that he was making progress with the powerful Lebanese businessman Iskandar Safa, who was to become the boss of *Valeurs actuelles* magazine, among others. Safa played a decisive role in the liberation of[69].

Why another team? Wouldn't it complicate negotiations?

Charles Pasqua gradually came to believe that Sheikh El-Zein's pipes were burst. He didn't fully trust him and didn't think he was up to the challenge. He clearly felt that the channel was bogus.

---

69. Born in Beirut, Iskandar Safa (1955-2024) was a Franco-Lebanese businessman and media entrepreneur. In 1992, he bought Constructions Mécaniques de Normandie (CMN). He also owned the Valmonde group of titles, including *Valeurs actuelles*.

Why?

He thought the project was stalled, but I thought the opposite. I knew he was in Lebanon almost all the time, making contacts, negotiating and negotiating. I understand that Pasqua, seeing things dragging on, wanted to set up a parallel team.

Nevertheless, Sheikh El-Zein called me every day to keep me informed of developments. I referred him to Jacques Foccart and Jacques Chirac, as well as to Jean-Pierre Bondil, Comptroller General of the French Armed Forces and deputy director of Michel Aurillac's cabinet.

Aren't you tempted to join the Pasqua team?

I didn't ask. Only once, in his office, did Marchiani suggest that I join her. He even put Iskandar Safa on the phone. We spoke in Arabic. First he asked me to come with them, then he asked me if I knew how to shoot. I refused, but I knew that he was regularly in Lebanon and Syria for negotiations.

Charles Pasqua is not cutting ties with Sheikh El-Zein.

On the contrary, as I would later learn, he kept several irons in the fire, as El-Zein kept him informed and, it seems obvious, passed on information to his own team. In 1987, he told me he wanted to return to Dakar and Abidjan.

He saw El-Zein once again at its center. I had chosen another interpreter, Dr. Kaouk, a Lebanese Shiite, reserve officer in the French army, who worked as a doctor at the French embassy in Dakar. He spoke better Arabic than I did, my good friend Kaouk.

For the first time, money is involved.

Let me stress this point: the only time money was mentioned was during this interview. Sheikh El-Zein has asked to be rewarded for his work. Until now, he had neither asked for nor received anything. Pasqua asked him how much and for what. His interlocutor immediately replied $3 million to finance infrastructure, schools and religious centers for underprivileged children in southern Lebanon. He said so in front of me. The Minister responded favorably on the express condition of obtaining the release of the hostages[70].

---

70. At the time, 18 million francs.

Sheikh El-Zein was instructed to continue his mission. Charles Pasqua left the center to cheers of "Vive Chirac!" and "Vive de Gaulle! We left for Abidjan, where he saw Sheikh Adnan Zalghout at the Hôtel Ivoire, then Nagib Zaher again, and Fouad Gandhour.

A ransom in the form of humanitarian projects.

It's obvious that this could be construed as a disguised ransom, even if, more intimately, I think that Sheikh El-Zein, a pious man, really intended this money, or part of it, for building schools. Months went by. I kept in touch with Pasqua. I also saw Jean-Charles Marchiani, whose children were very close to mine. Jean-Charles remains a friend and our families are linked.

The final event came on May 4 1988, four days before the first presidential election in France, when Marcel Carton, Marcel Fontaine and Jean-Paul Kaufmann were released, following the release of Jean-Louis Normandin and Philippe Rochot on November 27 1987.

To this day, I'm still puzzled by the outcome. Admittedly, the hostages owe their newfound freedom to the Marchiani/Safa tandem. There's no denying that. But much remains unexplained.

Shortly before I saw them on all the televisions in Beirut's Summerland Hotel, I received a call from Sheikh El-Zein telling me I was in a house with hostages. That's when I asked Jean-Pierre Bondil, who was a military man in the Gaullist sense of the word, to join me, begging El-Zein, in Arabic, to hand over Jean-Paul Kaufmann. But he didn't.

We were ready to fly to Cyprus to welcome the French. He cut the conversation short. That evening, the hostages were free. I couldn't stop wondering what route had been taken. I still do.

Later, Sheikh El-Zein will confirm that he is with the hostages.

I repeat: I was at my desk when he called me. I sent for Jean-Pierre Bondil. We put on the loudspeaker and I implored Sheikh El-Zein to put Jean-Paul Kaufman on the phone to provide me with tangible proof. He replied in the negative, but reaffirmed that he was indeed with them in the car—a Mercédès—that took them to the parking lot of Beirut's Summerland Hotel.

There, the Syrian secret service allegedly violently evicted him to get the Frenchmen out of the vehicle and into the establishment in the presence of Jean-Charles Marchiani. Sheikh El-Zein said:

"Your friend Marchiani pushed me around".

Did the Marchiani/Safa duo use Sheikh El-Zein to your detriment?

Jean-Charles Marchiani had no connection with him. I'm sure he didn't. Pasqua had to pass on information to him. Which didn't stop me from congratulating him the very next morning. It was indeed he who, the day before, was on the plane bringing back the hostages.

Charles Pasqua called me the next day to complain about the interviews Sheikh El-Zein was giving to the Lebanese and Arab media, claiming to be the father of the liberation. He was furious and called him a liar. He confided in me that he was "going to take care of him" and even asked me to intercede so that Abdou Diouf would withdraw his Senegalese nationality and diplomatic passport. The Senegalese president refused.

As soon as Charles Pasqua said: "We'll take care of it", what was my reaction? I immediately told Jacques Foccart. He asked me to bring him over from Beirut and give him a return Paris-Dakar ticket. That's when one of his teams brought him back to Paris. I had my secretary, Nathalie Ronce, carry his ticket for him, and I even asked her to wear a headscarf. In Dakar, Sheikh El-Zein continued to make numerous statements to the media, taking credit for the release.

All I knew all along was that Pasqua's networks, led by Jean-Charles Marchiani and Iskandar Safa, were very active and mobilized to secure the hostages' release. Well done! But I must pay tribute to Jean-Pierre Bondil.

Syrian and even Libyan intelligence services must have been aware of Sheikh El-Zein's level of involvement.

Certainly, and without informing me. They knew that El-Zein was seeing Pasqua at the Place Beauvau. My interpretation today is that Sheikh El-Zein gave sensitive, even vital, information to Pasqua's men, who used it to move forward without keeping me informed.

Who finally gets them released?

If we exclude this dirty trick, it's the Marchiani team. We have to be honest. They had the right contacts, in this case Syrian and Libyan intelligence, who weren't part of my network.

Where the matter gets murky is that Jean-Paul Kaufmann himself would later confide that Sheikh El-Zein was in the car in which he was let out. Why did he refuse to put the hostage on the phone? That remains a mystery to me.

Has he been instructed not to put Jean-Paul Kaufmann on the phone?

The most important thing is that the hostages' nightmare has come to an end.

Do you think you were bypassed in this case?

I think I've been double-crossed. We relied on my contact to glean information that was crucial to the progress of the case. But the aim was to free the hostages, and this was done. The day after May 4 1988, Jacques Chirac and Charles Pasqua welcomed them at Villacoublay airport.

Did you ever feel sidelined as a negotiator?

Once the hostages had been freed, Charles Pasqua asked me to intercede with Abdou Diouf to withdraw Sheikh El-Zein's diplomatic passport.

Why this request?

According to him, he tried to sabotage the negotiations.

In what way?

Probably by taking credit for the release of the hostages, in order to receive the expected sum, even though this operation had been unwound through another channel. It was following this request to withdraw my passport that I started receiving death threats from Beirut.

In *La Menace*[71], then in an investigation for *Libération* in 1990[72], journalist Pierre Péan, Jacques Foccart's biographer and a long-time

---

71. Pierre Péan, *La Menace*, Fayard, Paris, 1987.
72. "Otages: histoire d'une dette impayée", *Libération*, February 28, 1990.

friend of yours, asserts that the $3 million was never paid to Sheikh El-Zein after the hostages were freed. He even accused you of not having paid him.

I immediately alerted Charles Pasqua and Jean-Charles Marchiani to this. They advised me to "let it run its course".

Sheikh El-Zein accuses you of keeping the money.

The whole thing is grotesque and serious. Who was supposed to hand over this sum if not the French government? If it had been embezzled, they would have immediately lodged a complaint against me. But there was nothing. No trace of any accusation. Curious, isn't it?

This sum could have been handed over by the intermediaries, yourself or Marchiani.

And who would have given me this money? Can anyone claim to have given me $3 million? Not a soul.

Why didn't you file a libel suit against Pierre Péan?

I didn't even know such nonsense had been published, otherwise I'd never have met him again.

He has published an entire book on the subject and quotes you extensively. You couldn't ignore it.

I repeat: can anyone say that he handed over or transferred $3 million to me? Nobody, because all these rumors are unfounded. The only thing I managed to do after the hostages were freed was to get Sheikh El-Zein to come to Paris from Beirut so that I could give him his ticket back to Senegal. Once again, it was Foccart who broke the deadlock.

How could Sheikh El-Zein have obtained the hostages' release?

I don't have an answer to that question.

The hostage affair resurfaced two years later with new revelations by Pierre Péan. In *Mémoires impubliables*, his *post-mortem* book[73], he writes: "*In February 1990, Robert Bourgi was frightened. He received*

---

73. Pierre Péan, *Mémoires impubliables*, Albin Michel, March 2020.

threats from Beirut, which he took very seriously. He had, in fact, initiated the negotiations with Sheikh Zein that led to the release of Kaufmann, Carton and Fontaine on May 4 1988. Zein, who heads the Shiite community in Dakar, is very vocal against France and Bourgi. Bourgi obviously knows that I'm the journalist who has been closest to the truth in this case, and that I've already mentioned his role. I'm very suspicious when he brings me what I consider to be a very big state secret. But I soon received confirmation, both from Sheikh Zein and from former members of Aurillac's cabinet. On February 28, 1990, Libération's shocking front page headline about a photo of Sheikh Zein with Pasqua writing, was not at all tongue-in-cheek: on the bangs of essential contacts with Iran, secret negotiations had probably led to an agreement between France and the kidnappers of the Lebanese hostages. The chosen intermediary, Sheikh Zein, was to collect $3 million and pass it on to his Beirut correspondents. The sum promised by Pasqua was never paid, and this unfulfilled commitment may partly explain the September 19, 1989 attack on the UTA DC-10. Four whole pages follow, in which I tell the incredible story of Jean-Charles Marchiani, the great mastermind who **ultimately** *took in the hostages on behalf of France. I say that Marchiani did nothing more than brutally push Sheikh Zein, who had just received the hostages brought by the kidnappers to the parking lot of* Beirut's Summerland Hotel"[74]. **Péan confirms that you have indeed been bypassed in this affair.**

My answer is quite straightforward: I've never denied my role in this matter, nor the contacts I've made, including that of El-cheikh Zein. I've been explicit enough on the subject. The fact remains that I'm still trying to find out who freed the hostages. I mentioned the meetings between Zein and Pasqua in Dakar and Paris, closely followed by that with Abdou Diouf.

Once again, my doubts stem from the fact that El-cheikh Zein did not put Jean-Claude Kaufmann on the phone on the afternoon of May 4, 1988. I was stuck in Paris, obliged to follow all this from a distance. I can still see myself, in front of Jean-Pierre Bondil, asking him to confirm the number of hostages and insisting that he put me through to the journalist. "Eminence, put me through to the man with the glasses," I begged. Then

---

74. *Ibid*. p. 249 ff.

the line went dead. That same evening, like all French people, I would see the arrival of the ex-hostages at Summerland with Marchiani.

The next day, Sheikh El-Zein confirmed to me that he had been "hustled" at that very moment by Syrian intelligence men. Who freed the hostages? El-Zein? But it's also possible that the Marchiani/Safa team accelerated the release process. To sum up: I've never had proof that El-Zein, my main contact and emissary, was the last man.

Pierre Péan implies that, feeling cheated in this case, you are providing him with highly sensitive information on the explosion of the UTA DC-10 over the Ténéré on September 19, 1989, an attack that is allegedly linked to the non-payment of the $3 million. Here's what he wrote: *"Bourgi, who finds himself in a delicate position, telephones me from Libreville to tell me that he is ready to go further and give a long interview to* Libération. *On his return, I see him twice. His only concern at the time was to protect Chirac, who didn't know all the ins and outs of the affair [...]. We did a very long interview, a copy of which, annotated by Bourgi himself, is still in my archives. Overall, he confirms my investigation into the link between the non-payment of the ransom and the attack on the UTA DC-10. [...] The day before or the day before, he calls me to stop everything and to tell me the exact opposite of what he had told me the day before. Which boiled down to 'Pasqua didn't promise anything'. The road to the truth is long. One of Pasqua's policemen put the barrel of a revolver to his kidneys and asked him to stop talking about the hostage affair and to meet Pierre Péan.*

Very incomplete and riddled with errors. I knew Pierre, a friend, very well, and I held him in the highest esteem—may he rest in peace—but much of what he writes is false. I confirm once again that Charles Pasqua promised in front of me to hand over $3 million to Sheikh El-Zein if the hostages were released. When I was in Dakar, Abidjan or Lebanon, there was never any question of other matters. Let's put those 3 million in whatever terms we like. Initially, it was not considered a ransom. I'm delighted that the hostages have been released, but I can't confirm that their jails were opened with one of the keys to El-Zein. There was a lot of tension surrounding this issue. I can't deny that.

With serious threats against you.

One day in 1990, I was sitting in the bar of the Prince de Galles—not the Georges V—when Charles Pasqua's diplomatic adviser, Bernard Guillet[75], came up to me, accompanied by a man introduced as a "collaborator" of the Minister of the Interior. Guillet kissed me before the other man slipped his hand into his jacket and warned me:

> "It's time you stopped telling stories. You know what will happen to you if you continue to spread things about Pasqua."

I turned back to Bernard Guillet, stunned, and asked if this was indeed a death threat. The individual reiterated:

> "Stop hitting Pasqua."

So I was very explicit:

> "1. Bernard, listen to me. If anything happens to me, you seem to forget that I have protection somewhere.
> 2. That my in-laws are Corsican.
> 3. I'm going to warn people tonight."

After I left him, I rushed to Jacques Foccart to tell him what had happened. I then called Omar Bongo:

> "Dad, this is what just happened. These threats are not to be taken lightly. You know better than anyone that I've never spoken ill of Pasqua."

To which he replied:

> "I'll take care of it, son."

That same evening, he spoke to Pasqua on the phone. During the night, he asked me to go down to Libreville, telling me that the problem "had been settled with Charles".

---

75. Born in 1945, Bernard Guillet was Charles Pasqua's diplomatic advisor at the Ministry of the Interior from 1986 to 1988 and from 1993 to 1995, as well as at the Hauts-de-Seine General Council. Involved in several politico-financial affairs, including the financing of Rassemblement pour la France (1999-2007) and Angolagate. He was investigated by Judge Philippe Courroye in connection with the transfer of funds to the France-Orient-Maghreb association.

How else can you explain these threats, if not by the fact that the whole of Paris, especially journalists, believe that, having been cheated in this affair, you were about to deliver information on the UTA DC-10 bombing? A sort of revenge.

I knew nothing. As proof, the police never approached me and I was never questioned by any judicial authority or magistrate, even though there were many complaints from the victims' families in this case. This is the only answer I can give.

The only thing is, a few days after the hostages were freed, I received these threats on the phone. I lived on rue Saint-Dominique. As I've already mentioned, my uncle in Beirut then took over the business.

These threats come as a surprise, given that you are a friend of Bernard Guillet.

He even got me to join his France-Orient-Maghreb association, set up with Charles Pasqua. This earned me my first summons to Rue des Rentiers[76].

Why?

This association was in the crosshairs of Judge Philippe Courroye, due to suspicious movements of funds. I remember being questioned by Major Keck, who had been appointed by the judge. A good man. Immediately after my interrogation, having realized that I had been the victim of a frame-up, we went for a coffee. His daughter was taking her A-levels, as was mine. I bought that day's edition of *Le Monde* and what do I learn? The indictment of Bernard Guillet, notably for "concealment of misappropriation of corporate assets". Luckily for me, I had paid my membership fee by cheque. I immediately withdrew from this structure.

Why did you join this association when the members of the board were practically all in the crosshairs of the investigators?

I didn't know her. I wanted to help her, because I thought she was a reliable way of strengthening ties between Paris and the Maghreb. I was

---

76. Nicknamed the "Château des Rentiers", the financial brigade was historically located at 122, rue du Château-des-Rentiers, in Paris (13th arrondissement). Since 2017, it has been located at rue du Bastion (17th arrondissement).

at peace. I had paid 10,000 francs by cheque. You'll always find a trace of everything I've done in my career to do with money.

In everyone's eyes, I'm the perfect herald of Françafrique, yet my name doesn't appear in any of the major scandals linked to this system. From the Elf affair to Angolagate and the Biens Mal Acquis affair, Bourgi's name has never appeared. Curious, isn't it?

Why did Sheikh El-Zein put you in charge?
I had been his intermediary since the beginning of the affair. He knew that I had introduced Charles Pasqua to him and many other personalities.

Could it be that Charles Pasqua, having promised him the $3 million, passed the buck to you?
To say that this money stayed with me is shameful. You can imagine that if Pasqua had entrusted me with such a sum to give to Sheikh El-Zein, the latter would have immediately warned him in case of non-payment. And I would have been called to account. It's all part of a plot. One of the many that have marked my career.

The fact remains that Sheikh El-Zein has received nothing.
I can confirm this.

His discontent is therefore legitimate
Yes.

In his investigation for *Libération*, Pierre Péan claims to have interviewed Charles Pasqua, who denied any involvement on your part in the hostages' release.
I don't understand this attitude or these denials. It's pure fabrication. But why? I still don't know to this day. He met Sheikh El-Zein twice through me. Public meetings. My ice-age with Jacques Chirac is clearly linked to this episode. Jacques Foccart, who saw me as extremely upset by this climate, had to make his own inquiries. After learning the truth, he was responsible for the thaw with the Mayor of Paris.

Do you keep in touch with Sheikh El-Zein?
I never saw him again, not even when my family was in mourning.

Didn't he warn you about the DC-10 affair? Doesn't he tell you that something serious could happen if you don't pay?

He told me absolutely nothing, assuming he knew anything at all, since the affair moved on to Libya. On the other hand, I remember as if it were yesterday the death threats I received on the phone, then at the Prince of Wales.

Why don't the judges stick their noses into Club 89's activities and funding?

I have no idea. I've never been questioned or summoned on this point.

How do you view Charles Pasqua's role in this case?

In 2011, when I wrote about the financing of political parties by African heads of state in *Le JDD*, I asked to be heard by the financial division. I remember that, in the eyes of the magistrate who questioned me, two networks coexisted in Africa: those of Foccart and those of Pasqua.

Just as he had admitted that Foccart's galaxy was not involved in any interest in the release of the hostages, Pasqua's was "charged" by the judges.

As the setbacks of Bernard Guillet, Jean-Charles Marchiani and Charles Pasqua himself would later show.

What worried me most in this case were the blatant death threats. On the phone, they would ask me "where's the money?", while telling me to be very "careful". Fortunately, my uncle in Beirut managed to sort out the problem and tell these people that I had nothing to do with paying any ransom.

Although Jean-Charles Marchiani was part of the Pasqua team in the French hostage affair, you kept in close contact with him afterwards. In particular, you were one of his regular visitors at the Santé prison, following his indictment for a €1.4 million kickback received, between 1991 and 1994, as part of a deal between the Vanderlande company and Aéroport de Paris.

We were already basically friends. My wife is Corsican like Jean-Charles. Whenever they met, they talked about Corsica and Corsica. They would talk about their common acquaintances, such as Prefect Bernard Tomasini, Jean Tiberi and so many others. Our respective children grew

105

up together and are friends. Our families are intertwined. My wife and I used to spend long days in Saint-Florent, where Jean-Charles and his wife Christiane own a house. So it seemed natural and normal to visit Jean-Charles when he was going through legal problems. Judge Philippe Courroye gave us this opportunity. We would spend an hour talking to him in the voting booth. We'd ask him what we could do to help him, what cases or dishes we could bring him. But we weren't his lawyers. We never talked about the circumstances that led to him being charged.

Chapter 10: Crossing the Desert

Does the hostage crisis give you greater influence?

Not really, since a few days after their release, Jacques Chirac was knocked out by François Mitterrand in the presidential election. In this case, Jean-Charles Marchiani, with the help of Iskandar Safa, was a successful intermediary. I realized that after Nagib Zaher, I had bet on another unreliable personality.

Back at Paris City Hall after his defeat, Chirac asked me what I was going to do. Bernard de Montferrand suggested that I be appointed as a judge in an administrative court in Lyon. Horror! I kindly turned down the offer.

The same Chirac then asked me to work for him. Help! Fortunately, I refused. I would have found myself in the middle of the fictitious employment affair. I stayed with the RPR and the Club 89. Even Michel Aurillac had lost his constituency.

The day after the presidential election, his cabinet dissolved itself.

And quite violently too. He was stripped of everything overnight. No car, nothing. I said to him:

> "Michel, my car is here. The same as yours: a Renault 25 GTX. I'll give you a lift."

You then register with the National Employment Agency. A totally implausible and even humiliating drop-off point for you, isn't it?

But it's true, as my unemployment benefit statements attest. I clocked in every month for three years alongside foreign workers. But it was my fault. I had refused the magistrate's post and Chirac's offer to join him.

Nevertheless, I remained a delegate for Club 89 and continued to travel on my brother's behalf.

René, for whom you become legal advisor.

He was head of Medex Africa. He took me under his wing. I travelled all over the continent in search of contracts for the pharmaceutical industry. This enabled me to continue to cultivate my networks.

This was followed by a troubled period with Jacques Chirac.

I didn't hear from him for several years. I'm still trying to find out why. From 1990 to 1993, there was a polar cold between us. A terrible time for me. I bumped into him quite by chance, in January 1993, at a Club 89 meeting. He refused my handshake with a frightened look on his face. Jacques Foccart did what he could to reassure me that things would work out.

In the same month, however, you seal your reunion.

I found myself back at Club 89 when my secretary gave me an urgent call. It was him.

"Mr. Mayor, I was like a dying flower waiting for the sun," I told him.

Jacques Foccart was in on the secret. The next day, I was received in a salon at Paris City Hall. He came in. We embraced as if the years of tension had suddenly disappeared. I was as happy as a kid at Christmas. We then moved on to the Salon Bleu, where he spoke of a cabal against me. Foccart had apparently given him a clearer picture.

Whose cabal?

I wouldn't know. You journalists are funny. He advised me not to try to understand. I turned to the Dean, who confirmed that I wouldn't get any answers. We decided to work together again.

Wasn't this the result of the investigations into the attack on the UTA DC-10?

Jacques Foccart never said anything on the subject. I didn't even know if it came from France or Africa. But it must have been serious enough for Chirac to categorically refuse to speak to me for several years. This episode was particularly painful for me. It wasn't all so easy for me.

After his defeat in 1988, did Jacques Foccart express skepticism about Jacques Chirac's ability to one day occupy the Élysée Palace?

He never did. He remained loyal to him until his last breath, except that he no longer believed in Pasqua's polls, which had shown him to be the winner. By 1990, however, the schism between Pasqua/Séguin and Chirac was blatantly obvious. As proof of this, one morning I had Philippe Séguin, accompanied by his friend Étienne Pinte, for breakfast at my home. At the time, I lived on rue Saint-Dominique. He had this to say:

> "You know, Robert, Chirac promises a lot, but doesn't deliver much."

How do you explain this loyalty?

Foccart was a definitive Gaullist. He never doubted for a moment Chirac's ability to become president one day. Nevertheless, it should be remembered that he knew Édouard Balladur very well, having worked with him in Georges Pompidou's cabinet.

On this point, I'd like to reveal what few people know: before the first round of the 1995 presidential election, on April 23, Jacques Foccart informed Jacques Chirac of his desire to meet Édouard Balladur in the event of a second round.

I was personally responsible for organizing the meeting, with the help of Nicolas Bazire[77], Édouard Balladur's chief of staff and chargé de mission at Matignon, whom I scouted out at his home in Cité Vaneau. Enchanted by the proposal, he mentioned it to the Prime Minister. The lunch in question went remarkably well. It was a tête-à-tête. Balladur was exceptionally considerate towards his host, already overcome by illness. He walked him to the elevator, holding his arm, and then to the steps of Matignon.

And Foccart confided this to him:

> "Edouard, in the event that you are present in the second round, I want to assure you that I will bring you everything I represent."

That evening, we returned to Paris City Hall. Jacques Chirac was delighted with the lunch.

---

77. Born in 1957, Nicolas Bazire is a senior French civil servant and businessman. In 2020, he was sentenced to 5 years' imprisonment, two of which were suspended, in the Karachi affair, linked to retrocommissions in connection with contracts for the sale of frigates to Pakistan. He is appealing this decision. The trial is scheduled for June 2024.

Is the Pasqua/Séguin duo approaching you for African "affairs" in the run-up to this election?

Club 89 was the target of a veritable takeover attempt on his part. Michel Aurillac had been instructed by Jacques Chirac not to allow Philippe Séguin to sit on the board of directors. I mobilized all my networks and contacts to ensure that this was the case on the African side. All the members of the club's Abidjan branch voted against the appointment. The Pasqua/Séguin team knew of my loyalty to Chirac, but Pasqua was really trying to short-circuit the 89 Club, of which I was still the official tenant**.**

Are the same people from the Pasqua "networks" solicit African heads of state?

Of course, but this doesn't mean that these presidents have gone over the edge. Whether Omar Bongo, Abdou Diouf, Blaise Compaoré or Denis Sassou Nguesso, they remained Chiraquiens. But beware: in spite of everything, they showed a great deal of consideration for Pasqua, who was much appreciated. In Brazzaville, Libreville and even Ouagadougou, he felt right at home. Remember that it was in Burkina Faso, in September 1994, that he sent back some thirty individuals, mostly Algerians, detained in a military camp at Folembray, in the Aisne region, and considered to be "Islamists".

At the time, I met a lot of members of his "cell" in Africa whom I wasn't used to seeing. Daniel Léandri, for example, or François Antona. It wasn't always easy, but I had Omar Bongo's atomic umbrella over my head. It also has to be said that no French political figure could match the quasi-mystical dimension of Chirac, and especially Foccart, in French-speaking Africa.

Chapter 11: Phantom Lawyer, Real Lobbyist

Like Jacques Chirac, you were losing ground after the 1988 presidential election. You became a lobbyist.

I never lost momentum, as you say. In fact, my activities for Medex Afrique served as a cover. Behind the scenes, I continued to work for presidents such as Omar Bongo, Abdou Diouf and the others mentioned above. My working method was taking shape. I became close to people like Pierre Salinger. I continued to work a lot with Michel Aurillac, a new partner at Vovan & Associés, as a lawyer.

Your legend is built methodically.

For African presidents, I organized contacts with leading French politicians. I was the *go-between*. Even though the Left was in power, I pulled a lot of levers. I was an intermediary, an intercessor, a go-between. I started setting up a whole bunch of lunches, interviews and meetings at my office. For example, it was I who introduced Jacques Foccart to Laurent Gbagbo. It had to be done! On paper, this meeting was unthinkable.

Why become a lawyer?

Few people know this, but it was Foccart himself who put me on the trail at the end of 1992. He wanted me to obtain some sort of official status.

> "Robert, Medex Afrique and the ANPE have had enough! You're a doctor of law and you've taught. You need to formalize your activity. Take the lawyer's oath."

He had also found out that I was exempt from the course.

Isn't it rather because, since all future lawyers are subject to a morality investigation and a tax inspection, practising this profession is a way of clearing yourself of all suspicion?

I had nothing to reproach myself for, but after the cabal that Chirac had told me about, I have to admit that this in-depth morality—and tax—investigation came at just the right time. Indeed, it was not in vain.

If Foccart advised me to become a lawyer, it was because he wanted to protect me in some way. It gave a tremendous boost to my career. He knew perfectly well that I needed a different dimension.

Had you never thought of doing this job before?

No, I wanted a title, a function.

You took your oath before the Paris Court of Appeal on May 26, 1993. However, you will never plead.

Like many others, starting with Dominique de Villepin. I immediately set up my own practice on avenue Pierre 1er de Serbie. My wife was a lawyer, as was Michel Aurillac. I became more of a "lawyer-lobbyist". Numerous personalities and companies began to approach me. They were aware of my extensive address book. If there was a dispute, I would sometimes refer them to Catherine. I'd open the doors, she'd handle the files.

You continue your missions, like Roland Dumas on the left.

With one difference: I wasn't on the judges' radar...

From then on, you're Africa's contact in Paris.

I've become indispensable. I receive everyone: presidents, their staffs, their families, officials, senior civil servants, lawyers, representatives of state bodies, opponents and even religious dignitaries. My missions consist in passing messages that are more or less encrypted. I bypass official diplomacy, which, by the way, gets me into a lot of trouble.

How do you monetize your address book and intermediaries?

Based on the American model. It's nothing more or less than what lobbyists do in Washington. I had to make a living, I wasn't being philanthropic.

112

The higher up the hierarchy of requests, the higher the fees.

That's obvious.

Take the example of Pascal Lissouba, president of Congo-Brazzaville from 1992 to 1997, weakened and unappreciated by Paris for threatening to turn to the Americans. What "services" did he receive?

I first saw him at Omar Bongo's Moroccan salon. After bringing me to Libreville, he had arranged to meet me in this room. I can still see Lissouba sitting there, his hair white. A very cordial relationship quickly developed between us. I always had a good relationship with him, even if it embarrassed Denis Sassou Nguesso, who was very close to Chirac and father-in-law of Omar Bongo.

He was looking to restore his reputation in Paris.

With Michel Aurillac, in association with personalities such as Pierre Moussa, former head of the World Bank, we set up an operation aimed at restoring his image, in addition to a communications campaign. I opened every door.

Aurillac and Moussa were commissioned to carry out an audit of the Congo's public accounts, in which I did not participate. I'm not an economist or a financier. I know how to collect and spend money, but I don't know how to audit government accounts. I was in charge of communications and public relations.

According to journalists Antoine Glaser and Stephen Smith, this mission was billed at over $20 million[78].

It's all very, very, very exaggerated and makes you smile.

The operation obviously didn't come to fruition, but it was the original *deal*, with the *nec plus ultra* of a visit to General de Gaulle's tomb.

It was Jacques Foccart who accompanied him by helicopter. I'd whispered the idea to Pascal Lissouba and Claudine Munari over lunch at the Crillon. I told the Congolese president that it would be a good idea to go

---

78. Smith Stephen and Glaser Antoine, *Ces Messieurs Afrique 2. Des réseaux aux lobbies*, Calmann-Lévy, Paris, 1997, pp. 34-63.

to Colombey-les-deux-Églises. The Quai d'Orsay did a thousand and one contortions to scupper the trip.

It was unthinkable, *even more so* with Foccart on board. Can you imagine? Even sub-claquering, he was still fiercely opposed by diplomats. It was appalling. Fortunately, Pascal Lissouba categorically refused to make the trip without him.

A true rehabilitation.

So much so that Sassou Nguesso blamed me. He lived in his apartment on Avenue Rapp in Paris. He was living in a kind of golden exile after the Congolese national conference and his defeat in the August 1992 presidential election in Brazzaville. He worked on his return by consolidating his networks in France.

When I went to see him at his home, the day after Lissouba's move, he remarked:

"So, Robert, you're taking Lissouba to Colombey with Jacques?"

I replied:

"Denis, you have to understand certain things..."

Frankly, you have to know how to have fun. (laughs)

Chapter 12: Operation Rescue Mobutu

With Michel Aurillac, also a lawyer for the Accor hotel group, you repeat the same operation with Mobutu Sese Seko. The size of Zaire and its ailing president, discredited after the repression of the "March of Hope" in February 1992 and weakened by a rebellion, make this mission all the more sensitive.

This was a crucial issue. Michel Aurillac, Jacques Foccart and I constantly made it clear that it was in France's interest to safeguard Mobutu or, at the very least, to find a pacification solution with a cohabitation Prime Minister like Léon Kengo wa Dondo[79].

Bruno Delaye, head of the Élysée Palace's Africa unit, and his collaborator Dominique Pin, played a fundamental role in Mobutu's return to "frequentation". They understood what was at stake, even though the Zairean president was already weakened by prostate cancer. Bruno Delaye is the son of diplomat Raoul Delaye, one of Jacques Foccart's men and a great ambassador, particularly to Upper Volta. Bruno Delaye and Foccart conversed frequently.

It's no less important to say that Bruno Delaye always opened the doors of 2, rue de l'Élysée to me, unlike many other Africa advisors. I often had lunch with him. When I arrived at this address, the diplomats' eyes would glaze over. I was the wolf in the sheepfold.

How did you get to know Mobutu?

In the early 1990s, I met him through the Cameroonian businessman Henri Damase Omgba, who was very close to Paul Biya and Jacques Foccart. He passed away in 2013, aged 76. It was he who introduced me to

---

79. Born in 1935, Prime Minister from July 6, 1994 to April 2, 1997, then President of the Senate from 2007 to 2019.

Ngawali Mobutu in his apartment in Neuilly-sur-Seine, who introduced me to his father. He will be present on my trip to Gbadolite.

Do you already do favors for his family?

Obtaining visas, finding schools for the children... I looked after Bobi Ladawa, the Marshal's second wife. I arranged visits to the Bichat hospital to see Niwa, Mobutu's eldest son, who was seriously ill[80]. I couldn't do this without the approval of Jacques Foccart, who called Bruno Delaye and the Minister of the Interior directly, even though he was a leftist.

Mobutu was hated by the left.

Here again, Foccart played an essential role. How did he do it? By raising awareness among Jacques Chirac, now Mayor of Paris once again[81], of the importance for France of "keeping an eye on" Africa's largest French-speaking country and preventing its implosion. Which explains Foccart's trip with me to Gbadolite, Mobutu's pharaonic palace in the middle of the bush, in August 1994.

One of his last trips to Africa.

The ultimate "coup". This trip, on August 10 and 11, 1994, was preceded by that of the General Secretary of the Quai d'Orsay, Bertrand Dufourcq. I borrowed an Aeroleasing plane with Jean-Claude Pelois, Jacques Chirac's security officer. Leaving Le Bourget, we stopped off at Toulon-Hyères airport, where Jacques Foccart boarded. A nurse accompanied us, as he was already feeling quite tired.

Once in Gbadolite, Mobutu's protocol put us up in a villa, then we had lunch with the president, going over all the topical issues: his relations with France, especially with Rwanda, where since April a serious genocide had been taking place with millions of refugees in the east of the country; his relations with South African President Frederik de Klerk; and his relations with the new Prime Minister Léon Kengo wa Dondo, appointed a few days earlier on July 6.

---

80. Born in 1955 in Kinshasa, he died on September 17, 1994 at the Bichat-Claude Bernard hospital.
81. Jacques Chirac was first elected mayor of Paris in March 1977, then re-elected in March 1983 and March 1989 until May 16, 1995.

This trip to Gbadolite had been preceded, before Léon Kengo wa Dondo's appointment as head of government, by a meeting between the latter and Bruno Delaye and Dominique Pin at the Élysée Palace, and also with Jacques Chirac at Paris City Hall. I remember that Foccart asked the future Prime Minister to be a loyal and faithful collaborator of the Maréchal. He then telephoned Mobutu to assure him that all guarantees had been given by his head of government for a peaceful cohabitation. Then Chirac sent us to Gbadolite. Mobutu agreed.

I would like to point out that, although the French emissaries obtained the appointment of Kengo wa Dondo, it was not immediately a foregone conclusion. Opposing them were Honoré Ngbanda Nzambo, alias "Terminator"[82], Félix Vunduawe Te Pemako, Mobutu's cabinet director, and several generals.

During our interview with Mobutu Sese Seko, he also recounted incidents between his head of government and the Governor of the Central Bank of Zaire, who had been suspended from his post by the Prime Minister. Finally, he stressed his concern that the new government should succeed, while wishing Zaire a return to international prominence. For Foccart, Zaire was not a small country. It was vital, even vital, to save this regime in the face of the simmering Anglophone threat.

Apart from this lunch, there were other interviews. Over 7 hours in all. We had breakfast on August 11, from 8:30 to 10 a.m., followed by another extended lunch from 12:45 to 2 p.m. Mobutu hammered home the point that he had politically imposed Kengo wa Dondo on his supporters, on the political forces backing him at a time when the head of government's party was residual in the National Assembly. Then, recalling the importance of reviving economic policy, he dwelt at length on the forthcoming presidential election.

I remember perfectly that, while he was certain of his victory, he wanted an irreproachable control and observation process to be put in place. He was confident, as his party, the Mouvement populaire de la révolution (MPR), was the only one to cover the whole country. He felt at home

---

82. A dominant figure in Mobutu's security sphere, Honoré Ngbanda was Minister-Counsellor, Zaire's Ambassador to Israel, then Head of Intelligence from 1985 to 1990, before becoming the Zairean President's political advisor and Minister of Defense from 1990.

everywhere. He even told us that he was considering reappointing Jean Nguza Karl-i-Bond as post-presidential Prime Minister[83].

All these talks were part of the process of rehabilitating Mobutu. The United States resumed its cooperation after these visits. Belgium followed suit. The President of Zaire also spoke at length about Nelson Mandela, recalling that he had never ceased to support and finance him since his release from prison, and that he had received him at his home in Goma. He pointed out that Nelson Mandela's actions merited greater flexibility. Finally, he regularly expressed his fear of seeing Rwanda and Burundi fall into the English-speaking orbit. A fear shared by François Mitterrand.

How did the interviews with Léon Kengo wa Dondo turn out?

There were two: the first without the presence of the Head of State, and the second with Mobutu, his daughter Ngawali, her father's political advisor, and myself. The Prime Minister assured us of his loyalty to the Marshal. He put an end to rumours that he intended to run against him in the presidential elections.

He also assured me that he did not want to financially strangle the country in order to weaken the regime. His decision to thank the Governor of the Central Bank of Zaire was a response to his desire to put an end to the systematic plundering of this institution's assets by two clearly identified figures: Mobutu's chief of staff and one of his special advisors, who were making regular withdrawals at very short intervals in the "name of the President". Throughout my stay, I was particularly touched by Mobutu's consideration for me. He came to see me in person at my villa and drove the car I was in himself.

Chirac was not yet in power. Who convinces François Mitterrand of the need to restore Mobutu?

Jacques Foccart, with the decisive help of Bruno Delaye. In this capacity, he had already secured Mobutu's invitation to the 5th Summit of Heads of State and Government of Countries Using French in Common, held in Mauritius from October 16 to 18, 1993. The apotheosis, the real rehabilitation, was of course the invitation to the France-Africa summit

---

83. A native of Léopoldville and member of the MPR, Jean Nguza Karl-i-Bond (1938-2003) was First State Commissioner of Zaire (1980-1981) and Prime Minister from November 25, 1991 to August 15, 1992.

in Biarritz on November 7 and 8, 1994. It was there that the dimension of François Mitterrand became clear to me. He was bidding farewell to Africa. We had known for a long time that he was ill. More than 50 African heads of state were in attendance.

Have you known Jean-Christophe Mitterrand since Nouakchott?

Rather, in Lomé, when he was a correspondent for AFP. I saw him several times. I liked him. He also had an excellent audience in Mauritania, his other country of journalistic assignment.

On May 7 1988, the eve of the French presidential election, Michel Aurillac and I met at Pointe-Denis off the coast of Libreville. That same evening, during a meeting with Omar Bongo, the latter asked us:

> "So, who's going to pass?"
> "Mr. Chairman, my marabout says he's my father!" replied Jean-Christophe.
> "And what does Bourgi's marabout say?"
> "Dad, mine is much less optimistic" (laughs).

As with Pascal Lissouba and Congo-Brazzaville, Mobutu's rehabilitation came at a high price. An audit of the Bank of Zaire was carried out by Michel Aurillac. For your part, you set up communication campaigns.

Nothing could be more normal. Consult a general practitioner and you'll be charged €30. See an eminent professor, and it's €300. My contact levels were exceptional, but I didn't know how much Aurillac or Moussa received. I, on the other hand, knew what I was getting. And everything was duly declared to the tax authorities. I'm surprised that journalists in search of sensations have never investigated my income or delved into my tax returns. I'll make them available to them.

It was important for Mobutu, who had been dropped by the United States and Belgium, to remain in the French-speaking orbit.

Once again, this strategy owes much to Jacques Foccart's intervention, relayed by Bruno Delaye. Paris revives Mobutu.

When did his invitation to Biarritz become official?

From October 1994, a month before the summit. Bruno Delaye asked me to inform him personally that an invitation would be sent to him via the Zairean ambassador to Paris, Raymond Ramazani Baya[84]. François Mitterrand agreed.

You are multiplying your missions for the President of Zaire. Another one is being set up with the former American Africa man and diplomat, Herman Jay Cohen[85].

I met him through Pierre Salinger. I met him two or three times in the United States. He was already an official lobbyist. He came to Paris with a deep desire to meet Jacques Foccart, who was more than willing to receive him.

We wanted to make the Americans aware of the French approach to Zaire. Despite the excesses of the regime, we could not decently let this major French-speaking country in Central Africa go adrift, on pain of a sub-regional conflagration. Foccart was also working to rehabilitate Mobutu in the United States. It was there, for the first time, that I heard the name of William Lehfeld, US ambassador to Kinshasa, but above all the CIA's man on the spot.

You set up a communications contract between yourself, Herman Cohen and a certain Max-Olivier Cahen, a Belgian, son of the senior civil servant and diplomat Alfred Cahen, who was an intimate of Mobutu.

There was a contract, of course. I never met Ambassador Cahen, who had played a prominent role with Mobutu.

This contract amounts to $600,000, which you have divided equally among yourselves.

Affirmative, it was divided into three equal parts.

---

84. Ambassador of Zaire to France from 1990 to 1996. He later became his country's Minister of Foreign Affairs and International Cooperation.
85. Assistant Secretary of State for African Affairs under the Clinton administration, Herman Cohen founded Cohen & Woods International.

Do you approach the likes of Jimmy Carter?

No, we mainly saw White House personalities and a senator influential in African affairs.

How did Mobutu react when he arrived in Mauritius in 1993?

Very humbly. Having not seen his peers for a long time, he was apprehensive about their reception. François Mitterrand was extremely polite. So did Jacques Toubon, Minister of Culture and Francophony. He had lunch with the Marshal in his suite at the Royal Palm. Mitterrand then arranged to meet him in Biarritz.

Prior to the France-Africa summit, Mobutu received guests in his apartments on Avenue Foch in Paris.

Yes, and one man once again played a crucial role: Bernard de Montferrand, now diplomatic adviser to Édouard Balladur. Before the summit, I organized a lunch between him and Ngawali Mobutu at my office. On my recommendation, the Minister of Foreign Affairs, Hervé de Charrettes, also met with the Marshal on Avenue Foch. I had mentioned the importance of such a meeting to de Montferrand over lunch. For those who know this diplomat through and through, he almost choked, but he understood, from the look on my face, the importance of my request.

During the interview, President Mobutu, an extremely cultured man with a keen interest in the great French families, retraced the entire history of the Charrettes line. It was impressive. The minister was stunned:

> "Monsieur le Maréchal, I never knew you were so steeped in French culture."
>
> "It's not just culture, Mr. Minister. It's also about food and wine, both of which I adore. Robert knows all about them."

Then it was off to Biarritz with a few complications.

Why?

Minister, Jacques Toubon asked me for a favor before heading off to Biarritz:

> "I don't give a damn about taking a scheduled flight! Robert, couldn't you arrange a plane for me?"
>
> "Listen, Jacques, I'll give it a try."

I informed Mobutu, who immediately agreed. I'm not very fond of burying a man without saying what we owe him. And so Jacques Toubon, Minister of the French Republic, and his entire delegation, including myself, boarded a plane chartered by the President of Zaire himself!

Before the summit opened, I insisted that he go and thank him. Which he did, courteously and respectfully.

"Jacques, you have a friend in me," Mobutu told him.

Toubon, who had to prepare the big party afterwards, turned to me and asked me to come along with his advisor Maurice Portiche. I was surprised, as I was an unofficial personality. When we reached Daniel Jouanneau, head of protocol at the Élysée Palace, he greeted the minister and his advisor, then blocked my path:

"No, you're not coming in!"

Toubon asked why.

"These are instructions from Mr Juppé and Mr Villepin."

Villepin, whom I didn't know at the time.

Jacques Toubon pleaded with me to avoid a row. Shamefully, piteously, I returned to the Hôtel du Palais, where I waited for my fellow African heads of state in a room in Mobutu's suite. For the first time, I was denied access to such an event. And on top of that, on instructions. At 11 pm, Omar Bongo and his counterparts returned to the hotel. Mobutu was surprised not to have seen me. Anxious to save face, I said nothing. Omar Bongo, on the other hand, had suspected the incident:

"Son, you've been locked out, haven't you? The Tangani will never change."

The worst comes to the worst.

Jacques Toubon returns from the summit and approaches me:

"Robert, hop! We've got to get back on the plane. I've got to get back. I've got things to do in Paris."

We all flew back to Paris that evening on Mobutu's plane. During the flight, he apologized for the afternoon's tensions.

"Jacques, do you think this is normal? You, a minister in office unable to impose my presence on Jouanneau?"

He didn't react. The trip was quite painful. As the days went by, I related this misadventure to Jacques Foccart, who was not at all surprised. This kind of attitude did absolutely no credit to French diplomacy in view of the work I was doing.

And there was more to come.
Some time later, Toubon came back to inform me that, as he had to go to Armenia, he wanted me to get him a plane again. I therefore appealed once again to Mobutu's generosity, who chartered a Falcon 900. The entire French delegation flew to Yerevan in this aircraft.

Why doesn't the French Republic provide an aircraft?
I didn't ask myself the question. We set off from Le Bourget to the Armenian capital, where we stayed for two days with the crew. Mobutu took care of everything.

Why is Toubon asking to travel on a plane generously loaned by an African president?
The French should know that at that time many of their ministers, and not only them, were traveling—and not only—at the expense of what they described as "African potentates", not to say "bloodthirsty autocrats". I'm sick and tired of Mobutu being paid without knowing that. Does he pay for everything to go to Biarritz? To Armenia? Honestly.

Was there big money behind these trips?
It was a convenience. It allowed ministers to save money on their budgets.

What role do you see in Mobutu's return to the saddle?
I played my part, but it's obvious that my role was strengthened by the presence of Foccart and Chirac. Seeing that Bruno Delaye, in close contact with Foccart, regularly returned to the subject, François Mitterrand

123

understood the importance for Paris of not demonizing Zaire, a loyal ally of the West. In France, there was also considerable concern about the post-Mobutu era. He was then overtaken by illness and Laurent-Désiré Kabila's rebellion.

Chapter 13: 1995 in the Line of Fire

In the early 1990s, you worked regularly for Denis Sassou Nguesso, Omar Bongo, Gnassingbé Eyadema and Blaise Compaoré.

At that time, Omar Bongo sent me everywhere, including the United States, to improve his image and that of Gabonese governance. He appointed me as his *special adviser*. As far as Sassou was concerned, my missions were limited to France. I made contacts for various high-profile figures such as Jean-Dominique Okemba[86].

Jacques Foccart had asked me to take charge of Gnassingbé Eyadema, who was in free fall after showing his determination not to unlock his regime. We were at the height of the period of sovereign national conferences, which were bringing a real breath of democracy to French-speaking Africa. I went on several missions to Lomé.

I was also a frequent visitor to Blaise Compaoré, who had all the trouble in the world establishing his legitimacy after the assassination of Thomas Sankara in 1987, and because of his compromise with Liberia's Charles Taylor, whose rebellion he supported from 1989 to 1997, before being accused of juicy trafficking once Taylor was head of the country from 1997 to 2003.

What were your assignments?

Public relations of the highest strategic intensity. With Blaise Compaoré, for example, I had a very good relationship. He often included me in his travels with his wife Chantal. I remember accompanying him to the Poitou-Charentes region headed by Jean-Pierre Raffarin, who had organized a big party in his honor. The President of Burkina Faso was very keen

---

86. Nephew and "securocrat" of the Congolese head of state, he is the emblematic leader of the National Security Council (CNS).

on decentralized cooperation. He had a close relationship with the former president of the French Senate, René Monory. Loudun, the town of which Monory was mayor for many years, was twinned with Ouagadougou.

I also had Jacques Chirac receive him at Paris City Hall. I took Dominique de Villepin to the Bristol, his favorite Paris hangout. These were the other aspects of my work.

It was then that Nicolas Sarkozy joined forces with the Pasqua/Séguin duo[87]. What is your relationship with him?

We'd seen each other from time to time, but we weren't intimate. I first met him in 1982, as mayor of Neuilly-sur-Seine. Omar Bongo had asked me to enroll one of his protégés in a school there. He received me very kindly. He knew who I was. The little girl was enrolled in five minutes. He asked me to tell Bongo. I suggested calling him personally and giving him his number. He was already working the Foccart and Chirac way: straight to the point, without salamalecs or leg-pulling. I quickly realized that he would go far.

I saw the real Nicolas Sarkozy in 1985, when I was a project manager for the RPR. One day, I had to go to Rue de Lille, the party headquarters, for a meeting of all the project managers. I had come back specially from Abidjan. The appointment was set for 4pm. I arrived an hour early. Paulette Giry-Laterrière, Jacques Chirac's closest aide, asked me to wait. Then I heard a voice coming from Chirac's personal office. I turned to his secretary:

"Paulette, are you sure the mayor isn't here? I can hear someone."

She told me it was Sarkozy. Once in the office, I realized that he wasn't sitting in any visitor's chair, but in Chirac's! In front of his desk! I shouted at him:

"Nicolas, are you feeling well?"
"I play president."
"I don't know if I'll live to see it, but you will."

Events will prove me right.

---

87. Nicolas Sarkozy was Budget Minister and spokesman for the Édouard Balladur government from March 30, 1993 to January 19, 1995.

Are you continuing to mobilize the Shiite community in Africa?

This modus operandi had died out by the time I left Côte d'Ivoire. I no longer organized any collections or transfers, but went directly through the heads of state, who sent their emissaries to my office in Paris.

Presidents again called upon in the run-up to the 1995 presidential election.

Affirmative. As with every election, it was back to business as usual.

Who was involved in this vote?

The bulk of contributions came from Omar Bongo, Denis Sassou Nguesso, Blaise Compaoré and Mobutu Sese Seko.

For what amounts?

I don't have the exact breakdown by head of state, but I can say that the total contributions reached at least $10 million. So much so that one day, while I was in his apartments at the Palais du bord de mer[88], Omar Bongo asked me:

> "Son, what can they do with all this money I'm giving them?"
> "Dad, ask the principal. I don't know."

I mentioned the cost of an election campaign in France. He smiled.

What did you agree with the African presidential emissaries?

Either the money would be sent to the Élysée via one of these presidents, or the African presidents would send their emissaries to my office, and we would then go to the French presidency or to Jacques Foccart's office in Rue de Prony or Luzarches, always accompanied by Jean-Claude Laumond. Foccart continued to welcome us with coffee and this thought:

> "Is it consistent?"

Charles Pasqua is making more and more inroads on your land.

I didn't have any "land". Let's just say he courted the African presidents I worked with. In Brazzaville, Libreville and elsewhere, his "men" were always around. I saw people like Jean-Paul Lanfranchi. Lanfranchi, who

---

88. Name given to the Gabonese Presidency.

was close to Jacques Chirac, Omar Bongo and above all the Mobutu family, worked as a lawyer in Kinshasa. He was a great help to the Marshal during his desert crossing. We have to admit it. Other emissaries such as Daniel Léandri, François Antona, Jean-Charles Marchiani, and even Alfred Sirven, were also highly visible.

In the run-up to 1995, these members of the Pasqua network really got into the swing of things for candidate Balladur. They made a point of being friendly to several heads of state, including Omar Bongo and Denis Sassou Nguesso.

How much did these presidents donate?

I don't know.

Did Omar Bongo confide in you about this?

None of the presidents I worked with really opened up about their relationship with Charles Pasqua. They received his emissaries. When I met them, Jacques Foccart was obviously informed. I did know, however, that these presidents gave considerably more to candidate Chirac. Omar Bongo once told me that it was as much as double. The "donations" to Balladur were mainly to cover his back. Just in case...

Do you know how much money Omar Bongo reserved for Jacques Chirac?

Whatever the occasion, it was rarely less than 10 million francs, or €1.5 million.

How often during this period?

Two or three times a year. The contributions came from the presidents I've mentioned with varying degrees of intensity. Omar Bongo was the most generous. In fact, when the pace quickened in the run-up to an election, these presidents were always astonished, as the French state began to regulate and reimburse election campaigns in order to avoid excesses.

From 1988 onwards, and especially from 1995, the financing of political parties and election campaigns became increasingly regulated. Until 1988, there was no legal framework for such "donations". From that year onwards, a system was gradually put in place. In 1995, the French government banned donations from legal entities and companies. Individual contributions to political organizations were then capped at €7,500. In other words, from 1995 onwards, my missions became more complex. It wasn't the same music anymore.

However, you remain the organizer of these transfers.

it's always been me. In Paris, I was the point of contact for Bongo, Sassou, Mobutu and Compaoré for funds donated to the Élysée Palace, often on the occasion of official visits. For the 1995 presidential election, these presidents donated no less than 5 million francs. President Mobutu gave me 10 million francs, which I in turn gave to Jacques Foccart.

The progressive regulation of French political life means you're actually crossing a red line.

I responded to solicitations and requests for financing without asking myself any questions. I will denounce these practices later.

When did you start collecting for Jacques Chirac with a view to 1995?

As early as 1993, when the Mitterrand-Balladur cohabitation began. Pasqua's teams descended on African capitals, chanting that "Chirac's time was over". The polls were in Balladur's favor, as they were conducted by the Ministry of the Interior, headed by Charles Pasqua himself. To hear them tell it, Balladur was bound to win in the first round. Poor fellow…

Jacques Foccart was no fool. He spent his time discrediting and demolishing them. But as he was getting on in years, he was less and less mobile. I took over. He always believed in the victory of the mayor of Paris, even if the terrain seemed more favorable to his "friend of thirty years" turned adversary.

I'd like to remind you once again of the importance of the lunch between Édouard Balladur and Jacques Foccart on April 23, 1995, just before the first round of the presidential election. A veritable tacit pact was forged during this meeting. In the event of Balladur's victory, Jacques Chirac was to be given a seat in the hot seat. A very high position. Not necessarily that of Prime Minister—in fact, he would have categorically refused it—but a very high office. Nicolas Sarkozy, though close to Balladur, never knew anything about this meeting.

Jacques Foccart promised to join the Balladur camp in the event of a second round.

That was really what the deal was all about. With Jacques Chirac out of the way, a confrontation with the left became inevitable. There was talk of the entire Chirac entourage switching over to the Balladurians. I'll say it again: Jacques Foccart pledged to bring everything he could to the table, and that meant a lot of people, believe me.

Receiving African emissaries in your office does not prevent you from traveling to Africa.

We had to maintain contact and multiply our good offices. Jacques Chirac asked me to go and see Bongo and Sassou to make them understand that he urgently needed subsidies.

What about Senegal?

These issues were not discussed with Abdou Diouf, whose heart leaned to the left even though Jacques Chirac was godfather to one of his children. Abdou Diouf's name was never once mentioned in the RPR's financing operations.

Director of Cabinet for Alain Juppé, then Minister of Foreign Affairs[89], Dominique de Villepin is growing in stature. Is he beginning to grasp the scope of the system?

Allow me to illustrate my answer with an example: one day, I received in my office an investigative journalist from *Le Monde* who was working at the time at *Le Canard enchaîné*, and who has become my friend. In conversation, he said to me:

> "Robert, I can tell you that we don't like you at the Quai d'Orsay. I've just had lunch with Villepin and Philippe Martel[90]. Villepin told me he wanted to put bracelets on your wrists."

Very surprised, I asked why. Handcuffs, of course, never happened. But I had just learned that I was in his crosshairs.

---

89. Alain Juppé was Minister of Foreign and European Affairs in the Édouard Balladur government from March 30, 1993 to May 11, 1995.
90. Chief of staff.

Why do you think that is?

Before the presidential election, when I was on a financial mission for Jacques Chirac, I was made to understand that I was not to cross paths with him or meet him. The first contact between us took place at the beginning of 1995, as he was managing, among other things, the Zaire dossier and the pursuit of Mobutu's rehabilitation on Jacques Chirac's behalf.

He started calling me, asking me questions. I'd never set foot in the Élysée Palace before. This would happen, of course, on May 7 of the same year, once Chirac had won the election. Previously, I'd been content to provide him with notes, assessments and decipherments of certain African events and countries.

This election brought to the fore a veritable mille-feuille of networks. Foccart's, Pasqua's, the 89 Club's... What role for Maurice Robert?

I've never seen him with Foccart or Chirac.

Yet he was Foccart's main lieutenant.

Let me be clear: Maurice Robert never financed any African head of state. Rather, he was in charge of the Elf network. Charles Pasqua, on the other hand, relied on the Hauts-de-Seine department and on Daniel Léandri, a consultant with Sucres & Denrées (Sucden), a very prosperous group in Africa.

Is Pierre-Philippe, Charles Pasqua's son, playing a role?

To my knowledge, none.

Yet he is an advisor to the Mimran group in Senegal.

The only time I saw him was in the Charvet boutique. He came up to me and congratulated me on everything I was doing. He kissed me and even gave me a tie.

Long after the hostage crisis, I kept running into his father in Parisian hotels or, occasionally, at Omar Bongo's home. In Libreville, he always had this phrase that the Gabonese president never failed to pick up on:

"Ah, the Shiite again!"
"But Charles, what do you have against Robert?"
"What saves him is that he married a fellow countrywoman."

131

Like François Mitterrand, was Jacques Chirac a follower of the occult?

Readers should know that he was a great believer. He was into cosmogony and clairvoyance. As for François Mitterrand, it wasn't just Élizabeth Tessier, far from it. I saw Malian marabouts around him. His son, Jean-Christophe, was an enthusiast for mysticism, unlike his partner at the Élysée Palace, Guy Penne, who didn't believe in it at all.

Ditto for Jacques Chirac. He too was "followed" by two very important Malian marabouts close to Omar Bongo and Blaise Compaoré. Shortly before the 1995 presidential election, I remember being asked to welcome one of them at Roissy-Charles de Gaulle airport. I put him up in a discreet hotel near Place Beauvau.

Who introduces and sends him these marabouts?

The closest African presidents, starting with Omar Bongo. The one I welcomed to Paris was his personal marabout. At the time, at the Palais du bord de mer, there were not only Beninese, but also countless Senegalese and Malians, starting with Mamadou Diop, Secretary General of the Presidency.

Was this a suggestion from these heads of state, or a specific request from Chirac?

Jacques Chirac was a firm believer. We were close to the vote. It must have been early April 1995. One night, Jean-Claude Laumond took me home. We picked up the marabout in question and took him to Paris City Hall. And there, outside Laumond's presence, I witnessed a surreal scene: he took both of Chirac's hands before launching into a stream of incantations and cabalistic words that I partly understood, some of which were taken from the Koran. He looked at Jacques Chirac and let him know that while he had been predicted defeat in 1988, this time he was guaranteeing victory. After the ceremony, Jacques Chirac telephoned the Gabonese president to say:

> "Omar, I just finished with our friend. It's good for me, thank you. If I'm elected, I'll call you first. Which he did."

It should also be pointed out that the heads of state who "followed" him in this respect demanded that he himself buy the animals that had to be sacrificed on African soil to help him. I didn't know where the money went, however.

Before the presidential election, does Jacques Chirac have a plan for Jacques Foccart?

He wanted him at his side, but Dominique de Villepin thwarted his plans. It should be noted that Villepin killed Foccart, whose methods he did not appreciate. He even feared them. Except that he quickly adopted them as soon as we started working together. Foccart didn't like Villepin either, whom he nicknamed "Villepinte".

What advice did Jacques Foccart give Jacques Chirac after his victory in 1995?

Those he had already given him during the first cohabitation period from 1986 to 1988. He has always been very close to Chirac. He was one of the first historical barons of Gaullism to join and support him from 1976 onwards.

What was this advice? To maintain personal and family ties with African heads of state. To be able to devote time to them. I remember he drew up a detailed organization chart of the relatives and families of the leading figures. Their pedigree, the names of their wives and children, with dates of birth, as well as their school and university careers. He informed Chirac of deaths, marriages and baptisms.

He had suggested that, as far as his schedule would allow, he should make two or three phone calls a day to the most influential people to check up on them. He attached great importance to this, and Jacques Chirac always respected his instructions. Personal relationships had to take precedence over more political ones.

The level of rapprochement that French leaders were once able to establish with their counterparts on the continent has totally disintegrated. That's why, for years now, the Franco-African relationship has been slowly but surely withering and dying. I'm probably the last person in French political circles to be able to call any French-speaking African president at any time.

Once Jacques Chirac was elected, it was a cold shower for the Doyen as he learned that he would not be returning to 2, rue de l'Élysée, but to 14, at the Etat-major particulier.

When he heard the news from Chirac, he asked Catherine and me to come and stay with him. For the first time since I'd been with him, I saw him shed angry tears and utter the phrase:

133

"I'm going to teach this little boy who Foccart is. Treating me like that."

I was speechless. And to keep Robert Bourgi speechless, you have to go really hard. Catherine managed to calm him down. Villepin said straight out that he didn't want him at the Élysée, can you believe it? Foccart had his office a little further away. He never went there. It was Chirac's chief of staff who brought him diplomatic dispatches every day.

Villepin is also blocking your way to the Africa cell.
Worse! I was the plague incarnate.

Aging and ill, was Foccart still powerful and influential? Who did he still have around him? Who did he rely on?
No one would be able to say what Foccart's constellations were. He had connections absolutely everywhere.

After his victory, Jacques Chirac made Blaise Compaoré the guest of honor at his first national holiday as president, on July 14, 1995. Was this in gratitude for his financial support?
He had participated in the financing, but his contribution was much smaller than that of Omar Bongo or Denis Sassou Nguesso. However, the Chirac couple had close ties with the Compaoré couple. Chantal Compaoré had a definite influence on the new French president. She even had a title of nobility, as she was born Terrasson de Fougères. In a way, she embodied the Franco-Ivorian haute bourgeoisie, speaking exquisite French that was a far cry from that of Bernadette Chodron de Courcel.

Now that your office has become the nerve center of Franco-African relations, are you approached by the intelligence services?
I've never seen them.

Aren't they trying to get information from you?
I repeat: I never met the RG or the DGSE. Some of my contacts or the personalities I rubbed shoulders with were certainly part of it, but a guy in my office ostensibly announcing himself as an agent of the services was never seen, even though I was a close friend of Prefect Robert Broussard

when he was on the rampage in Ajaccio and Paris[91]. And I knew Philippe Massoni very well[92]. They never questioned me.

It is customary to say that African heads of state form a closed "club". They all know each other, see each other frequently, talk to each other, exchange views and clear up issues. Like Jacques Foccart, you become their gateway to France. Who calls on you the most?

Without question, Omar Bongo, even when it came to trinkets. Once Jacques Chirac was at the Élysée Palace, he always wanted to talk to Dominique de Villepin, the new Secretary General of the French Presidency, whom he nicknamed "Mamadou", after the former Secretary General of the Gabonese Republic, Mamadou Diop from Senegal. He was constantly calling me to ask me to tell "Mamadou" this or that.

In fact, he didn't need anything. He wanted to maintain contact with Paris. Dominique de Villepin, an extraordinarily intelligent man, quickly understood the importance of these informal relations. The two men began to talk regularly on the phone, just in case. Except once, when Omar Bongo asked me more seriously to take charge of a file concerning Gabon's relations with the Bretton Woods institutions (World Bank and International Monetary Fund). The power was with Villepin. I would inform him of the request, and he would intervene with the relevant minister.

How did you get on with your "cohabitation" with the Élysée's Africa unit, which you bypassed?

Apart from Bruno Delaye, the only Africa advisor to the French presidency with whom I regularly rubbed shoulders was Bruno Joubert under Sarkozy. The two of us often had lunch together, although we didn't always agree on France's African policy. I held this diplomat in high esteem, but he had too many certainties stamped Quai d'Orsay. He could never stand the informality of bilateral relations. And the Africans paid him back in spades.

You were even behind his departure from the Élysée Palace.

That's true.

---

91. Born in 1936, Philippe Broussard was Prefect Delegate for Police in Corsica (1983-1985) and head of the Central Border Police Directorate (1992-1996).

92. A senior French civil servant and police officer, Philippe Massoni (1936-2015) was notably Central Director of the Renseignements Généraux (1986-1988) and Prefect of the Paris Police (1993-2001).

Chapter 14: "The Heir"—the Chirac Years

When Jacques Foccart died on March 19, 1997, Jacques Chirac installed you as his successor and asked you to work with Dominique de Villepin.

We all gathered at the Luzarches cemetery for the funeral, after a grand ceremony at the Église Saint-Louis des Invalides and in the courtyard. There was a large turnout, but surprisingly few African presidents, with the exception of Abdou Diouf, Pascal Lissouba, Teodoro Obiang Nguema Mbasogo and Didier Ratsiraka.

At Luzarches, I arrived in Jacques Toubon's car, when Dominique de Villepin's secretariat informed me that Jacques Chirac would be seeing me that evening, at 7:30 pm, at the Élysée Palace. The same Villepin who only wanted to handcuff me.

As we left the cemetery, Chirac called out to me:

> "Robert, how I understand your suffering. Your wreath of flowers is almost as big as mine."

I reminded him of what the deceased meant to me.

That evening, in Villepin's office[93], which I was seeing for the first time, Chirac joined us in paying tribute to the memory of the deceased:

> "God, what a sad day. How I loved that man. What an exemplary servant of the State! To think that he was a close friend of the General's from 1946 onwards, and that he was with me right up to his death."

Then he said how pleased he was that I'd met the General Secretary, even though I'd taken great pleasure in telling him the story of the brace-

---

93. Michel Lunven, *Ambassadeur en Françafrique*, Guéna, 2011.

lets in a humorous tone. Chirac burst out laughing and the interested party replied:

"Robert, let's move on!"

And Chirac spoke more solemnly:

"Robert, Jacques has left. From now on, apart from me, your only contact for African affairs will be Dominique."

He turned to Villepin and asked him to work with me in complete confidence, before unpacking my pedigree and that of my father, pointing out that I had been involved in African affairs long before many others.

He then clearly asked me to retrieve all Jacques Foccart's files from both rue de Prony and Luzarches. It was a delicate mission. On Rue de Prony, there was Odette and the police on duty in front of the building. In Luzarches, the gendarmes were also in front of the villa. Jacques Chirac suggested I go on this mission with Fernand Wibaux. I had to recover what there was to recover: documents, letters, correspondence, missives... Jacques Foccart had built up a library over half a century. There were archives, countless letters, mission letters, tickets.

Potentially compromising files?

François Wibaux and I made a date to "clean up" the rue de Prony. He was waiting for me at the café and didn't want to come up. He preferred me to collect everything and hand over the documents.

"Mr. Ambassador, we both have a mandate for this mission," I friendly reminded him.

Odette, who had been personally informed of our visit by Chirac, was waiting for us. All the documents were ready, contained in bags. I didn't know what they were. I went back down to find Fernand Wibaux, who took charge of returning everything to the Élysée Palace.

What was in the bags? RPR financing memos? Evidence of bribes?

As much as the RPR operated a "cash machine", I've always fed the Françafrique "fantasy machine". A machine that, it has to be said, was very well maintained by the press on the basis of very little information. Constant inventions, interpretations and suppositions.

Readers should understand that at no time did I know or look at what I was carrying. I was given a mission: to carry a bag, a suitcase, envelopes, confidential mail from point A to point B. That was it. That was the end of it. On the other hand, if Jacques Chirac had asked me to retrieve such documents, it was because he naturally knew what they contained. So did Odette.

We then headed for Luzarches, where the house was surrounded by gendarmes. Fernand Wibaux pulled out his Élysée advisor card. We climbed into the "Case à fétiches" and moved everything we could.

Did you know exactly what you were looking for?

We took documents, archives, quite a few things we'd been asked to retrieve, and I don't think it was about The *Adventures of Tintin*.

Documents that could worry Jacques Chirac or the RPR?

Only he knew. After Luzarches, I parted company with François Wibaux. He returned to the Élysée Palace to entrust all these archives to Villepin.

> "I thank you, comrade, the mission was accomplished very well," he said.

How long did you stay in Luzarches?

Two good hours and a good hour on rue de Prony.

Did you bring only files?

Yes, there must have been every period of Foccart's life: the Resistance, Overseas France, the period of General de Gaulle, Georges Pompidou...

Aren't these files being returned to the national archives?

No, certainly not.

Why did presidents such as Omar Bongo, whom Jacques Foccart had installed, not attend his funeral?

Honestly, I have no explanation. Jacques Chirac, on the other hand, was remarkable with his magnificent ceremony at Les Invalides.

Do you have any feedback from Chirac's secret missions?

Two or three days later, I received a phone call from him asking me to come to Villepin's house. I can still see him in his shirt-sleeves and tie behind his desk. He said to me:

> "Robert, I have a certain amount of money at my disposal. Who should I give it to? As someone who was very close to Jacques, who do you think we should thank for having been with him all these years?"

I immediately mentioned Odette and her niece, whose name escapes me; the chauffeurs; the gardener at the villa in Luzarches; the staff at his house in Cavalaire-sur-Mer.

Jacques Chirac was taking notes, and I could see that he was writing down a sum on a sheet of paper. I couldn't make out the exact amount, but to this day I'm confused by the story. He kept asking me if I wasn't seeing someone else:

> "Who accompanied Foccart to his final moments in Cavalaire?"
> "Mr. Chairman, I can't think of anyone else who deserves to be rewarded in this way."

He stared at me, thanking me, before standing up and saying:

> "This is your home. I'll be there whenever you need me, whenever you want me."

Didn't you understand his insistence?

With the nerve that is mine, I asked him why he had insisted so much on the "who else do you see?", pointing out:

> "Mr. President, if it's me you're thinking of, I've given everything for Mr. Foccart, but don't ask for anything. You know everything I've done for him, especially when you were at the Fort de Brégançon and I was preparing your visit for him."

Do you still not know how much?

Totally.

Who was responsible for getting the money to the staff?

I don't know, not me.

How has the legacy of Foccart, the real Foccart, been managed?

He was not a landowner and, contrary to popular belief, had no personal fortune. He asked no one for a salary. Many of his friends enabled him to live with dignity.

Are you trying to recover objects from the "fetish hut"? Trinkets? Souvenirs?

His notary called me shortly after his departure. He had no children, but an astronomical number of godchildren. He had thought of me and left me a statue. It was a Virgin, the figurehead of a Portuguese ship sunk three centuries ago, which I had noticed.

When I was at his place, I used to say to him all the time:

"Dean, this Virgin is magnificent."

He said nothing, but retained everything.

Have you been approached by historian Jean-Pierre Bat, who is in charge of the Foccart collection at the French National Archives, for his work[94]?

Never.

Is it true that you visit his grave in Luzarches every year to put flowers on it?

I go there every year, and not just once, but once every two months with my wife Catherine, equipped with the utensils needed to clean it. We're often accompanied by our children, if they're available, and we have lunch at an inn where I used to meet Jacques Foccart and Odette Leguerney.

Did his death precipitate the absorption of the Ministry of Cooperation into the Quai d'Orsay and the de facto disappearance of the Rue Monsieur?

This process began long before, with the death of Houphouët-Boigny, who was opposed to it. Édouard Balladur immediately endorsed the

---

94. Author of *Le syndrome Foccart. La politique française en Afrique de 1959 à nos jours*, Folio Inédit Histoire, Paris, 2012.

Chapter 14: "The Heir"—the Chirac Years

devaluation of the CFA franc. The demise of Jacques Foccart facilitated the demise of Rue Monsieur. Jacques Chirac was African only because of him. With Foccart gone, opposing this left-wing reform was no longer a priority.

What did Jacques Chirac think of the already ambitious Nicolas Sarkozy?

He never criticized or demolished Nicolas Sarkozy in front of me, not even during the second cohabitation, when he was Budget Minister and government spokesman. However, Omar Bongo told me that, during a dinner with Jacques Chirac in 1994, the latter had told him that Sarkozy had made the wrong choice.

That same year, Omar Bongo received Nicolas Sarkozy at the Crillon. I was present at this three-quarters of an hour meeting. The strong man of Libreville called me into his office and said:

> "In Africa, we can't stand betrayal. I told Nicolas that Chirac had been a father to him. Following Balladur was a serious mistake."
> "Omar, you're wrong. He'll get through to the first round," retorted Sarkozy.
> "Nicolas, I've known Kennedy, Ford, Carter, Reagan, de Gaulle, Pompidou, Giscard, Mitterrand... and I'm telling you that Chirac will be elected, because the French don't like people who look down on them."

At the time, Nicolas Sarkozy was stubborn in his certainty.

Your image is the stuff of fantasies among journalists, activists and other intellectuals who are quick to cut you down to size. You're described as an "occult" or "sulphurous" figure, an opportunist making money off the backs of Africans. Yet you have filed very few libel suits.

I wasn't interested in that, and it's worth remembering that I was the primary source for journalists, the real ones, whether they specialized in Africa or French politics, starting with my great friend Claude Angéli, boss of *Le Canard enchaîné*, whose wedding I was the best man for.

The only complaint was lodged by Francis Szpiner, my lawyer at the time, against Michel Lambinet, owner of *La Lettre d'Afrique*. This was in May 1995. He had written that my proximity to Marshal Mobutu had enabled me to trade in diamonds. I attacked immediately.

Another complaint was lodged in 2004 against Jean-Pierre Béjot, founder of *La Dépêche Diplomatique*.

I don't even remember. No interest.

You remain a very close associate of Omar Bongo. Just before the 1995 presidential election in France, his name was involved in a pimping affair linked to the delivery of his Smalto suits to Libreville. This was one of his very first "affairs" on French soil. How did he react?

Very, very badly. He was accused of delivering his costumes accompanied by call-girls, but also, and above all, of being a carrier of the AIDS virus.

Are you in charge of clearing this up?

What's more, I'm the one who goes to the American Hospital in Neuilly to fetch Bongo's medical file, which clearly states that he is not infected with the virus, and he demands that this fact be made known.

It's no secret that Omar Bongo loved women. It's no secret that he had almost sixty children of his own. Many emissaries, both Gabonese and foreign, talked about his interest in women. I personally asked him about the Smalto suits. He categorically denied the presence of women during deliveries. He repeated this to Jacques Chirac during his visit to Paris in May 1995.

The AIDS affair proved more devastating.

He was much more affected than the suits. He asked me to give his medical report to the "doyen" of the Zimbabwe club in Paris, who was none other than Claude Angeli. I went to see him, showing him this authentic file certified by the American Hospital in Neuilly. *Le Canard* published an article exonerating Bongo, but he was extremely distressed by the rumors.

On the evening of Jacques Chirac's victory, he threw a big party at the Crillon.

I was obviously there with Fernand Wibaux and Colonel Costes. Pascal Lissouba was there. It was the first evening before the "normalization"

143

of the Smalto suit affair. Omar Bongo received other personalities in the days that followed. I didn't set up this visit.

The next day, he met Charles Pasqua's "people": Étienne Leandri, François Attala and Jean Taousson, then Elf's André Tarallo and Philippe Jaffré, the successor to Loïk Le Floch-Prigent at the head of the company.

I never met Philippe Jaffré in any African capital. On the other hand, I did witness a number of grand effusions between Le Floch-Prigent and Sassou Nguesso in Brazzaville. The Congolese president owes a huge debt to Elf, particularly in financial terms, for his return to power.

Did you know Jean Taousson, who is very active in Gabon?

By no means. The most active in the sub-region was, as I mentioned, the pro-Chirac lawyer Jean-Paul Lanfranchi. He had the President's confidence and was later Pierre Castel's personal adviser. Jean-Paul Lanfranchi was undeniably involved in Mobutu Sese Seko's defense vis-à-vis the French authorities.

This member of the Pasqua network also looked after the Marshal's relatives in France. The Foccart and Pasqua clans had surprisingly joined forces to save Mobutu.

Jacques Chirac enthrones you as Foccart's successor even though you have nothing in common. Jacques Foccart worked to defend France's strategic interests. You, on the other hand, are a lobbyist with a formidable presence in Franco-African circles, but working for your own personal interests. Why does this image of "Foccart's heir" stick to you?

Indeed, there's no comparison. The character is unique. The mold that created him was used only once, and broke when he died. Personally, I've never claimed to be his "heir", for the simple reason that he doesn't have one. The expression "heir to Foccart" is yet another invention of journalists. Nevertheless, I'm clearly using his modus operandi, particularly when it comes to financing the French political right. The way he taught me. He showed me his working methods. With Fernand Wibaux, we were the last representatives of Maison Foccart. If there is a legacy, it's in behavior and attitude. The unofficial, discreet side, but still influential.

Wherever there were African presidents in France, I was there. Jacques Chirac, Nicolas Sarkozy and a host of French ministers, political and economic leaders passed through me to pass on messages and sensitive mail, without me having any official mission.

I used to go to African capitals at their request. When I'm referred to as a lobbyist, it's also because of all the senior politicians who use this title on purpose. It's only my personal proximity to many African heads of state that has enabled me to carry out these missions. Jacques Chirac, Dominique de Villepin, Jacques Toubon, Nicolas Sarkozy, Claude Guéant... they have all, at one time or another, called on my services because of my status and influence. The proof is in the fact that I took part in all their trips and meetings on African soil.

When he disappears, how are his "networks" rebuilt? Are they perishing?

But there are no "Foccart networks"! Yet another legend! There are honorable correspondents and personalities on whom he relied. On the other hand, I've never known anyone who could say: "I belong to the Foccart network". The only people I was close to were Maurice Robert and Jacques Godfrain. But we didn't work together at all.

How did your partnership with Villepin come about?

From 1995 to 1997, we only exchanged notes. He called me "Maître". It was only after Foccart's death, when Chirac asked me to work alongside him, that he started calling me "Camarade". A kind of entry into his circle. We worked together in total confidence. He knew how close I was to Chirac.

How did you work with him? At night? At night?

I saw him two or three times a week. I'd pass by Avenue de Marigny with "Chambertin" as my code name.

Why "Chambertin"?

Because the only time I ever had lunch with Villepin was at the restaurant Le Bar au Sel, near the Quai d'Orsay. We were with Georges Ouégnin. The sommelier arrived to ask what we wanted to drink. Villepin launched into an admiring diatribe about "le vin de l'Empereur", Napoleon's favorite wine. Napoleon drank it daily, even in exile.

Villepin, who only appreciated this wine, decided to christen me "Chambertin". For his secretaries, the code became this sweet nickname. That's why you won't find any trace of Robert Bourgi in their diaries.

Do you prefer to meet in the evening?
Starting at 7:30 pm. I exceptionally parked my car—I was the only one allowed to do so—on the sidewalk of Avenue Marigny, in front of the last gate before the Faubourg Saint-Honoré. The police, always forewarned, accompanied me directly to his offices.

The burning issues are Zaire and the fall of Mobutu, but also Denis Sassou Nguesso's desire to return to Brazzaville and, later, serious matters such as the Beach disappearances[95].
The Two Congos were a constant preoccupation. We talked about all the latest African news. The Ivory Coast, with its too-weak Henri Konan Bédié, was also starting to worry us.

You knew all the players in Congo-Brazzaville. Is Dominique de Villepin asking you to play a role in this matter?
Of course, starting by introducing him to the protagonists. At the time, Denis Sasssou Nguesso was still in Paris. He met a lot of people. Don't forget that I also knew Pascal Lissouba very well, thanks to Omar Bongo. Villepin's main request was to introduce him to the important people around Sasssou Nguesso. I mentioned people like Jean-Dominique Okemba.

The guardian of the temple and boss of the secret services.
More than that: alongside Denis Sassou Nguesso, he holds the sceptre and is mystically linked to the ancestors. He's also the regime's very own paymaster. A ruthless man who doesn't hesitate to describe himself as such. Follow my gaze.

I set up his first meeting with Dominique de Villepin, in his office. Sassou had not yet returned to power. They introduced themselves as Admiral and Secretary General, before quickly calling each other by their

---

95. Between May 5 and 14, 1999, Congolese refugees crossed the river between the two Congos to return home. When they reached the river port of Brazzaville, known as the "Beach", they were sorted. At least 353 of them disappear.

first names. It was then that Jean-Dominique Okemba told his counterpart that he never called me Robert, but "Complice".

Exiled in Paris, will Sassou Nguesso meet President Jacques Chirac?

Very regularly. I visited him in his apartments and accompanied him several times to Jacques Foccart's home. He also saw Jacques Toubon, Minister of Justice and Keeper of the Seals, at the Chancellery in Place Vendôme[96]. At the same time, I kept in touch with Pascal Lissouba on the recommendation of the Gabonese President.

France was pro-Sassou at the time.

All the way. Pascal Lissouba was beginning to come under the influence of his entourage. He was stubborn and turned to the Americans. Jacques Foccart strongly influenced Chirac on this issue.

Do we know that Paris is supporting Sassou Nguesso's return financially, and even militarily?

Jacques Foccart had arranged for Elf to provide financial assistance to Sassou Nguesso, who was also helped by Omar Bongo and other of his peers, including, of course, Angola's José Eduardo Dos Santos. Franceville was the hub of this aid, particularly for arms deliveries.

On the other hand, I've had no contact with the Angolans. My first meeting with José Eduardo Dos Santos was during Nicolas Sarkozy's visit to Luanda, in May 2008, as part of the rekindling of bilateral relations against the backdrop of Angolagate.

Are you being asked to reason with Pascal Lissouba?

No. However, Jacques Chirac and Dominique de Villepin expressly asked me not to cut ties with him. When I flew to Brazzaville on Air France, Omar Bongo was systematically informed of my meetings. And he would always have me flown to Libreville, where I would give him an even more detailed account of my meetings.

---

96. Jacques Toubon was Minister of Justice and Keeper of the Seals in the Alain Juppé government from May 18, 1995 to June 2, 1997.

Jean-Yves Ollivier, a businessman in Brazzaville in particular, is also well-connected and well-received in African palaces. With the exception of Southern Africa, where you don't operate, you share the same relations and "work" in the same countries. What is your relationship with him?

I didn't know him very well. Brazzaville was the only capital where we crossed paths most often. We sometimes flew together, side by side in first class. He even opened up to me by giving me telephone contacts. During these trips, we didn't hesitate to open up to each other. He even told me we were neighbors, since he lived at 16, avenue Pierre 1er de Serbie.

I can't hide the fact that we were very discreet with each other. We never talked about our missions, but we kissed each other Mediterranean-style every time we met.

Weren't there parasites between you in certain capital cities?

I sometimes asked the presidents I knew about his activities. Denis Sassou Nguesso was very fond of him, as were Omar Bongo and Jacques Foccart. His openness to southern Africa is undeniable. It's said that he had an easy time signing numerous contracts, particularly in the arms industry, but I always refrained from asking him questions on these subjects.

He keeps you at a safe distance and never hesitates to tackle you.

We were from two different worlds. He had occasion to charge me here and there. Like him, many felt that I was far too present with Chirac, Foccart, Villepin, Bongo and Sassou. Too much, too much, too much!

In his book, *Ni vu ni connu. Ma vie de négociant en politique de Chirac et Foccart à Mandela*, published in 2014[97], he asserts: "[...] intermediaries, honest or dishonest, as in any profession, exist everywhere, always have existed and always will, since they are the indispensable links in the system, capable of penetrating the often opaque decision-making centers to identify the best interlocutors. It's a service that, like any other, pays for itself. I make a good living from it. To do that, you don't need suitcases of black money, to bribe, to be

---

97. Jean-Yves Ollivier, *Ni vu ni connu. Ma vie de négociant en politique de Chirac et Foccart à Mandela*, Fayard, 2014.

bribed, to transfer kickbacks from one end of the planet *to the other"*[98].
What does this thought inspire in you?

She makes me laugh...

Alongside Congo-Brazzaville, the other major issue for the Chirac era, until the 1997-2002 cohabitation, was Zaire.

After the rehabilitation operation mentioned above, Mobutu Sese Seko became increasingly ill from 1995 onwards. Having still not met Dominique de Villepin face-to-face, I told him that, as Mobutu was in Lausanne undergoing treatment for prostate cancer, it would be a good idea to pay him a visit as Secretary General of the Élysée Palace. Objectively speaking, Mobutu didn't give the impression of being able to see Zaire again in his lifetime.

Jacques Foccart had given two sound pieces of advice on this matter: that Mobutu should be able to maintain contact with Étienne Tshisekedi, his historic opponent, and, above all, that he should consider strengthening the capabilities of his army by appointing General Donatien Mahele Lieko Bokungu, nicknamed "Le Tigre", to head the general staff. He was assassinated in May 1997. It should be noted that it was Foccart who proposed this scenario.

Dominique de Villepin went to Switzerland and reported back to Foccart on his return. Mobutu agreed to both proposals, except that the nomination of Donatien Bokungu was rejected, for obscure reasons, by Kongulu Mobutu, Mobutu's son nicknamed "Saddam Hussein".

France concretely supports the regime's survival.

Yes, one day I was at Foccart's house. He had Mobutu call him directly on the Élysée switchboard, who told him that his army was in great distress. Laurent-Désiré Kabila was being strengthened by the Ugandan and Rwandan regimes. The Zairean president then asked the DGSE's Service Action (SA), which Foccart had created under de Gaulle, to intervene.

At rue de Prony, I saw Jacques Foccart call Jacques Chirac to ask him to make a thousand SA men available to the regular Zairian army. I still remember the arguments used:

---

98. *Ibid*, p. 242-243.

"Jacques, the Americans are behind Kabila. This great French-speaking African country is going to escape us. There's not a moment to lose. You need to be able to mount an operation using the SA. A thousand men would be enough to overpower Kabila's troops."

Jacques Chirac informed Alain Juppé, Prime Minister and statutory head of the DGSE, who opposed the operation.

The doctrine in vogue was to limit French militarism in Africa.

Above all, he didn't like Mobutu. But it's true that Paris, still traumatized by the post-Rwandan genocide context, was reluctant to get involved militarily. What's more, go and make Juppé understand Zaire's geostrategic interests. He didn't like Mobutu, just as he didn't like Robert Bourgi...

I then went to Dominique de Villepin, who replied:

"Comrade, there's no need to insist, there will be no intervention".

That's when it all fell apart. With Foccart's thousand men, the destiny of this great country would have changed radically. Laurent-Désiré Kabila's men would have been defeated, even discomfited.

You accompanied Mobutu until his death.

I'm always overcome with emotion when I talk about him, because I was in the best position to know what he brought to France. After his operation in Lausanne, he returned to his villa in Roquebrune-Cap-Martin, in the south of France. In conversation with him, he confided the following:

"Robert, France is letting me down and Jacques [Chirac] has a short memory. You're witness to that. I don't blame Juppé, he wasn't necessarily aware of it. Villepin is relatively new and was kind enough to come and see me in Switzerland. But Chirac..."

That's when I saw that he was literally floating in his clothes, with difficulty walking. I was holding his arm and, as you know, I was also on the plane that brought him back to "Kin" after another month's hospitalization in France.

A triumphant return.

In March 1997, a million people were waiting. So did Kengo wa Dondo, the whole government and the constituted bodies. But once on the tarmac, the doctors on board the plane told Mobutu that he didn't have the physical strength to walk down the catwalk. All the officials were told to head for the presidential residence in the capital. The people of Kinshasa remained at the airport, still hoping to see their leader. It was here that Mobutu, held on the left and held on the right, slipped discreetly into a car to reach his villa. He gave his famous speech, in which he burst into tears.

Then came the final attempt at negotiation, in early May 1997, on the *Outenika*, in the presence of Laurent-Désiré Kabila and Nelson Mandela, in Pointe-Noire. But Kabila's troops were in Kinshasa. It was all over.

Did you attend the Outenika **meeting on behalf of France?**

I had no mission statement and didn't need one. I was in Mobutu's cabin. That's all there was to it. I was there when Nelson Mandela arrived. That's when I saw "Madiba" for the first time. Ngawali Mobutu was also there. Mandela said to Mobutu:

"How are you my friend?"

Realizing that his interlocutor was unable to give him his arm, Mandela helped him into the conference room where Kabila was waiting. The latter scorned him copiously. Mobutu knew the game was up.

He then headed for Gbadolite. His last circle allowed him to board a plane bound for Lomé just as elements of the Division Spéciale Présidentielle (DSP), the Praetorian Guard created by Mobutu himself, attempted to shoot down the aircraft. For Gnassingbé Eyadema, the guest was too cumbersome. It's not easy to keep Mobutu at home. Mobutu ended his days in Rabat, where he died in September 1997.

It was from your office that he asked you to end his days in France.

This was after the futile *Outenika* negotiations. Back in France, I received a call from his aide-de-camp, Colonel Hilaire Motoko Elabe, the last commander of the DSP's security battalion, who never let go of his boss. He put me through to a Mobutu with a barely recognizable voice, asking me, as a favor, to be allowed to return to France to die in Roquebrune-Cap-Martin.

151

"Of the two Jacques, there is only one left who can grant me this favor. I'm counting on you."

But to do so, we needed to request authorization. I called Villepin and explained the situation to him, recalling all the actions, primarily financial, taken on behalf of France. He didn't ask for anything. Just to spend the rest of his life there. Half an hour later, Villepin told me that Jacques Chirac had listened to him willingly, while asking Alain Juppé to make a decision. And Juppé replied:

"Let him die somewhere else!"

That evening I broke the news to Colonel Motoko, who had this typically African reaction:

"Hey, master, even this..."

Unfortunately, with Jacques Foccart gone, the levers on Africa at the Élysée suddenly became much less powerful.

How is it that Jacques Chirac asked his Prime Minister to arbitrate on such an issue?
Because, in reality, he often lacked courage. And because Mobutu no longer represented anything.

Who gets his exile in the Cherifian kingdom?
It was Jacques Chirac, intervening with King Hassan II.

Why doesn't France welcome him?
Because of Juppé's incomprehensible veto, he was able to free up so much room for maneuver thanks to the space left by Foccart's departure. I remember that, at the time, the French press ran the headline: "Foccart is dead, Mobutu's tomb is open!" It was no longer the main news story.

Before the dissolution of the National Assembly in France, followed by parliamentary elections, Jacques Chirac obtained his repatriation to Morocco. All those close to the Zairean president received special treatment in the pure tradition of the Cherifian kingdom. I spoke to his aide-de-camp every day about his health. Some days, he would say on the phone:

"Dad is very tired, he won't be able to talk to you. It's no good."

I understood that his health was deteriorating rapidly.

Was Villepin already very aware of Africa?

Through his knowledge of books and his time at the Quai d'Orsay, yes. But from our first meeting, I introduced him to people. I established direct, friendly and fraternal contacts with Omar Bongo, Denis Sassou Nguesso, Blaise Compaoré, Amadou Toumani Touré, Laurent Gbagbo, Gnassingbé Eyadema, you name it.

In addition to Marshal Mobutu, you're involved with the entire Congolese political class.

It's an exaggeration to say it, but I've forged ties with Étienne Tshisekedi[99] whom I met in Brussels in the early 1990s, at Jacques Foccart's request, when Zaire was experiencing serious political instability. His son Félix, President of the Democratic Republic of Congo (DRC) since 2019, brought me to his father. In May 2024, I attended one of his conferences in Paris, having been invited by his protocol. I'm always welcome in the former Zaire. But at the time, nothing was going right in this country on the brink of collapse. A great leader, Étienne Tshisekedi was already the Marshal's historic opponent, and was even for a time his Prime Minister—for barely a month in 1991, then from August 1992 to March 1993. He returned to the post in early April 1997. He always told me of his genuine willingness to cooperate with Mobutu, but the latter's entourage, starting with his Praetorian Guard, wouldn't hear of it. Hence the Kengo option we put forward. If the Mobutu/Tshisekedi alliance had held, Laurent-Désiré Kabila would undoubtedly have had less room for manoeuvre.

As a close friend of Jean-Pierre Bemba, you went so far as to visit him in The Hague.

His father, Jeannot Bemba Saolona, the boss of the Zairian bosses, was a key figure in the Mobutu galaxy. It was with him that I met Jean-Pierre, who was like a son to the Marshal. He was very interested in French politics, with a keen interest in the Chirac/Foccart duo. We never stopped

---

99. Étienne Tsisekedi (1932-2017), president of the Union for Democracy and Social Progress (UDPS), was the historic opponent of Mobutu Sese Seko.

seeing each other and our respective wives. This friendship naturally led me to visit him several times in The Hague, where he had been imprisoned for acts for which he was not even responsible. Hence his release[100]. He has always been extremely confident about his country. He is currently Deputy Prime Minister, and I must emphasize his perfect collaboration with the Congolese President.

Why visit Bemba and not Gbagbo?

Every time I saw Jean-Pierre, I stayed for at least two hours. Naturally, we talked about Laurent. My brother Albert visited him very frequently. Why shouldn't I? For the simple reason that ill-intentioned spirits, in the diabolical sense of the word, never ceased to pass me off as a conspirator against him, and that I had sided with the rebels to such an extent that he was convinced. For the Bourgi family, he remains a brother. I can't wait to see him again, and I hope that when he reads this book, he'll know the role I played as his defender and peacemaker, working with the Chirac family and others to calm things down.

---

100. Vice-President of the DRC from 2003 to 2006, and founder of the Mouvement de Libération du Congo (MLC), Jean-Pierre Bemba was convicted of "war crimes" in 2016 by the International Criminal Court (ICC) before being acquitted two years later in June 2018.

Photo Album n°2

In 1986, in the Glam Falcon 20 taking Minister Michel Aurillac to Gabon with his advisors André Mousset and Christian Sabbe. My back.

*In 1987, with Michel Aurillac,
Rue Monsieur.*

*The day I was sworn
in as a lawyer, in 1993,
with my wife and
my Gabonese friend,
Noël Bayot.*

*On a visit to Gabon in 1993, the Dalai Lama passed through
the French residence in Libreville. I'm in the company of Ambassador
Louis Dominici (right) and Stéphane Martin, the future director
of the Musée du Quai Branly—Jacques Chirac.*

*President Omar Bongo's special envoy to the United States,
I was received at New York City Hall with Michel Teale, in 1994.*

157

President Mobutu Sese Seko welcomed me to Gbadolite in 1994.

Back in Cotonou in 1996, I was reunited with President Mathieu Kérékou.

158

Jacques Foccart photographed in the privacy of his apartment on rue de Prony with his parrot "Coco".

With his indefatigable secretary Odette Leguerney, Jacques Foccart enjoyed a sea outing off Cavalaire-sur-Mer.

159

*A few months before his "departure", in March 1997, Jacques Chirac
elevated Foccart to the rank of Grand Officer of the Legion of Honor.*

With my friend Laurent Gbagbo, in 2000, in Abidjan.

*In 2001, with my friends Georges Ouégnin and Émile Boga Doudou,
Côte d'Ivoire's Minister of the Interior, assassinated in September 2002.*

In 2002, with Blaise Compaoré and my "brother" Georges Ouégnin.

161

Alain Juppé, President of the UMP, visited Libreville in April 2003, with Pascal Drouhaud, head of the party's International Relations Department, Omar Bongo and Virginie Aubin, Juppé's Chief of Staff.

Alassane Ouattara greets my wife and daughter Sophie, in 2006, at a Children of Africa Foundation event.

Speech by President Sarkozy at the presentation of my Légion d'honneur in September 2007.

Distinction pinned to jacket.

163

With Bernard Debré, Renaud Dutreil and Patricia Balme, in 2007.

In 2007, with the ambassadors of Gabon and Senegal,
Jean-Marie Adzé and Doudou Salla Diop respectively.

In 2007, with Pierre Bédier and his wife.

In 2007, in the presence of Najr Abi Assi, political advisor to the President of the Lebanese Republic, who attended the presentation of my Légion d'honneur.

165

In 2007, with Claude Guéant and Ivorian ambassador Eugène Allou and his wife.

In 2007, with Jean-Dominique Okemba, Denis Sassou Nguesso's "securocrat" and head of Congolese intelligence.

In 2008, we celebrate Michel Aurillac's 80th birthday with his wife, Martine, at the Bristol.

In 2008, I found myself in Nouakchott with the influential Mohamed Ould Bouamatou, during General Mohamed Ould Abdel Aziz's presidential campaign.

167

With Jean-Philippe Gouyet and Philippe Bohn at the 2010 Africa-France Summit in Nice.

With Karim Wade, Abdoulaye's son and Minister of State.

In 2010, I reintroduced Karim Wade to President Sarkozy in his office at the Élysée Palace.

Autographed photo and tribute from "Papa".

Chapter 15: Laurent Gbagbo, an Unexpected Donor

The Ivorian political scene began to teeter with Henri Konan Bédié's disputed presidential election on October 22, 1995, two years after the death of Félix Houphouët-Boigny. You knew Laurent Gbagbo very well. What about Alassane Ouattara?

I knew him too. He was an opponent at the head of the Rassemblement des républicains (RDR), while "HKB" was working hard to block his way up the political ladder. He would receive me in his villa in Mougins, in the south of France, or I would see him in his apartment on Avenue Victor Hugo in Paris. I accompanied him on a visit to Dominique de Villepin when the latter held the Foreign Affairs portfolio[101].

How does Paris view Henri Konan Bédié?

Jacques Chirac made an effort to support him in the memory of Félix Houphouët-Boigny, but there was never any chemistry. The same goes for Jacques Foccart. As for Alain Juppé, he always considered, right from his trip to the 89 Club, that he wasn't working hard enough.

On the other hand, and this needs to be known, I organized a meeting between Laurent Gbagbo and Dominique de Villepin just before his victory in the presidential election of October 2000, in the complete ignorance of Jacques Chirac, President of the Republic.

How did Jacques Chirac and Villepin react to the fall of "HKB" in December 1999? Did they see it coming?

No one saw General Robert Guei coming, not even Fernand Wibaux or Michel Dupuch, who had been stationed in Abidjan for a number of

---

101. Dominique de Villepin was head of French diplomacy from May 7, 2002 to March 30, 2004.

years. In 1999, the cohabitation had been in place for two years, with Lionel Jospin as Prime Minister. Jacques Chirac suggested that the French army, present in Port-Bouët, intervene to save the regime. The head of government opposed the idea.

A helicopter was waiting for Bédié on a runway in Port-Bouët. He joined him in an armored vehicle. Georges Ouégnin wanted to climb aboard. Bédié refused, and left for Lomé with only his family. France took note of the coup but did not recognize it.

Are you "activated" at this moment?

Of course I knew him. I knew General Guei for a long time. I called him "Bob". He summoned me and George Ouégnin. No one ever knew. He gave us a letter for Jacques Chirac. We gave it to Villepin.

About what?

It was a request for recognition. It was obviously rejected. In Paris, nobody wanted to hear about this general, the first military putschist in Côte d'Ivoire.

In the months leading up to the *putsch*, Laurent Gbagbo relied on you to open up to French right-wing networks.

I went even further, in the early 1990s, when I introduced him to Jacques Foccart himself, when he was still an opponent. He had this to say:

> "Mr. Gbagbo, if President Houphouët-Boigny saw me, I don't know what he'd think, but I'm convinced that the future is in your favor."

Later, after the demise of the "Old Man", Foccart would ask me to discreetly introduce him to Villepin, as he felt that he was going to be an important figure. This was just before the fall of Henri Konan Bédié. Laurent Gbagbo came out of the interview extremely "joyful", as he himself put it.

Back then, when he came to France, he stayed at the Ibis at Porte d'Orléans. In other words, a very spartan hotel. To prepare for the meeting, I invited him to the Tsé Yang restaurant opposite my office. Villepin asked me to come along that evening to take his "special whisky" and talk about the leader of the Front Populaire Ivoirien (FPI). In power in Abidjan, Henri Konan Bédié knew nothing of this meeting. The meeting was scheduled for the following day at the Bristol bar.

On D-Day, I picked up Gbagbo at his hotel in my car. The big guy arrived at 7 p.m. sharp. The meeting was very cordial. Côte d'Ivoire is not just any country for France in Africa. All the major groups and hundreds of companies are based there. With his usual frankness, Laurent Gbagbo explained to his interlocutor that he sincerely didn't think he would come to this meeting. Villepin's response:

"That's not knowing me very well."

The conversation began, and we had very little time. Gbagbo felt that Henri Konan Bédié was at an impasse, on a slippery slope even with his openly xenophobic concept of ivoirité. He was certain of winning the 2000 presidential election. A good premonition. The next day, Villepin asked me to come back "with the person we'd seen the day before" for lunch at the Élysée Palace, in the President's private apartment on the 1st floor, on the Rue de Marigny side.

Côte d'Ivoire's main opposition leader lunches at the Élysée Palace.
A three-way lunch: Villepin, Gbagbo and myself. Laurent Gbagbo thanked him for his courage in receiving him, while reminding him once again that he was facing the future president of Côte d'Ivoire.

Beyond your friendship, why are you helping Laurent Gbagbo, a man of the left, a member of the Socialist International and a personal friend of your brother Albert, as well as personalities like Guy Labertit, the Socialist Party's "Mister Africa"?
Because I had a lot of sympathy for him. In fact, Albert congratulated me on my work in helping Gbagbo open up to him the networks of the French right-wing then in power, at least at presidential level. A Gbagbo-Villepin meeting in the heart of the Élysée Palace was an enormous risk.

Didn't this lunch leak?
Villepin told Chirac, who was furious:

"Bourgi's making a mess again!"

But I was cleared. With Villepin, the two men hit it off perfectly. They would call each other regularly thereafter.

What about Alassane Ouattara?

Jacques Chirac and Villepin never received him. Chirac didn't like him at all. Nor did his wife, Dominique Folloroux-Ouattara, whom he considered "intriguing".

In 2000, France nevertheless had great difficulty in recognizing Laurent Gbagbo, elected under conditions he himself described as "*calamitous*".

It was at this time that Georges Serre[102], Foreign Minister Hubert Védrine's "Mister Africa", contacted me. The Minister of Cooperation, Charles Josselin, under Védrine's supervision, was in Libreville. The next stop was to be Abidjan, but the trip would have been impossible without Gbagbo's explicit recognition. Georges Serre, who would later become a great ambassador, notably to Côte d'Ivoire, told me to talk to Villepin to get Paris to go along with it. I went straight to the Élysée Palace, via the Secretary General's private secretary extraordinaire, Nadine Izard, to ask to see him.

I remember it was a Thursday. Villepin asked me to go to Abidjan, while informing me that Jacques Chirac would recognize Laurent Gbagbo the following Monday morning. As soon as I arrived in Abidjan, I had dinner with the new presidential couple. On the Monday in question, Villepin informed me that Jacques Chirac would be joining Gbagbo at 9 a.m. Abidjan time. I ran to his house. Security let me into his room, where I can still see him shaving in his bathroom. I warned him:

"Chirac will call you!"

At the appointed hour, the phone rings. On the other end, his French counterpart says:

"My call is worth recognition".

The scene was unbelievable. Gbagbo hugged me and kissed me. I took the opportunity to point out to him that Georges Serre had been a great

---

102. Born in 1952, with a degree from the Institut national des langues et civilisations orientales (Inalco) and a doctorate in African studies from the École des hautes études en sciences sociales (EHESS), Georges Serre was Africa advisor to French Foreign Minister Hubert Védrine from 1997 to 2002. He later became French ambassador to the Democratic Republic of Congo (DRC), Cameroon and Côte d'Ivoire. At the end of his career, he became advisor to Rodolphe Saadé, head of the CMA-CGM shipping group.

advocate for him. He thanked him too. This is how Paris recognized him: in his bathroom, in front of his mirror!

His first visit to France, in June 2001, was not without its problems either.

He had come from Brussels and was waiting for a green light from Jacques Chirac to travel to Paris. I can confirm that Villepin used all his powers of persuasion to ensure that his welcome was in keeping with the protocol due to a head of state. The meeting went smoothly.

Villepin then visited Gbagbo at his hotel, and I can tell you it was a far cry from the Ibis at Porte d'Orléans. I had informed him that his host loved Strathisla whisky. Gbagbo immediately had some delivered. On arriving at his hotel, Villepin remarked:

> "Tell me, Laurent, how do you know it's my favorite whisky?"
> "Robert is there, he knows everything."

I still have a bottle from 1963, which Villepin gave me as a present.

Why didn't Chirac like his Ivorian counterpart *a priori*?

He swore by "Houphouët". There was, between these two men, a feeling of filiation. He never strayed from that path.

During this meeting, Dominique de Villepin considers asking the new Ivorian president to support the RPR.

He had been thinking about this since our meeting at the Élysée Palace, when he took me aside to tell me not to forget 2002. The subject was a delicate one, of course, as Gbagbo was profoundly left-wing and his party a member of the Socialist International. I asked him to trust me and let me address the issue when the time came.

Is this the very first time that Villepin has raised the issue of financing an election campaign with African funds?

Yes.

How do you explain the fact that Villepin, who wanted to handcuff you, seems to be gradually embracing this system?

He had no attraction for this type of process. However, at the Élysée Palace from 1995 to 2002, he saw a lot of money flowing in from many countries south of the Sahara. Above all, he became aware of Jacques Chirac's attraction to money. Could he alert him? Raise his awareness? Restrain him? Give him moral lessons? The two of them had been so familiar for so many years.

How do you convince Gbagbo to resort to a practice that goes against his principles?

I made him understand that he had a reliable ally in the French presidency in the person of the Secretary General, which was no mean feat. Then I asked for a tête-à-tête. He immediately understood what I was talking about. I didn't know if he was going to finance the left and the Jospin camp, but I made him understand that it would be a good omen to support Jacques Chirac. He remarked:

"Robert, I'm going to betray my side, but I'll do it."

I set up a lunch in a private room at the La Pérouse restaurant, whose owner was an acquaintance of mine, and paid for the meals of all the French and Ivorian security personnel. Omar Bongo, a great lover of this kind of juicy detail, wanted to be kept informed almost minute by minute.

Lunch has begun. The whisky and Chambertin helping, Laurent drank, Dominique drank, I drank and, at one point, Villepin looked at me. We had agreed on the right moment. I turned to our host:

"Laurent, I'm going to talk to you the way I've been talking to all the leaders of the French right for years. You need to help Chirac with his campaign. Earlier, you gave me your agreement, can you confirm it to Dominique?"

This he did, and confirmed to Chirac during his other official visit to France in December 2001. The funds were handed over by his collaborator Eugène Allou, head of protocol, on December 13 to be exact.

A new entry in the circle of contributors.

Omar Bongo, Denis Sassou Nguesso and Blaise Compaoré were already regular members of this *select* "club".

Why call on Gbagbo, a man deeply rooted in the left?

Because Jacques Chirac needed money! And Côte d'Ivoire is an ultra-privileged partner of France, with means. It is France's leading

176

trading partner south of the Sahara and the world's leading cocoa producer. It's an agricultural powerhouse.

True, but why solicit a president he didn't like?

Jacques Chirac did not initiate this request directly, Villepin did. The nuance is fundamental. Chirac loved money! No matter who they came from. He was irresistibly attracted to money. It's that simple, and that's what you journalists still fail to understand.

Was this a risky operation for you?

When Villepin approached me, he was well aware that the risks involved were minimal, if not non-existent.

In an interview with journalist François Mattei, while serving his sentence at the International Criminal Court, Laurent Gbagbo explains: "*It was 2001. Villepin and Bourgi asked me to spill the beans for the 2002 elections in France. [...] It was the price to pay for peace in Françafrique. [...] I'm not proud of this episode. I thought I'd gained the room to maneuver I needed to advance our objectives. [...] They didn't come back. I wouldn't have accepted. They knew that. Later, Chirac would say that I had missed it, claiming that I had let the information slip.*"[103]

Dominique de Villepin asked me to get a contribution from Laurent Gbagbo, which I did. To convince him, all I had to do was remind him that I had brought him into the Élysée Palace while Henri Konan Bédié was still presiding over the destiny of Côte d'Ivoire. He gave me the green light for lunch at La Pérouse. Laurent Gbagbo is anything but stupid or naive. He knew full well that the question of financing would sooner or later be put on the table.

When I approached him over lunch, he stared Villepin straight in the eye and confirmed his contribution. But it was true that it went against his convictions. He was doing it because "Houphouët" and Henri Konan Bédié had done it before him. He hoped that this "effort" would bring him a certain tranquility in his relationship with Paris. Something French leaders have never respected.

---

103. Laurent Gbagbo and François Mattei, *Libre. Pour la vérité et la justice*, Max Milo, 2021, p. 57.

How was the delivery carried out?

On December 13, 2001, Eugène Allou came to my office in a car belonging to the Ivory Coast embassy in France. He was carrying $3 million. The money was in Puma bags. I wanted to wrap it in paper. I then went to my daughter's room to get some posters of mini-Austin, of which she was a fan. For the record, I had just given her one! We wrapped the 3 million in these large glossy papers before placing them in two unmarked bags. Then I made an appointment with Villepin to hand over the funds.

We arrived at the Élysée via avenue de Marigny. Nadine Izard was waiting for us. Eugène Allou was carrying the bags alone, constantly asking if we had far to go. The poor man was at the end of his tether.

Arriving in Villepin's office, this long-time political fighter at Laurent Gbagbo's side reminded him that the man he served was loyal and of his word, but that he shouldn't be tickled too much. He insisted that Laurent Gbagbo was not "Baoulé", but "Bété", an ethnic group that was the victim of serious massacres in the wake of Côte d'Ivoire's independence. Villepin got the message, or at least he showed he did.

The two men would see each other often thereafter.

Between May 2002 and March 2004, Villepin made frequent visits to Abidjan as Foreign Minister. It was during one of these meetings, in 2002, between the three of us, that Gbagbo confided to him that he didn't feel at ease with his northern border. According to him, Blaise Compaoré was "getting a bit too agitated". He expected a neutral position from France. Villepin assured him that he was symbolically putting him under his protection.

Once back in Paris, he wanted a debriefing. He wanted to know what was going on in the North. I gave him the necessary explanations, all the more easily as I knew Blaise Compaoré perfectly. I pointed out to him that Alassane Ouattara was often seen in Ouagadougou, which was not by chance. Blaise Compaoré confirmed to me that he felt closer to Alassane Ouattara than to Laurent Gbagbo.

Chapter 16: New Money from Burkina Faso

You're close to Burkina Faso, and your contact there isn't just anyone: he's Salif Diallo, the man who made Compaoré politically.

He was the confidant, the Sherpa. He was more direct, rougher and less devious than the Burkinabe president. During our exchanges, he implied bluntly that if he could get rid of Gbagbo, he wouldn't hesitate. It has to be said that Gbagbo's victory has had a devastating effect on Côte d'Ivoire's Burkinabè community, which numbers several million people, particularly in the cocoa plantations.

Did you pass this on to Villepin?

Naturally, it was even Salif Diallo who encouraged me to do so.

In addition to his influence on the President of Burkina Faso, he was his emissary for the transport of funds from Ouaga.

In the run-up to the 2002 presidential election in France, *bis repetita*! The "chiraquie" asked me once again to collect money. The President of Burkina Faso was one of the most assiduous donors, even though he admitted to me that the coffers were not overflowing. In November 2001, I arranged a major fund-raising event with Salif Diallo in Ouagadougou, before he himself came to Paris. He was staying at the Sofitel Champs-Élysées where I went to pick him up. And there was a very big problem: the money wasn't in bags or briefcases, but in djembes!

> "Big brother, the boss said it had to go unnoticed. He came up with the idea because Villepin loves music."

It was Sunday, November 18, and the two of us stood in front of four drums filled with dollars: 3 million in total. I was incredulous. Villepin was due to meet him that evening. We got into a car from the Burkina Faso embassy. Salif Diallo is very tall, and the djembes didn't all fit in the trunk.

How did you go about it?

He asked me to take my own car, but as I'd just had a herniated disk and didn't want to touch the money, I asked my son Olivier, a strong lad, to accompany me. As usual, everyone was warned. This time, we went straight into the courtyard of the Élysée Palace. The gendarmes didn't seem at all surprised. And there my son and Salif Diallo were, with Nadine Izard's help, getting the djembes out of the car. Just imagine the scene: the gendarmes, the bailiffs in their clothes...

We made our way up to Villepin's office with our djembes packed to the rafters. He greeted us and asked the usual questions about the amount. Salif Diallo apologized because the money was in dollars. The Secretary General of the Élysée then went to fetch Jacques Chirac:

"Mr. Chairman, your visitors have arrived."

He showed up in a shirt and tie, without a jacket:

"So dear friends, how are you?"

The four djembes stood in front of him. It was like being at a Bob Marley concert. When he spotted my son, he hesitated for a moment, thinking he was a journalist.

Was this the first time he'd been involved in your operations?

Yes, Chirac asked the usual questions about his studies and so on. Then I asked Olivier to wait in Nadine Izard's office.

Four of you in the President's office.

He only had eyes for the djembes and barely looked at Salif Diallo. He did, however, ask him how his president, Blaise Compaoré, was doing. Salif Diallo again apologized for the motto. Then Chirac looked quizzical, not knowing where the money was supposed to come from. The djembes had been sealed at the bottom, and the skin had to be cut off. He turned to me to see if I was equipped to do this. I told him I wasn't.

180

Fortunately, Nadine Izard arrived with a large pair of scissors in hand. Salif Diallo, who had the bearing of a lord, wondered if he'd landed in an asylum. I'll never forget that scene.

Once the first djembe was opened, it was turned upside down and a shower of dollars fell to the ground. All small denominations of $5 and $10. I can still hear Chirac's remark:

> "He's going strong, Blaise. He's only given us small bills. What are we going to do?"

With that, I told him that my mission was over, as was that of the emissary. We asked for leave. We "asked for the road", as they say in Africa.

Why do you think African elites have compromised themselves in this way at the heart of the French presidency?

It was political clientelism in the original sense of the word. France was still very influential in Africa. But my theory, the one that will motivate my interview with *JDD*, is that Africans were still prisoners of an inferiority complex. Whether they were dealing with French presidents, ministers or deputy ministers, they felt inferior. Things have changed for the better. Jacques Foccart respected them much more than Jacques Chirac.

Notwithstanding a few sensitive operations, such as bankrupting Guinea-Conakry as soon as it gained independence, or assassinating opponents such as the Cameroonian Félix Moumié.

Africans felt inferior, weaker. The number of meetings I've attended, where I've seen simple French "ministraillons" address African heads of state, or solemnly make commitments to them without ever fulfilling them, is incalculable.

> "Your file, your negotiations with the IMF, I'll talk to the head of state about it…"

Nothing followed. As for the Africans, they continued to be solicited and to give and give and give. Real cash cows. I was becoming increasingly exasperated.

181

When did you first meet Blaise Compaoré?

In 1986, when I was working with Michel Aurillac. Then Minister of Justice and Keeper of the Seals in Thomas Sankara's government, but above all the mastermind and No. 2 of the Burkinabe revolution led by the National Revolutionary Council (CNR), he had stayed in a private hotel. I was impressed by the man. He was a very handsome man. I didn't see him in Ouagadougou at the time. Instead, I was received by Thomas Sankara himself, on the recommendation of one of my former students in Abidjan: Ablassé Compaoré. On the other hand, I took my first steps with "Beau Blaise", for whom I would later work until my interview with the *JDD*.

Did you work with his inner circle, including his brother François[104], Alizéta Ouédraogo[105] and General Gilbert Diendéré[106]?

You couldn't say I was part of his clan, or even his family. I knew the very likeable, cultured and courteous François Compaoré. I used to see him in Ouagadougou, and he never hesitated to come and say hello to me at my office. But that doesn't mean I was intimate with the Compaoré family. I vaguely met Gilbert Diendéré. As for Alizéta Ouédraogo, I'm hearing about her for the first time with your question.

A contributor to the financing of the RPR and very close to Félix Houphouët-Boigny, who introduced him to his future wife, Blaise Compaoré was very pampered by the Chiraquie. He sometimes made sumptuous gifts to Dominique de Villepin, such as a bust of the Emperor purchased for nearly €80,000.

---

104. Nicknamed the "Little President", François Compaoré, born in 1954, was special advisor to the President of Faso under Blaise Compaoré. A powerful and influential figure, he is suspected of having ordered the murder of journalist and press director Norbert Zongo, in December 1998. A refugee in France since the fall of his brother in October 2014, his extradition to Burkina Faso, requested by ministerial decree in 2020, was cancelled by the French justice system at the end of 2023.

105. François Compaoré's mother-in-law, Alizeta Ouédraogo is a businesswoman who prospered in many sectors (import-export, public works, hides and skins, etc.) under the Compaoré presidency.

106. General and Blaise Compaoré's private chief of staff, Gilbert Diendéré was behind a coup d'état on September 16, 2015, which attempted to overthrow the transitional government presided over by Michel Kafando. In 2022, he was sentenced to life imprisonment for his role in the assassination of Thomas Sankara on October 17, 1987.

It was 2004, and Villepin was at the Quai d'Orsay. At the time, Compaoré and I met very frequently to discuss current affairs, as well as the weather. I always mentioned Villepin's passions. For example, I suggested to the President of Burkina Faso that it would be a good idea to give him a gift related to the Emperor.

I knew the Galerie de Souzy, which specialized in Napoleonic art and whose owner I frequented. It's near Place Beauvau. There, I spotted an object showing Napoleon on St. Helena, his hand on a globe. It told the story of his destiny. I mentioned it to Compaoré, who immediately wrote me a check. My son Olivier and the gallery owner's son presented the gift themselves to Compaoré at the Ministry of Foreign Affairs. The invoice appears in the appendices to this book. On the other hand, I have never been to an auction room at the request of an African president to make a purchase.

Is Compaoré offering himself "protection" at a time when Ivorian rebels are setting up their rear base in Ouagadougou?
He was generous, but didn't link this kind of gesture to calculations.

You don't give an object worth more than €75,000 to a French politician without an ulterior motive...
I don't think he had any. I've always condemned his support for the Ivorian rebels, but I wasn't a minister, let alone President of the Republic.

Did he approach you or call on you after his fall in October 2014?
I didn't hear from him after my interview with *JDD*. Meanwhile, Alassane Ouattara came to power in Côte d'Ivoire. I haven't seen him since either, for reasons I'm still struggling to understand. I bump into Dominique Ouattara from time to time in Parisian restaurants, at Flandrin or Stresa. She's always very courteous to me, which never prevents me from asking her when her husband intends to extend an invitation to me.

Chapter 17: Villepin: The Betrayal

Salif Diallo is President Compaoré's emissary. Who were the other presidents you worked with? You mentioned Eugène Allou, Jean-Marie Adzé, Karim Wade and Pascaline Bongo.

To begin with, there was me, the chief emissary of the presidents, with whom I was familiar. I called them by their first names and was on first-name terms with them, with the notable exceptions of Omar Bongo, Abdou Diouf, Abdoulaye Wade and Gnassingbé Eyadema. All their emissaries were very close to me.

On this point, allow me to spare a special thought for Pascaline Bongo, despite our distance over the last few years. May she know that I love her as one might love a sister. I remember the many missions, sometimes complex and complicated, entrusted to her by her father. I've always admired her intelligence, her sophisticated education and her culture, and I'll never forget the warm welcome she received from the French authorities. Omar Bongo was always where his daughter was. She was his totem. I never went on a mission with Ali Bongo. Conversely, Pascaline was present at all meetings and interviews. One day, on the 5th floor of the Palais du bord de mer, I asked Bongo about his relationship with his children. He told me that his son, already a minister, had a hair in his hand.

Another emissary: Karim Wade, my nephew. I haven't always been kind to him, but he should know that I'm like an uncle to him. I love his children as much as I love my own and my grandchildren. I've been on many missions with Eugène Allou: what a character and what loyalty to Laurent Gbagbo! Gabon's ambassador to France, Jean-Marie Adzé, carried out missions for Jacques Chirac and Dominique de Villepin. With Maixent Accrombessi, Gabon's "co-president", relations were more delicate. I enjoyed watching him speak whenever he came to Paris, but unfortunately he never did what I asked him to do with Ali Bongo: relax his power and his regime, leave the press alone, respect opponents, ease the pressure... He didn't listen to me.

Who were the African presidents who contributed to the 2002 presidential election?

Denis Sassou Nguesso, Omar Bongo, Laurent Gbagbo, Blaise Compaoré and Abdoulaye Wade. Presidents whose payments I also knew. I think I can say that for this campaign, nearly $10 million was paid out.

Following in the footsteps of Laurent Gbagbo and Blaise Compaoré, Omar Bongo also made a contribution during his visit to France in February 2002.

He donated $3 million. We were at the Élysée General Secretariat. Omar Bongo was accompanied by Pascaline. Jacques Chirac, Dominique de Villepin and myself were there. That was the time when I began to feel really uneasy about these practices, especially after the djembe sequence.

Laurent Gbagbo president, you take care of his visibility in France, where he is on an official visit in December 2001. As part of his meeting with Jacques Chirac, he went to the Académie française, where he was received in private session by Hélène Carrère d'Encausse, the perpetual secretary. Why such a trip?

He met with Jacques Chirac and Dominique de Villepin. I wanted to make his visit even more special by welcoming him to the Académie française on December 7. I enlisted the help of my friend Laurent Personne, a direct collaborator of Maurice Druon and Hélène Carrère d'Encausse. A loyal Chiraquien and Gaullist, Laurent Personne was a true friend. Laurent Gbagbo was also welcomed by the Paris Bar thanks to the intervention of another friend, the lawyer and President of the Paris Bar, Francis Teitgen.

In September 2002, Laurent Gbagbo's feared rebellion launched its offensive on Abidjan. He called on France to come to the rescue by activating the Military Defense and Cooperation Agreements. However, Jacques Chirac refused to come to the rescue.

I remember as if it were yesterday a meeting on this subject at the Quai d'Orsay in Dominique de Villepin's office[107], the day after the offensive, in the presence of Salif Diallo, Alassane Ouattara and yours truly. It was early evening. At the end of the meeting, Villepin called Jacques Chirac, who instructed him not to stop the rebels until a buffer zone had been established in Bouaké.

The lunch at La Pérouse immediately came to mind, as did the entire content of the meeting between Villepin and Gbagbo. France facilitated the rebels' advance before calming them down by imposing a demarcation line. Jacques Chirac clearly refused to send French troops against Guillaume Soro's men.

This news led to an increasing number of meetings at the Quai d'Orsay with Dominique de Villepin. These meetings, particularly in early 2003, were generally attended by Salif Diallo, representative of the President of Burkina Faso, and representatives of the rebellion, but without any representatives of the Ivorian authorities. What exactly is being said? Is Villepin trying to influence the rebels or put Gbagbo on the spot?

As soon as Gbagbo was elected in October 2000, Paris was disloyal to him, but I could do nothing about Jacques Chirac's decisions or those of personalities such as the Secretary General of the Élysée Palace or the head of diplomacy. Numerous meetings were held at the Quai d'Orsay as soon as the rebel offensive began. I passed on messages, which earned me the reputation of being seen as a traitor by the Ivorian side, even though I was being reprimanded by the French president. Politics is all about low blows. Nicolas Sarkozy knew this closeness. In fact, I was behind his first meeting with Laurent Gbagbo at the UN in New York in September 2010.

Hence a real sense of betrayal.

I had many tense discussions on this subject with Villepin, who each time used as a pretext France's new military doctrine in Africa: Lionel Jospin's grotesque "ni-ni"; no longer intervening while remaining

---

107. Secretary General of the Élysée Palace from 1995 to 2002, Dominique de Villepin was Minister of Foreign Affairs from May 7, 2002 to March 30, 2004, then Minister of the Interior, Internal Security and Local Freedoms from March 31, 2004 to May 31, 2005, and finally Prime Minister from May 31, 2005 to May 17, 2007.

present; the end for Paris of its role as "Africa's policeman", etc. I reminded him, however, that Laurent Gbagbo had helped France financially, with real largesse in return for commitments. All the same, I reminded him that Laurent Gbagbo had helped France financially, with real largesse in return for commitments. Villepin took refuge behind the raison d'État.

In fact, anti-French resentment quickly grew in Côte d'Ivoire, where he had to visit several times, notably in January 2003. For this trip, I had arrived the day before to have dinner with the furious Gbagbo couple. Simone warned me:

"You see your Villepin, he's going to have to deal with me tomorrow."

She even accused me of covering it up.

The next day, the welcome at the presidential residence was absolutely terrible. An army of naked women covered in kaolin awaited the Minister of Foreign Affairs. Symbolically, it was a declaration of war. When women are painted like that, nobody touches them. Not even the military, police and other forces of law and order. Villepin was heckled because they refused to let him pass. I convinced Laurent Gbagbo to go and get him in the courtyard of the residence.

The three of us were Gbagbo and Villepin. The founder of the Front populaire ivoirien (FPI) lashed out violently at his interlocutor, asking him if, by any chance, he didn't take the Ivorians for "Colonial Negroes?" Referring to the rebellion, he referred to the generals' coup d'état in Algiers and asked if de Gaulle had accepted it. He immediately called for an end to the financing of this rebellion by Compaoré et al.

After this visit—it was never mentioned—Villepin was to go to Bouaké to meet French soldiers, which Gbagbo took as a declaration of war, an explicit support for the rebels. I tried to dissuade him, but in his superb mood, Villepin went north anyway. From then on, Laurent Gbagbo knew where he stood. Then came the Marcoussis conference, where he was literally humiliated by having to accept a government comprising representatives of the rebels.

Is Élysée relying on you to convince Blaise Compaoré to stop supporting Guillaume Soro?

No. Jacques Chirac and Dominique de Villepin knew where I stood and that I was close to Laurent Gbagbo, even if the latter questioned my friendship. I'd like to reiterate here that, even if I was surrounded by personalities who didn't appreciate him, I never betrayed him at any time.

It was Eugène Allou who prepared Laurent Gbagbo's visit to Marcoussis.

Sensing that the trap was about to be sprung on the Ivorian president, I expressly asked him to dissuade his boss from coming. Everyone was in on it: the Élysée Palace, the Quai d'Orsay... He insisted on coming anyway. For him, it was the ultimate humiliation. Villepin went so far as to threaten to "break his arm" if he did not accept the proposals that emerged from the conference.

What was Dominique de Villepin's state of mind during these payments?

After Jacques Foccart's death, Jacques Chirac asked us to continue his mission, to take on his role. Financing for Africa had existed since the creation of the RPF. Villepin found himself trapped in a kind of historical logic, with, what's more, a president who was very sensitive to this continent. The Élysée general secretariat therefore logically remained the point of passage for African presidents to reach the French head of state.

Was your relationship with official diplomacy always so tense during Jacques Chirac's first term in office (1995-2002)?

You can't say that, because I didn't care at all. In fact, I was completely indifferent. The only diplomats I met regularly at 2, rue de l'Élysée were Bruno Delaye and Bruno Joubert.

In his book, *Un ambassadeur en Françafrique*, Michel Lunven, who served in the Central African Republic among other posts, describes you as "*intriguing*". He claims to have you "*particularly in his sights*", accusing you of disrupting official diplomacy. He even opens up to Dominique de Villepin, who tells him not to worry, as he has "*a file against you*" and knows that you no longer have access to the Élysée Palace.

(Laughs) Why has this file never been released?

The diplomat finally admits that Villepin is lying, even acknowledging that you would later become his shadow advisor at Matignon.

Which is just an extension of what was happening at the Élysée Palace. I accompanied Villepin all the way up the political ladder. From the Élysée General Secretariat to Matignon, via the Quai d'Orsay and the Ministry of the Interior.

Like Michel Lunven, are there any other diplomats out there trying to give you a run for your money?

They didn't have the capacity at all. Once again, the only one I had any contact with was Bruno Joubert. We got on so well that he offered me some wine from his native region, Chablis 1st Cru. I still have two boxes of it in my cellar.

Why does Villepin claim to have a *"file"* against you?

I still wonder. Why did he continue to work with me until 2007?

Despite your collaboration, did he continue to distrust you?

Not at all, since I assisted him in all his portfolios. At the Élysée Palace, I saw him at least once a week. At the Quai d'Orsay, two or three times a week. The same at the Interior Ministry and Matignon. My diaries attest to this. All dates are reproduced in the appendices of this book.

In the run-up to the 2002 presidential election, the flow of African funds began to pick up again against a backdrop, as we have seen, of drastically tightened regulations on the financing of political parties in France. In November of the same year, the resounding Elf trial exposed Françafrique at its most obscure and reprehensible. This atmosphere contributed to your distancing yourself from the Chirac camp.

Elf trial, from which, incidentally, Bourgi's name is absent. You won't find any trace of it. There was a clear break with Villepin, even though I continued to see him and rub shoulders with him until he left the Prime Minister's office in May 2007. Our relationship began to deteriorate when the judges started to take a close interest in Africa and the financing of certain countries such as Gabon and Congo-Brazzaville.

This was the genesis of the "Biens mal acquis" affair, for which I was never questioned by a single judge. Eva Joly herself confirmed this during a debate organized with me by *Mediapart* in January 2023[108]. Nevertheless, associations and private individuals in France were lining up complaints against African presidents, their families and their assets. The climate was undoubtedly deteriorating.

After the 2002 presidential election, the money shipments continued. For example, Jean-Dominique Okemba handed over €500,000 in March 2004 and January 2005 during his visits to the Élysée Palace.

After some ten million dollars for the 2002 elections, contributions continued. But, in the minds of African presidents, these were "gifts". As a journalist who has specialized in Africa for many, many years, you know as well as I do that this is a common practice on the continent, and one that is widespread among presidents. It's the norm. It has even given rise to the neologism "gift-giving".

African presidents saw nothing wrong with these practices. They gave money as if it were a piece of art. It was to show their affection, but also to maintain a certain level of influence. They knew they could buy a form of non-interference, even complacency, on the part of France in their internal affairs. French politicians were, in a way, indebted to them. These contributions enabled these heads of state to obtain certain "services" in return, and to defend certain issues while maintaining strong ties with Paris.

In February 2011, Jean-Dominique Okemba was awarded the Légion d'honneur by the French ambassador to Brazzaville, Jean-François Valette. Are you behind this decision? Is it a way of consolidating your networks?

Absolutely not, but the man, a convinced Francophile, rendered enormous services to France. This distinction was well deserved.

Omar Bongo gives another €1 million during a visit to France in October 2004. Why such large sums outside any electoral campaign?

Once again, I've never tried to find out. I assume that they met the operational needs of the RPR in its broadest sense, and subsequently of the Union pour un mouvement populaire (UMP)[109] and their senior staff.

---

108. "Total Day", *Médiapart*, Cité Fertile de Pantin, January 28, 2023.
109. Chirac party created on November 17, 2002.

In the years following the 2002 presidential election, Robert Bourgi was increasingly described as *persona non grata*.

As always, I was the target of bitter people who were jealous of my level of relations.

Despite this, the period is becoming increasingly delicate. The delivery system is gradually coming under fire from the judges.

Press articles and investigations into Françafrique were piling up. It was a flood.

A climate that accelerated your break with Villepin at the end of 2005.

October 10 to be precise. He asked to see me in the afternoon. The head of his private secretariat, the famous and fabulous Nadine Izard, picked me up in her own car at the Monceau Fleurs store in Les Invalides. The appointment alone struck me as strange. It was the first time I'd been with the Prime Minister. I used to come myself and park in the courtyard of Matignon, as I would later do with François Fillon.

I got into Madame Izard's mini-Austin to drive to the Hôtel de Matignon on rue de Babylone. It was also the first time we'd taken this route. I was introduced to the Pavillon de musique. I didn't know the place. I was to frequent it regularly with Fillon.

I was settled in, and there was a small fireplace. Then Villepin came in wearing a tracksuit. He'd just been jogging in the garden. As usual, he offered me a whisky before sitting down opposite me:

> "Robert, like me, you read the press, the indictments, the judges, the Elf scandal, Bongo, Sassou and so on. And since we know that you're our link with all these heads of state, I've decided to distance myself a little, because it's starting to smell a bit sulphurous".

Was he working for Jacques Chirac?

I have absolutely no idea.

What exact expression did he use for fund deliveries?

"It's starting to smell like sulfur."

I asked him to clarify his thoughts.

192

"Robert, the money, the briefcases, the funds... It's all starting to come out, to surface and become too visible."

He even added very prosaically:

"If the judges question me and stick a finger up my arse, it'll end badly!"

Villepin didn't know it yet, but he was about to get his hands on the real Bourgi.

"Dominique, what money are you talking about? It's been like this between us for years. How many emissaries have I sent to your office at the Élysée, Place Beauvau, the Quai d'Orsay and now Matignon? The money you took didn't smell of sulfur."
"If that's the way it is, we'll stop, it's over!"

Why such a knee-jerk reaction? It's understandable that politicians are starting to protect themselves at a time when Africa is becoming the judges' playground.

Don't get me wrong: if Villepin had asked me to stop everything in a normal, courteous way, I would have understood and accepted. But he asked me to do so in a perfectly cavalier manner, and what's more, with a lack of respect for the donors. Bongo and Sassou had been helping to finance the dark side of French political life for years, and suddenly I was told that their money smelled bad, that it stank, that these presidents had become infrequent and that I, moreover, had become a character to be shunned. It was a barrage of reproaches. It unsettled me and shocked me deeply.

His reticence is understandable in view of the increasingly thorough investigations being carried out by the judicial authorities.

There's an art to it, and that's not knowing my character.

"Let's stop everything," I said.

I stood up abruptly to head for the exit when he ran after me. I held him at bay:

"Get the hell out of here. You piss me off, do you understand? You piss me off!"

Once through the gate, he was still trying to catch up with me. The gendarme on duty watched in disbelief. You never heard Bourgi scream. I kept shouting:

"You're pissing me off!"

I set off again on foot, as I had no vehicle. As I was walking along, ruminating on my anger, I called Bongo, who was beside himself. His reaction was:

"Son, calm down. Ah, is that so? Well, we'll stop everything and I'll let BP know".[110]

I then cancelled all the sensitive lines on my cell phone. Bourgi was no longer reachable. Then I called Patricia Balme, a close friend of Serge Dassault, who went on to join Renaud Dutreil's cabinet under the Fillon government, and who is above all a childhood friend of Nicolas Sarkozy, with whom she used to stick up RPR posters and campaign. I've always kept excellent relations with her. We saw each other again recently on the subject of the Senegal crisis, since she was in charge of President Macky Sall's communications[111].

I described the scene to him. Reaction?

"They don't know what they're doing, and that's not knowing you very well. You know what I'm going to do, Robert? I'm going to call Nicolas."

I went home and told my wife not to put anyone on the phone, including God the Father if he called on behalf of Villepin.

In your interview with the *JDD*, journalist Laurent Valdiguié asserts that Villepin is invoking the "presidential councils on the moralization of public life" to ask you to stop. He's following instructions.

---

110. "BP": Father-in-law, nickname given to President Denis Sassou Nguesso by Omar Bongo. Denis Sassou Nguesso, whose eldest daughter Édith Lucie (1964-2009) married the Gabonese president in August 1990. This union produced two children: Omar Denis Junior Bongo Ondimba and Yacine Bongo Ondimba.
111. Interview conducted on February 12, 2024 ahead of Senegal's March 24 presidential election.

As I was saying, he's always talked out of both sides of his mouth. For example, he was certain of Sarkozy's political demise with the Clearstream affair. He couldn't stop laughing:

> "That's it, we've got him, we're going to fuck him, we're going to stuff the midget!"

It was Villepin's flowery language that would later inspire me to use the same language during the François Fillon suit affair. I didn't even know who he was talking about. I didn't even know Nicolas Sarkozy's nickname. He continued:

> "He has a Swiss bank account, it's proven. He's dead!"

He wouldn't stop. One day, he asked me to come to Place Beauvau to pass on the information in *Le Canard enchaîné*, and wanted me to intervene directly with Claude Angeli. I told him this:

> "Dominique, you've received him several times. You know him perfectly well and have his contact details. It's obvious that I'd never tell him that kind of bullshit."

I added that the whole thing was going to backfire on him. And it did.

For Nicolas Sarkozy, under pressure from the Chirac/Villepin duo, you're a real catch.

I hadn't seen him since our first meetings at Club 89. He wasn't part of my first circle. He was Minister of the Interior at the time. Patricia Balme made an appointment for me. I went to Place Beauvau, where he introduced me to Claude Guéant, his chief of staff:

> "Robert, Patricia told me everything. You see, we serve them and they throw us away. We saw each other years ago, but even if I wasn't in the loop, I know what we owe you and what you've done for our family. You've walked through the doors of this office, and now it's yours. Your knowledge of Africa is invaluable, but you should know that I refuse to accept any money from African presidents."

He gave me his cell phone before letting Cécilia in to make the introductions. She remarked:

195

"Ah! the famous Robert Bourgi!"

He walked me to my car, and I confirmed that I was going to join his first circle. He immediately invited me to a meeting at the Bristol with Patricia Balme.

What do you bring to the table?

All my contacts, my relationships, my knowledge of the psychology of each African politician, their pedigree and their career. Every time a president traveled to Paris, I set up a visit, an interview, and attended every audience, whether large or small. I warned him that attending tête-à-tête meetings was a must for me. He had no problem with this, quite the contrary. I attended audiences with Denis Sassou Nguesso, Omar Bongo, Abdoulaye Wade, Blaise Compaoré and all the others when he was still Minister of the Interior.

Why switch to Nicolas Sarkozy if he refuses to accept any money from African presidents?

Firstly, I wanted to make a mockery of the Chirac camp, which stabbed me in the back. Secondly, it should be pointed out that my job was not simply to organize fund transfers. I was involved in political strategy. I deciphered African contexts. I acted as an intermediary. I facilitated contacts at the highest level. I intervened with heads of state in trouble with France, starting with Laurent Gbagbo.

Do these tensions go all the way back to Jacques Chirac?

I don't know.

Why doesn't someone like Omar Bongo pick up the phone and ask him directly?

Same answer.

Omar Bongo remains omnipresent in French politics. He follows all current events very closely.

I illustrate this interest and his influence by his intervention in the appointment of Jean-Pierre Raffarin's successor to Matignon, in May 2005. This is an important point. It was a fierce battle. Dominique de Villepin was Minister of the Interior, Internal Security and Local Freedoms; Michèle Alliot-Marie was Minister of Defense; Nicolas Sarkozy was Minister of Finance, and so on. Competition was fierce. It was during this period that the Gabonese president received Nicolas Sarkozy at Le Meurice during a visit to Paris in March 2005. I attended the meeting. Omar Bongo promised to intervene to make him Prime Minister.

By intervening with Jacques Chirac?

Yes. The problem is that Villepin asked him for the same thing: support to win the job.

"Dad" suddenly out of step.

He wondered how he was going to do it. I advised him to meet with him. He was frank, confiding in me that he supported Nicolas Sarkozy, while at the same time undertaking to speak to Chirac about him. So he backed him twice, knowing that in the end, the decision was obviously up to the President of the Republic, who, as everyone knows, opted for Villepin.

I heard the news at Le Meurice in front of Omar Bongo, who had been informed by Jacques Chirac over the phone. He sounded doubtful:

> "Jacques, you can't run again and you're unwell. Why not put Nicolas in as Prime Minister?"

Why did she like Nicolas Sarkozy so much better?

He appreciated his direct style. Forgive my frankness, one day he confided in me a little directly:

> "Robert, the difference between Nicolas and Dominique is that the former has balls like me. I would never have been appointed by Léon Mba if I hadn't had them. On paper, others were better qualified, but I got the job."

Following your incident with Villepin, are African presidents siding with you in favor of Nicolas Sarkozy, given that Jacques Chirac will not be standing for re-election in 2007?

On learning of my initiative, Omar Bongo called Nicolas Sarkozy to congratulate himself on my rapprochement, while referring to the "grave error" of the Chirac camp. Meanwhile, the calls to my office

197

were incessant. Villepin was pestering me. After a few days, everyone knew I'd gone over to the other side. Chiracism was mortified. Panic on board! They no longer had any crisp, strategic information from south of the Sahara.

Once again, I can't be reduced to transferring funds. I was doing political work. With this affair, "Chiracism" no longer had any feedback from African presidents—the real ones, not the ones with the diplomatic tongue in cheek.

What's disturbing is Jacques Chirac's lack of reaction, knowing that he's preparing Dominique de Villepin for 2007.

After ten days or so, my wife convinced me to get back in touch with him. We met again, as in the good old days.

"It's all forgotten, Comrade! Let's not talk about it again."

On the other hand, I reaffirmed that there would never be another African sub. I punctuated the interview as follows:

"I'm no longer your African, which means I'm no longer the President of the Republic's African, but Sarkozy's African. You need to know that!"

But that doesn't mean you're cutting your ties for good.

I continued to work for Villepin, feeding Nicolas Sarkozy much more seriously with sensitive information. I fed him with my interviews.

But the breach of trust is total.

And it comes from me, not her. I was with Villepin right up until the day before he left Matignon. He continued to see me, but I was no longer wanted. The break was irreversible.

You're at loggerheads with Dominique de Villepin. Are other members of his entourage trying to pacify the situation?

Not at all, but once he was appointed Prime Minister, he immediately phoned Omar Bongo to thank him and tell him that I would always be welcome at Matignon. Which was the truth. But trust was broken on my side.

What are the prognoses of the same heads of state for 2007?

It's worth noting that shortly after Villepin was installed at Matignon, Omar Bongo and Denis Sassou Nguesso made a joint visit to Paris, during which a sort of conciliabule took place to gauge who might succeed Chirac as candidate for the Right.

What did it involve?

Shortly before this visit, Omar Bongo had asked me in Libreville to organize a breakfast at Matignon with "Mamadou" as soon as he landed in France. I was very surprised, because, like his Congolese counterpart, he never started his audiences before 10 a.m. I'm sure he'd be delighted. More importantly, a head of state, *a fortiori* the oldest president of French-speaking Africa, doesn't travel to Matignon. It therefore seemed important, even urgent. I conveyed this request to the new Prime Minister, who asked.

Arriving in Paris, Bongo and Sassou, son-in-law and father-in-law, set down their bags at Le Meurice, then disembarked at Matignon with honors and the Republican Guard. A breakfast for four: the two presidents, Dominique de Villepin and the little Bourgi, who came with his car parked in the park.

Extraordinary scene. Villepin was seated between the two heads of state, with me right in front of him. After the customary greetings and courtesies, he asked Omar Bongo about the purpose of the meeting:

> "Dominique, Jacques (Chirac) is ill, so let's think about what's next. As Matignon, you're in the best position for the Élysée. I argued for Nicolas (Sarkozy), but also for you. You won, very well. Now let's think about the future. Are you ready to kill the father? Declare yourself a candidate? You'll win and, with us, you'll have the support of the whole of Africa".

Villepin is tested.

Of course he did. He asked for time to think while turning to me:

> "Comrade, what do you think?"

I couldn't go against Bongo and Sassou. I told him to run, knowing in my heart that he wouldn't for lack of courage.

You play on both levels.

By design. I knew the character intimately. He wasn't going to declare himself. One day in 2006, I had a meeting with him at Matignon. When I arrived outside his office, I recognized his voice and that of Sarkozy. They were shouting at each other. They were both shouting. That day, I realized which of these two political animals was the dominant one. The one 25 centimetres shorter was undeniably the stronger.

As with "Houphouët", Omar Bongo's interference in Franco-French politics remains considerable.

As soon as Villepin was confirmed at Matignon in May 2005, he asked me to join him at Le Meurice. Before a meeting with Jacques Chirac, he wanted to propose a list of the future government. The list is reproduced in the appendices of this book.

I took a sheet of paper bearing his effigies—El Hadj Omar Bongo— and he asked me to write down: minister such-and-such, name; minister such-and-such, another name and so on. And there Bongo was, unrolling the entire government of France! I was writing under his dictation. He called his aide-de-camp to tell his secretary to prepare a letter:

> "My dear Jacques, while we wait to meet again, I'll have Robert bring you the composition of the future government I'm proposing," and so on.

Another incredible detail: not only did he draw up a list of favorites for the Villepin government, but in the days that followed, he invited them all to his suite to meet and greet them. I can still see Jean-François Copé, François Fillon, Pierre Bédier, Michelle Alliot-Marie, Renaud Dutreil, Philippe Douste-Blazy... He didn't receive them individually, but in groups, as if at school, to make them understand that they belonged to the rising generation and that it had been his custom, since de Gaulle and Pompidou, to get to know the new faces. He asked them in turn to introduce themselves. François Fillon was asked to state his identity and CV, followed by Jean-François Copé. It was surreal.

Bongo commented:

> "I think you'll be part of the government."

In the meantime, I had forwarded his letter to Jacques Chirac's personal secretary. When you look at the Villepin government's list of June 2, 2005, it's more or less the same as the one Bongo had put together. Even Renaud Dutreil has been promoted.

He is yet another example of the short-circuiting of official diplomacy. Secretary of State for SMEs, Trade, Craft Trades, Liberal Professions and Consumer Affairs in the Raffarin I and II governments[112], Minister in the Raffarin III[113] and Villepin[114] governments, Renaud Dutreil obtained your intervention to be received by Omar Bongo in Libreville, in March 2004, against the advice of the Élysée Palace.

He was visiting Gabon. Incidentally, his plane went off the runway on landing. He was due to meet Gabon's no. 1 on arrival, but the meeting was cancelled. The next day, I learned from Pascaline Bongo, her father's chief of staff, that Michel de Bonnecorse had personally intervened with Jean-Marc Simon, the French ambassador in Libreville, to prevent Renaud Dutreil from being received at the Palais du bord de mer. The diplomat was embarrassed.

Why?

Diplomatic jealousies and because Bonnecorse learned from Jean-Marc Simon, who was doing his job, that I was there. As usual, I was always on the sidelines of ministerial visits, but never far away. I was always careful to stay out of the way, managing to follow all the hearings.

I went to see Bongo:

> "Dad, I organized this trip. You received Renaud Dutreil at Le Meurice in Paris, a minister I hold in high esteem. Take a look at him."
> "Robert, listen: Bonnecorse pisses me off. There's danger every time he sees you somewhere. I'm going to get your Dutreil."

How did Michel de Bonnecorse react?

I don't know, and it's not my problem at all.

---

112. From May 2002 to March 2004.
113. March 2004 to May 2005
114. From June 2005 to May 2007.

Chapter 18: Nicolas Sarkozy: The New Friend

In May 2006, Nicolas Sarkozy toured West Africa as Minister of the Interior, on the theme of "selective immigration". A stopover in Cotonou was important in that it enabled him to develop his African policy should he win the 2007 presidential election. He announced a clean break with Françafrique, while exorcising "*the networks of another era*".

I had absolutely nothing to do with this tour, but of course I reminded him of my four-year stay in Benin and its indelible memories. He was planning to denounce Françafrique, but asked me not to take offense. To which I replied that Benin being the "Latin Quarter of Africa", the Beninese would be all the happier for it.

He was supported by his advisor David Martinon, a "little" Bonnecorse who would later be appointed ambassador to Afghanistan. Bonnecorse, who would later be appointed ambassador to Afghanistan. He was the shadow of his master. When he knew I was with Nicolas, we gave him painkillers to keep him going. He was with the President in Cotonou, but I already knew all about his declaration of a "pseudo" break with Françafrique.

You're also trying to save the Dutreil soldier by appealing to Omar Bongo.

In vain. He served in the governments of Jean-Pierre Raffarin and Dominique de Villepin from May 2003 to May 2007, and wanted to run again with Nicolas Sarkozy, but Sarkozy would have none of it.

Sensing the danger, he activated all his contacts and asked me to bring "Papa" in to have a word with the new president, before whom I went to plead his case. He was an intelligent lad, and well liked by

African presidents. But Nicolas Sarkozy told me this, two points, open quotation marks:

"I don't want it!"

I made it clear that this was a personal request from the President of Gabon.

"Tell Omar I don't want him in my government!"

I failed to save him, even though I had put all my energy and affection into it.

Nicolas Sarkozy seems to be adopting a different approach to African issues, giving the impression that he wants to clear up a number of problems: Djibouti, by receiving Élisabeth Borrel, the widow of Judge Borrel, for the first time at the Élysée; Côte d'Ivoire, by smoothing out tensions with Laurent Gbagbo; and Angola, by visiting Luanda in 2008 to warm up bilateral relations tarnished by Angolagate and the Falcone affair. What did you think of this approach?

Whether in his behavior or in his attitude, he wanted to get everything out in the open, bypassing official channels. How many times did I have to go and explain to African presidents that he wanted to put everything on the table? No more hidden funds, nothing!

I briefed him on all the rotten dossiers surrounding these presidents and all the reproaches they levelled at France. I alerted him to potential deteriorations in the bilateral relationship due to sensitive issues such as the "Biens mal acquis" affair. He was aware of all the dark sides of this relationship, which could be damaging. That's why he wanted to renew France's African policy.

Two examples illustrate my point. During his tête-à-tête with José Eduardo Dos Santos, he openly mentioned the management of Sonangol, the powerful public company in charge of managing the oil sector, which had been criticized by international institutions. It was a daring move in the context of the times. In Brazzaville, where he was visiting in March 2009, he asked Denis Sassou Nguesso, at a dinner organized in his honor, not to run again for a third term of office deemed unconstitutional. I was on the same wavelength.

When he came into contact with Omar Bongo, he also always spoke the truth. Why this freedom of tone? Precisely because he owed these presidents nothing, refusing their money. He was also heavily involved in the Angola scandal, with several men from the Pasqua network, of which he was a political protégé, being implicated.

Staying with Gabon, the "Biens mal acquis" affair was born around this time. In March 2007, several associations filed a complaint in Paris concerning Omar Bongo's real estate holdings—33 apartments—in France. In November of the same year, the opening of a preliminary investigation infuriated the Gabonese president, even leading him to threaten to close RFI and "unleash" anti-French demonstrators in Libreville. The investigation was shelved, but re-launched in July 2008 following the publication of a report by *Transparency International*, **which led to new complaints. How did he react?**

I didn't intervene in any way in the "BMA" affair, apart from faithfully relaying his counterpart's anger and the seriousness of the situation to President Sarkozy. Omar Bongo had sent me the following message:

> "Tell Nicolas that if this continues, I'll come out of my silence and name all the French personalities who have benefited from my largesse, in particular to acquire real estate in Paris".

At the same time, he threatened to kick out all the French, starting with the economic groups. Nicolas Sarkozy wondered whether he would carry out his threats. I reminded him of the serious anti-French events of 1990 in Libreville and Port-Gentil.

"Bongo, you'd better not piss him off," I pointed out.

He phoned to remind him that, having been close to Charles Pasqua and former mayor of Neuilly, he knew better than anyone what services he had rendered to French public and political figures.

He insisted, however, that he had no leverage over the justice system, illustrating his point with the conviction of several figures such as Alain Juppé and the interests of the same justice system for Jacques Chirac when he was mayor of Paris.

A distance is established with Paris.

Bongo was ulcerated. Even his visits to the American Hospital in Paris became rarer. He died not in France, but in Spain, in June 2009. It was this episode that determined my appearance in *Le JDD* two years later. I didn't suddenly go mad that day. Someone naturally asked me to speak out.

In June 2022, former Miss France Sonia Rolland was indicted for *"concealment of misappropriation of public funds, corruption and misuse of corporate assets"* **as part of the "Biens mal acquis" affair. She was accused of having accepted an apartment in Paris, in the 16th arrondissement, worth €600,000, offered in 2003 by Édith Lucie Bongo.**

Omar Bongo never mentioned this type of operation or transaction in my presence, but it's obvious that he was always giving gifts. It never stopped. He would confide in me: "Son, I've just received such and such". Knowing his prodigality, it was a confession every time. No need to draw me a picture.

One day, I flew back from Libreville on one of his personal planes. I flew with Sonia Rolland and lawyer François Meyer, close to the Palais du bord de mer. You don't get on Omar Bongo's plane by chance. It's up to the reader to follow my gaze. Sonia Rolland confirmed the existence of this apartment to the judges, claiming to have been gullible…

The mirage of a break with Françafrique was quickly realized when Omar Bongo visited the Élysée Palace on May 25, 2007, almost as soon as Nicolas Sarkozy took office.

The visit was organized "my way", informally, with the prior agreement of the new president and Claude Guéant.

The day before, the President of Liberia, Ellen Johnson Sirleaf, was received. In reality, it was a diversion to make the visit of the doyen of French-speaking African heads of state and a "baron" of Françafrique more palatable.

Of course it was. When the Quai d'Orsay learned that Omar Bongo was about to be received as the first African head of state, there was an extraordinary outcry. Nicolas Sarkozy asked me, via Claude Guéant, to explain to the Gabonese president why he would only be the second to receive such honors after his Liberian counterpart. He understood.

Bongo and Sarkozy were close. Immediately after voting in the presidential election in France, I flew to the South-West to join a friend. I was staying at the Grand Hôtel in Saint-Jean-de-Luz when Nicolas Sarkozy was declared the winner. The first phone call he made was to Omar Bongo, who called me back and said:

"Son, thank you!"

That's all there is to it. It's up to the reader to follow my gaze.

All the more so as his visit was followed by that of his father-in-law, Denis Sassou Nguesso, confirming Sarkozo's ambiguity.

Here too, I was at the helm. I was able to interest Claude Guéant in Africa thanks to this type of travel and this art of evolving in the informal.

Does he see these visits as problematic? Are these heads of state, who can be criticized internally, received without qualms?

On the contrary, he considered them to be very useful to France.

It's hard to believe you when you say they didn't take part in financing Nicolas Sarkozy's campaign, because that was their modus operandi.

But that's the truth, and that's what my lobbying work is all about. Nicolas Sarkozy and Claude Guéant trusted me completely. I explained to Omar Bongo and Denis Sasssou Nguesso that the new French president would refuse any funding from them. There was never any African money going to him. Never, never, never! And I can't believe that there could have been any financing from south of the Sahara without going through me, given that I've been organizing the convoying of funds or the arrival of African emissaries in Paris for almost thirty years.

Omar Bongo was always giving to everyone, without being asked. Didn't he naturally offer funds to Sarkozy's teams without Sarkozy's knowledge?

At the risk of repeating myself: when I switched to his camp in October 2005, Nicolas Sarkozy expressly told me that he would oppose any transfers of African funds. All these presidents understood this very well. Incidentally, I would point out that if such financing had existed, it would have been known a long time ago, given the development of cases such as Biens Mal Acquis.

In 2011, Mike Jocktane, a former advisor to Omar Bongo and Ali Bongo's deputy chief of staff, claimed in an interview that the former Gabonese president had financed this campaign[115].

For over a quarter of a century, all funding from the Gabonese presidency to Paris and all money destined for France from Omar Bongo's pockets went through me. I was the only channel. I therefore formally maintain that, as early as 2005, Nicolas Sarkozy took a clear position by refusing to accept money from African presidents. He wanted to turn the page radically. This Jocktane tells stories.

How much cash did Gabon's No. 1 give out at the end of his audiences?

I don't know, but his generosity was universal. He always distributed this *cash* in Krafts envelopes. What I do know, however, is that he had his audience files well in hand, and had been doing so since the day before. He obviously knew who he was going to receive, and so, together with his most trusted men, his official aide-de-camp and his private aide-de-camp, he made up the sum accordingly. Bongo never touched the money. He planned ahead and had the sum prepared.

I think it's safe to say that, on the African level, every head of state passing through Libreville to ask for an audience at the right time, the amount didn't go below 500 million CFA francs, or €800,000 today. He only gave this sum to presidents of countries in varying degrees of need, especially those in West Africa. Don't think that he gave such sums to Paul Biya or Denis Sassou Nguesso, who didn't need them at all. He helped opponents too. This amount could rise when these same heads of state were campaigning. Having heard it from Bongo's side, I know that for Abdoulaye Wade's 2007 presidential campaign, he sent, via Karim Wade, 1 billion CFA francs (over €1.5 million). Ministers of all African countries received a minimum of 100 million CFA francs, or €150,000.

---

115. Violette Lazard, "Les mallettes de Bongo à Sarkozy : l'interview qui accuse", *Libération*, November 22, 2011.

He was always telling me:

"You see, Son, they all ask me for assignments, but I know why they come."

Whatever the status, it never went below 50 million CFA francs, about €80,000.

For Gabonese visitors, it was more modest. He didn't give all the time, but it didn't go below 5 or 10 million CFA francs.

As for Bongo's generosity towards French political figures, as I said, his generosity went everywhere. In my political camp, of course, and elsewhere. Some personalities, like Bernard Kouchner, are even in the public domain.

Did Omar Bongo distrust or abhor certain characters?

He didn't like certain people. Forgive me for not naming names. I rubbed shoulders with over a hundred personalities in his office. He was very fond of Roland Dumas and Jacques Chirac, whom he saw as accomplices, friends, kids, like at school. He loved Villepin, whose intellectual dimension impressed him. He introduced him to fields other than politics. He also liked Nicolas Sarkozy.

For the rest, he received because he had to receive. He was in his role. However, his main quality was to get people talking, to unravel secrets. He knew how to break down the armour of his interlocutors, and was quick to detect those of average ability. We knew when he'd had enough. He'd cut the conversation short. When he put his right hand on the bottom of his face to make it go from right to left, everyone knew to cut the conversation short and end it. He also adored Antoine Veil, Simone Veil's beloved husband. He respected him enormously. But the one person he loved above all others, and who somehow made him dream and travel through time, was Foccart. You need to have seen Bongo take the Doyen by the hand to direct him to be convinced.

Africa is omnipresent on the presidential agenda. In addition to his visits to the Élysée Palace in May 2007, Sarkozy made his first African tour in July, visiting Libya, Gabon and Dakar, where he delivered a speech whose post-colonial arrogance made it a landmark event. Were you aware of the content of this speech?

Initially, he was scheduled to make a stopover in an English-speaking country. This was postponed until South Africa, in 2008, which he approached through the military prism and his desire to rethink France's presence in Africa.

I persuaded Nicolas Sarkozy to go to Libreville, as it was symbolically important to greet the longest-serving French-speaking African president on his first tour. It had long been an unwritten rule, given the importance of African "Wisdom". This was the case under President Félix Houphouët-Boigny. Omar Bongo followed suit.

I discussed these stages with Nicolas Sarkozy, avoiding, as usual, the issue of Libya, an area I didn't cover at all. I briefed him on Dakar, in constant contact with Abdoulaye Wade and his son Karim. He didn't say a word to me about the Dakar speech. All I knew was that he would be delivering it at Cheik Anta Diop University, and that the Senegalese president would be in attendance. I was expecting a basic "you are the most beautiful, the most brilliant" speech.

I was in Libreville to prepare for this stage. I followed the speech from a distance. I knew there was a tête-à-tête planned with Abdoulaye Wade. Omar Bongo called me to ask if Nicolas Sarkozy had been drinking or if he was in his right mind. When he arrived in Libreville, Omar Bongo received him for a tête-à-tête. He had a box of his favorite chocolates brought in, before curtly apostrophizing him:

> "It's a good thing I wasn't in the amphitheatre in Dakar. But how can you talk like that? Africa? Not enough history? Who wrote this speech? Henri Guaino? Who the hell is he? You're going to look for someone who can't put Gabon on a map when you've got Robert with you? Do you know who his African history teacher was at the Lycée Van Vollenhoven in Dakar? Joseph Ki-Zerbo. And you call on Henri Guaino. You'll be paying for it throughout your term of office."

Weren't you alerted to the content of this speech?

No, for the simple reason that its author held it back as much as possible. Sarkozy's advisors discovered it in Dakar. In Libreville, during the meeting with President Bongo, he also asked me for my opinion on his speech. I told him he should never have made it. France is still paying for that speech.

What did Abdoulaye Wade think?

That same evening, when all the African media were talking about it, he called Omar Bongo, very distressed:

> "Omar, it was very hard, I'm offended. Sarkozy explained to me that he had read the speech in the car on the way to the university. He was only able to change it at the last minute."

During the same official visit to Gabon, the French Head of State announced the partial cancellation of the debt of this country, considered by the United Nations to be a middle-income country. Why such a "gift"? Are you behind this decision? Who is suggesting it?

In Libreville, he confirmed the promise made to Omar Bongo at the Élysée Palace in May. Since Georges Pompidou and even de Gaulle, it has been customary for French authorities to show a certain generosity towards Gabon. Nicolas Sarkozy spoke of a "gesture" towards Gabon during his meeting with Omar Bongo in Paris. And he did.

This is in keeping with the great tradition of the French Republic towards Libreville. President Bongo's first plane was a gift from France. The Transgabonais received real support from Paris too. It was important to maintain the bonds of friendship with this key country in France's presence in Africa.

When you join the Sarkozy camp, Claude Guéant is introduced to you. He is a discreet and, it seems, efficient man. The two of you hit it off.

Right away. When I met him at the Ministry of the Interior, we talked at length and often had lunch together. The man was subtle, fine and discreet. I introduced him to Africa. He immediately understood and grasped the threads of the business.

Like most high-ranking civil servants a little cramped in their suits, you seduce him with tales of exotic Africa.

More than that, because he knew the importance of the Franco-African relationship. He had the para-official and paradiplomatic knowledge on which this relationship is based. That no longer exists today. I told him about the players. Influential personalities. I'd give him their ethnic and family backgrounds, and explain how to approach them. He was extraordinarily skilful. After that, what happened to him was a different matter.

Your relations with the Élysée cell headed by Bruno Joubert, which Nicolas Sarkozy abolished, were more cordial until the serious disagreement that arose during the 2009 visit to Paris of Mauritanian President Mohamed Ould Abdel Aziz.

I consider Bruno Joubert to be the best Africa consultant of the last thirty years.

However, it was Michel de Bonnecorse who appointed him to this position.

Anyway, I had the best relationship with him.

What makes this diplomat different from the others?

He exuded real charisma and culture, despite his "old France" side, which, in my opinion, is no pejorative. He loved Africa. What separated us was that, at times, he tended to distort the psychologies of his influential players.

Are you charged for your services? How much?

I didn't have a fee schedule.

You continue to live off *lobbying* contracts.

From lobbying contracts, but above all from my income—declared—which was at the discretion of the heads of state I worked for. I didn't draw up fee invoices based on missions or time spent with these presidents. It was all-inclusive. They gave me what they wanted.

How much did Omar Bongo give you per year?

Almost 50,000 euros a month plus extras. He was ahead of Denis Sassou Nguesso, Laurent Gbagbo, Blaise Compaoré, Abdoulaye Wade and Marshal Mobutu. I made a very good living. It wasn't by the ladle, but by the barrel.

It's easy to see why Omar Bongo and Denis Sassou Nguesso are omnipresent in the Franco-African set-up.

This long predates my activities. Let's not forget that the three poles of Françafrique are Dakar, Abidjan and Libreville. Sassou came on board, all the better for having become Omar Bongo's father-in-law by marriage. They never left each other's side. They traveled together or both arrived at international conferences. Every summer, they even went to Spain for a spa treatment.

Did you receive any emoluments from the French government for which you performed this service?

None, not even plane tickets.

Even though you had no official function, you still worked for the Élysée Palace.

I have never received a penny from the French state, and I defy the best investigators to find any payment from the French authorities into my bank accounts.

Yet you served him through your missions as *missus dominicus*.

I paid for my own plane tickets and hotels. I received money from African heads of state and, as I said, I never had any complaints.

In September 2007, you convinced Laurent Gbagbo, who was still your friend, to come to the United Nations General Assemblies to meet the new French head of state. An important step after the years of tension with Jacques Chirac.

Why New York? Because I felt the ground was more neutral than in Paris. A presidential election had been due to be held in Côte d'Ivoire since 2005. The situation was totally deadlocked. We were heading for a blank mandate.

We set up this visit with Claude Guéant. Everyone doubted that it would take place. I knew from Laurent Gbagbo himself that he would come. The meeting went well, even though Sarkozy insisted that a presidential election had to be held.

You helped to warm Franco-Ivorian relations by arranging for the two men to meet again at the Europe-Africa summit in Lisbon in December of the same year.

213

Absolutely. I never went into the files. I stayed on the symbolic level. I convinced Laurent Gbagbo to obtain peace with Paris by making gestures towards the tricolored groups. That's what's been done since de Gaulle. Chirac and Sarkozy followed the same line. Since Jacques Foccart, French companies have been favored. As a fine psychologist, he understood that this was a guarantee for Hexagone. That's why the interests of groups like Bouygues and above all Bolloré were preserved, even encouraged. In April 2008, the Ivorian authorities awarded Bolloré the concession for the container terminal at the autonomous port of Abidjan. Laurent Gbagbo even organized a decoration ceremony for him. But all this has to be weighed up.

This makes me all the more comfortable in asserting that the behavior and attitude of the French authorities towards him created his "radicalization". Gbagbo was by no means anti-French, but he is a man with a culture and a backbone. He's not a soft fudge. Paris considered him an adversary from the outset. That was a mistake.

What do you mean by that?

France didn't spare him or understand him. He was literally humiliated at Marcoussis. His human nature was profoundly violated. It started with Villepin and the misguided relationship between Alassane Ouattara and Blaise Compaoré. I was a faithful visitor to the President of Burkina Faso. I saw the constant comings and goings of Guillaume Soro and all his lieutenants. It was so obvious that Ouagadougou was being used as a rear base for the rebellion. Paris, which knew better, did absolutely nothing to help Gbagbo.

I even warned Nicolas Sarkozy. It has to be said, however, that despite his closeness to Alassane Ouattara, he played the game right up to the 2010 presidential election. What happened during and after that election is another matter.

Chapter 19: The Chirac Legion of Honor

In September 2007, you were awarded the Légion d'honneur by Nicolas Sarkozy, following a decision endorsed by Jacques Chirac.

Thanks to my friend Patricia Balme, a member of the cabinet of Renaud Dutreil, a minister I liked a lot, but whom, unfortunately, as I said, I couldn't catch. Patricia Balme informed me that I should apply for the Légion d'honneur before the end of the Chirac mandate. Which I did. The first application was rejected by Michel de Bonnecorse.

As Jacques Chirac's Africa advisor, he's decidedly not fond of you. Already, when he was appointed Michel Dupuch's successor in 2002, he was instructed to keep you at a distance. As for the Légion d'honneur, he decided to torpedo your first application, deeming it to be "*complete bullshit*".

Nonsense. Once again, I don't need to go to 2, rue de l'Élysée to see my contacts. It would have been quite the opposite. But I don't blame him. Why was my work with African states so successful? Precisely because I had no official cover while, as an advisor to the Élysée Palace, he advanced with the pompous and terribly boring solemnity that the presidents in question didn't appreciate. At the French presidency, they have never understood, and never will, the political habits and customs of African palaces, and the importance of informal, personal relationships in dealing with this continent.

Will you take another chance?

I submitted a second application. And I find it quite astonishing that President Chirac signed a decree awarding me this Legion and that his advisor on Africa, who supervises the list when it comes to personalities

215

connected with that continent, couldn't stop him. How is it that Renaud Dutreil's first attempt was rejected, but the second was successful while Bonnecorse was still at the Élysée Palace?

Renaud Dutreil's office apparently managed to slip your name into the list of nominees at *the last minute*, at Easter 2007.

I'm willing to believe what my friend Patricia Balme told me: we were on vacation, and therefore relaxed, and half an hour before the closing of the lists, Robert Bourgi's name managed to slip through. I'm nonetheless delighted to have been awarded the prize, and equally delighted that Renaud Dutreil was ultimately able to give it to me.

However, I still find it curious that Jacques Chirac should sign such an important document while Michel de Bonnecorse kept a watchful eye on things. When the file arrives at the Élysée Palace from the Chancellery, it is strictly controlled by the Élysée General Secretary and the Head of State's aide-de-camp. The list then goes to Bonnecorse himself.

According to Patricia Balme, you're more of a stickler for this distinction.

Is she the one who fills in the application, yes or no? The decree signed by Jacques Chirac awarding it to me was obtained on the second attempt. But it has to be said that this was made possible thanks to the friendly and affectionate maneuvering of Patricia Balme and Renaud Dutreil, who slipped my name in shortly before the closing of the lists. So it was Jacques Chirac who awarded it to me and, ironically enough, Nicolas Sarkozy who awarded it to me.

Why would Jacques Chirac have agreed to award it to you, knowing that you had won the enemy camp?

I don't know, but he signed the decree. As soon as I knew it had been published in the Journal Officiel (J.O), I announced it to Nicolas Sarkozy, who said:

"He gave it to you, but I'm going to give it to you."

In September 2007, he hangs it on your lapel.

It was June/July 2007. He was an elected official and was already receiving me regularly. One day, I reminded him not to forget to give me this title. He then called Claude Guéant, who called in the chief of protocol. In the President's office, the Chief of Protocol unfurled the list of ceremonies and their dates, as well as the names of the recipients. As far as I was concerned, he announced a date in August. Nicolas Sarkozy stared at him:

> "You wouldn't think it, but Robert Bourgi decorates himself. Find me an evening when he'll be the only recipient."

He announced the day of the handover, on his return from the United Nations General Assemblies in September 2007.

You're an essential cog in the perpetuation of Françafrique, even though, according to you, funding for African presidents has come to a screeching halt under Nicolas Sarkozy. How do you explain this declared desire to break with the past, while at the same time decorating yourself a few weeks after his victory?

It's pure Sarkozy. Before his investiture and swearing-in, he called me at my office on rue Saint-Dominique to tell me that he wanted to meet with me, like all future ministerial candidates. But he didn't want to mix me up with all those people.

He wanted me to be his personal guest at his swearing-in ceremony, and to be placed in the family square. As soon as they saw me arrive on D-day, the journalists were stunned. That's when I spotted Villepin and said to him:

> "You're like a bastard on Father's Day".

Another contradiction: Nicolas Sarkozy decorates you while at the same time bringing to the forefront personalities who, like Jean-Marie Bockel[116], intend to destroy Françafrique.
There was a real friendship between us, and it endures.

It can't explain everything, *especially* when it comes to political and diplomatic issues.
Nicolas Sarkozy is no fan of diplomats or official channels. They are imposed by the French political system and by the presidential office, but

---

116. Appointed Secretary of State for Cooperation and Francophony in François Fillon's government on June 18, 2007.

this has never been his cup of tea. I think he's made this point sufficiently clear. Otherwise, he would never have decorated me. De Gaulle himself had a holy horror of diplomatic reflexes.

In his speech, he asks you to participate in France's foreign policy *"with efficiency and discretion"*. He adds that, as far as the cult of secrecy is concerned, you are *"a teacher"*, while advising you to *"stay in the shade so as not to get a sunburn"*. A sunburn you'll get in September 2011, with your interview in *Le JDD*. He adds: *"You know, Robert, that passion torments"*. What does he mean by that?

Every time a diplomat from the Quai d'Orsay or the Élysée Palace scuttled or criticized me, I called him or her or complained to Claude Guéant. It irritated me, tormented me. I'd had enough. That's the underlying meaning of his remark.

Why was he so keen to award you the Légion d'honneur?

Although it was imposed by the calendar, he wanted to make it a kind of "publicity". With me, he was symbolically exacting part of his personal revenge on the Chiraquie, particularly Dominique de Villepin.

A rarity: I was the recipient of the Légion d'honneur's smallest award, and the only one in the Élysée party room, where the President had authorized me to invite as many guests as I wished. Unlimited attendance! There was a huge turnout: African ambassadors, political leaders, ministerial advisors, friends...

Chapter 20: Who wants Jean-Marie Bockel Dead?

At the beginning of 2008, during his greetings to the press on "rue Monsieur", the historic headquarters of the Ministry of Cooperation, the new Secretary of State for Cooperation and Francophony, Jean-Marie Bockel, intended to sign "*the death certificate of Françafrique*", while referring to the "*predation*" of certain African leaders.

It was terrible, and the reaction was swift. This conference signed his political death warrant.

Who made it fall?

Definitely Omar Bongo. That same evening, he phoned me to ask who this "raving lunatic" was. I hadn't yet read what he'd said. I was sent the report before he told me to ask Nicolas Sarkozy to thank him:

"You have to tell Nicolas to go away!"

He was wound up. Fifteen minutes later, the same warning shot from "BP".

"Chief—he always called me Chief—go see Nicolas right away!"

I ran to the Élysée to make it clear how unhappy these presidents were, while summing up Bockel's remarks as "unmitigated bullshit". I also felt targeted by this statement, but I was used to it. On the other hand, with Omar Bongo and Denis Sassou Nguesso, in the middle of the Elf affair and at the start of the Biens Mal Acquis affair, it didn't go down well at all.

Surprisingly, Nicolas Sarkozy quickly agreed to their request.

We came very close to a diplomatic incident with several "friendly countries". To defuse the situation, he was quick to ask Claude Guéant

219

if he could think of anyone to take Bockel's place. Guéant thought for a moment:

> "I do have someone who went to Côte d'Ivoire once: Alain Joyandet. I don't know if he knows anything about Africa, but Robert can always introduce him"[117]. (laughs)

How did Bockel come to this decision?
Very, very badly. He didn't last a year. It was March 2008, and he had been appointed in June 2007. Nevertheless, Nicolas Sarkozy asked me to get in touch with him. It was the highly networked Philippe Bohn, Senior Vice-President of the European Aeronautic Defence and Space Company (EADS), who arranged the meeting. We met in a private room at Chez Laurent, a restaurant just a stone's throw from the Élysée Palace. In addition to Philippe Bohn, we were joined by his partner and friend Jean-Philippe Gouyet, Head of Africa and Maghreb at EADS[118] and Bernard Squarcini[119], a true Corsican like my wife.

It was there that I met the poor, recently dismissed Secretary of State. We got to know each other very well, though, and exchanged a few words man to man. He was a military man. We saw each other regularly when he was Secretary of State for Justice, from June 2009 to November 2010, still in the Fillon II government. Since then, we've been the best of friends.

A friend with few grudges, he was the first French personality to send a wreath of flowers to the Gabonese embassy in France, on the announcement of Omar Bongo's death in June 2009.
Exactly.

What was Nicolas Sarkozy afraid of to react so quickly?
His motto has always been:

---

117. Former RPR national secretary in charge of new technologies, member of the RPR then UMP political bureau, mayor of Vesoul from 1995 to 2012, deputy then senator for Haute-Saône, Alain Joyandet was Secretary of State for Cooperation and Francophony from March 18, 2008 to July 4, 2010.
118. Philippe Bohn and Jean-Philippe Gouyet were Senior Vice President and Africa and Maghreb Director of EADS (future Airbus Group).
119. Bernard Squarcini was Director of Territorial Surveillance in 2007, then Central Director of Domestic Intelligence (DCRI) from 2008 to 2012.

"I don't want any problems with African presidents, and I don't want the veil to be lifted on certain practices."

How do you explain a French president agreeing, at the request of an African counterpart who carries no extraordinary weight in world geopolitics, to get rid of a member of his government?

Omar Bongo was the stuff of legend. Nicolas Sarkozy knew all about it. He had known him since he was mayor of Neuilly. "Papa" had been in office since General de Gaulle. That's no mean feat. His influence on African issues was considerable, including at the United Nations. If, for example, Bongo asked African states to support France on a resolution, there was no arguing about it.

Gabon is a small country, but its president was able to sort out a lot of conflicts. He was involved in African diplomacy. From the release of Nelson Mandela to the civil war in Congo-Brazzaville, not forgetting peace talks, he was at the helm everywhere on the continent and knew everything. Nicolas Sarkozy, on the other hand, has always had a cowboy streak. He always wanted to solve problems quickly.

It was Claude Guéant who broke the news to Jean-Marie Bockel. Nine months after his appointment, he was reconverted to Secretary of State for Defense and Veterans. It's a shame what happened to him. He thought the Cotonou speech had made history. But only David Martinon believed that...

How did you hear about the Philippe Bohn-Jean-Philippe Gouyet duo?

We became friends at various meetings. Both are Gaullists. They're first-hand informants. After Nicolas Sarkozy lost the primary, I made an agreement in my office between all these people, including Claude Guéant, to support François Fillon.

On the other hand, there are a number of episodes that suggest that Franco-African relations are on the up. Alain Joyandet's induction into Omar Bongo's home on April 13, 2008.

African and French audiences need to know how this demining operation went. Once Jean-Marie Bockel's departure had been made official after his deplorable press conference on Rue Monsieur, dictated by the

221

inimitable David Martinon, Nicolas Sarkozy asked me to have dinner that very evening with Alain Joyandet to inform Omar Bongo and Denis Sassou Nguesso.

We met at the Bristol. After meeting him, I put Omar Bongo on the phone. He was flabbergasted. A head of state on the line like that, he couldn't believe it. He wasn't used to it. He promised his illustrious interlocutor to reserve his first visit for him. I did the same thing with Denis Sasssou Nguesso. The press hadn't even been informed yet. I think I remember giving the scoop to journalist Jean-Michel Apathie.

Once Alain Joyandet was officially appointed to his post on March 18, 2008, he was besieged by an armada of journalists wanting to know what role I had played in his appointment. Being related to many of them, I thought of a press trip to Libreville. The interviews started in mid-air.

Once they had landed in the Gabonese capital, the journalists had no visas. However, presidential cars were already waiting for them on the tarmac. They understood nothing. The next day, we all went to see Omar Bongo, whom I had already briefed on the questions he would inevitably be asked. He was a director. He wanted to restore his prestige and make sure people understood that he was still the "boss", to the point of being able to unseat a member of the French government, as was the case with Jean-Pierre Cot, François Mitterrand's Minister for Cooperation and Development, at the request of Félix Houphouët-Boigny[120].

Journalists were ecstatic, and Bongo was peppered with questions. Supposedly dead, Françafrique was back with a vengeance. A French Secretary of State kissing the hand of Africa's most senior president under the spotlight and the microphones was unprecedented. I reveled in it. Then it was our turn to go home. Omar Bongo was in his imposing armchair. Alain Joyandet sat opposite him, Claude Guéant on his right and the tiny Bourgi on his left. Bongo asked the newly-appointed minister if he was happy, while hoping he wouldn't do a Bockel. And Alain Joyandet reassured him:

"Mr. President, I have received instructions".

---

120. François Mitterrand's Prime Minister for Cooperation and Development, Jean-Pierre Cot was forced to resign on December 8, 1982, twenty months after his appointment on May 22, 1981, under pressure from several African presidents, including Félix Houphouët-Boigny. He was criticized for having made a radical break with current practices in Franco-African relations.

Translation: "It's going to be a step backwards!" At the end of the interview, Omar Bongo let in all the French press, including a team from Canal+, who had been waiting outside. Alain Joyandet and Claude Guéant were "trapped". What else is there to say?

After Alain Joyandet's forced resignation following suspicions that he had illegally obtained a building permit for his house in Port-Grimaud and had flown to Martinique on a private jet for more than €116,000, there is talk of Jean-Marie Bockel's return to Coopération. With Claude Guéant, you would have defended such a scenario.

I beg to differ. There were many candidates, including Bernard Debré, Anne Marie-Idrac and even Thierry Mariani, but the Guéant-Bourgi duo never played this card. In the end, Henri de Raincourt, a "marquis" of no substance whatsoever, won the job.

Between your Légion d'honneur and Jean-Marie Bockel's dismissal, you are perpetuating the logic of the predominance of unofficial links to the detriment of diplomacy. The Minister of Foreign Affairs, Bernard Kouchner, has virtually no influence on Africa, which remains the "reserved domain of the reserved domain" that is the Presidency of the Republic.

Stripped to shreds in a book by Pierre Péan[121], Bernard Kouchner has had no African dimension whatsoever, apart from, at best, the Rwandan issue. Africa was an even more reserved domain under Nicolas Sarkozy.

In the same way that Omar Bongo got Jean-Marie Bockel's head thanks to you, you brought up Abdoulaye Wade's strong dissatisfaction with the French ambassador to Dakar, the writer Jean-Christophe Ruffin, whom you succeeded in getting recalled in June 2010. How did this work out?

In the simplest terms: Abdoulaye Wade called Radio Bourgi. I was on my way to the airport to join my wife in Corsica. Arriving at Orly, I received a feverish call from him:

> "My nephew, how are you, what are you doing?"
> "Uncle, I'm going to join my family in Corsica."

---

121. Pierre Péan, *Le monde selon K*, Fayard, Paris, 2009.

"It's out of the question! You're going back to Paris immediately. Ruffin has changed his nationality, becoming Senegalese and one of my opponents. I don't want to see him anymore. I can't allow the French ambassador to play against me. I want him out!"

So that was another Bockel affair. I cancelled my trip before rushing to Claude Guéant's house. Abdoulaye Wade wasn't the dean in terms of longevity, but in terms of age. So respect. The Secretary General of the Élysée Palace and I explained everything to President Sarkozy in his office. He had this to say:

"Again? What the hell, is it always like this?"

I replied that things had changed over the last thirty years: before we changed heads of state, now we change ambassadors...

Appointed to this post in August 2007, with responsibility for Gambia, Jean-Christophe Ruffin had previously chaired the NGO Action contre la Faim. He had a "developer" streak and assumed a certain freedom of tone that deeply displeased the Senegalese authorities. Since taking office, he had called for dialogue with the opposition. He criticized President Wade for his frequent travels, as well as his project for a statue of the African Renaissance, which he considered costly. His predecessor, André Parant, who occupied 2, rue de l'Élysée at the time, had also run into trouble in Dakar for criticizing the dynastic temptations of the Wade clan. With Jean-Christophe Ruffin's departure in the bag, President Sarkozy asked me who I thought should replace him. Traditionally, I'm not close to diplomats, but during my last visit to Brazzaville, President Sassou Nguesso complained about the local ambassador, Nicolas Normand.

Nicolas Sarkozy had this to say:

"Really? Even over there?"

I knew Nicolas Normand, because every time I visited the Congolese capital, I went to the ambassador's residence—a kind of pilgrimage—since it was De Gaulle's hut. He was also the son-in-law of Roger Fauroux, a former minister under François Mitterrand. At Nicolas Sarkozy's request, I had to announce his appointment to Dakar at the same time as Ruffin's departure. Nicolas Normand, who lives on the Place du Panthéon in Paris, close to Laurent Fabius, was all the more delighted as the Quai d'Orsay had already "tipped" him for Djibouti after Brazzaville. Dakar is a fine post.

Later, I'll be his godfather when he receives the Cross of the Legion of Honor. I presented it to him. At the ceremony, Roger Fauroux said to me:

"But how happy I am to finally meet Monsieur Robert Bourgi!"

At the Quai d'Orsay, they must have choked.
I think there was a general distribution of antidepressants.

At the time, Nicolas Sarkozy was preparing *L'initiative 2010 pour l'Afrique* **to celebrate the fiftieth anniversary of independence.**
Jacques Toubon was asked to prepare the event. He had been one of Dominique de Villepin's atonement victims when he was an advisor to Jacques Chirac at the Élysée Palace, but it wasn't me who slipped his name in. However, Nicolas Sarkozy knew full well that all heads of state visiting Paris consulted me at their hotels. The atomic bomb of 2011 had not yet been dropped.

In 2009, a French observation mission was set up for the presidential elections in Congo-Brazzaville, at a time when Sassou Nguesso's regime was in the crosshairs of the European Union, which was refusing to send anyone. This operation involves personalities such as lawyer Emmanuel Carlier, Patrick Gaubert, Jean-François Mancel and Jean-Marie Fourgeoux. Are you one of them?
I wasn't involved. It wasn't one of my missions. And even if I had been offered it, I would have refused. I wasn't interested.

For fear of being exposed, given the nature of the regime?
No, because I was on the best of terms with Sassou, but I never joined a group. I always worked solo, that was my line. I never deviated. "Secret de deux, secret de toujours. Secret of three, secret of all", Jacques Foccart was always telling me. I made that my maxim.

In 1998, however, you organized an observer operation for the presidential elections in Gabon.

There were personalities like lawyer Francis Szpiner and magistrate Georges Fenec. It was the first truly pluralist presidential election in this country. They were able to do their work in complete freedom. But, to be honest, at that time, no one had any real clout against Bongo.

Many other French personalities were appointed to observe elections in Africa. However, the exercise was open to question. One example is Jean-Paul Benoît, a lawyer and European deputy whom Omar Bongo wanted to appoint as French ambassador to Libreville in the 1990s. With his partner Jean-Pierre Mignard, a personal friend of François Hollande, he defended Alassane Ouattara and the Ivorian state in the trial against Laurent Gbagbo at the International Criminal Court (ICC) in The Hague. This former colleague of the Minister of Cooperation, Pierre Abelin[122], was a member of Club Zimbabwe, to which you belonged. What was this about?

It was a club born in the late 1970s, out of meetings, friends and conversations. The honorary president was Omar Bongo himself. In addition to Jean-Paul Benoit, other members included Christian Casteran[123], Jean-Marc Kalflèche[124], Claude Angeli, the Gabonese Albert Yangari Ngorouma[125] and yours truly. Whenever Omar Bongo came to Paris, he made sure we got together for a chat and a meal. We'd talk about current affairs.

Thus, the director of *Le Canard enchaîné* belonged to what might today be described as an informal *think tank*, chaired by Omar Bongo himself.

Absolutely.

Nicolas Sarkozy's victory marks the return of his friend Patrick Balkany to the Franco-African village. The Levallois-Perret mayor's "African activities" were not new, as he had carried out several

---

122. Pierre Abelin (1909-1977) was Minister for Cooperation in Jacques Chirac's government from May 1974 to January 1976.
123. Journalist specializing in African issues, died in 2016. Author of *Omar Bongo, Confidences d'un Africain*, Albin Michel, Paris, 1994.
124. Journalist specializing in Africa, notably for *Le Figaro*, died in 2001.
125. A journalist by training, Albert Yangari Ngorouma (1943-2023) was director of Radio-Télévision Gabonaise 1 (RTG1) and the government daily *l'Union*. Deputy Director of Omar Bongo's private office, he was also Secretary of State for Public Relations and then for Tourism.

missions in the 1990s on behalf of Édouard Balladur, then Prime Minister. With Nicolas Sarkozy, he is particularly interested in the mining sector in Mauritania, the Democratic Republic of Congo (DRC) and Guinea. How do you see this renewed interest?

I immediately wondered what he was up to and what he could possibly be doing on African issues. I knew him, of course, as I knew all the constellations in the Sarkozy galaxy. He wanted to see Mohamed Ould Abdel Aziz to discuss iron ore with him. Apparently, he had a few interested contacts in this sector.

The Mauritanian president received him when he visited France in autumn 2009. I think it was the shortest audience he ever gave: ten minutes, watch in hand! Patrick Balkany left much faster than he had expected. He came for business. He got nothing. I've never been associated with his "business", but I've always had a great deal of affection for him and his wife, Isabelle.

Didn't his activism worry you?

No more than that, although one day when I was talking to him at the start of his term of office, President Sarkozy tested me:

> "I'm being harassed by Patrick, whom I adore, who wants to be appointed Minister for Cooperation. He wants a portfolio. What do you think, Robert?"

I alerted him to the fatal error of such an appointment and the reactions it would inevitably provoke. Patrick Balkany knew nothing about African affairs. He'd been given a diplomatic passport, which was more than enough.

Caught for his activities on the continent between 2007 and 2012, he was indicted for "tax fraud laundering", "corruption" and "corruption laundering". At the time, judges Renaud Van Ruymbecke and Patricia Simon were interested in his mining activities in the DRC and his relationship with businessman Georges Forrest. Were you aware of this?

He effectively entered Africa via the mining sector. That's what he wanted to do in Mauritania and Guinea. But I knew nothing about his methods or contacts. Only the judges can answer that. He was doing business or looking for business. I don't know if he succeeded, but both in Mauritania and Gabon, he broke his back. Nicolas Sarkozy asked me to have Omar Bongo receive him during his visit to Libreville in July 2007. He wanted to show his friend that he had intervened on his behalf with his Gabonese counterpart, without going any further. He clearly completed his request by saying:

"Robert, I'm asking you this, but don't push it any further..."

I asked Omar Bongo to receive him, but the meeting was not to lead to anything concrete. In fact, Balkany left the presidential palace empty-handed. He's still waiting to hear about African affairs.

He allegedly brought Georges Forrest a contract, pocketing a $5 million commission in the process.
I knew no more than that.

Another mission during the Sarkozy mandate, this time to Madagascar, where you travelled on behalf of Louis Dreyfus Commodities.
I met Louis Dreyfus through Abbas Jaber, a French-Senegalese-Lebanese businessman whose father was close to mine and for whom I was an advisor-lawyer. We hit it off. He wanted access to Africa. I must say I never received a single cent from him. I took advantage of this mission to speak with Andry Rajoelina, then president of the transition.

In addition to African presidents, you've worked for a number of French groups.
I worked for Bolloré and Air France. The company paid me 10,000 francs a month, or 1,500 euros. That was under the Chirac and Sarkozy mandates. They called on my services and contacts to solve certain problems in Gabon, Beirut and Dakar. For example, I would lobby the presidents to obtain new services. I used to take Guy Delbrel, the company's long-standing director of international affairs, to see Abdoulaye Wade, Omar Bongo and so on. I'm very fond of him too. Good father, good grandfather, good husband. When we have lunch or dinner together, we don't look at the number of calories or the blood alcohol level. For Bolloré, I tried to open doors, notably in Guinea, for his tobacco business. He put his plane at my disposal. I paid him every month. In his tobacco division, my correspondent was the delicate and intelligent Pierre Imbert.

Photo Album n°3

*President Mobutu Sese Seko honors me
with his friendship and affection.*

In 2002, in Marbella, President Denis Sassou Nguesso, who unfortunately turned his back on me after my interview in the JDD.

In 2004, another meeting with Denis Sassou Nguesso at the Hotel Bristol.

In 2005, my wife and I, with Omar Bongo Ondimba, at the Pavillon d'Armenonville.

With the much-missed Henri Lopès, in 2008.

231

In 2009, with Hajj Hussein Teffaha,
a Shiite imam from southern Lebanon.

With the delightfully intelligent Chantal, "Coco" Sassou Nguesso, daughter of the Congolese president and influential advisor to her father, in charge of public relations and communications, as well as President Sarkozy.

233

With Catherine in Syria, in front of the mausoleum of Sitt Zeinab
(revered daughter of Imam Ali, Commander of the Faithful),
in preparation for my visit to Iran in 2010.

*In 2010 in Teheran, with Iranian President Mahmoud Ahmadinejad,
before starting negotiations for the release of Frenchwoman Clotilde Reiss.
Greeting me, he said that Shiites were present everywhere, including
in the Senegalese presidency.*

Negotiations begin under the watchful eye of Ayatollah Khomeini.

235

In 2010, lunch on the heights of Damascus with General Mohamed Nassif (white hair), head of the Syrian secret service. By my side, my brother and friend Hassan Hejeij, a Lebanese national with great influence in that country.

In 2010, Alain Joyandet, Secretary of State for Cooperation and Francophony, with businessman Mohamed Ould Bouamatou, my son Olivier and my "brother" Jean-Paul Fayot. Jean-Paul Fayot.

My old friend Jean-Paul Fayot, an active member of the Republican Right and a renowned dental surgeon who has practiced in Marseille, Nice and Abidjan. We've known each other since the "Van Vo" high school. He has accompanied me throughout my family and professional life.

On January 19, 2013, my dear friend Jean-Claude Darmon was made a knight of the Legion of Honor by Nicolas Sarkozy. I find myself in good company with Michel Drucker, Claude Lelouch and Gervais Martel, President of Racing Club de Lens.

In 2020, I introduced the yet-to-be-inaugurated president of Guinea-Bissau, Umaro Emballo Sissoco, to President Sarkozy, in the company of businessman Kamel Benali.

239

Many political leaders always come to meet me.
Here Jordan Bardella, President of Rassemblement National,
with David Rachline, Mayor of Fréjus, in 2022.

In 2023, an audience with President Macky Sall, with a delegation from
the Nouvelle génération d'entrepreneurs (NGE), an economic organization.

In 2024, Nicolas Sarkozy invited my friend
Mohamed Ould Bouamatou and his son to his office.

In Eric Dupont-Moretti's Paris office,
in 2016, when he was defending my interests.

At the Petit Palais, on Dakar's corniche, I'm the first guest of Amadou Ba, candidate for the Alliance pour la République (APR) in Senegal's March 2024 presidential election.

Generation Bourgi: all my grandchildren.

243

Annual pilgrimage to the tomb of General de Gaulle at Colombey-les-Deux-Églises.

Chapter 21: Putschists at the Élysée Palace

In August 2008, General Mohamed Ould Abdel Aziz's coup d'état in Mauritania was closely followed by the Élysée Palace, creating several diplomatic mini-crises. A few weeks after the *coup*, you introduced a relative of the new strongman in Nouakchott, businessman Mohamed Ould Bouamatou, to Claude Guéant. How did the meeting come about?

I had lived in Mauritania for over two years, teaching at the École nationale d'administration in Nouakchott, but I didn't know this influential businessman and cousin of General Mohamed Ould Abdel Aziz. I met him a few days after the coup, through my friend Abbas Jaber.

He contacted me while we were both on vacation in Saint-Tropez. He wanted to introduce me to him. Mohamed Ould Bouamatou came to my hotel to explain the reasons for the *putsch*, arguing that the overthrown president, Sidi Ould Cheik Abdallali, although legitimate, had become very unpopular.

By taking this step, he clearly hopes that the new regime, which has been ostracized by the international community, will be endorsed, *a fortiori* by Nicolas Sarkozy in his capacity as President of France and the European Union.

Yes. He also asked me to arrange for the Chief of Staff of the Mauritanian army, General Mohamed Ould Ghazouani[126], who had been dismissed by the defeated president, to be received at the Élysée Palace. I asked him for 24 hours. I then asked Claude Guéant for a meeting.

---

126. Mohamed Ould Ghazouani was elected President of the Islamic Republic of Mauritania on August 1, 2019 and re-elected on July 1, 2024.

He immediately agreed to receive the businessman, in my presence and that of General Mohamed Ould Ghazouani. The Chief of Staff had been introduced to me just before the audience. I had previously organized a breakfast at the Bristol, to which all these people were invited, as well as Karim Wade and Alain Joyandet. Alain Joyandet was quite embarrassed, as he had no official request for an audience.

With this interview in the heart of the Élysée Palace, you are working to legitimize a regime born of a coup d'état.

The interview went very well. At least at first. Karim Wade withdrew at the very beginning because, as Minister of State, he did not wish to appear as a stakeholder in the case. From the outset, Mohamed Ould Ghazouani made a very strong impression on me. His eyes were Persian blue. A haughty bearing. He explained in detail the reasons for the *putsch* and gave an overview of the situation on the ground, pointing out that the junta was backed by the big families—the big tents—of Mauritania.

This discussion, together with my deciphering of the situation, won over Claude Guéant. The Élysée's Africa advisor, Bruno Joubert, joined us after half an hour. He seemed absolutely horrified by the scene. A diplomat coming face to face with a putschist general: imagine the scene! I reaffirm what I said earlier: Bruno Joubert was, in my opinion, the best Africa advisor to the French presidency in the last twenty-five years, but the situation was not lacking in piquancy. He wondered what trap had been set for him.

Mohamed Ould Ghazouani repeated the same speech and the same thoughts. Claude Guéant asked Joubert for his opinion. Ulcerated, the diplomat replied rather curtly:

> "Mr. Secretary General, the European Union rejects the power of General Mohamed Ould Abdel Aziz. It is inconceivable that the President of the Republic could accept this situation. Moreover, General Mohamed Ould Ghazouani was one of those who precipitated the fall of President Abdallali."

Which was the truth.

It's hard to argue the contrary. Mohamed Ould Ghazouani was indeed a "putschist" received at the Élysée Palace. His reaction was terrible. He glared at the diplomatic adviser, telling him not to speak to him like that.

Seeing that the situation was becoming tense, Claude Guéant turned to Alain Joyandet, Minister for Cooperation, to ask him what he thought of the Mauritanian context.

The poor guy was in over his head (laughs). He agreed with me that the *putsch* was motivated by the unpopularity of the outgoing regime. The meeting ended. Claude Guéant reaffirmed that I would continue to liaise with Paris. We then returned to the Bristol, this time for lunch. Bruno Joubert left the meeting very preoccupied.

Yet another illustration of the serious short-circuiting of diplomacy.

Admittedly, the most important figures in the new Mauritanian regime all passed through me. They could not decently approach the Quai d'Orsay, on pain of being turned down.

This *putsch* was rejected by the European Union and the United States. Don't you have any qualms about introducing its main perpetrators to the French presidency?

None at all. I followed my master's teachings on the subject.

This marks the beginning of the end for Bruno Joubert as Africa advisor to the Élysée Palace.

Nicolas Sarkozy is back from his vacations. Claude Guéant had obviously kept him informed of the meeting and its tone. He summoned me to ask me what I thought of it in person. After making several contacts in Nouakchott, I reaffirmed the importance of playing the Mohamed Ould Abdel Aziz card. Claude Guéant was on the same line.

Then the tensions with Bruno Joubert came up. I told Nicolas Sarkozy that his behavior towards Mohamed Ould Ghazouani had struck me as discourteous, not to say improper. The latter later confided to me that he had almost come to blows.

I felt that the President of the Republic was taking my side. He called for the release of President Sidi Abdallali, while waiting for the 2009 presidential elections. This did not prevent him from receiving candidate Abdel Aziz at the Élysée Palace in June of the same year, a few weeks before the election, which acted as official recognition.

Prior to the elections, Claude Guéant met Mohamed Ould Ghazouani again in February 2009, accompanied by Mauritanian Foreign Minister Mohamed Ould Mohamedou, in the presence of DGSE Director Érard Corbin de Mangoux and yourself.

Absolutely.

Why is the head of the DGSE here, and why with you? This is one of the very few interviews you'll be attending in this format.

I didn't care about the head of the DGSE. The interview was primarily with Claude Guéant in his capacity as Secretary General of the Élysée Palace. Nevertheless, we were witnessing the rise of Islamic terrorism in the Sahel. Mauritania was one of the first countries to be affected, following a suicide bombing outside the French embassy in Nouakchott in June 2009, and above all the death of four French tourists two years earlier, in December 2007. In other words, the "Mauritania" file was quickly entrusted to the services rather than to the Quai d'Orsay.

After this meeting, Claude Guéant contacted Mouammar Kadhafi, Chairman of the African Union (AU), who recognized the new Mauritanian regime.

I was not informed of such a call. I found out later from General Ghazouani.

Does Gaddafi's position convince France to legitimize Mohamed Ould Abdel Aziz?

You could say that.

In France, many movements are speaking out against this *putsch*, including in the National Assembly.

I was panned by the press, but I did my job.

In June 2009, Mohamed Ould Abdel Aziz was received in Paris.

I didn't organize anything. We had breakfast with him on a Saturday morning. Claude Guéant, Mohamed Ould Bouamatou and myself were present.

Do Mauritanians pay you?

I've never received a penny from them.

How can you explain your involvement, spending so much time and energy on a mission with zero pay?

I always worked under my own influence. I was always marked 20/20. I was known to be very close to Nicolas Sarkozy and Claude Guéant. I was the only person capable of resolving requests for meetings on Africa that had not been formalized at the highest level of the French government, without having to use the diplomatic corridors. After Mohamed Ould Abdel Aziz's victory, Alain Joyandet represented the President of the Republic at the swearing-in ceremony. I was present in Nouakchott, but always in an unofficial capacity.

How did Bruno Joubert's downfall come about?

As soon as Claude Guéant confirmed his departure, President Sarkozy decided to replace him. He's hyper-reactive. A reptilian. When he decides to do something, he does it quickly. He demanded that we find him a place to stay, and asked for my opinion. I begged him not to involve me. Bruno Joubert will get the French embassy in Morocco.

What was his mistake? Tackling the illegitimate chief of staff of a foreign country?

Let's give credit where credit is due: Bruno Joubert was a great diplomat, but he paid dearly for his cult of diplomacy with a capital "D" and his cult of ethics with a capital "E". On the other hand, when it came to the scourge of the scales, his analysis was naturally the right one.

How did he take it?

So bad that I never saw him again. He always thought I was the cause of his troubles. For the record, ten years later, I attended the funeral of his father, whose death I'd learned of by perusing the obituary pages of *Le Figaro*. As a friend, I went to the church on avenue Franklin Roosevelt to attend the funeral service. As I approached him to kiss him, he pushed me away in front of the entire congregation. I returned to Catherine, who had accompanied me, before leaving the scene, vexed. After recounting this episode to Nicolas Sarkozy the following day, he again remarked:

"You see, Robert, that's what diplomats are all about."

Like his predecessors, Nicolas Sarkozy is radically contradicting himself when it comes to African policy, between the rhetoric of a desire for change and political pluralism and the actions taken. Receiving at the Élysée Palace a general who was behind a coup d'état, a few weeks before the presidential elections for which he is running, sets an unfortunate precedent.

He was totally at ease with this kind of contradiction.

Bruno Joubert was replaced by André Parant, another great diplomat with a prestigious African pedigree.

I knew him, but never went to talk to him. Once again, I was dealing with the Good Lord. No need to go through his advisors.

Elected in July 2009, Mohamed Ould Abdel Aziz came to Paris in November. He did not attend the dinner organized in his honor at the Quai d'Orsay, preferring instead to host guests at Le Meurice, including Foreign Minister Bernard Kouchner. He organizes these dinners himself, to which the head of French diplomacy is invited. Bernard Kouchner insisted that Alain Joyandet not attend. The Minister for Cooperation refused to follow this instruction, asking Claude Guéant to arbitrate.

And with good reason: Alain Joyandet felt he was the personal guest of the new Mauritanian president. I was one of the lucky guests. Claude Guéant asked that both ministers take part in the meal. At the very start of the dinner, Kouchner came over to greet me warmly.

"The station manager sends his regards, Bernard," I said.

Why this line of humor?

For months, he'd been telling anyone who would listen that he didn't know me and had only greeted me once in his life on an airport tarmac. But I had known him for a long time, notably through the highly profitable studies he had carried out for Gabon and Congo-Brazzaville on the creation of an insurance and social security system.

A clash ensued: he finally refused to attend the dinner and left the room to avoid appearing with a president he felt was not legitimate.

It's Kouchner, no more, no less. In line with his ethic: the socialist ideal with its many variants…

How did Mohamed Ould Abdel Aziz react?
He said nothing.

And Alain Joyandet?
As Minister for Cooperation, he played the game. He fulfilled his duties.

And Nicolas Sarkozy?
He thought it was Kouchner. He never appreciated or supported it. For him, it was a prize of war. Nothing more.

Bernard Kouchner has taken liberties with his ethics, working for two presidencies that are highly questionable from a democratic point of view.
It bears repeating: it was Omar Bongo who paid for both studies. The one for Gabon and the one for Congo. He paid €800,000, the amount discussed with Bernard Kouchner at his private hotel in Paris, rue Edmond Valentin, in the 7th arrondissement, during his visit to France in May 2007. For this meeting, the Gabonese president had requested my presence. As soon as he saw me entering the room, the head of diplomacy was astonished. Omar Bongo formally asked me to stay. Then he said to Kouchner:

> "Bernard, I had you prepare what you asked for the work done. Do you want it now?"

Embarrassed, he replied that Omar Bongo would be in Paris for several days, so he would have the opportunity to see him again. The President of Gabon informed him that his aide-de-camp, General Flavien Nzengui-Nzoundou, would contact him. He then left.

> "But Dad, you've put me in quite a situation," I remarked to the Gabonese president.

He then asked me to ensure that Nicolas Sarkozy was informed that evening of the content of this discussion.

251

A calculated rush.

And with good reason: the next day was the cabinet meeting. No sooner said than done: everything was scrupulously reported. At the cabinet meeting the next day, Nicolas Sarkozy greeted all his ministers, before asking Kouchner if his meeting with President Bongo at 8 p.m. sharp the previous evening had gone well. I was told that the head of the Quai d'Orsay was livid. His work was obviously not worth what he charged and received.

Chapter 22: The Death of the Father

How can you explain such a close relationship with Omar Bongo?

We first met in 1982, during a lively conversation on the subject of twins. He was concerned, as twins ran in his own family. This phenomenon, especially monozygotic twins, fascinates people in Africa. He put me on the spot.

He was wildly truculent and hard-working, unlike other African presidents. We'd talk about politics and life. This relationship gave rise to so much jealousy and enmity towards me. I was fiercely opposed by people close to him, by French people, by colleagues. I complained, but he didn't care.

Any examples?

One of his advisors, Liliane Marat, with whom he'd had a child, phoned me one day in a panic, claiming that Michel Teale, his political director of staff, whose father was Léon Mba's aide-de-camp, was spreading the word at the presidency about a relationship she'd have with me. For Teale, we were a couple. I arrived in Libreville and dotted all the i's and crossed all the t's, swearing to the contrary on my parents' grave. Michel Teale was summoned. When he arrived in the presidential office, he could only see Omar Bongo, as I was sitting in a large armchair with my back to him. The Gabonese president asked him:

"So, Bourgi slept with Liliane. Can you confirm it?"

Michel Teale approached and caught sight of me. After a man-to-man conversation, he admitted he had lied. Omar Bongo called Pascaline to terminate her functions. Then he summoned Liliane Marat and asked her to dine with me over a nice sauce-feuille dish.

You were talking about her gynaecology?

We never talked about women, I wouldn't have allowed myself. My upbringing forbade it.

Hard to believe...

It's true that he'd often make laudatory comments about such-and-such while watching television, for example, but that's where it ended.

What is your relationship with the "Corsicans" of Gabon? One immediately thinks of the Tomi brothers.

The only time I ran into Michel Tomi was after Ali Bongo's victory in 2009. He had helped him campaign a lot, notably by making his planes available. I wasn't close to this network. Nevertheless, Gabon was the hub for the movement of African funds. I tried to maintain the best possible relations with Charles Pasqua's close associates, including Daniel Léandri and Jean-Charles Marchiani.

In 2009, there were two major events: the death of Édith Bongo in March, followed in June by the death of your African spiritual father, who had been ill for several months. Did you discuss Edith's death with him and with Denis Sassou Nguesso?

No, but Denis Sassou Nguesso knew that I knew. Before his wife left, however, Omar Bongo gave me this very important message:

> "Son, you know how attached I am to Maman Edith. She's in Rabat for treatment. Nicolas needs to know that Bernard Debré will never look after us again. He's talked too much about his state of health."

I've avoided dwelling on the subject until now: the statements made to the press by Bernard Debré, former Minister for Cooperation, were a major factor in his decision to seek treatment in Spain, where he died. He knew he was ill well before his wife's deteriorating health. Maman Edith's death precipitated his own, but he had been suffering longer. I knew everything. He had cancer of the digestive tract. Every time he went to Rabat, he asked me to come. He was terribly affected by his wife's illness and had changed enormously.

He makes you his moral legatee.

In April 2009, a month after Edith's departure, he asked me to come to Libreville to entrust me with something absolutely crucial:

> "You see, Fiston, at the end of Jacques Chirac's presidency, I came to Paris several times and was never received. But you know what I did for him, just as I did for Pompidou, Giscard d'Estaing and all the others over the last forty years. I was no longer received during my last trips to France. The excuse was that Jacques was tired... Nonsense. I ask you for one thing: that you be my memory. You know everything and everything has passed through you. Let me know when the time comes."

This confession will determine my interview with the *JDD*.

Are the French authorities, through their departments, aware of Omar Bongo's illness, alongside that of his wife?

President Sarkozy knew exactly what was going on and what was being said when I visited both Rabat and Libreville.

Do Ali or Pascaline keep you informed?

While his father was hospitalized in Barcelona, Ali Bongo himself underwent emergency surgery at the American Hospital in Paris for intestinal and digestive problems. The only visitors allowed were Claude Guéant and Robert Bourgi. He had agreed with the Secretary General of the Élysée to travel together to Barcelona to see his father. But Bongo's illness suddenly worsened. In Spain, he didn't see a single French personality. Not even me. He took me on the phone.

Many people are holding you to account for publicizing his disappearance at a time when the Gabonese people were trying to hold back as much information as possible.

I received a call from Ali Bongo at night informing me that "Papa" was leaving. I had to inform Claude Guéant and President Sarkozy. It was he who informed me of the departure, after which I was perhaps able to inform a few journalists.

Appointed Minister of Defense in 1999, Ali Bongo had been preparing for the supreme office for some time.

I started coaching him in June 2008, at his father's request. He wanted Nicolas Sarkozy to receive him at the Élysée Palace, but this was not possible at first. However, he was able to meet Claude Guéant for breakfast at the Bristol and Bruno Joubert at 2 rue de l'Élysée. Nicolas Sarkozy will not see him again until early 2009, at the insistence of the Gabonese president.

One scene illustrates the disintegration of Franco-African relations. In June 2009, Jacques Chirac and Nicolas Sarkozy stood in front of Omar Bongo's coffin in the heart of the presidency in Libreville. At the same time, booing and virulent criticism of the two French presidents resounded from the crowd: "*Go away, we don't want any more of you! Manganese, oil, wood... you've looted everything, you've taken everything from us*"[127]. Was it a sign of organized exasperation, as the Gabonese know so well how to do?

I was there during these "incidents". It wasn't premeditated at all, but, on the contrary, the mark of a real weariness. France, through its judges and the press, had not stopped bashing Gabon in the years leading up to "Papa's" departure. The Gabonese couldn't take it anymore. I'd been feeling this resentment for several years. Exasperated, Omar Bongo often complained:

> "Tracfin goes out of its way for us Africans. On the other hand, all the Tangani who receive our money are never concerned!"

That's why he asked me to be his memoir, which justified my media outing. You journalists always thought I'd opened up to the press to get back on my feet because I was supposedly losing ground. Well, I didn't. I had received this confession and it was my duty to respect it.

What was Nicolas Sarkozy's reaction to this unprecedented rebellion?

He was horrified at having to pay so much for the legal woes of Omar Bongo and his entire clan.

---

127. Jérôme Bouin and Tanguy Berthemet, "Sarkozy and Chirac booed at Bongo's funeral", *Le Figaro*, June 16, 2009.

You unambiguously support Ali Bongo for the August 2009 presidential election. As you explained in the columns of *Le Monde*: *"In Gabon, France has no candidate, but Robert Bourgi's candidate is Ali Bongo. But I'm a very close friend of Nicolas Sarkozy. Subliminally, the voter will understand"*[128]. **What do you think of Robert Bourgi? Do you feel the same complicity as with your father?**

Omar Bongo asked me to introduce him to the "Château", which I did in 2008. In reality, he wanted an alliance with his daughter Pascaline. From my three decades of closeness and complicity with him, I learned this: Pascaline was by far his favorite. During all my tête-à-tête meetings, only she was allowed to follow the conversation. Confidential and sensitive missions were entrusted exclusively to her and Jean-Marie Adze. Bongo always told me that, apart from him, my contacts in Libreville were to be limited to Chantal Myboto, Laure Gondjout and Pascaline. One point. One line.

You have often stated in interviews that Ali Bongo was illegitimate, in reference to the 2009 presidential election, and that his father had been ill-advised to choose him.

I stand by what I said. He was pushed into it by default because he was the eldest of the boys. His father had a clear preference for his daughter.

Nevertheless, he was prepared for the presidency.

Given the choice, Omar Bongo would not have hesitated for a second to appoint Pascaline. Who was also present at the Gabonese president's side during his international travels? Pascaline, never Ali. In fact, I felt closer to her, but my position quickly became untenable as tensions between brother and sister escalated after 2009. Pascaline had been appointed High Representative of the Presidency, but dissension quickly took over.

In addition, Ali Bongo, who operates in the Anglo-Saxon style, is keeping all the barons of the old regime at arm's length, including former Economy and Finance Minister Paul Toungui, Pascaline's husband. He distanced himself from Paris, preferring to open up to new partners, starting with the Singaporean group Olam, whose local

---

128. Raphaëlle Bacqué, "Robert Bourgi, Françafrique veteran", *Le Monde*, August 30, 2009.

representative, Gagan Gupta, quickly became an intimate of the new presidential couple. An era is coming to an end for you.

The relationship seriously deteriorated after a year.

Criticized for not being as generous as his father, does Ali Bongo turn you off?

He paid me €1 million every year, from 2009 to 2013, into my business account for lobbying contracts. This is easily verifiable. But I sensed a real deterioration from the moment his chief of staff, the Beninese Maixent Accrombessi, began to turn him away from all those close to his father, and especially from France. That's when I started asking myself serious questions.

Did you know Maixent Accrombessi when he was Chief of Staff to Ali Bongo, Minister of Defense?

I knew him when Ali Bongo became president. He had extraordinary power. The new head of state swore by him. He was under his influence, and this went far beyond politics and business. There were mystical practices between them. Ali Bongo secretly traveled to Benin for voodoo masses. Priests would come to Libreville.

Maixent Accrombessi also came to my office whenever he was in Paris. Incidentally, this annoyed me, as he smoked non-stop during the interview. He called me "Uncle". One day, I turned the conversation to voodoo, reminding him that I had lived in Benin and that I was under the protection of a renowned marabout who had given his name to a street in Ziguinchor. Just to let him know that I was unreachable, which he knew full well. However, it was he who effectively pushed me aside from 2013 onwards.

Date on which you approach opposition.

With one nuance: during all this time, I never severed ties with the tenors of the former regime, whether Jean Ping, Paul Toungui, Jean-Pierre Lemboumba-Lepandou, Chantal Myboto or Raymond Ndong Sima, including declared opponents such as André Mba Obame. You have to understand that, like his late father, I wanted to ensure that a dialogue could be established with his opponents. I was in favor of intermediation, which Ali Bongo didn't appreciate.

He had openly asked me to cut all ties with these people, to which I replied with a phrase from his father: "you must never close the door and windows to let in air from elsewhere". I respected this saying, which displeased Maixent Accrombessi to no end. From then on, they cut me off.

Hence your increasingly virulent stance towards him.

Because he was under the diabolical sway of Maixent Accrombessi and no longer listened to anyone but him. The situation was becoming really worrying. By his attitude, he did everything he could to make me the spokesperson for his opposition.

When did you last travel to Libreville?

In November 2015, after three months of polar cold. Ali Bongo contacted me again, because he wanted to see me again. I travelled to Libreville, where I had a two-hour face-to-face meeting. He clearly wanted me back. It's true that, with the August 2016 presidential election approaching, it was better to have Bourgi on his side than on the side of the contemptuous supporters of his regime. He wanted me to stop meeting his enemies. Personally, I wanted to get everyone around the table. Ali replied that he wasn't the person to talk to and that there was a Mediator of the Republic for that. I was stunned.

It was during this visit that he chartered his personal plane for me to fly to Franceville to pay my respects at "Papa's" grave. Back in Libreville, another audience. He asked me to see Accrombessi. The next day, the pro-government Gabonese press turned on me. The atmosphere remained very degraded. The violence with which Bongo-fils handled the 2016 post-presidential election proved me right in my distancing. He still had Jean Ping's residence bombed, an unprecedented act in this country.

Are you called upon during this post-electoral crisis? Did Jean Ping, whose residence was attacked by the Presidential Guard, ask you to intervene with the Head of State?

I'd like to make it clear that I never sought to prevent Ali Bongo's candidacy, even if I had a personal opinion on the matter. He was Omar Bongo's eldest son. He bore his name. I couldn't work to push someone else, even though I was very fond of André Mba Obame. In fact, Omar Bongo once told me that if he had to choose between his minister and securocrat and his own son, he wouldn't have hesitated.

259

Inwardly, as I've already confided, he would have hoped that Pascaline would have been able to run. Alas, a woman at the helm of Gabon, even in 2009, was a complicated proposition. But the tandem scenario never took off. As soon as he came to power, Ali Bongo quickly marginalized and ousted his sister.

Unfortunately, I couldn't campaign for anyone else, especially as Omar Bongo had introduced him to Nicolas Sarkozy and Claude Guéant. So, in 2009, I pushed. After three years, however, Ali Bongo stopped all contact with me. Maixent Accrombessi, a veritable Cardinal de Richelieu, did the rest to poison my relationship.

Hence your support for Jean Ping in the 2016 presidential election.
He really won this election, while François Hollande didn't budge. I had supported his candidacy. Before the election, numerous negotiations took place in my office between the leading opposition figures, including Jean-Pierre Lemboumba-Lepandou, Jean Ping, Zacharie Myboto and Jean-François Ntoutoume Emane.

After the totally bogus results showing Ali Bongo as the winner, all these worried opponents called me. I escalated the matter to Nicolas Sarkozy. Alas, he had left the Élysée and my networks in Holland were weak. I even took part in demonstrations on several Saturdays in a row in front of the Gabonese embassy in France, on Rue Raphaël, sometimes even alongside Jean-Luc Mélenchon.

In May 2017, Emmanuel Macron clarified France's position by openly recognizing Ali Bongo's power, having given him "President" as soon as he arrived at the Élysée Palace, despite a general outcry from the European Union (EU).

Did you feel the hold of Sylvia and Noureddine Bongo?
I never really got to know them. I met Sylvia Bongo when she was young, through her father Édouard Valentin, the local RPR boss whom I affectionately nicknamed "Doudou"[129]. I didn't really see her again until her husband was sworn in, in 2009.

---

129. A businessman close to Omar Bongo, Édouard-Pierre Valentin (1939-2019) was notably the head of the Ogar-Vie insurance company, the leading insurance company in Gabon, where he settled in the 1970s.

Were you surprised by the coup d'état that deposed Ali Bongo in August 2023?

Not at all, because I've always said in the press that his regime was going to end badly, given its radical nature. You can criticize Omar Bongo all you like, but his system guaranteed social peace. He redistributed and knew his country like no one else. Not a single echo from the smallest village in the smallest province of Gabon escaped his notice.

With his son, it was Caesarism, omnipotence and totalitarianism. We'd been estranged since 2015. I didn't even hear from him when he suffered his stroke in 2018, in Saudi Arabia. The hatches were permanently battened down.

You are quick to recognize this *putsch*.

It was liberating. Ali Bongo's power had been mummified since his serious health problem.

Were you surprised by how quickly it fell?

The most surprising thing is that it comes from Brice Clotaire Oligui Nguema. He's always been discreet. Omar Bongo considered him one of the best. He trusted him completely. I always enjoyed talking to him.

Have you met him since his coup?

Of course we have. We had indirect contacts. I sent him a letter of congratulations. He had read my interviews in the Senegalese press. He sent me an extremely warm letter, published in this book.

During his visit to Dakar in early 2024, we also chatted, much to the astonishment of his entourage, whom I didn't know. The new Director of Protocol confided in me that he had never seen Brice Clotaire Oligui Nguema pay so much attention to one of his interlocutors. I gave him some advice. But I haven't been back to Gabon. For the moment, he's making no mistakes. I wouldn't be surprised to see him at the helm of Gabon one day. I wish him all the best.

Chapter 23: Clotilde Reiss Freed

More than twenty years after your mediation in the Lebanon hostage crisis, you are back on the Clotilde Reiss case. In 2009, this young academic and nuclear specialist was arrested and imprisoned in Teheran. She was accused of leaking documents (e-mails, photos...), notably from the Green Movement, which was protesting against the re-election of the ultraconservative Mahmoud Ahmadinejad. She was also accused of being a spy and a DGSE agent. As soon as she was arrested, French diplomacy and the media went into overdrive. At the same time, several mediations were organized, including one by Senegalese President Abdoulaye Wade, who was close to Iranian interests and at the time President of the Organization of the Islamic Conference (OIC). You didn't get involved in the case until very late, in March 2010, two months before the Frenchwoman's release. How did this happen?

Mahmoud Ahmadinejad was visiting Senegal and Abdoulaye Wade was head of the OIC. This mediation, which I followed closely, could never have succeeded.

Why?

There was one major difference between the two men: the Iranian was a fundamentalist Shiite and the Senegalese president a Sunni. I immediately grasped the angle of attack: the religious. I made an offer of service to the Senegalese president and his son, Karim, citing my origins. We then set up a mediation team comprising Karim Wade, Madické Niang, head of Senegalese diplomacy, and myself. Once in Paris, I informed Claude Guéant and Nicolas Sarkozy of my efforts. The latter stared at me, perplexed:

"I don't believe it."

"Why Nicolas?"

"Lulla failed, Erdogan screwed up, our services got nothing, our diplomacy ditto. I don't see how a Senegalese-Bourgi mediation could succeed."

"There's one thing you don't understand: I'm a chitte and I've mastered the art of negotiation."

Karim Wade and Madické Niang joined me in France and we received the green light from the Head of State, with this clarification:

"Robert, you'll be working without a net. The local ambassador will remain in the dark. No diplomatic passport, no official letter. Everyone knows how close you are to me. If the Senegalese presidency notifies Teheran that you're part of a mediation, the Iranian services will immediately understand."

Beforehand, you make a detour via Syria and Lebanon to activate your networks.

I made a preparatory trip to both countries from March 12 to 14, 2010. In Beirut, I met several Hezbollah officials, who then took me to the martyrs' cemetery, where Sayed Hassan Nasrallah's own son was buried.

I insisted that my wife, a devout Christian, accompany me. She had to wear a headscarf to enter the cemetery, where she said her prayers, punctuated by signs of the cross, in the presence of security and numerous Muslim women dressed head to toe in black. At the end of the prayers, these women embraced her effusively and presented her with flowers. An emotional moment.

The following day, March 13, we left for Damascus, where I developed my argument with several Syrian officials so that they could put pressure on Teheran. As it happened, President Bashar al-Assad had just received Mahmoud Ahmadinejad and Hassan Nasrallah. It was an opportune moment to plead the cause of the young Frenchwoman.

Claude Guéant was in constant contact with me. With the green light from the Syrian president, he was able to speak with General Mohammed Nasif Kheirbek[130]. I did the translation. The Secretary

---

130. Mohammed Nasif Kheirbeik (1937-2015) was Syria's Director of Internal and General Security and Deputy Vice-President for Security Issues.

General of the Élysée found the words that touched the security boss. As we were leaving, he told us he was going to report back and wished us good luck in Teheran. I would like to take this opportunity to thank my brother and friend Hadj Hassan Hejeij, a Lebanese businessman with close ties to Gabon, for his discreet and effective role during these visits. However, I would like to remind you that, as he was leaving, General Nasif confided in me:

"You know, Brother, Arabs are all Gaullists."

You are in Tehran from March 29 to April 1, 2010.

We'd been put up in a magnificent hotel overlooking the snow-capped mountains and a sublimely blue mosque. I was awakened by the sound of the muezzin. We were officially welcomed by the local Quai d'Orsay and a host of ministers. A lunch was offered in our honor before we left for the audience.

As translator, the Iranian president had called on a young former Sorbonne student who had an admirable command of the language of Molière. I was astonished, as I naturally wanted to exchange ideas in Arabic, but Iran's No. 1, we were told, could only express himself in Farsi (Persian). You bet...

Karim Wade handed him a message from his father setting out the purpose of the mission before introducing me, reminding him of my Lebanese, Muslim and Shiite pedigree. We agreed on the precise moment when I would take over.

My turn arrives. After the usual courtesies, I remind the Iranian president of my close ties with Nicolas Sarkozy and my two pilgrimages to Mecca. I attacked him directly through a religious prism:

"Mr. Chairman, President Wade is the supreme moral authority among African heads of state. Not only because of his age, but also because of the respect due to his rank. He was my teacher at the University of Dakar, in 1965 and 1966. I never worked with the French services. I have never seen a member of the DGSE, and I solemnly affirm that President Sarkozy is neither an enemy of the Arab cause nor of Iran. The proof: I'm his friend and at his side."

I continued on my way:

265

"You must know the Koran better than I do, but let me remind you of a hadith from the Prophet—*salla l-lahu alay-hi wa sallam* (May the peace and blessings of Allah be upon him and his family)."

"Go ahead."

"The Prophet—*salla l-lahu alay-hi wa sallam*—was staying with his favorite daughter, Fatima, known as "The Rose", wife of Imam Amir al-Mu'minin, the Commander of the Faithful. He was taking a nap while his two grandchildren, Hassan and Hussein, were playing right next to him. Not wanting them to disturb this rest, Fatima spanked them. The Prophet—*salla l-lahu alay-hi wa sallam*—then stood up and told her never to raise a hand to her children again, because when a child suffers, the throne of God is shaken. And right now, Mr. President, God's throne is being shaken in Iran."

He looked at me and asked:

"Why?"

"Because a child is suffering right now. The Frenchwoman is not a spy. Would a spy take photos? Would he send e-mails? A child's pain would shake God's throne, and it's happening in Teheran. Your duty is to free her. I appeal to Shiite dogma."

At that point, I whispered to Karim Wade that the case was well underway. Madické Niang remained as mute as a carp. He must not have understood anything. Mahmoud Ahmadinejad asked us how long we were staying. Karim Wade added that, although he was a Sunni, he too was devoted to God.

After the Shiite dimension came that of Islam. After three hours of talks, Mahmoud Ahmadinejad stood up and I stopped in front of him—I had prepared everything—and said:

"Mr. President, above you is a portrait of Ayatollah Khomeini. With your permission, I would like to say the prayer for the dead. I am the eldest member of this assembly. According to tradition, I will therefore stand before you."

He was particularly sensitive to this gesture. Then I gave him a hug. I could see that my words had been listened to religiously, so to speak. We left. A little later, the interpreter came to our hotel to tell us that Mahmoud

Ahmadinejad had reported to the leader Ali Khamenei and that we could announce, as a matter of principle, the release of the Frenchwoman. I asked him to keep quiet with the French ambassador.

When we arrived in Paris, we reported to Claude Guéant and President Sarkozy. Karim Wade made a wonderful case for Clotilde Reiss. Nicolas Sarkozy continued to shout "Inch allah". He still didn't believe it. In May 2010, the Iranian president called his Senegalese counterpart to confirm an imminent release. Clotilde Reiss arrived in Villacoublay on May 16.

This illustrates the indispensability of unofficial mediation. On the instructions of Jean-David Levitte, Nicolas Sarkozy's diplomatic adviser, André Parant had nevertheless seen fit to halt Abdoulaye Wade's mediation, preferring to open up other channels for negotiation.

The indispensable role of secret emissaries. On the plane, Clotilde Reiss wanted to know who had been behind her release and who she should thank. On arrival, Nicolas Sarkozy suggested I meet her, but I declined.

Were you compensated for this mission?

But no! I wanted to win a bottle of wine, a grand cru, a case of champagne, but nothing. Nothing at all! We did much better: I was suspended from my Legion of Honor for five years for words deemed inappropriate towards François Fillon.

Was a ransom paid?

Not much more, but Abdoulaye Wade and his son have been particularly active on this issue.

How do you explain your detour to the Central Bank of Iran during your stay in Tehran?

I have no memory of such a visit. The only factor that won Teheran's decision was Abdoulaye Wade's letter and my "Shiite to Shiite" intervention.

Chapter 24: Crisis in the Ivory Coast

The other big story of 2010 was the run-off presidential election in Côte d'Ivoire in November. This election triggered a merciless war, in the truest sense of the word, between the former Prime Minister and President of the Rassemblement des républicains (RDR), Alassane Ouattara, who was declared the winner by the Independent National Electoral Commission (CENI), but whose victory was contradicted by the Constitutional Council, which declared Laurent Gbagbo, the incumbent president after a blank mandate, the winner. How is Nicolas Sarkozy tackling this thorny issue?

He could no longer stand Laurent Gbagbo, whom he considered to be acting in bad faith. Personally, I deferred to the Ivorian Constitutional Council, which had declared him the winner of the election. Nicolas Sarkozy has always known that I've been following this issue closely since Jacques Chirac's time in office. I always briefed him fully on developments in the Ivorian situation, knowing that I held many cards. I was close to Laurent Gbagbo. I knew Alassane and Dominique Ouattara well, seeing them in their apartment on Avenue Victor Hugo in Paris.

I was close to Blaise Compaoré, whose role in the affair had been more than a little murky. Above all, I knew what France owed Gbagbo and what he had paid for Chirac, notably with his unlikely endowment to the RPR. I had introduced him to Jacques Foccart, then taken him to the Élysée Palace when he was just an opponent.

So I had all the contacts on both sides during this serious crisis. As the fighting became increasingly violent, President Sarkozy asked me to come to the Élysée Palace to talk some sense into "my friend" Laurent Gbagbo. Laurent Gbagbo. He was very annoyed, even incensed, but proposed, as I mentioned earlier, a status for former heads of state. The decision of the

Ivorian Constitutional Council was of absolutely no importance to him. And to see Sarkozy's anger was quite something.

His position has always been clear: the organization of the presidential election. As Claude Guéant was due to visit Côte d'Ivoire on October 3, 2010, shortly before the election, I told him how to approach the man, to listen to his nationalism and above all his popularity, particularly in Abidjan. I was not listened to. Laurent Gbagbo cried "treason" when he spoke of me, but I had nothing to do with it. I was his lawyer for years. The French authorities never appreciated it, for reasons that escape me.

On the evening of the second round, I maintained that he had been elected. A close friend of Alassane Ouattara, Nicolas Sarkozy took up the cause of the CENI. As far as he was concerned, Laurent Gbagbo had to "go", as he put it. He fulminated. This position was confirmed to me during an interview at the Élysée Palace in early December 2010, as the post-electoral crisis loomed.

He whined in his shirtsleeves:

"Your Gbagbo is a real pain in the ass!"
"But why do you say my Gbagbo? I know all the other protagonists too. He is the victim of a miscalculation on the part of our country."

He wanted me to persuade him to leave power, to get the hell out. In agreement with his European and Western partners, he was even prepared to offer him all the courtesies due to a former head of state: a chair in history at a French university; a monthly salary of 30 million CFA francs[131], paid by the Ivorian presidency; close protection... In short, the whole package!

I then went back to Claude Guéant's office to phone Laurent Gbagbo, who was sworn in on December 4, 2010. His aide-de-camp told me he was "as wound up as ever". He still took me, very annoyed:

"So Bob, what's up?"
"Laurent, we've known each other for over twenty years. You're my family's 'Uncle', and I'm calling you from the office of the Secretary General of the Élysée Palace. I've just come from the office of the President of the Republic. Here's what he proposes."

---

131. Approx. €45,000.

"Bob, listen carefully: tell Sarkozy I'll be his Mugabe. I won't do it. I will not capitulate! I'm going to storm the Hotel du Golf, and I understand that you're no longer my friend."

I was extremely saddened by this. We returned to President Sarkozy's office, where he was waiting for us on a sofa. On hearing that his proposals had been rejected, I remember him jumping up and down:

"Starting tomorrow, I'm glazing it!"

The rest is history.

Is this the only interview you had with Gbagbo during this period?
Yes. His arrest by Alassane Ouattara's forces, aided by rebel and French forces, was not long in coming. I never heard from him again.

After several weeks of fighting in the capital, Alassane Ouattara leaves the Hôtel du Golf. Laurent, Simone Gbagbo and many of their relatives are arrested. Alassane Ouattara is sworn in on May 21, 2011 in the presence of President Sarkozy. A ceremony you're not welcome to attend.
I was invited by Dominique Ouattara, who informed me by telephone, as architect Pierre Fakhoury can confirm. The timing was perfect, as I was to be part of the delegation.

Half an hour after this phone call, I received a very embarrassed call from Claude Guéant, asking for my understanding and apologizing. Alain Juppé, Minister of Foreign Affairs, had blocked my way. He didn't want me at the swearing-in ceremony. The request was passed on to President Sarkozy.

Why?
Someone should tell me before I die why he was always so angry with me. I was always fair to him. I concocted trips for him all over Africa (Ivory Coast, Gabon, Senegal...) on behalf of the Club 89, of which he was general secretary, a club that I never stopped financing thanks to the African presidents. I financed the RPR, of which he was also general secretary and then president. I asked Karim Wade to charter a personal plane for some of his missions. I got him to review the troops in Dakar

on June 18, 2003, at a time when he was already in trouble with the law, culminating in a conviction for "taking an illegal interest" in the Paris City Council's fictitious employment affair.

Why were you put on the scale?

But let me have an explanation before I leave this earth! Where have we seen a French politician condemned by the courts, whom I have invited to Gabon and Senegal, with the status of head of state and official dinners, behave in such a way? He remains an enigma. Dominique Ouattara herself sent me a verbal apology.

When Alain Juppé took over the Ministry of Foreign Affairs in 2011[132], he intended to *"break with Françafrique"*. Reacting to your interview with the *"JDD"*, he explains in *Le Monde*[133] that he doesn't feel concerned by your revelations about the financing of Club 89 by African presidents, while adding that he understands that you don't appreciate it since it's reciprocal...

This deserves nothing but indifference on my part, given what I've done for him and what I've described in the preceding pages. The reader has made up his mind about the character.

Did he shun you for fear that you, Claude Angeli's personal friend, might know too much about him?

He wouldn't have been wrong. For example, when it came to his apartment on rue Jacob in Paris, I was the first to know the source who revealed the whole story[134]. The reason is simple: she approached me to get in touch with Claude.

---

132. Alain Juppé was Minister of Foreign Affairs twice: from March 30, 1993 to May 11, 1995 in the Édouard Balladur government, and from February 27, 2011 to May 10, 2012 in the François Fillon government.

133. Brice Pedroletti, "Alain Juppé doesn't feel 'concerned' by Robert Bourgi's accusations", *Le Monde*, September 13, 2011.

134. In its June 28, 1995 edition, *Le Canard enchaîné* revealed that Alain Juppé, Minister of Foreign Affairs in the Balladur government, had for several years been occupying a 181 m² city-owned apartment on rue Jacob in the 6th arrondissement, at a rent of 12,000 francs (€1,600). Another apartment had also been made available to his son, Laurent, at a discount of 1,000 francs on the rent, on the instructions of Alain Juppé himself. The Paris public prosecutor conditionally closed the case, citing an offence of interference.

This famous *"great misunderstanding"* that you later evoked in Bordeaux, when you met Alain Juppé for a book signing in January 2016.

When I went to the Mollat bookshop in Bordeaux, on January 23 to be precise, my daughter Clémence, who was studying in the hypokhâgne class at the Lycée Michel de Montaigne, asked me to accompany her to a Juppé conference. I had warned Nicolas Sarkozy beforehand so that he wouldn't be surprised. I was seated at the back of the room with my friend Jean-Paul Fayot, a dental surgeon, former professor of dentistry at the University of Medicine in Abidjan and General Secretary of the Club 89 in Abidjan.

At the end of the conference, I accompanied my daughter to the book signing, with a dozen books purchased at the door. Clémence asked me to come forward. Juppé gasped when he saw me. It must be said that there was a team from Yann Bartès' *Petit Journal*, which didn't help matters.

I greeted him:

"Alain, it's time to clear up this great misunderstanding between us."
"No problem, come and see me at my office on boulevard Raspail. Let me know as soon as you arrive in Paris."

I then phoned his secretariat. No answer, of course. We're both from 1945, and at our age, people don't take out long-term loans any more.

What are you referring to when you speak of a *"misunderstanding"*?

I wanted to tell him who had stabbed him in the back for his apartment on Rue Jacob. No one ever knew, not even him. It was Philippe Martel, his chief of staff when he ran the Finance Department at Paris City Hall. He wanted to expose the whole affair. I was very close to Philippe, even when he was working for Alain Juppé at the Quai d'Orsay. In early 2013, he switched to Marine Le Pen, because he'd had enough. He had left the RPR in 1997[135].

---

135. An Énarque and senior civil servant, Philippe Martel was a close associate of Alain Juppé from 1988 to 1994, first at Paris City Hall and then at the Quai d'Orsay. He was one of seven fictitious employees at Paris City Hall, earning him a 14-month suspended prison sentence in 2004. An RPR activist, he left the party in 1997. At the beginning of 2013, he switched to the Front National and became chief of staff to Marine Le Pen. Philippe Martel passed away in November 2020.

He approached me to introduce him to Claude. I was taken aback, because usually, when you want to meet the director of *Le Canard enchaîné*, it's to drop a thermonuclear bomb. It didn't fail. I set up the meeting at the Grand Hôtel Intercontinental, now the Westin Paris Vendôme, on rue de Castiglione.

Was the fictitious jobs affair weighing on him?

He told us he wanted to settle the score. As usual, Claude took notes in a small notebook. After the meeting, we both left for the Hôtel Régina, stunned by these revelations. He then called the secretariat of Alain Juppé, then Prime Minister, to confirm the information. No reply. The article came out. Philippe, no longer with us, couldn't stand Juppé. He paid for it, and paid well.

Will he try to bring you closer to the Front National?

He took steps to get me closer to Marine Le Pen, which I always refused. I didn't even intervene in Jean-Marie Le Pen's visit to Libreville in 1988. It was fabricated by General Louis Pierre "Loulou" Martin[136], a close associate of the Front National boss who was behind several Gardes présidentielles in Africa, including the one in Gabon. I ran into Le Pen-père at his funeral in 2004. "Loulou" was a Foccart man. I liked him a lot.

---

136. Louis Pierre Martin (1924-2005). Commander of the Foreign Legion, he took part in the Second World War, as well as in the Indochina and Algerian wars. He took part in the generals' *putsch* against General de Gaulle in 1961. A close friend of Robert "Bob" Denard, he created the Gabonese Presidential Guard in 1970. He was made Grand Officer of the Legion of Honor in 2004.

Chapter 25: A Candidate for the AFD

Like Nicolas Normand, you not only appoint diplomats, but also the CEO of the Agence Française de Développement (AFD), as Dov Zerah did in June 2010.

I met him through my friend Abbas Jaber, who had introduced me to Mohamed Ould Bouamatou in Saint-Tropez. Both came to my office two years before Dov Zerah was appointed. A member of the UMP party, he was president of the consistory and had headed the Compagnie française pour le développement des fibres textiles (CFDT, later Dagris). He was a municipal councillor in Neuilly-sur-Seine. He had long been interested in the position of CEO of AFD. It was traditionally a left-wing stronghold. He asked me to support his candidacy. I asked him why he should go through me.

"Abbas told me that you were very close to President Sarkozy."

I promised him I'd take it up with the higher-ups. It has to be said that this support was not without interest for Abbas Jaber's business. Dov Zerah left me his CV, which I slipped to President Sarkozy in the course of a conversation:

"Nicolas, there's this person, Dov Zerah, who would be very interested in the French Development Agency".

When consulted, Claude Guéant mentioned other profiles already in the pipeline. Nicolas Sarkozy nevertheless gave the lead to Dov Zerah. The file followed its course. He called me almost every day, as if this was the only priority for the President of the French Republic. I advised him to calm down.

One evening, it was a Friday, I received a call from Claude Guéant confirming his appointment by the Council of Ministers and asking me to inform the person concerned. I called Dov Zerah on his mobile a good twenty times. No answer. At midnight, he called me:

> "But Robert, what's going on?"
> "I've been trying to reach you for over twenty times!"
> "But Robert, it's Shabbat! I couldn't pick up the phone."
> "I'm talking to the future boss of the AFD!"
> "No, really? Champagne, please! I'll come and see you tomorrow."

And we celebrated his appointment with Abbas Jaber. Nobody thought for a moment that he was going to win the job, but the choice didn't appeal to me any more than that. I'd been in my role as a lawyer-lobbyist. On the other hand, Abbas Jaber sincerely believed that this would bring him more opportunities in Africa, as AFD finances many projects in his field, which is agriculture. He was banking on it.

Dov Zerah had confirmed it to him, and I was Abbas Jaber's advisor. Over lunch at Chez Nini, a kosher restaurant in the 17th arrondissement, with plenty of boukha and company, I confided in him:

> "Dov, I'm Abbas' lawyer. He got you this prestigious job through me, so you have to deal with him."
> "There's no problem, Robert."

Well, if Abraham, Moses, Jacob and Aaron were able to do business, Abbas got absolutely nothing during Dov Zerah's three years in office! Nothing! And as for me, I never heard from him again. So I made this confession to my friend:

> "Abbas, I'm more than ten years older than you. In every language in the world, there's a word: tomorrow. He will pay dearly."

I might as well tell you that I spent my time tearing him down. He only served one term.

Is it enough for ambitious personalities to be recommended to you for you to defend their case? Has giving your trust so blindly ever exposed you?

There's one thing you have to understand: I'm an Oriental, an African and a Frenchman all rolled into one. Three civilizations and three systems of thought live within me. When I'm with Abbas Jaber, I see his father with mine. They arrived in Senegal at almost the same time, both naked as worms at the beginning of the last century. I see his father in my father's office. Those images never leave me. He's like my little brother. Incidentally, he's not just anybody. His business is extremely serious.

You've ensured that it will lead to the privatization of Dagris.

Naturally. He won the case, but not without difficulty. The ex-CFDT was a veritable nest of spooks. Jacques Foccart had discreetly placed all his men there. The French government wanted to sell this jewel.

Abbas, who was already active in oilseeds, approached me about this project. I made President Sarkozy aware of this interest. At his request, Claude Guéant listed the bidders for privatization in front of us, to which President Sarkozy replied: "You can add Mr. Abbas Jaber, a friend of Robert's". Abbas Jaber was the surprise winner, because there were several rounds. Nobody expected it.

The Ministry of the Economy and Finance even cancelled the operation for the first time. Does this mean that the process has been rigged?

I don't know about that, but once again, Abbas Jaber's candidacy was not at all far-fetched, given his area of competence and expertise. Dagris managed the cotton sector in several French-speaking African countries. This enterprise enabled him to structure his group, which would later become Advens-Geocoton, in a formidable manner.

From March to October 2011, a military operation led by a coalition of countries, under the aegis of the UN, led to the fall of Muammar Gaddafi. Have African presidents expressed their concerns to you, given the Libyan leader's popularity south of the Sahara?

I've never been involved in North African affairs. Omar Bongo asked me to tell Nicolas Sarkozy to stop criticizing Gaddafi. Jean Ping, who chaired the African Union's commission, told the French president himself. It was Bernard-Henri Lévy who won his support, for reasons that still elude me to this day.

Are you making him aware of the dangers of Western intervention and the possible implosion of this country, with irreparable damage to the sub-region?

I passed on Omar Bongo's message. Many other African presidents have alerted him. But he preferred to rely on a philosopher when it came to African geopolitics. Comprenne qui pourra.

From the outset, he was very proactive in mobilizing his partners. You don't see this as a desire to settle old scores with the Libyan leader, do you?

The case has been before the courts for years. I won't get into that kind of debate.

Based on an extremely detailed and documented investigation by *Mediapart*.

It's up to the judges to decide. If you ask me what I think about this affair, I'm absolutely and firmly convinced that Nicolas Sarkozy has nothing to do with the Libyan financing affair. Why is that? The day after an exhausting several days in police custody, his secretary, Sylvie Burgel, called me to say that he wanted to see me. I was very surprised by this request, as I knew he was tired and very affected. He asked me if I knew anything about all this, having organized the financing of African presidents for almost thirty years. He seemed taken aback.

Yet he was the only one to be taken into custody.

I refer to what he solemnly told me in October 2005:

"I don't want a penny more from Africa".

Even less so from Gaddafi, although I can't imagine that he wasn't lavish in his largesse towards certain French political figures. Muammar Gaddafi, you'd shake his hand and hit the jackpot if he felt you were corruptible.

In reality, Nicolas Sarkozy is being accused without any proof. Gaddafi's beloved son, Saïf al-Islam Gaddafi, leader of the Libyan Arab Jamahiriya, played a fundamental role with his father right up to the end. If he'd had the slightest proof of financing, do you think he wouldn't have mentioned it immediately, given the conditions of the Libyan leader's disappearance? I'd like to add that I've seen journalist Fabrice Arfi in my office several times regarding this case. I told him the same thing. That I knew nothing. Moreover, my name, as in all the other files, is totally absent. I'd like to take this opportunity to point out that *Médiapart*, no more than any other French media, has never published or highlighted any alleged movement of funds from sub-Saharan Africa to Nicolas Sarkozy. Nor has any judge. This proves that the transfers stopped in 2007.

There are testimonies, notably from businessman Ziad Takieddine.
I'll leave him to you! He found me an affair with President Sarkozy in Senegal. Nonsense. I sent him a message in my own way: from Beirut. He never mentioned my name again.

He accuses Nicolas Sarkozy, then denies it, before asserting that the same Nicolas Sarkozy is behind this reversal. It's just grotesque, it's not serious. Politics is too important to indulge in such foolishness.

You were appointed by the Ivorian government to defend it in a dispute with Noël Dubus. Did you know this controversial figure, mentioned in Ziad Takieddine's retraction concerning the Libyan financing of Nicolas Sarkozy's 2007 presidential campaign?
The Ivory Coast ambassador to France did indeed appoint me as his lawyer. He wrote an explicit missive published in the appendices of this book. I had heard about this individual, his bad reputation and his propensity for generating "business". So much so that I personally called Omar Bongo to inform him of my constitution by the Ivorian state and to ask him to forbid this individual access to Gabonese territory. This was done.

In his book _Les visiteurs du soir_[137], Renaud Revel devotes an entire chapter to you. According to him, you were very friendly with Nicolas Sarkozy, warning him against _the "irresponsible" BHL_. BHL. He portrays you as frozen, even tetanized, as he unrolls his war plan concocted by the philosopher in front of you, even as African presidents express their deep concern. How do you explain his blindness?
Renaud Revel, whom I was delighted to meet for a few hours in preparation for his book, has had a great deal of difficulty with the truth. As I mentioned earlier, certain heads of state, most notably Omar Bongo, expressly asked me to make Nicolas Sarkozy aware that he was on the wrong track with his assessments and analyses of Muammar Gaddafi.

---

137. Renaud Revel, _Les visiteurs du soir : ce qu'ils disent à l'oreille du président_, Plon, 2020.

The French president did not heed this advice, as it was he who took the final decision to strike at the Libyan leader, with the support of NATO and UN forces.

Behind this decision: Bernard-Henri Lévy. I know him personally. We spent many long hours talking together. I even owe him a debt of gratitude for showing me a beautiful spot on the Côte d'Azur with a lovely private beach. When we got together, we talked about the Middle East and Africa. He's a cultured and curious boy. However, I criticize him for taking himself a little too much for the revolutionary André Malraux, whose "dandy" side he only embraced. A physical and sartorial dandy, with his hair always impeccable, his shirt immaculate and his shoes always beautifully shined.

But the Malraux of *Conquérants* was more than just an armchair revolutionary. It's all well and good to take journalists and press agencies to Afghanistan, Libya, Sudan... But there are certain languages, outfits and postures that need to be respected in order to grasp local contexts and realities more subtly. At the time, I don't think Alain Juppé really appreciated his intervention. You can say what you like about Alain Juppé, but he doesn't play with the truth when it becomes dangerous.

Revel also explains that Libya is the *"dossier of your life"*. You want to turn the tide of history against this philosopher who seems to have *"marabouté"* the French president.

What nonsense! Libya was never a strategic issue, for the simple reason that it did not fall within my area of intervention. At Omar Bongo's request, I abjured Nicolas Sarkozy not to intervene to defeat the Gaddafi regime.

Claude Guéant is also involved in this investigation into Libyan financing of Nicolas Sarkozy's 2007 campaign, in particular for a €500,000 transfer to his personal account following the sale of two Flemish paintings.

Nicolas Sarkozy also asked me about the affair, asking if I knew anything about it. If I had, I would have immediately warned Claude. In fact, I find it rather strange that a man who has been Minister of the Interior, Secretary General of the Élysée Palace, Director General of the French National Police and Prefect could land such a sum in a private personal account. A sum on which he paid no tax. If he'd warned me, I'd have told him right away to stop this nonsense.

Have you kept in touch with him?

Claude is three months older than me. He was very weakened by his incarceration at the Santé prison. I never let him down. I kept his esteem and affection.

He's bouncing back in Africa, following in your footsteps. After becoming a business lawyer, from 2012 he carried out numerous assignments alongside his son-in-law, banker Jean-Charles Charki. He works on behalf of groups such as China's Citic Construction SA LDT in Côte d'Ivoire.

I went once with them to Gabon, in December 2012, during Ali Bongo's term of office. I gave them access to the country. We met the president and Maixent Accrombessi. For the rest, he doesn't need my services, because he's well known. His address book is thick.

Chapter 26: Media Bomb

On September 11, 2011, *Le JDD* published one of your landmark interviews, which, in the words of *Le Monde*, set *"the Republic on fire"*[138]. Under the headline *"J'ai vu Chirac et Villepin compte les billets"* (*"I've seen Chirac and Villepin counting bills"*), you pull the pin out, exposing all the practices and movements of money from Africa, methodically supervised by you over several decades. Why come out of the woodwork and why on this date?

The time had come to empty my bag. Firstly, because of the promise made to Omar Bongo at the end of his life, to be his memory when the time came. But, above all, because I could see all the presidents I'd worked for stunned under the hammer of French judges. They couldn't take it anymore. Not a day went by without the indictment of one person or another, and even the arrest of high dignitaries in public, at French airport customs. The press went into overdrive. Everything from south of the Sahara was rotten, and everything from the West was worth its weight in gold.

For years, I'd helped convoy millions of euros in cash for leading French politicians, who enjoyed total impunity. Omar Bongo told me that he had always financed Gaullism. He was fed up with investigations detailing his wealth in France. I was the only witness to all this. I wanted to redress the balance.

When exactly do you decide to open your box of secrets?

From a conversation with Pierre Péan, whom I saw several times a month and who was completing an investigation into the movement of

---

138. "Robert Bourgi, l'ancien 'M. Afrique' qui met le feu à la République", *Le Monde*, September 12, 2011.

funds within the French Republic[139]. I told him I wanted to "confess". It was he who directed me to *Le JDD* and to Vincent Valdiguié, who had been trying for years to pin a case on me without ever finding anything. He got the interview of his life. He couldn't sleep.

Why wait more than two years after Bongo's death?

Time for reflection. In the summer of 2011, I decided to reveal everything. My wife tried in vain to dissuade me, insisting that I was still friends with many African heads of state and that they would turn away. But Bongo's message resonated with me. In Gabon, Ali Bongo was far from his father's image. It was no longer my era.

Isn't this interview timed to coincide with your fading star? Your Gabonese protector is no longer there. Nor is Laurent Gbagbo. In Paris, you are *blacklisted* by Alain Juppé. The Left is preparing to return to power.

Where did you see my star fading? I was still very close to many other current and future heads of state, such as Compaoré, Sassou Nguesso and Macky Sall.

Your statements are splashed all over the place. Did you ask Nicolas Sarkozy for a green light?

Absolutely not, on the contrary, he was surprised. As soon as the paper came out, he phoned me early in the morning to find out what had got into me. He asked to see me the same day, in the afternoon, letting me in for the first time through the Coq entrance instead of the rue du Faubourg Saint-Honoré.

He was waiting for explanations. I reminded him of my commitment to the late President of Gabon, and of his weariness at the iniquitous treatment meted out to African dignitaries, while more than half of the French political class was not clean.

Readers and observers have been quick to associate President Sarkozy with the financing system you denounce. Did he blame you?

---

139. Pierre Péan, *La République des mallettes. Enquête sur la Principauté française de non-droit*, Fayard, Paris, 2011.

Not at all. The proof is that he has kept his friendship and confidence in me. I've just had a minor operation. He called me every day[140].

African presidents are directly affected by your revelations. President Blaise Compaoré's emissary, Salif Diallo, is one of the first to speak out.

Because they never knew the reason why I made that exit. What's more, he knew perfectly well that I was telling the truth. Blaise Compaoré has not lodged a complaint. In fact, there were none, with the exception of Jean-Marie Le Pen. Jacques Chirac and Villepin threatened me, but never acted on their threats. A consummate professional, Jean-Pierre Elkabbach told Villepin shortly after my interview that he had one month to lodge a complaint. I'm still waiting for it.

Didn't you warn any African president beforehand?

No, they would have strongly discouraged me from talking.

With this interview, you give the impression of attacking a system that has fed you. To "spit in the soup".

I don't feel that way at all.

Are you aware of the *de facto* turning point in your career? A "man of the shadows" who steps so far into the light is no longer credible. He even becomes unattractive, not to say dangerous.

It's true, African presidents turned their backs on me overnight. I never heard from them again. This was the case, for example, with Denis Sassou Nguesso, for whom I had enormous esteem. I suffered, not financially, but personally. They all cut ties, but I had the sensation of freeing my conscience.

In this interview, you talk about "*gifts*" to Villepin. What were they?

Mainly books, African objets d'art or objects linked to Napoleon, such as the statue of the Emperor I mentioned, the invoice for which is reproduced in this book. Mobutu gave him a staff of the Maréchal d'Empire. He received African masks of exceptional quality.

---

140. Interview with Robert Bourgi, April 10, 2024.

After this *outing*, many doors closed. Are you still entrusted with missions?

Gabon paid me until 2013. I continued to work for Senegal and for several French groups. I advised Imperial Tobacco, Advens...

After your interview, you start work on your *memoirs* with journalist Laurent Valdiguié. Nicolas Sarkoy reads the first pages and explains that, if they are published, half the French political class will disappear.

That's an exaggeration. I kept him up to date, talking to him about the issues involved, including, of course, the question of African financing, which has been raised here with you. He asked me not to go ahead with the book by blocking the final press proof. And I threatened to take legal action, via my lawyer, if the text was ever published.

Why?

As the interviews progressed, I realized that Laurent Valdiguié, who had been recording me for two years, was gradually leading me to accuse Nicolas Sarkozy of having been bribed by African presidents, which, I would remind you for the umpteenth time, is totally false, false and false. His questions were biased. His transcriptions were not faithful to my words. One day, I got angry and put an end to our collaboration.

You reread the manuscript. What was so incriminating about it?

Nicolas Sarkozy didn't want us to keep coming back to the subject of financing African presidents. He asked me not to publish it.

Was it Libya-related?

Absolutely not. He still cherished the hope of being re-elected. He simply didn't want any false amalgams. I repeat: Nicolas Sarkozy refused from the outset to finance any of these presidents. That's why he was always able to tell them the truth during his five-year term. He had this leeway because, unlike his predecessor, he owed them nothing. Do you honestly think that if Nicolas Sarkozy had been financed by Africa, he would have been able to deliver his famous speech in Dakar?

Chapter 27: Wade: One Term too Many

As we saw in the Lebanon hostage affair, you have a close relationship with Abdou Diouf.

They go back well before the release of the French hostages, to our first meeting in 1986, when I was working in Michel Aurillac's office. I used to go to Dakar two or three times a month. It's worth remembering that Michel Aurillac had met President Diouf in 1960, when he graduated from the École nationale de la France d'outre-mer (Enfom). He was already close to Léopold Sédar Senghor, and later presided over one of the chambers of the Supreme Court headed by Isaac Forster[141]. He had a real predilection for Senegal.

With Abdou Diouf, discussions lasted up to two hours. We discussed all Senegalese and international political issues. In my modest capacity, I was one of those who persuaded this Head of State, a member of the Socialist International, not to abstain in the United Nations vote on New Caledonia. The UN, I would remind you, was pushing for a decolonization process. He was tempted to abstain, but François Mitterrand and his Prime Minister Jacques Chirac took a dim view. Jacques Foccart was sent to Dakar to change his mind.

Michel Aurillac had also asked me to speak. Bruno Diatta, the Senegalese presidency's emblematic chief of protocol, had my return flight to Paris delayed long enough for me to develop my arguments. In the end, Abdou Diouf followed France. Thereafter, I continued to rub shoulders with him even when I was no longer an advisor on Rue Monsieur. Even so, we weren't intimate. I was not close to his family or his children.

---

141. A Senegalese jurist, Isaac Forster (1903-1984) was the first judge from sub-Saharan Africa to be elected to the International Court of Justice, in 1964.

What do you remember about the character?

He reflects the confidence placed in him by Léopold Sédar Senghor. He had all the qualities: intelligence of mind, class, culture. And he was so pleasant. I really enjoyed seeing him. We're neighbors in Paris. I sometimes catch a glimpse of him.

What was your relationship with Abdoulaye Wade, the historic opposition leader of the Senegalese Democratic Party (PDS)? Did you know him for a long time?

With Abdoulaye Wade, it was a different story. As far back as I can remember, he was a friend of my father. They met in the late 1950s. He was a lawyer with a practice in Dakar, and had excellent relations with my father.

A few years later, my younger brother, Rassek Bourgi, interned at the firm. To this day, he considers him his mentor. Almost a second father. Even though I've sometimes had my differences with Abdoulaye Wade and his son Karim, I have respect for this great figure. Who wouldn't? No Senegalese would.

Did you know Karim Wade when he was young?

I'd be lying if I said I knew him when he was young. The first time I spoke with him was after his father came to power in 2002. We always had lunch together when he came to Paris. I had very strong opinions about him. But those who are close to him, those who know him and those who know him well know that our esteem is mutual. He's my "little one" in the strongest sense of the word. The time has come for him to serve his country, especially after the unlikely changeover we have just witnessed with the arrival in power of Bassirou Diomaye Faye[142].

Why support Abdoulaye Wade in 2000 and not the Socialist Party candidate? Was it political conviction, the PDS being a member of the Liberal International?

I felt that Abdou Diouf's time had passed. Twenty years was a long time.

---

142. Born in 1980, member of PASTEF and public finance inspector by profession, Bassirou Diomaye Faye will succeed Macky Sall on April 2, 2024.

To what extent are you making use of your contacts to support Wade's bid for the presidential election? Are you close, for example, to his friend Alain Madelin, who was a minister under both Jacques Chirac and Édouard Balladur?[143]

Obviously, I used my contacts to get my French political friends to take a very close interest in this personality and his candidacy. I told them he deserved their full attention. Of course, I knew he was backed by Alain Madelin, but I didn't play along with him to help Wade win.

At a luncheon at the Élysée Palace in September 2001, Abdoulaye Wade confirmed financial support for the 2002 presidential election in France. You confirmed this operation to *JDD* before retracting your statement. Why did you do this?

President Wade did indeed promise a contribution. In April 2002, he handed over $1 million in the office of the Secretary General of the Élysée Palace. The money was contained in a briefcase. Why did I withdraw? I had great respect for Abdoulaye Wade, who had been a friend of my family for over fifty years. After the *JDD* interview appeared, he called me from New York, where he was attending the UN General Assembly. He had some touching words for my parents and the Bourgi family. I agreed to his request to retract my statement. Today, I maintain that he took part in financing this presidential election.

In 2002, journalist Jean-Marc Kalflèche, a member of the Zimbabwe club, wrote a book on Abdoulaye Wade, published by Lafont: *Wade, une vie pour l'Afrique*. Were you behind this project?

I got to know Jean-Marc very well as part of the club chaired by Omar Bongo. He had an extraordinary pen. But I didn't initiate this project.

In May 2003, Alain Juppé was in Libreville and Dakar as President of the Union pour un mouvement populaire (UMP). You got President Wade to make a pass at Camp Dial Diop.

---

143. Born in 1946, Alain Madelin, President of Démocratie libérale, was Minister for Industry, Post and Telecommunications and Tourism in Jacques Chirac's government from 1986 to 1988; Minister for Enterprise and Economic Development in Édouard Balladur's government from 1993 to 1995; and Minister for the Economy and Finance in Alain Juppé's government from May to August 1995.

As always, I followed both trips informally, but played a leading role in their organization, particularly as regards the program. I still hold Alain Juppé in high esteem, but I'll be frustrated if I have to leave this earth without ever knowing why he always kept me at a distance. He had just been convicted in the case of fictitious employment at Paris City Hall. I asked the two presidents to treat him with the utmost respect, as Juppé's entourage and "friends" were beginning to grumble. Everything went splendidly. Karim Wade mobilized a plane to pick us up in Libreville. He was on the plane with Juppé's imposing delegation, which included Martine Aurillac, wife of Michel Aurillac, then a member of the Paris parliament whom I love dearly.

In Dakar, Abdoulaye Wade pulled out all the stops for Alain Juppé, who was even given a parade at Camp Diop on May 8th. He reviewed the troops. He was very touched by the gesture. It's my duty to say what only I have heard and experienced with Alain Juppé, Abdoulaye Wade and Karim Wade.

Before the official dinner, the Senegalese president had organized a tête-à-tête with the UMP leader on the 2nd floor of the presidential palace. That day, I admired President Wade's ability to use the right words with his host, asserting, as a former lawyer and law professor that he was, that his conviction would soon be forgotten and that he remained a central political figure in France.

What do you do for Abdoulaye Wade? How do you get on with his communicators, including Anne Méaux, head of Image 7?

The invaluable Anne Méaux looked after the image of Abdoulaye Wade, his son and, more generally, that of Senegal. She honored me with her friendship, which was shattered by the François Fillon suit affair. If I ever get the chance, I'll explain myself to her. With President Wade, I had neither plans nor precise missions. He called on me whenever he needed me.

You take Karim Wade in hand. You introduced him to Nathalie Kosciusko-Morizet, Nicolas Sarkozy's Minister of Ecology, Development, Transport and Housing. On what issues?

I introduced him to many of Jacques Chirac's and Nicolas Sarkozy's ministers, such as Nathalie Kosciusko-Morizet when she held the

Transport portfolio. It's no secret that I have a special affection for her and her grandfather, Ambassador Jacques Kosciusko-Morizet. I enjoyed chatting, lunching and dining with her. I deeply regret that she has left the political arena in France.

Superior in spirit, she loved to serve the state and was respectful of institutions. In fact, her intellectual superiority was a handicap, as she could appear to have no mercy for mediocre minds. And in the world of politics, mediocrity is commonplace.

I remember the weekends we spent together as a family, whether in Essonne or at her home near Sainte-Mère-Église, where we never stopped talking. She could have had an even more prestigious political career. She should know that she still has a role to play in that respect.

How do you feel about Abdoulaye Wade's unprecedented bid for a third term in 2012?

He was sure of going through in the first round. I arranged for Nicolas Sarkozy to meet Karim, who, as I said, warned him of the fatal error this candidacy would have on his father's image. But he wouldn't budge, convinced that his father would take a third ride without a hitch. The rest is history...

An attempt that marks your break with the Wade camp.

We fell out around this time in 2011. I kept telling Karim that his father had to avoid fighting too much.

With Abdoulaye Wade playing a dangerous game, you're getting closer to Macky Sall.

From the moment he came into conflict with President Wade. He had retreated to his home after being ousted from the perch of the presidency of the National Assembly, and when he began to weave his web in very good intelligence to take the supreme power in 2012.

During a trip to Senegal, I was, as usual, in a presidential car, and went to visit him. He was no longer in office. The driver reported the visit to the higher-ups. Abdoulaye Wade gave me a memorable dressing-down that very evening.

"One of two things: either you're with me, or you're not!"

As a result, I distanced myself. Macky Sall had also been introduced to me by the excellent Pascal Drouhaud, former head of international relations at the RPR and, it should be noted, a long-standing personal friend of the future Senegalese president. I always enjoyed talking to him.

Chapter 28: Confidences

Why do certain French-speaking African countries elude you—or why do you shy away from them—when their presidents are presumably knocking on your firm's door? We're thinking of Chad's Idris Déby Itno, Central Africa's Ange-Félix Patassé and François Bozizé, Niger's Mamadou Tandja, Guinea's Alpha Condé and Mali's Amadou Toumani Touré and Ibrahim Boubacar Keïta.

I've known and rubbed shoulders with countless other presidents. I never met Ange-Félix Patassé in the Central African Republic, but at the Bristol during his visits to Paris. He always offered me a glass of Bordeaux 1er Grand Cru. I met François Bozizé two or three times at Marshal Mobutu's house. Alpha Condé, on the other hand, is a very old acquaintance. He used to visit my office when he was an opponent, but once he was president, from December 2010 onwards, nothing. Alpha Condé will always remain Alpha Condé. But I would go so far as to reveal that he has always been a member of our family council. He's even the dean. My father was very fond of him. My brother Albert adores him. I wish the reverse were true.

I saw "ATT" regularly in Bamako, Dakar and Paris. I liked him very much. He was always very friendly to me. I used to meet "IBK" in the courtyard of my office. Why was that? He was very close to Anne Lauvergeon, who lived in my building. He came to visit her whenever she was in Paris, as they say in Africa.

What was your relationship with Gnassingbé Eyadema, whom Jacques Foccart asked you to look after? He was very close to Jacques Chirac. Do you go through Charles Debbasch for your missions?

I knew Eyadema well, but I never conveyed funds from Togo, even though Jacques Foccart was very fond of him. He received me very early. I used to meet Charles Debbasch at the palace in Lomé, but nothing more. I didn't "work" with him. He was close to the Togolese president, but not in the same way as my links with Omar Bongo.

With Eyadema, we weren't joking. Our relationship was warm, but not at all complicit. I'm not aware of any financial assistance from him to Jacques Chirac. Perhaps directly via Jacques Foccart.

Why not intervene in Cameroon? No emissaries to Paul Biya?

I visited the country a few times on the recommendation of Jacques Foccart. But I've never had any particular predilection for Paul Biya.

You receive many opponents and other personalities. We've seen you with Cellou Dalein Diallo and Anicet-Georges Dologuélé. What services could you render them?

I supported Cellou Dalein Diallo. I sometimes met him in Dakar, but I didn't see him much more than that. For these opponents, I operated as usual. I opened doors and made contacts.

In Africa, Freemasonry is "the network of the network". Do you belong to a lodge?

Not in the least. I didn't even attend Ali Bongo's enthronement as Grand Master of the Grande Loge du Gabon (GLG). I've never worked with them, but I've always found myself frequently at the table of more or less illustrious Freemasons.

What are the main character and psychological traits of the heads of state you know or have known?

Unfortunately, I wasn't very close to Félix Houphouët-Boigny, whom I met for the first time in 1978 at Foccart's request, in order to offer him my thesis. I spent three long hours with him. What a character! He was simply extraordinary. I can understand why de Gaulle, who was rather stingy with compliments, described him as an exceptional political mastermind. A man of uncommon distinction with a very distinctive voice. He didn't speak, but whispered. He anticipated everything. Everything that is happening today in Africa or in the Near and Middle East was already in his speeches.

How could we fail to mention the charismatic Omar Bongo? Our meeting in Libreville in 1982, at a meeting of the International Association of Francophone Mayors (AIMF), sealed a great filiation. I was a professor at the University of Law in Abidjan. Jacques Chirac made the trip and introduced me to him. We hit it off immediately, so much so that he asked me to stay an extra day, even though I was due to return to Côte d'Ivoire. I asked the dean of the faculty, Francis Wodié, for permission.

Nobody knew me in Libreville. I was going there for the first time. As I said, Omar Bongo immediately guessed that I was a monozygotic twin. He was fascinated by these questions. Let me remind you: twins in Africa have a real power of attraction. A fascination. From that day on, a very strong bond was born between us. Over time, this friendship developed into a family relationship. I've never known a more generous man. I'm not necessarily referring to money, but to the heart. It was in 1986 that he asked me to call him "Dad".

A little anecdote about generosity: one of its fiercest opponents came to see me at my office to talk about serious personal problems, not political ones. He asked me to intervene. I phoned Bongo to explain his opponent's situation. He agreed to come to his rescue, asking me to withdraw a large sum of money from the bank, to which he added a "bonus" to support his opponent's newspaper. Here's Bongo. Contrary to popular belief, he didn't like going out or partying. He had a unique way of talking, of making you laugh. His use of humor was his trademark. He was unique.

My relationship with Blaise Compaoré, whom I met when Thomas Sankara visited Paris in 1986, was more complex. Although pleasant and attentive, I felt he was a more calculating character. I worked with him until 2011, the date of my interview with *JDD*. I really got to know him in his Paris apartment, where he spent a lot of time with Chantal. He had a quality that few African heads of state possess: punctuality. He was interested in French history. He knew that I had mastered certain events. I would tell him about them. I also went to meet him in Ziniaré, his native village some fifty kilometers from Ouagadougou, where he rested at weekends, surrounded by his many animals.

I understand that he impressed his collaborators and opponents alike: he had a look that was both terrifying and enticing. We often phoned each other in the evening. If I had the opportunity, I'd be delighted to see him again, despite what I may have said about him in connection with the assassination of Thomas Sankara. He was not absolved of all responsibility for that tragic event.

Abdou Diouf was also a master of punctuality. He always received me at the General Secretariat, not at the Senegalese Presidency. The eminent Bruno Diatta would come to fetch me and introduce me. President Diouf was already waiting for me outside the door. I always enjoyed talking to him. He was very aware of his responsibilities and had a perfect command of his files. He was always precise, meticulous and methodical. He adored Jacques Chirac, while showing great respect for Jacques Foccart. In a word, Diouf was a class act.

I first saw Denis Sassou Nguesso when I was working with Michel Aurillac. He gave me the freedom to maneuver. I never stopped meeting him as president or as an opponent. I visited him four or five times a week in his apartment on Avenue Rapp. I always considered him a dandy and never hesitated to point this out to him. I often saw him in Europe, in Italy and Spain. His wife, Antoinette, was utterly delightful. I don't think I'll ever live those moments again. The man is very tough. He holds on to power in the strongest sense of the word. He worshipped Jacques Chirac, but had a soft spot for Nicolas Sarkozy.

I saw Idriss Deby Itno very often, both in N'Djamena and in Paris. He was always smiling, but I kept my distance from him, even when we kissed or held hands. The character didn't really lend itself to friendship.

Abdoulaye Wade, who came to power late in life and of whom I had been a student, was profoundly African and Senegalese, but was never, in my eyes, an African president. He remained a lawyer and a professor. His personality and phrasing were impressive. He has always been close to my family. He's like a father to my brother Rassek. I liked the way he approached and dealt with issues. He often met Nicolas Sarkozy, when the latter was minister, at the Senegalese residence in Paris. He would talk to him as if he were a student. The conversation would drag on and on. I knew that Sarkozy, by nature impatient, was only waiting for one thing: to leave. I haven't seen him in years, and neither has Karim. If he would call me, which he won't, I'd already be at his place in Versailles.

As for Laurent Gbagbo, he remains my friend, my brother. The tragic post-electoral crisis of 2010/2011 and all the gossip have driven us apart. Very close to my daughter Sophie, he was a member of my family even before he became president. He had written me a letter from the prison where Félix Houphouët-Boigny had sent him. I frequented him when we worked in Abidjan. He used to visit me at the Hôtel Ivoire when I was in Abidjan. He didn't deserve what happened to him. He was never left alone. He had the stature of a Patrice Lumumba, carrying high the values of Africa and always seeking a form of respectability, which is to his credit. Let him know that I never betrayed him. I've done a lot for him.

How did you manage the relationship between Omar Bongo and Denis Sassou Nguesso from the moment the latter became the father-in-law of the former? Did you tread lightly?

Their relationship was very strong, but there was an obvious difference in status. While both were heads of state, Omar Bongo was the oldest French-speaking president in Africa. Caution was called for. Well, I always managed to navigate the river of their relationship without too many problems. I kept in mind that everything I did in Congo-Brazzaville was known to President Bongo, and vice versa. Whenever I was in Brazzaville, Bongo always sent his plane to bring me to Libreville. I've never had any complaints about the Bongo-Sassou kinship, but be careful and measured.

Chapter 29: A Felon named Fillon

Six years after your thunderous outburst on African presidents' money, you're once again rocking the French Republic in 2017, in the midst of the presidential campaign, with a fatal blow to François Fillon, candidate for the Les Républicains party. After *Penelopegate*, which dangerously weakened Nicolas Sarkozy's ex-Prime Minister, *Le JDD* reveals that you "gifted" the election favorite with two Arnys suits worth a total of €15,000. You signed his death warrant at a time when his campaign was based on probity, exemplarity and transparency.

Several facts have matured my thoughts. First, his speech in Sablé-sur-Sarthe, in August 2016, in which he linked two notions that were absolutely antinomic and shocking to me: "De Gaulle" and "mise en examen". Secondly, his attack on Nicolas Sarkozy, even though the latter kept him on as Prime Minister for five years. Whether we like it or not, and despite the fact that he constantly called him a "mollusk", five years isn't nothing.

President Sarkozy made Fillon politically. Who was he before his appointment? Nothing. He had been nothing more than a mere technical minister. Not even the holder of a sovereign portfolio. Nicolas Sarkozy was always trying to get rid of him and replace him with Jean-Louis Borloo, but a lot of people came to his defense. The day after his speech, François Fillon and I had breakfast at the Ritz, during which I told him verbatim that he was really messing up. He admitted that, caught up in his militant enthusiasm, his words had gone beyond his thoughts.

"I disagree with what you said, François," I hammered.

If it had been a Sarkozy-Fillon duel, my choice would have been quickly made. The fact remains that he came out on top in the right-wing primaries, fair and square, so I made this remark to him at the end of the interview:

"You're the favorite, you have to be properly dressed".

I went to Arnys to order two suits. The store already knew him. I asked his boss to send him his master tailor. All the media coverage of this affair was an afterthought, but it's worth noting that I'd been enjoying buying him clothes for several years. Made-to-measure shirts, ties. We'd been seeing each other since the early 1980s. We were very close. There was no calculation on my part.

How did Nicolas Sarkozy react to the Sarthe speech?
He confided in me that he was affected and shocked.

Did he influence your decision to "trap" his former head of government?
I've said it a thousand times: he had nothing to do with my decision. You journalists should stop systematically seeing Sarkozy's shadow or paw in everything you say or do.

Under what circumstances did you meet Fillon?
With Jacques Foccart. We went to see Joël Le Theule, Minister of Defense, for whom he worked[144].

When you were offering these suits—in effect, influence peddling—did you already have an idea in the back of your mind?
At first, even though I was angry with Fillon, I didn't want to hurt him. But the weeks went by. The man I'd seen two or three times a week for so many years suddenly became unreachable. I kept sending him messages, text messages and phone calls. He stopped answering and even avoided me. Not a word of thanks for the costumes, can you believe it?

His staff, starting with his campaign manager and former prefect, Patrick Stefanini, formed a security cordon around him.

---

144. A native of Sablé-sur-Sarthe, Joël Le Theule (1930-1980) was Minister of Defense in Raymond Barre's 3rd government in 1980.

I couldn't care less about his team, as I did with Chirac and Sarkozy. Incidentally, Patrick Stefanini resigned in December 2016. Then one day, while I was in a bistro on rue Cler, near his home, opposite my fishmonger's, a text message from Fillon arrived. I was in the company of someone who had been put in the confidence of the anger that was rumbling:

> "Hello, Robert, my head is under water. Let the weeks go by and we'll get together for a St Julien".

Fillon has a predilection for this wine, which is not booze. I had the person in question read the message. She had this to say:

> "He's dead."

I went home and showed the message to my wife:

> "My God, he really doesn't know what he's doing".

He was starting to put his head on straight after *Penelopegate*, so I made my decision.

To *"fuck"* it, as you put it.
Absolutely. Nicolas Sarkozy invited me to lunch. I read him the message. He took his head in both hands and asked me what I was going to do. I told him he'd never be president.

What reaction?
He knew that nothing would stop me. He warned me against thinking about the collateral damage to our political family. He certainly had a thousand and one reasons to get his ex-Prime Minister in trouble, but he strongly advised me not to go through with it.

Does he suspect what's about to happen?
I immediately contacted Laurent Valdiguié to give him this new scoop. I hadn't hung up before he was already in my office, pen in hand. My secretary had prepared a copy of the invoice. He hadn't even finished going through it when he commented:

> "Fillon, it's over".

After *Penelopegate*, you're back with a vengeance. Why were you so sure of your facts? That these suits, even for €15,000, were going to ruin his candidacy for good?

Because when, in a presidential campaign, you keep talking about ethics, transparency and the high cost of living, and you accept €15,000 suits, you know it's all over. I've put the final nail in his political coffin. From then on, Laurent Valdiguié did his job. Unlike the historian Frédéric Turpin, who wrote an entire book on Jacques Foccart without ever contacting me![145]

He contacted François Fillon to cross-check his information and to warn him of what he was about to publish. On the Friday and Saturday before the article was published, he and Anne Méaux, his communicator and head of Image 7, to whom I was close because she was under contract to President Abdoulaye Wade, flooded me with messages. I was at the Bristol with my grandchildren. I finally decided on Fillon. He begged me not to reveal my identity or answer any journalists. I refused, but told him he had no one to blame but himself.

I'm not begging for an audience! I never asked him for anything. He, on the other hand, owed me a great deal. Even his good friend Jean de Boishue[146] was able to say on BMF TV that he was entirely responsible for the situation and the final crash. Money, lucre... I knew he was greedy. Worse: stingy. He was invited everywhere by everyone without ever paying a penny. That's just his nature.

Are you aware that you're on the verge of imploding your political family?

I have no regrets. I missed François Fillon, man to man, and badly too. The rest didn't really matter to me.

Valérie Pécresse received only 4.78% of the vote in the first round of the 2022 presidential election.

That's not bad, is it? Anne Hidalgo didn't exceed 2%. (laughs)

---

145. Frédéric Turpin, *Jacques Foccart. Dans l'ombre du pouvoir*, CNRS Éditions, Paris, 2015.
146. Born in 1943, Jean de Boishue is a senior civil servant. An associate professor and RPR member, he was a Member of Parliament, Secretary of State for Higher Education, General Councillor for Essonne (1988-2001) and Mayor of Brétigny-sur-Orge in the same department (1984-2001).

Would you do the same today?

There's no need to redo anything, there's nothing left to do.

What was Nicolas Sarkozy's reaction to the article?

He phoned me and said, "Thank you, my Robert". Although he didn't cause the fall, he wasn't unhappy about it. In the streets of the 16th arrondissement, where I live, passers-by would stare at me nastily and apostrophize:

> "Ah, we can tell you've done a fine job. Are you pleased with yourself, master?"

The aftermath of *Penelopegate* proved me right. The same people came back to me to tell me that I had been right in the end, while calling François Fillon a "sad sire". Not only did they learn that he paid his wife handsomely to do nothing, but that he had been reimbursed for his son's wedding expenses and the rent on his student room. Pathetic.

No news from him after that?

Nothing. On the other hand, all the African presidents' aides kept congratulating me:

> "Hey, Big Brother, really, you're too strong. Nicolas is avenged!"

On every TV show, you boast of having "*fucked*" a former French Prime Minister. Do you regret this language?

The French should know that this flowery language is widespread and commonly used by their political class. Does Villepin use a more polished vocabulary when he claims to want to "bourrer le nabot" when talking about Nicolas Sarkozy?

He doesn't say so publicly.

I was just satisfied to have disqualified this candidate. That's what I wanted. I achieved my goal, even though my comments led to my being stripped of my Legion of Honor for five years. I got it back on March 9, 2024.

François Fillon wasn't the only one to be "gift-wrapped" in clothes. That's your oriental side.

303

That's my temperament, without calculating or having an idea in the back of my head. I gave François Fillon little gifts, just as I used to give them to African personalities. I'm not going to name anyone, but I gave many, many, many gifts. I'd already given François Fillon a blazer in 2014, and some pants… Always from Arnys.

After this affair, you ask to be heard.
Via my lawyer Éric Moutet. It took some time. I was summoned to the OCCLIF[147] as a simple witness. I went to Nanterre where I was questioned by the head of the department, Commissaire Divisionnaire Guillaume Hézard. It was April 4, my birthday. He offered me a coffee and a chocolate.

I pointed out that he was acting on a rogatory commission from the "implacable" judge Serge Tournaire, and asked him when I would see him. Hézard replied that the judge wouldn't need to talk to me, as he was already fully aware of what I'd done.

"We have the means to know everything," he was quick to add.

What happened to the costumes?
François Fillon's security officer brought them back to my office, after the program during which journalist David Pujadas completely pilloried him[148]. They hadn't been cleaned and weren't even in their original cover.

Distinctive feature: they still had halos under their arms. I then sent them to Guillaume Hézard, asking him to donate them to the Little Sisters of the Poor on Avenue de Breteuil.

Didn't you play several games well before the right-wing primaries on November 27, 2016? In 2014 and 2015, you paid the UMP led by Nicolas Sarkozy, but also Force républicaine, François Fillon's movement, €7,500 to each of the two formations by way of support. These sums earned you a suspended prison sentence of one month and a €2,500 fine in 2018 for exceeding the authorized limits.
Nicolas Sarkozy knew that I'd been very close to François Fillon for over thirty years. One day, he didn't hesitate to point out that I was seeing a bit too much of him for his taste, which was not untrue. We would see each

---

147. Office central de lutte contre la corruption et les infractions financières et fiscales.
148. *L'Émission politique*. Guest: François Fillon, France 2, March 23, 2017.

304

"They Know I Know Everything"

other at my office, in top Parisian restaurants, at the Force républicaine headquarters, and so on.

I supported François, but with the secret idea of getting him to drop out of the primary. I even instigated a lunch between him and Nicolas Sarkozy at a restaurant under the Alexandre III bridge, whose chef was the same one Fillon had had at Matignon, to try and break the tie.

It was a first approach. Just before the primaries. But Fillon wouldn't budge. Feeling he could win, he was living his hour of glory. On the other hand, I was totally unaware of the legal provisions governing the financing of political parties. I was sanctioned for that.

Although close to Nicolas Sarkozy, you were quick to criticize him after his speech in Grenoble in July 2010. You consider his statements on immigration, Islam and the immigration/crime link to be clumsy.

And I stand by it. The day of the speech, I was having a drink with Jean-Marie Bockel at the Georges V. My reaction was to say that he was going to lose all the suburbs and the binational vote in the 2012 presidential election. This text was inspired by Patrick Buisson, his political advisor who would switch to the populist far right, first with Nicolas Dupont-Aignan and then with Éric Zemmour, after working with François Fillon for the 2016 primaries[149].

By supporting both Nicolas Sarkozy and François Fillon, you're dealing your cards in such a way that you'll be remembered at the goodwill of the potential winner.

I'm in no way motivated by opportunism. I loved Nicolas Sarkozy above all else. I was with François Fillon, a man I'd spent a lot of time with during my career. I couldn't consider this relationship as secondary and put an end to it for purely electoral reasons. To be honest, if I'd wanted to be opportunistic, I'd have played the Alain Juppé card instead. He's always been the favorite on the right. You must stop attributing to me obscure calculations of political opportunism.

---

149. Born in 1949, Patrick Buisson was a journalist and essayist. Political advisor to Nicolas Sarkozy from 2007 to 2012. He died in December 2023.

Chapter 29: A Felon named Fillon

In the run-up to his trial in 2020, François Fillon confessed to having made two mistakes in relation to the suit affair: *"having accepted them"* and *"having given his trust to someone who didn't deserve it"*[150].

A particularly ill-timed and discourteous remark considering what our relationship was. This affair would never have happened if he'd behaved properly, like a true gentleman. I thought, conversely, that we were friends. I always enjoyed meeting him, talking to him. And now, all of a sudden, this man gives no sign of life as soon as he is nominated for the 2017 presidential election. As if I didn't exist anymore.

I'm made of flesh and blood. I have a brain, nerves and muscles and, above all, a memory. He didn't even answer my messages anymore. Suddenly, I was a plague. And even if his entourage had warned him about our association, his attitude was inexcusable.

Are you aware of the moral decay of the French right?
Nicolas Sarkozy warned me:

> "My Robert, I'm asking you to take the measure of your punishment, because you risk blowing up the whole of the right".

Looking at him, I warned him that God himself would not make me reverse my decision. Just as he was determined to vitrify Laurent Gbagbo, I was determined to pulverize Fillon.

How do you feel about his announcement, in early 2023, that he was retiring from political life?
Pity.

By claiming to have *"fucked"* a former head of the French government, you sparked an outcry from the Paris Bar Association. In early 2019, after a hearing before its disciplinary board, you were banned from practicing law for a year, six months of which were suspended. Your lawyer at the time was Éric Dupont-Moretti. How did you meet him? Your meeting coincided with the rise in African cases for the man who was not yet Minister of Justice and Keeper of the Seals. Are you behind some of his cases?

---

150. *Vous avez la parole,* France 2, January 30, 2020.

I met him for the first time following my interview with the *JDD*, which had already earned me a summons from the Conseil de l'Ordre. For the Fillon affair, I had preferred my old friend Pierre Haïk, who very kindly refused to defend me. Ditto Thierry Herzog, who was much more inelegant. Pierre Haïk referred me to Éric Dupont-Moretti, who took my case.

From then on, we maintained close ties of friendship and trust. We saw each other often, including in Corsica. I had him received in Dakar by Macky Sall. He defended me in relation to Jean-Marie Le Pen's complaint, as well as my financing of Nicolas Sarkozy and François Fillon, for which he had called me a "big ass". I was a familiar face in his Paris office.

After his appointment to the Chancellery, I worked with his assistant, Antoine Vey, who defended me as best he could before the Conseil de l'Ordre. As soon as he was appointed to Jean Castex's government in July 2020, however, he sent me a message to the effect that it would be preferable not to see each other again. It has to be said that I had 14 bank robberies to my credit, 152 indictments, 1,002 searches and 162 convictions, including one with three years' imprisonment...

When I think I used to frequent the Chancellery when Jacques Toubon and Jean-Marie Bockel were its tenants. In short, I've suddenly become infrequent there too. We haven't seen each other since that appointment.

Did you present him with any African files?

As for the connections I made when he was still "Acquittator", I introduced Éric Dupont-Moretti to Maixent Accrombessi, Ali Bongo's chief of staff, who was concerned by the Marck affair. He became Gabon's lawyer, although it didn't go very far. I also put him in touch with the Congolese Moïse Katumbi Chapwe, who was in trouble with Joseph Kabila's regime.

I introduced him to Patricia Balme in connection with the Frenchman Michel-Thierry Atangana, imprisoned in Cameroon for several years as part of the Épervier anti-corruption affair. And one day, when I happened to meet Jean-Dominique Okemba at the Bristol, I told him how much I liked this "black dress".

I understand that Denis Sassou Nguesso tried to offer him some business. I also established contact with the Equatorial Guinean ambassador to France, Miguel Oyono Ndong Mifumu, without knowing anything about the developments of this meeting. Eric knows how to be a secretive man...

Chapter 30: Behind the Gold of the Republic

In 2012, after Sarkozy's mandate, did you try to get closer to personalities close to François Hollande?

Under no circumstances am I seeking to do so. It's not my political family, even though I obviously know many of its protagonists. During François Hollande's very first trip to Africa, to Senegal and the Democratic Republic of Congo, in October 2012, journalist Thomas Sotto invited me to a Europe 1 morning show to comment. I suggested that François Hollande, if he wished to leave his mark on France's African policy, should invest himself personally with his African counterparts to avoid the temptation of unlimited mandates.

For the rest, my interventions became more discreet. I went my own way. I continued to introduce political and economic leaders to Nicolas Sarkozy. I took care of Senegal. I received opponents from Gabon, etc.

How do you feel about Emmanuel Macron's decision to suspend your Legion of Honor? Did he want to keep you at arm's length by sending out a signal towards Françafrique, which he, like his predecessors, wanted to do away with, right from his first trip to the continent, to Ouagadougou, in November 2017?

I didn't do anything against this decision and didn't hold any grudges. On the other hand, my wife, rather disappointed, had to untie all the red ribbons from my jackets.

Did Emmanuel Macron deliberately attack the "ambassador" of Françafrique to make a point?

In 2017, François Fillon had to win. When Emmanuel Macron trashed him, he knew perfectly well that I had played no small, albeit indirect, part in his victory. He enjoyed a boulevard, and I was no stranger to it. Some people even imagined that I had deliberately ousted the LR candidate to give him a chance to break through, which is not true. When he came to power, it was undoubtedly important for him to clarify things, in particular by aligning himself with General Benoît Pugat, to keep me at bay. General Pugat has just been revealed by the *Mediapart* website to be the target of a corruption investigation into the awarding of Legions of Honor[151]. We're in the middle of a vaudeville.

Were you, in spite of everything, inclined to approach the Macron camp?

But I'm not! Just as you've never seen me chase François Hollande.

Even via Jean-Marie Le Guen?

Another rumor. I never approached Jean-Marie Le Guen—in fact, quite the opposite. It was he who wanted to meet me through the architect Pierre Fakhoury. Fakhoury organized a dinner on January 14, 2010 at the home of lawyer Pierre Haïk with Claude Guéant, Jean-Christophe Cambadellis, Jean-Marie Le Guen and myself. Pierre Fakhoury whispered to me that he wanted to meet the "Cardinal"[152]. The Right was still in power, but I don't know what Le Guen's plans were. It has to be said that I know a great many politicians of all stripes, and they know me. I don't shy away from any relationship. They often see me and come up to me to say hello.

This was recently the case with Emmanuel Macron's Prime Minister, Gabriel Attal[153], on a beach in Ajaccio. I met Jordan Bardella through the mayor of Fréjus, David Rachline, during a vacation in Saint-Raphaël. I was in a restaurant. They recognized me and invited me to their table. We had a nice drink and talked a lot. I've seen them both on several occasions. Jordan Bardella is a highly intelligent man who thinks things through and has ambitions for France. Between him and me, the points of disagreement were obvious, but nothing profoundly dissimilar. We exchange messages regularly. I don't see the danger of his rise.

---

151. Antton Rouget, "L'ancien chef d'état-major de l'Élysée visé par une enquête pour corruption", *Mediapart*, April 9, 2024.
152. Nickname given to Claude Guéant.
153. Interview conducted on May 30, 2024.

In any case, the political family to which I've belonged for over 50 years is brain-dead. Since Nicolas Sarkozy's defeat in 2012, I've distanced myself from this formation, to which I still made a financial contribution until recently, but I stopped a year ago. I had placed a lot of hope in Emmanuel Macron, but the disappointment is huge. Both internationally and domestically. We are absent from the Arab political scene. Let's not even talk about Africa, which we've totally lost. I think Jordan Bardella has the chance to give our country new strength, hope and solidity.

Apart from Jean-Marie Bockel and Roland Dumas, do you have any other links with Socialist figures? Michel Charasse comes to mind.

As I said, I didn't know Roland Dumas very well, even though he was a close friend of Omar Bongo for almost thirty years, as journalist Christian Casteran recalls in his book, *Confidences d'un Africain*, written with the Gabonese president[154]. I have maintained and continue to maintain a whole host of relationships with leaders of the French left. Jean-Marie Bockel, of course. The story of his downfall is now well known. But since the mediation of Bernard Squarcini, Philippe Bohn and Jean-Philippe Gouyet, I've been honored by his friendship. He is a man of courage and a true patriot. His son fell heroically in Mali.

In *Les visiteurs du soir*, Vincent Revel also portrays you as the self-proclaimed bag-bearer for *"a host of political parties, from the RPR to the PS, via the UMP and the PC"*[155].

These are Revel's obsessions, nonsense! What's more, in Cameroon, a country I've hardly ever set foot in. Nonsense. Once and for all: I've never been a porter, a term I don't appreciate. I've spent my life accompanying the emissaries who carried them—the nuance is significant—usually to right-wing personalities. And they were never suitcases in the true sense of the word. More like sports bags, briefcases, satchels in a pinch.

At the time, and until the laws of 1988, then 1990 and 1995, the financing of political parties was authorized. Other laws were subsequently passed, in 1995 and 2013, which tightened up the system, and I'm not saying that we shouldn't have juggled a bit more.

---

154. Omar Bongo, *Confidences d'un Africain: entretiens avec Christian Casteran*, Albin Michel, 1994.
155. *Les visiteurs du soir*, p. 306-307.

I've played the role of accompanist, but never for other parties. Never, never, never. I was, however, in the confidences of certain heads of state. Of course, I knew that Valéry Giscard d'Estaing and François Mitterrand were spoiled for choice. But I didn't direct funds on behalf of the PS, let alone the PCF. Renaud Revel needs to stop rambling and romanticizing all the time.

You mentioned a number of funny episodes with Jean-Marie Le Pen, who didn't hesitate to insult you in the media after your interview in the *JDD*, in which you accused him of having received funding from Omar Bongo for his 1988 presidential campaign. In fact, he was the only person to win his libel suit against you. Why did you mention Le Pen's name? Was it a mistake? A lapse of memory?

He filed a lawsuit, which I lost. I was defended in this case by Éric Dupont-Moretti, obviously much less at ease defending Robert Bourgi than major criminals. All I have to say is: "Mr. Le Pen, you know that I know". Other personalities, including his closest collaborator Lorrain de Saint-Affrique, have won legal actions against him. I'm not even talking about the statements made by the former Prime Minister of Gabon, Jean Eyeghe Ndong, who confirmed these funds came from Gabon[156]. Curiously, no complaint has been made against him.

Of all the French political figures you've rubbed shoulders with, who has left the strongest impression on you?

In fact, there are four, and I can't decide between the first two: Jacques Foccart and Jacques Chirac. The former is my personal favorite. Then, each with their advantages and qualities, Dominique de Villepin and Nicolas Sarkozy, despite my disagreement with the former. These four personalities are flamboyant and impressive in their culture. It's true that I had a falling out with Dominique de Villepin, but how could I fail to be moved by his charisma, his loquaciousness, his speech at the United Nations? Even if our relationship is no longer the same, we say hello to each other when we bump into each other in restaurants. Long after the

---

156. "Un dirigeant africain évoque des valises pour Le Pen", *Le Journal du dimanche*, September 28, 2011.

JDD interview, in March 2012 he even sent me a copy of his book *Seul le devoir nous rendra libres*[157], with a beautiful dedication.

You remain formal with some of them, such as Dominique de Villepin, while adopting the familiar with others, such as Nicolas Sarkozy. How do you explain this?

It came instinctively, naturally. Villepin called me "Camarade", but we were always on familiar terms. We never felt the need to be on first-name terms. Same with Alain Juppé.

Over the course of your "career", you've developed a particular modus operandi: you've always stuck to the main collaborator of Presidents Chirac and Sarkozy, their sherpa, whether it's Jacques Foccart or the Élysée secretaries-general, the target chosen to make your "business" bear fruit. Was this a deliberate strategy?

It's not a deliberate strategy, but the fruit of circumstances and encounters. When I met Jacques Chirac, it was through Jacques Foccart, whom I'd been seeing for a long time. Chirac naturally introduced me to Dominique de Villepin, Secretary General of the Élysée Palace. When I switched to Nicolas Sarkozy, it was he who introduced me to Claude Guéant.

After his term of office, Nicolas Sarkozy also became something of a lawyer-lobbyist, particularly in Africa, which is unprecedented for a former French president. On the continent, he defends the activities of the Accor hotel group, of which he was appointed independent director in 2017 and reappointed in 2019, a group in partnership with the *Qatar Investment Authority* to develop its business on the continent. He also supports his friend Dominique Desseigne, head of the Barrière group. He represents other economic entities such as Michaël Fribourg's Chargeurs group, a former employee of his Minister of Industry, Éric Besson. He defends the interests of online betting company Beltic. Finally, he cultivates his relationship with several presidents, including Alassane Ouattara and above all Paul

---

157. Dominique de Villepin, *Seul le devoir nous rendra libres*. Editions du Cherche Midi. Paris. 112 pages. 2012.

Kagamé, with whom he promotes French economic groups. Are you helping him in this conversion?

Not at all. As a former French president turned lawyer, he didn't need my help to develop his activities and address book in Africa. He never spoke to me about it, and never asked me for anything. He relies on his brilliant young diplomatic adviser, Pierre Régent. On this subject, I'd like to digress for a moment to say that he was deeply affected by his official trip to Kigali in February 2010, after 16 years of diplomatic estrangement, during which he acknowledged the "serious errors of assessment" and "blindness" of the French authorities at the time, in the face of the genocidal dimension of the Habyarimana regime.

I was part of that journey. Having always known him as a warrior, I can still see his face completely mined at the Genocide Memorial, facing that mountain of skulls. He told me that what he had seen was just "appalling". Watching him carefully over lunch with Paul Kagamé, I could see that the Rwandan president was changing the way he looked at France. Relations were undeniably warming up.

You introduce Nicolas Sarkozy to personalities visiting Paris, such as President Obiang Nguema Mbasogo, but also, in January 2020, to Umaro Sissoco Embalo, who has not yet been recognized by his country's Supreme Court as the new President of Guinea-Bissau. You meet him accompanied by Moroccan businessman Kamel Benali.

It was Macky Sall who asked me to introduce him to Nicolas Sarkozy. Macky Sall and Emballo had been friends for a long time. For this meeting, I was approached by Ali Attyé, the Guinea-Bissau president's factotum and a Shiite Muslim, whose family is close to mine. I knew absolutely nothing about Guinea-Bissau. I asked Nicolas Sarkozy for a green light, and he said:

"OK, I'll come to make you happy".

I didn't worry about Emballo's non-recognition or whether it would bother President Macron. Nicolas Sarkozy is well-versed in the issue and didn't raise any objections. He joined us in a hotel lounge. Kamel Benali wanted to take part in the interview, but refused. He just put himself in

314

the picture (laughs). I saw him again recently, having lunch with Francis Szpiner. He likes all those Szpiner circles...[158]

A lawyer with a keen interest in Africa, which was for a time your own.

I met him more than twenty years ago, by chance, at the presentation of a Légion d'honneur to a colleague. Mayor of the 16th arrondissement from 2020 to 2023, before becoming a senator, he defended me in a private matter, but he is above all a friend. On the other hand, I haven't supported him in any of his African projects.

In early 2019, Nicolas Sarkozy succeeded in arranging an unlikely mediation between Guinean President Alpha Condé, in conflict with Israeli businessman Beny Steinmetz, head of Beny Steinmetz Group Resources (BSGR). Did he put you in the loop?

President Sarkozy never discusses his African affairs, or any affairs whatsoever, with me. He has surrounded himself with his adviser from the Quai d'Orsay, Pierre Régent, whom he particularly appreciates, as I do. He sometimes attended our meetings. A very discreet and intelligent presence. But most of the time, I'm alone with Nicolas.

You are the friend and source of many journalists specializing in French politics and Africa. You've even helped some of them in a difficult situation.

Real journalists have always followed me on my peregrinations. I had no secrets from some of them, starting with Claude Angeli. I saw him at least once a week. We'd go over the big issues of the day. I put him above all others. For me, he's in a class of his own. It's a mark of his confidence that he chose me to be his best man at his wedding to his charming wife, Stéphanie Mesnier, also a journalist. We're both getting on in years, but at over 90 years of age, I'm still impressed by the relevance of his analyses and the sharpness of his judgments.

---

158. Defending former Central African President Jean-Marie Bedel Bokassa before the Bangui Assize Court, Francis Szpiner is also known as a lawyer for Abdoulaye Wade, Djiboutian President Ismaël Omar Guelleh and the State of Djibouti in the case relating to the 1995 assassination in that country of Judge Bernard Borrel ; the State of Senegal against Khalifa Sall and the former Socialist Minister for Cooperation, Christian Nucci.

I miss other journalist friends like Jean-Marc Kalflèche. I even feel like saying to him: "Your absence, Jean-Marc, weighs heavily on me". He had a sharp eye for Africa. I was very fond of Christian Casteran and Daniel Carton, journalists at *Le Monde* and *Le Nouvel Observateur*. For those who also cover Africa, I have enormous respect for the Antoine Glaser-Stephen Smith duo, who regularly consulted me for their respective investigations or as part of the preparation of their books. I even helped Stephen Smith out of a tight spot during the presidential elections in Gabon in August 2009. I was at Disney World in Orlando, USA, when I received his call for help. He had just been arrested by Ali Bongo's henchmen in the bush. He asked me to intervene. After telephoning Ali, he was freed and taken to the Congolese border. Informed by me, Denis Sasssou Nguesso took over and resolved the situation.

Finally, there's Pierre Péan, despite a few articles or books that might have upset me or that I might have found unpleasant. Our friendship was sincere. I got to know him in the 1980s through my brother Albert, when he published two books, including *Affaires africaines* on the Omar Bongo regime[159]. This book provoked a serious crisis with France. The Gabonese president was threatening diplomatic relations. Jacques Foccart was no longer in office, but did his best to calm things down.

Pierre Péan whose life you would have saved.

Until now, this episode has remained unknown. Albert and I often dined with Claude Angeli, Jean-Marc Kalflèche, who nicknamed me the "Gaullo-Gaullian", and Pierre. Foccart was well aware of the relationship between Péan, who was not on my political side, and the Bourgi family. We laughed a lot. He was subtle, critical and humorous.

One evening in 1984, Foccart asked me to come to rue de Prony, telling me that *Affaires africaines* was too explosive. He had clearly instructed me to warn Pierre Péan.

> "I have learned from Pierre Debizet[160] that something is afoot against this journalist."

---

159. Pierre Péan, *Affaires africaines*, Fayard, 1983.
160. Pierre Debizet (1922-1996), a former member of the French Resistance who was awarded the Croix de Guerre and the Médaille de la Résistance, was one of the leaders of the RPF's order service, before becoming a key figure in the Service d'Action Civique (SAC), an organization disbanded in 1982. He is accused of being behind the 1978 murder of communist and anti-colonialist activist Henri Curiel. See Les "missions africaines de M. Debizet" by Laure Greil Samer, *Le Monde*, August 1, 1981.

316

"I hope, "Doyen", that those with a grudge against him don't come to an end."

"Let him know."

Which I did. We met at the Hôtel Élysée Ponthieu, near Avenue Matignon. I urged him to put the pedal to the metal, while making it clear that Foccart was in charge. There was clearly a "contract" on Pierre Péan's head, and in the end he would not be bothered. I would see him often thereafter, giving him a great deal of first-hand information, which he would not hesitate to use to the detriment of my interests and personal comfort. The Lebanon hostage ransom is a case in point. I often took him to Foccart's house. He was one of the few journalists invited to Luzarches. Underneath his Robin Hood exterior, Pierre had a tender heart. I regret I contracted covid at the time of his funeral[161]. I'll miss his pen and his laugh.

The only problem I had with journalists was with Vincent Hugeux when he was a senior reporter at *L'Express*. He'll deny it, but he used to come and see me at my office. He too owes me a debt of gratitude in Gabon. I remember that, during one of Omar Bongo's presidential campaigns, we travelled around the country on the Transgabonais. The president was accompanied by André Mba Obame. As we slowed down on the approach to a station, the Minister of the Interior, suddenly spotting the journalist through the window, shouted:

"Patron, it's the French journalist who's always criticizing us. We've got to stop him!"

As I knew both Hugeux and the methods of the Gabonese state, I was quick to tell Omar Bongo that such a decision would be eminently dangerous for the bilateral relationship and would do his country no credit. Vincent Hugeux should know that I saved his ass. We saw each other afterwards, but, like Alain Juppé, I'd like someone to tell me one day why he always held a grudge against me.

All your life, you've sat at the finest tables. What's your favorite restaurant?

Without hesitation, Le Pavillon, by Yannick Alléno, on the Champs-Élysées, and the restaurant at Le Bristol when it was run by Éric Frechon,

---

161. Born in 1938, Pierre Péan died on July 25, 2019.

who has just left. I was extremely fond of this restaurant. Le Flandrin, too, on avenue Henri Martin in Paris's 16th arrondissement. A sort of "HQ" for my wife and me. We have our napkin rings there. I like to go to l'Ambroisie, place des Vosges, a restaurant long run by Bernard Pacaud, as well as Stresa, rue de Chambiges, in the 8th arrondissement. I also enjoy my friend Sam's Chez Waknine.

Although Muslim, you've also tested the biggest bottles.

I scrupulously respect the values of the Muslim religion, while remembering that I'm a Shiite, but not a cutthroat. I've visited Mecca twice, and I drink wine and spirits. I don't count the whiskies I've shared on memorable evenings with Villepin or Charles Pasqua.

In my cellar, among dozens of bottles, there's still the 1963 malt that Dominique gave me. I've told my children never to open it. On the other hand, I've always forbidden myself to drink alcohol in front of or in the company of Muslim personalities, a fortiori heads of state. Only Omar Bongo, Sassou Nguesso and Mobutu chose the best vintages for me.

How do you respond to your detractors who believe that your love of Africa is primarily driven by greed?

I won't even comment. Let's avoid falling into the grotesque.

What are your most vivid and painful memories?

Sartre said, "*I am a man made of all the others, who is worth them all and worth anything.*" I've been extremely happy, both professionally and personally, when I defended my thesis with Pierre Dabezies, a Free French Cadet whom I admired; when Jacques Chirac won in 1995; and when Nicolas Sarkozy won in 2007. Another happy moment was the success of my children.

I experienced moments of great distress: the death of my mother in 1960 and that of my younger sister Rassika on July 17, 1967. I was terribly sad when Jacques Foccart died. A whole part of my life was absorbed by this event. I won't forget Chirac's reassurance. I was also saddened by the death of Omar Bongo in 2009. It brought tears to my eyes.

Antoine de Saint-Exupéry said that "the child is the father of man". I know countless people, but I'd like to take this opportunity to mention all those brothers and sisters who, as children, teenagers and students, left me with lasting memories. First, the Lebanese industrialist who made his fortune in Dakar, Mohamed Bourgi aka "Moe". As far back as I can remember, he's there. He retired to Nice. His mother, Mama Assem, was a cousin of my parents. We've known each other for 72 years. An admirable man above all values. In elementary school, Sophie Mezzadri and Marie-Josée Riedlin were great friends, as was Jacqueline Audic.

I still have friends from my high school days at "Van Vo" in Dakar, such as Viviane Marchi, the daughter of one of my teachers, and her brothers Don Jean and Christian. Pierre Cave, whose father was a radiologist at Dakar University Hospital. The Bohuon brothers, from Brittany. The eldest, Jean-Malo Bohuon, ended his career as a magistrate in Nanterre. With his brother Yves, they were my tennis buddies. I'm also thinking of Marc Lapeyre and Hervé Dufour, son of my law professor at Dakar University, who ended his career at Nice University.

I can't fail to mention here my unfailing friend Jean-Paul Fayot, whom I met in 1958 at the "Van Vo" high school in Dakar. A renowned dental surgeon in Marseille, Nice and Abidjan, an active member of the UNR, then the RPR, the UMP and LR, he has accompanied me throughout my family and professional life. He remains very active in Les Républicains. All these people never cease to populate the affective lobe of my brain.

As the organizer of the transfer of African funds to the RPR and, indirectly, to its founder, what scene particularly impressed you?

This man touched and impressed me deeply during my "career". I admired him. I sometimes go to the Montparnasse cemetery to pay my respects. I can't imagine him gone. There's a scene I remember quite often, which makes me laugh every time. It was in the winter of 1994. We were in his huge, splendid office at Paris City Hall. I had arrived in the courtyard of honor in a car from the Gabonese embassy in France, only to be greeted by the ever-faithful Jean-Claude Laumond, who led me into Jacques Chirac's waiting room. The door opened, and I saw him smiling in his shirtsleeves:

"Hello, Robert."
"Good morning, Mr. Mayor."

Here we are in his blue den, with a crackling fireplace.

319

"How is President Bongo? He's very confident that I'll win."

"I can confirm this, Mr. Mayor, he confirmed it to me again by telephone a short while ago, and I'm sending you this as a token of my affection."

I handed him a satchel containing 1 million francs divided into ten small packets of 100,000 francs, which he placed on a table. It's the first and only time in my life that I've touched a satchel with African money myself. After moving to his armchair, he slipped on his jacket, tucking in 4 packets, 2 in each pocket.

"Mr. Mayor, this is far too visible, you need to unload."

Which he did before raising his arms high.

"And now? Can you tell?"

I couldn't help myself. We burst out laughing. Then he called Laumond to hand him the two packages he'd taken out of his pockets, whispering something in his ear. Laumond left the office with a friendly, knowing wink.

Putting an end to decades of political activity, I'm reminded of the phrase attributed to William Shakespeare:

> *"Truth always triumphs, but its victory is slow and difficult. Like the ancient goddesses, it takes its time, and the time of the gods is not the time of men."*

You embodied Françafrique for decades. Do you have any regrets?

I was a privileged player and witness to this system. In my memoirs, I mention, among many other things, the financing of French political parties, especially on the right of the political spectrum. I organized these movements for several decades, proudly carrying out these missions. I couldn't help it, but it gradually became a source of discomfort for me, which led me to denounce it. I wanted it to stop. The whole world came down on me, including those who were behind the convoys. But *"Ainsi va le monde"*, as journalist Vincent Hervouët so aptly puts it[162].

---

162. Vincent Hervouët, *Ainsi va le monde*, Albin Michel, 2014.

Conclusion: France is Grateful to Africa

In the aftermath of independence for the former colonies of French-speaking Africa, France strove to maintain a vertical relationship with this "historic bloc" on the ashes of the Franco-African Community, which had been plagued since its inception in 1958 by the non-adhesion of Guinea's leader, Ahmed Sékou Touré, and the gradual obsolescence of this system from 1960 onwards. Despite this context, for France, maintaining close relations with these newly autonomous territories was essential for a number of reasons: to guarantee access to strategic energy resources; to secure captive markets for its manufactured goods; to enhance its international aura; to preserve its rank as the "greatest of the middle powers"; to maintain its linguistic influence via the French-speaking world; to perpetuate its militarism; and to preserve this zone from the East-West conflict of the Cold War era.

After the shock of the decolonization of sub-Saharan Africa, which he had neither wanted nor anticipated, and to better preserve the growth of this industrious France, General de Gaulle set about installing heads of state at the head of these countries who were in every way sympathetic to his vision, his international plans and the well-understood interests of these new partners. In the minds of the French authorities, any backsliding on these issues would have been to the detriment of the Hexagone, and immediately compensated by the action of other powers on the African continent, starting with the Soviet Union.

Until the early 1990s, this clientelism was essentially supported, developed, animated and embodied by one man: Jacques Foccart. Inhabited by the raison d'État, this small, frail man, as discreet as he was powerful, maintained the cohesion of this "pré carré", in the original sense of the word, even at the cost of actions or "instructions" that were

321

totally outside the institutional and republican sphere. Two long-term leaders undoubtedly helped him in this post-colonial undertaking: Félix Houphouët-Boigny and Omar Bongo Ondimba.

As a land of resistance to the Nazi and Vichy enemies, French-speaking Africa did more than just preserve captive markets and well-understood interests. It also contributed to the health of French political life by financing its parties and personnel of all stripes in the aftermath of the Second World War. Robert Bourgi, and before him his father Mahmoud, was one of the privileged witnesses to this cornucopia on the right of the political spectrum. The account of this wise and prudent "logistician" of innumerable cash convoys is all the more instructive. For the first time, it provides a precise description of the modus operandi, players and emissaries involved in these movements. It also reveals the importance of the Lebanese and Middle Eastern communities in Africa, a fact too little known to explain part of Jacques Chirac's attachment to this other part of the world.

Despite increasingly drastic laws on the financing of political parties and election campaigns, these contributions and "gifts" have long endured in the murky silence of Africa's nightlife, until they have completely withered away, in the image of France's African policy.

But in this long-standing relationship of mixed interests, the "client" has not always been who you might think. By funneling millions of CFA francs to Paris, in response to "solicitations" from French politicians, many African presidents have managed to buy themselves internal peace, their political survival, but also the calculated indulgence of Paris regarding the absence of civil liberties or real democracy in their countries. In this sense, they have benefited, in return, from the system they have helped to nurture, even, in the case of Omar Bongo, going so far as to influence certain decisions taken by the French state.

This clientelism explains the close, ultra-personal ties between François Mitterrand and his counterparts south of the Sahara, and especially Jacques Chirac, who was backed by a very strong network in Africa. The constant financial support provided by this network sheds new light on the privileged treatment Blaise Compaoré, for example, received from France. Invitation as guest of honour to Jacques Chirac's first Bastille Day ceremony in 1995, organization of the France-Africa summit in Ouagadougou in December 1996, and induction into the Académie des sciences d'outre-mer are just some of the courtesies extended to Burkina Faso, a country of only relative strategic importance. What about the positioning of the French state apparatus in relation to other states? Whether in Gabon or Congo-Brazzaville, the powers that be have long been able to count on its extreme unction. And with good reason.

In addition to regulations governing the financing of political parties, this system has also been undermined by regime changes in France and, more importantly, by judicial activism. In November 2010, the Criminal Division of the French Supreme Court (Cour de Cassation) authorized judges to investigate the assets accumulated in France by three African presidents, triggering a change of direction. This unprecedented move even explains their disenchantment with France, symbolized by the death of Omar Bongo, champion of Françafrique, in Spain.

For the people of Africa, on the other hand, the profligacy and largesse of their presidents in the French political arena raises more serious questions. Illustrating the "politics of the belly" so dear to the political scientist Jean-François Bayart, these millions of euros in prebends and glittering estates were as much funding that escaped the development of their countries. In this respect, the emergency situation in which many of the continent's French-speaking states find themselves (health, infrastructure, schools, industry...) is no stranger to the siphoning off of their national economies, often to the benefit of Franco-African practices.

At a time when the progress of scientific research, the militancy of certain associations and memorial initiatives (restitution of works of art looted during the colonial period, creation of historians' commissions, etc.) are enabling them to reappropriate their history, Africans, young and old alike, are becoming increasingly aware, if that were still necessary, of the role, involvement and even compromise of their leaders with the Fifth French Republic. Such is also the didactic vocation of this book.

F.L.

Appendices and Documents

From Jacques Chirac's first years as head of the Rassemblement pour la République (RPR) in December 1976, to Brice Clotaire Oligui Nguema's coup d'état in Gabon in August 2023, Robert Bourgi's professional life and involvement in Franco-African relations spans almost half a century. The sheer volume of personal notes, diaries, letters and confidential correspondence accumulated over this period would have merited two additional volumes to the present Memoirs.

However, some 150 of them have been carefully selected and are reproduced in these appendices. Eclectic and never-before-published, they shed light on or reinforce the points made in this book, while confirming Robert Bourgi's close ties with many of the key figures of the Fifth Republic, starting, of course, with Jacques Foccart.

Readers will find everything from Jacques Chirac's correspondence to activities within the Club 89; a letter sent by Laurent Gbagbo from his cell in Yopougon prison in 1992; the Villepin government's list of May 31, 2005, written in Omar Bongo's own hand before being handed over to President Chirac; and a photocopy of the €75,000 check issued by the Burkinabe presidency for the purchase of a bust of Napoleon, a gift intended for the same Dominique de Villepin.

Robert Bourgi's handwritten personal notes are rarer. These decipher sensitive African news or report on Bourgi's regular meetings with African heads of state. Far from bypassing the analyses of current diplomats or Quai d'Orsay officials, these documents prove, if proof were still needed, the multiplicity of sources on Africa that go back to the highest levels of the French state in order to gain a better grasp of the continent's inner workings and dynamics.

Last but not least, these appendices contain Robert Bourgi's diaries. The sheer number and multiplicity of these annotated appointments are proof of the extent to which the man described by a US Department of State dispatch, revealed by Wikileaks, as "the leading figure in Françafrique" was able to penetrate, even permeate, the corridors of the Élysée Palace and the ministries, offering advice, comfort or, more generally, receiving, like the Prince's advisor, the grievances and confidences of his interlocutors.

Appendix 1: First correspondence between Jacques Chirac
and Robert Bourgi, October 8, 1976.

Jacques Chirac

PARIS, le 8 Octobre 1976

Cher Monsieur,

Votre lettre m'a beaucoup touché et
je vous remercie de ce témoignage d'amitié et de
confiance.

Malgré mon éloignement actuel du
Gouvernement, soyez assuré que je ferai en sorte
de continuer à servir notre pays et à défendre
les idées auxquelles vous et moi nous croyons.

Je vous prie de croire, Cher Monsieur,
à l'assurance de mes sentiments les meilleurs.

J. Chirac

Monsieur Robert BOURGI
Assistant en Droit

Parc Berthault "Les Palmiers"
2000 - A J A C C I O

Appendix 2: Correspondence between Jacques Foccart and Robert Bourgi, then in Benin, following the latter's meeting with President Félix Houphouët-Boigny on April 28, 1978.

JACQUES FOCCART
95, Rue de Prony
75017 Paris
Tel. 227-11-27

447/78

PARIS, le 26 Avril 1978.

Cher Ami,

J'ai bien reçu votre petite carte du 12 Avril et vous en remercie.

J'étais, en effet, à Abidjan le 15 Avril ; j'étais même parrain à un baptème où se trouvait le Président HOUPHOUET, baptème qui a eu lieu dans l'après-midi. Je regrette de ne pas avoir su que vous étiez là car je vous aurais vu avec plaisir.

Je suis très heureux que vous ayez eu un bon contact avec le Président de la République de Côte d'Ivoire. C'est, en effet, un homme exceptionnel qui est très simple et très humain et qui a une vision des problèmes politiques tout à fait remarquable.

Je suis peiné des nouvelles que vous me donnez de votre Père. Il ne peut hélas en être autrement.

Bien Amicalement

328

Appendix 3: Announcement of Mahmoud Bourgi's death, April 10, 1979.

Ses Enfants

ont la douleur de vous faire part du décès de leur Père

Mahmoud BOURGI

Officier de l'Ordre National du Mérite Français

Officier de l'Ordre du Cèdre Libanais

Chevalier de l'ordre National du Mérite Sénégalais

décédé dans sa 81eme année le Mardi 10 Avril 1979

à l'Hôpital Principal de DAKAR

Ses Obsèques ont été célébrées le Mercredi 11 Avril 1979 à Dakar

---

Appendix 4: Tribute by Claude Hettier de Boislambert after the death
of Mahmoud Bourgi, April 10 1979.

CLAUDE HETTIER DE BOISLAMBERT

PRÉSIDENT DE LA COMMISSION NATIONALE DE LA
MÉDAILLE DE LA RÉSISTANCE
GRAND CHANCELIER HONORAIRE
DE L'ORDRE DE LA LIBÉRATION

51 bis, bd. de Latour-Maubourg
75007 Paris · Tél. : 705 35·15

Appendix 5: Condolences from Admiral Philippe de Gaulle following the death of Mahmoud Bourgi on April 10, 1979.

4 Avril 1979

PHILIPPE DE GAULLE

VICE-AMIRAL
D'ESCADRE

Très sensible au décès du vieil et fidèle ami du Général de Gaulle que fut Monsieur Mahmoud Bourgi, prie Monsieur Robert Bourgi son fils, ainsi que sa famille, d'agréer l'expression de ses pensées très attristées et de ses sentiments fidèles de bien vive sympathie.

Appendix 6: Letter from Jacques Foccart to Robert Bourgi, May 2, 1979, Mauritania, in tribute to Mahmoud Bourgi.

JACQUES FOCCART
95, Rue de Prony
75017 Paris
Tél 227-11-27

446/79

Cher Ami,

      J'ai trouvé, rentrant de voyage, votre lettre du 13 Avril m'annonçant la triste nouvelle du décès de votre Père, mon Ami Mahmoud BOURGI, survenu le 10 Avril à Dakar.

      C'est, en effet, un très vieil et fidèle ami que je perds. Il me rappelle les souvenirs des temps héroïques du Gaullisme en particulier ce qu'on appelle "la traversée du désert". Nous n'étions pas si nombreux et nous étions en butte à beaucoup d'obstilités. Il a toujours été à tous moments l'Ami fidèle du Général de GAULLE et il l'a maintes fois prouvé.

      J'imagine qu'il a dû être accompagné à sa dernière demeure par une foule immense car sa loyauté et son sens de l'amitié lui avaient valu l'estime de tous.

      C'est avec un profond chagrin que je pense à lui et c'est de tout coeur que mon épouse se joint à moi pour vous adresser à vous-même et à tous les vôtres nos bien sincères condoléances et l'assurance de notre profonde sympathie.

Bien Amicalement vôtre

Monsieur Robert BOURGI
Boîte Postale 121
Nouakchott   Mauritanie

Appendix 7: Letter from Ambassador Raphaël Léonard Touze, May 14, 1979, in tribute to Mahmoud Bourgi.

AMBASSADE DE FRANCE
AUX PHILIPPINES
—
L'AMBASSADEUR

Manille, le 14 mai 1979

Cher ami

    J'ai reçu il y a quelques jours votre lettre du 13 avril m'annonçant le décès de votre père. Cette nouvelle nous a beaucoup frappés, ma femme et moi. Nous gardons, en effet, malgré le temps - il y a déjà seize ans que nous avons quitté Dakar - le meilleur des souvenirs de votre père. C'était un homme d'honneur, un grand ami de la France, et je me suis réjoui, pendant mes trois années de Consul général à Dakar, qu'il ait bien voulu me compter parmi ses amis. Sa perte sera profondément ressentie par de nombreux Français, au même titre que par sa famille.

    Voulez-vous, cher Ami, accepter de ma femme et moi nos plus sincères condoléances et les transmettre autour de vous.

    A Nouakchott vous avez comme médecin notre fils Jean-Etienne que vous avez connu en culottes courtes à Dakar.

    Ma femme se joint à moi *pour un adieu, à un* *et avec votre, nos meilleures amitiés.*

Raphaël Léonard TOUZE

Monsieur Robert BOURGI
Boîte postale 171
NOUAKCHOTT Mauritanie

Appendix 8: Letter from Jacques Foccart to Robert Bourgi, October 23, 1979, regretting the latter's inability to attend a major symposium on *General de Gaulle's African policy*, organized in October 1979 by the Centre d'études d'Afrique noire (Cean) - Institut d'études politiques de Bordeaux (IEP). The proceedings (421 pages) were published in 1981 by Pedone.

JACQUES FOCCART
95, Rue de Prony
75017 Paris
Tél. 227-11-27

PARIS, le 23 Octobre 1979.

738/79

Cher Ami,

A mon retour d'un voyage que je viens de faire à Abidjan, j'ai trouvé votre lettre du 8 Octobre.

Nous avons, ma femme et moi, séjourné à Abidjan du 1er au 17 Octobre et je suis justement rentré pour participer au Colloque de Bordeaux.

J'ai moi-même beaucoup regretté de ne pas vous rencontrer.

Nous avons parlé de vous à Bordeaux et nous avons été désolé que vous ne puissiez être des nôtres. Si j'avais su que vous veniez d'arriver à Abidjan, je serais certainement intervenu auprès de M. Michel DUPUCH pour qu'il vous autorise à vous absenter. Je suis certain qu'il l'aurait fait.

Les travaux ont été intéressants et je dois dire que les rapports qui ont été présentés étaient assez près de ce que je considère comme la vérité de la politique du Général de GAULLE en Afrique. Bien entendu, ils ont donné lieu à des discussions qui ont permis aux témoins et aux acteurs de cette grande période d'apporter des rectifications. Il est apparu que c'était un excellent travail que de confronter les points de vue et de demander des corrections à ceux qui ont été les artisans de cette page d'histoire.

J'ai été frappé, en ce qui me concerne, par le fait que chez beaucoup d'Africains et également beaucoup d'universitaires français l'image de Jacques Foccart, homme mystérieux, et responsable des principaux coups d'Etat est restée très forte. J'ai pu remettre les choses au point sur un certain nombre de sujets et en particulier sur les interventions militaires françaises, pendant la période où j'étais en fonction.

M. Mathieu EKRA, qui représentait le Président HOUPHOUET-BOIGNY, a fait un discours d'une conception ...

. . . .

Monsieur Robert BOURGI
Boîte Postale 28 11
ABIDJAN   Côte d'Ivoire

334

qualité et il a fait connaître à l'assistance le message
verbal que lui avait confié le Président HOUPHOUET, à cette
occasion. C'était très émouvant. J'espère que nous en aurons
le texte. Je n'ai pu, pour ma part, rester jusqu'à la fin
car je devais prendre l'avion.

En terminant, je voudrais vous remercier,
cher Ami, de la pensée si sympathique que vous eue pour moi
et pour ce que j'ai pu faire. Je voulais vous dire également
que je pense souvent à votre cher Père qui aura été, pour moi,
l'exemple de la fidélité gaulliste de la terre africaine.

Merci encore -

Bien Amicalement

Jacques FOCCART

JACQUES FOCCART

Le 30 Septembre 1980

382/81

Cher Henri,

J'ai bien reçu vos lettres du 22 et 23 Septembre, retransmises à CAVALAIRE, puis à PARIS.

En ce qui concerne la première, je vais voir la semaine prochaine Jacques CHIRAC et j'insisterai pour que vous fassiez partie du Club 89. Vous y avez en effet votre place et votre expérience sera très utile.

Pour la seconde, je vous ai dit au téléphone mon point de vue, qui n'a pas changé. Une intervention serait totalement inefficace, mais bien entendu, j'en parlerai également à Jacques CHIRAC dans l'esprit que vous souhaitez. Je partage en effet tout à fait votre opinion.

Bien à vous

J. FOCCART

Monsieur Robert BOURGI
01 B.P. 2811
ABIDJAN 01

République de Côte d'Ivoire

336

Appendix 10: Letter from Jacques Foccart to Robert Bourgi, October 20, 1980, on the centenary of Brazzaville. Jacques Focart is already talking about Russia's influence in Africa.

JACQUES FOCCART

95, Rue de Prony
75017 Paris
Tél. 227-11-27

PARIS, le 20 Octobre 1980.

556/80

Cher Ami,

Merci de votre lettre du 12 Octobre qui me donne vos impressions sur les cérémonies de Brazzaville. Ceci correspond en tous points au récit que j'ai eu de différents côtés. Je crois même savoir que les Russes ont été fort mécontents de tout ce qui a été fait en faveur de la France alors qu'ils considèrent que ce n'est plus de notre "zone" mais de la leur.

Mon prochain voyage à Abidjan a été retardé. Il se situera vraisemblablement un peu avant la fête nationale c'est-à-dire aux environs du 5 Décembre. Je ne manquerai pas de vous informer.

Croyez, cher Ami, à mes meilleures sentiments.

Bien à vous

Monsieur Robert BOURGI
01 B.P. 36 11
ABIDJAN 01
---------- Côte d'Ivoire

337

Appendix 11: Letter from Marie-Antoinette Isnard, national delegate for French nationals living abroad, dated February 28, 1981, asking Robert Bourgi to approach the RPR representative in Côte d'Ivoire, after having expressed his willingness to support Jacques Chirac's candidacy in the 1981 presidential election.

COMITÉ NATIONAL DE SOUTIEN A LA CANDIDATURE DE JACQUES CHIRAC

7 RUE DE TILSITT (PLACE CHARLES DE GAULLE) 75017 PARIS. TÉLÉPHONE 755.97.15

Paris, le 26 Février 1981

123 Rue de Lille
75007 PARIS

N/Ref. 2192

Cher Professeur,

    Monsieur Jacques CHIRAC me charge de vous remercier pour le soutien et l'attachement que vous lui témoignez, vos encouragements; croyez le bien, lui sont particulièrement précieux.

    Je vous demande en tant que Déléguée Nationale des Français de prendre une part active au Comité de Soutien qui vient d'être créé à ABIDJAN et de vous mettre en rapport avec :

    Monsieur GIACOMONI
    01 B. P. 1745
    ABIDJAN 01 - Tél. 35 70 05 ligne directe : 35 77 12

qui jusqu'à présent a assumé les fonctions de Délégué, représentant le R.P.R. en Cote d'Ivoire.

    Naturellement, le Comité de Soutien à la candidature de Jacques CHIRAC est indépendant du R.P.R., car Jacques CHIRAC est le candidat de tous les français soutenus par le R.P.R., mais non candidat du R.P.R. Ce Comité sera le rouage essentiel au sein duquel se regrouperont toutes les bonnes volontés qui, avec vous et dans l'enthousiasme, se battent pour le succès de notre candidat.

    Je vous demande d'être l'interprète auprès de Madame Catherine BOURGI et de la remercier également pour son soutien.

    En restant à votre disposition pour tous renseignements complémentaires, je vous prie de croire, Cher Professeur, à l'assurance de mes sentiments les meilleurs.

Marie-Antoinette ISNARD
Déléguée Nationale des Français
de l'Etranger.

Maître Robert BOURGI
Professeur de Faculté de Droit
B. P. 3811
ABIDJAN

338

Appendix 12: Letter from the RPR delegate in Côte d'Ivoire, dated March 7, 1981, confirming Robert Bourgi as chairman of the support committee for Jacques Chirac's 1981 presidential candidacy.

RASSEMBLEMENT POUR LA REPUBLIQUE

DELEGATION DE COTE D'IVOIRE

01 BP 1745 ABIDJAN

Monsieur Robert BOURGI

01 BP 3811

ABIDJAN 01

Abidjan, le 7 mars 1981

Cher Compagnon et ami,

Vous avez bien voulu accepter de présider le Comité de soutien en Côte d'Ivoire pour la candidature de Jacques CHIRAC.

Ce témoignage de fidélité et d'enthousiasme nous est très agréable et nous sommes persuadés que le dynamisme qui vous caractérise vous permettra avec toute l'équipe constituée autour de vous de faire une propagande active dans les milieux de l'électorat français de Côte d'Ivoire.

Notre mouvement est tout à fait conscient de la très importante tâche qui est la vôtre et mettra tous les moyens dont il dispose à votre service pour la faciliter.

Croyez, Cher Compagnon et ami, à notre très cordial encouragement et à nos sentiments dévoués.

LE DELEGUE,

JX CIACOBONI

cc/ Comité National de J. CHIRAC

Appendix 13: Letter from Jacques Chirac thanking Robert Bourgi for his support, March 12, 1981.

Jacques Chirac

Paris, le 12 mars 1981

Mon Cher Compatriote,

J'ai le plaisir de vous confirmer que je viens d'aviser, conformément aux prescriptions légales Monsieur le Ministre des Affaires Etrangères de votre désignation, par mes soins, comme délégué habilité à contrôler toutes les opérations de vote, de dépouillement et de décompte des voix dans le bureau de vote pour lequel vous avez donné votre accord.

En vous remerciant pour le concours que vous m'apportez de la sorte, je vous prie d'agréer, Mon Cher Compatriote, l'expression des mes sentiments les meilleurs.

Monsieur Robert BOURGY
B.P. 3811, ABIDJAN
COTE D'IVOIRE

Appendix 14: Letter dated April 24, 1981 from Claude Le Breton, Consul General of France in Abidjan, confirming Jacques Chirac's appointment of Robert Bourgi to oversee electoral operations at several polling stations in Abidjan, for the 1981 presidential election.

REPUBLIQUE FRANÇAISE

CONSULAT GENERAL DE FRANCE
à ABIDJAN

01 B. P. 1385   ABIDJAN, le

N°.......................................

ATTESTATION

Le Consul Général de France à Abidjan certifie que Monsieur Robert BOURGY a été désigné par Monsieur Jacques CHIRAC pour le contrôle des opérations électorales aux bureaux 1 à 5 du Centre d'Abidjan lors de l'élection présidentielle du 26 avril 1981./.

Fait à Abidjan, le 24 avril 1981.

Claude LE BRETON
Consul Général de France

JACQUES FOCCART

333/81

Cher Henri,

J'ai bien reçu vos lettres des 12 et 16 Juin.

J'avais eu connaissance en effet de l'article de Philippe DECRAENE et j'avais apprécié l'éloge qu'il faisait de votre remarquable travail.

Je ne manquerai pas de remettre dès demain en mains propres à Jacques CHIRAC la lettre que vous lui destinez.

Voilà enfin terminé cette longue période électorale. Le verdict a été très sévère ! Nous avons payé pour la façon dont Monsieur GISCARD D'ESTAING a conduit le pays pendant 7 ans, en manquant tout à fait de psychologie et en considérant depuis les premiers jours que les Gaullistes étaient les ennemis à abattre. La leçon malheureusement n'a pas servi puisque j'ai entendu hier au soir dans un débat télévisé Monsieur PONIATOWSKI déclarer que GISCARD était le recours et désigner (sans le nommer toutefois) que l'adversaire c'était Jacques CHIRAC.

Nous allons voir comment François MITTERAND va gouverner. Il risque d'être embarrassé par une majorité trop forte et un Groupe qui ne sera pas facile à conduire.

Je souhaite que nous soyons capables de mener une opposition intelligente et que nous entreprenions une réorganisation de notre Mouvement qui reste au demeurant plein de vie, (j'ai distribué de nombreux carnets d'adhésions depuis le 10 Mai).

J'ai eu tout à l'heure un appel téléphonique de René qui m'a dit qu'il allait vous rejoindre demain. Je suis touché par la fidélité de votre famille.

Veuillez présenter mes hommages à Madame BOURGI et croyez, Cher Ami, à l'assurance de ma fidèle amitié.

Bien Amicalement

J. FOCCART

Monsieur Robert BOURGI
B.P.3811
01 ABIDJAN
COTE D'IVOIRE

Appendix 16: Personal letter of thanks from Jacques Chirac to Robert Bourgi for his support and involvement in the 1981 presidential election campaign in France (June 5, 1981).

Jacques Chirac

Paris, le 5 Juin 1981

Cher Monsieur,

Vous avez bien voulu m'apporter votre soutien et je tiens à vous en remercier personnellement.

J'attache, en effet, le plus grand prix à votre témoignage de sympathie et je suis très sensible à votre confiance qui me donne la force et l'espoir dans l'avenir.

Elle me sera précieuse pour continuer à défendre les idées auxquelles je crois et qui un jour, je le sais, l'emporteront.

Avec ma reconnaissance pour votre témoignage,

Je vous prie d'accepter, Cher Monsieur, l'assurance de mes sentiments les meilleurs.

Monsieur Robert BOURGI
Parc Berthault
Les palmiers A.
20000 AJACCIO

Appendix 17: Letter from Jacques Chirac dated June 25, 1981, counting on Robert Bourgi's support in Côte d'Ivoire.

Jacques Chirac

PARIS le 25 juin 1981

Cher Ami,

J'ai été très sensible à votre lettre du 16 juin, et je vous remercie de tout coeur pour l'efficacité de votre aide, et la fidélité de votre témoignage .

Nous allons en effet reprendre le combat, et j'aurai plaisir à vous rencontrer lors de votre prochain passage à Paris.

Je continue à compter sur vous et sur votre action dans ce beau pays de Côte d'Ivoire.

Je vous prie de bien vouloir accepter, Cher Ami, l'expression de mon très fidèle et cordial souvenir

Monsieur Robert BOURGI

01 B.P. 3811

ABIDJAN 01   Rép. de Côte d'Ivoire

"They Know I Know Everything"

Appendix 18: Letter from Pierre Dabezies to Robert Bourgi, September 18, 1981, requesting Jacques Chirac's explicit support following the invalidation of his candidacy for parliament.

ASSEMBLÉE NATIONALE

RÉPUBLIQUE FRANÇAISE

LIBERTÉ · ÉGALITÉ · FRATERNITÉ

PARIS, le 18/9/81

Cher ami

J'ai lu votre article et le trouve excellent

Plus je vais, plus je pense qu'il serait infiniment dommageable si, par malheur, j'étais "invalidé", que Chirac se croit obligé ([par certains] de son entourage ...) de défendre trop Dominati Je serais obligé de lever l'étendard gaulliste, et de monter un comité de soutien Gaulliste ... tant le soutien de mon adversaire contre moi serait caricatural. Je ne le souhaite pas. Si vous avez un mot à dire, dites le / car certains RPR qui ressentent étrangement à l'UDF, font entendre leur voix à l'hôtel de ville.

A bientôt. Bien fidèlement

Appendix 19: Letter from Jacques Foccart, dated November 19, 1981, informing Robert Bourgi of Jacques Chirac's support for his entry into the Club 89.

JACQUES FOCCART

PARIS, le 19 NOVEMBRE 1981

Cher Ami,

        Je m'excuse de n'avoir pas répondu plus tôt à votre demande concernant le CLUB 89.

        J'en ai parlé à Jacques CHIRAC qui estime que vous seriez une très bonne recrue et j'ai eu l'occasion également d'en parler avec Alain JUPPE qui, bien entendu, serait très heureux de vous compter parmi les membres de ce club. Adressez-lui un petit mot dans ce sens :

        - Monsieur Alain JUPPE
         Direction des Finances de la Ville de Paris
         17, Boulevard Morland
         75004 PARIS

        Je profite de l'occasion pour vous signaler que je serai à Abidjan du 1.er au 12 décembre. Je descendrai à l'Hôtel Ivoire.

        J'espère avoir le plaisir de vous voir.

        Croyez, Cher Ami, à l'assurance de mes meilleurs sentiments.

Bien à vous

J. FOCCART

Monsieur Robert BOURGI
01 B.P. 3811
ABIDJAN 01

"They Know I Know Everything"

Appendix 20: Message of friendship from Michel Aurillac, Club 89 president, November 4 1982.

CONSEIL D'ÉTAT

Paris, le 4 novembre 1982

PALAIS-ROYAL 75100 PARIS R P
TEL. 261.52.29

Bien cher Ami,

Ce petit mot, dans la hâte d'un retour à l'actualité parisienne me déivre à nouveau vous dire encore merci pour la qualité de votre accueil, sa chaleur et l'efficacité de votre organisation.

Nous nous réjouissons Martine et moi de vous revoir bientôt à Paris à l'occasion du colloque, avec Catherine et les Fayot.

Petit changement de date pour la soirée amicale. Je préside un dîner debout les 25, Voulez-vous nous réserver la soirée de Vendredi 26 - Rendez-vous chez nous 10 rue Masseran à 20 heures.

Amitiés de votre ménage au vôtre.

Appendix 21: Robert Bourgi, who still lives in Abidjan,
is named as the "tenant" of the premises at Club 89, avenue Montaigne
(November 26, 1982).

Paris, le 26 novembre 1982

Je soussigné, BOURGI Robert, demeurant actuellement
à Abidjan (Côte d'Ivoire), immeuble Niargon, appartement
1632, Riviéra 2, 01 BP 3811, donne tout pouvoir à Monsieur
Michel SCHNEIDER, afin de me représenter et d'agir en mon
nom avec l'E. D. F.-G. D. F. et les Postes et Télécommunications
pour ce qui concerne mon installation dans l'appartement
loué à mon nom 45 Avenue Montaigne, PARIS 8e, 6ème étage
à droite.

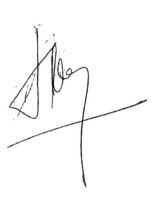

Appendix 22: Letter from Alain Juppé, Club 89 General Secretary, to Robert Bourgi, October 25, 1983, on his trip to Côte d'Ivoire.

Paris, le 25 octobre 1983

LE SECRETAIRE GENERAL

Nos réf. : AJ/AC

Cher Ami,

J'ai bien reçu votre lettre du 11 octobre et je vous confirme ma venue à Abidjan du 26 décembre au 2 janvier.

Le programme que vous suggérez me convient parfaitement. Je souhaiterais qu'on puisse y glisser un entretien avec les responsables R.P.R. des Français de l'Etranger, sans donner bien sûr à ce contact la dimension d'un grand show politique.

Si cela ne pose pas trop de problèmes d'organisation, je vous indique que je viendrai probablement accompagné de mes deux enfants.

En attendant une reprise de contact sur ce programme, je vous prie d'agréer, Cher Ami, l'assurance de mes sentiments les meilleurs.

Cordialement

Alain JUPPÉ

Monsieur Robert BOURGI

BPV 179
ABIDJAN 01
COTE D'IVOIRE

45, AVENUE MONTAIGNE 75008 PARIS TÉL. : 720.61.33

Appendix 23: Correspondence between Jacques Foccart and Robert Bourgi, December 14, 1983, concerning Alain Juppé's visit to Côte d'Ivoire.

JACQUES FOCCART
95, Rue de Prony
75017 Paris
Tel. 227-11 27

le 14 Décembre 1983

568/93

Cher Henri,

Pardonnez-moi de ne pas avoir répondu plus rapidement à votre lettre du 20 Novembre, mais j'ai été très bousculé par deux séjours en COTE D'IVOIRE puisque j'y suis retourné du 7 au 11 pour le jumelage de YAMOUSSOUKRO. **et Lagarches —**

Merci en tout cas de votre lettre dont les termes m'ont beaucoup touché. Je suis moi-même toujours très heureux de vous rencontrer.

En ce qui concerne le rendez-vous que vous aviez demandé pour Monsieur O. je n'ai pas fait d'intervention suite aux indications que vous m'avez données par la suite.

Pour Alain JUPPE , j'en ai parlé au Président HOUPHOUET qui est tout à fait d'accord pour le recevoir. Georges OUEGNIN est prévenu. J'ai également indiqué au Secrétariat d'Alain JUPPE que le Président le recevrait. Je vous laisse donc le soin de prendre le rendez-vous avec OUEGNIN.

Pour votre réception du 27 Décembre, je ne vois pas **des** *compatriotes que je pourrais vous indiquer afin que vous les ... Vous les connaissez en effet tous et bien mieux que moi ! —*

Merci également de l'envoi ... qui est fort intéressante et dont je pourrais ... par la suite.

. . . . . .

J'ai donné une interview au " FIGARO MAGAZINE " que vous avez peut être lue. Le Président BONGO m'a téléphoné. Il est très heureux de cette interview et en a semblé réconforté. Je l'ai fait parce que je sentais que le climat était resté mauvais malgré tout ce qu'on en dit. Nous devons donc tous faire un effort pour l'améliorer.

Je reste à votre disposition et vous prie de croire, Cher Ami, à l'assurance de mes meilleurs sentiments.

Bien Amicalement à vous deux

J. FOCCART

Monsieur Robert BOURGI

01 B.P. 3811
ABIDJAN 01

Côte d'Ivoire

Appendix 24: Letter from Michel Aurillac, dated January 26 1984, asking Robert Bourgi to explain the situation in Gabon and the deterioration in relations with France.

Michel Aurillac

Paris, le 26 Janvier 1984.

Mon Cher Robert,

J'ai bien reçu les propositions du Club d'Abidjan, concernant sa participation à la définition de la stratégie de gouvernement. Elles me paraissent tout à fait satisfaisantes, je vous en remercie, et vous prie de transmettre mes remerciements à toute l'équipe.

Nous verrons les modalités lors de notre entretien le 6 Février. Dans cette perspective je voudrais que vous soyez prêt à me faire le point du projet de voyage au Gabon. Ce voyage est jugé de plus en plus nécessaire. Je vous rappelle les dates envisagées : du 17 au 22 Avril. Si la détérioration du climat Franco-Gabonais vous paraît nécessiter une accélération du programme, je pourrais à la rigueur envisager de faire le voyage entre le 2 et le 11 Avril, la durée restant fixée à 4 ou 5 jours.

J'ai aussi été invité par notre ami de Port-Gentil ce qui alourdit mon programme, mais cela me paraît indispensable étant donné l'importance de la colonie française dans la capitale du Gabon. En vous remerciant de vous préoccuper de ce projet, je vous prie, mon Cher Robert de partager avec votre épouse, nos amitiés.

J. Aurillac.

Monsieur Robert BOURGI   Michel AURILLAC
01. BP. 179 ABIDJAN.

P.S. *Bien reçu votre dernière lettre. N ... ...*

Appendix 25: Letter of recommendation from Omar Bongo to Jacques Chirac concerning Robert Bourgi's political commitment, personality traits and desire to see him teach at the University of Libreville (March 16, 1984).

République Gabonaise
Union Travail Justice

Le Président de la République

LIBREVILLE, LE 16 MARS 1984

Mon Très Cher Ami,

J'ai l'honneur et le plaisir de Vous faire savoir que, grâce à mon Ministre Conseiller Personnel, j'ai été amené à faire la connaissance de Monsieur Robert BOURGI, Professeur de Droit à ABIDJAN, l'un des animateurs de Votre Club 89 aux dernières Assises duquel, j'ai délégué des personnalités gabonaises.

J'ai depuis, accordé deux audiences à Mr. Robert BOURGI à Libreville et l'ai invité récemment, avec sa jeune épouse, à prendre part aux manifestations ayant marqué le 16ème Anniversaire du Parti Démocratique Gabonais et de la Rénovation dont il cons- titue l'instrument privilégié.

Monsieur Robert BOURGI porte à Votre personne une très grande admiration et une profonde amitié nourries, l'une et l'autre, autant aux sources du Coeur qu'à celles de la Raison. C'est un Jeune homme très sérieux et très intelligent, connais- sant assez parfaitement l'homme Africain et bien au fait de l'évolution et des grands problèmes de notre Continent, dans son interdépendance avec l'Europe, et plus particulièrement avec Votre Pays, la France. C'est en outre un garçon simple qui suscite assez facilement estime et attachement de la part de ceux qui l'abordent sans idées préconçues et sans arrières-pensées. Ce sont là des qualités qui sont d'autant précieux qu'ils devien- nent rares dans les milieux qui nous sont familiers.

Monsieur Jacques CHIRAC
Maire de PARIS

- F R A N C E -

./2

Le Président de la République

Si Vous n'y voyiez aucun inconvénient, peut-être pourrais-je être amené, dans un proche avenir, à demander à mon Ministre compétent que des cours de Droit public, de sociologie politique, d'Histoire ou des idées politiques (africaines) soient amenagés pour lui.

Il pourra, comme Professeur missionnaire, venir les dispenser dans Notre Université Nationale.

Je Vous prie d'agréer, Mon Très Cher Ami, l'expression de ma haute et très amicale considération./-

EL HADJ OMARS BONGO

Appendix 26: Jacques Chirac's reply to Omar Bongo, May 23, 1984.

Jacques Chirac   Paris, le 23 mai 1984

       Cher Monsieur le Président,

               Vous avez bien voulu me faire savoir que vous aviez été amené à faire la connaissance de M. Robert BOURGI, Professeur à la Faculté de Droit d'Abidjan.

               Tout le bien que vous me dites de Robert BOURGI ne me surprend pas, car j'estime personnellement beaucoup ce jeune professeur, dont la compétence professionnelle le dispute à une grande connaissance de l'Afrique et des Africains. C'est également un homme qui a su parfaitement assimiler la pensée du Général de GAULLE et la traduire dans les différentes actions qu'il mène pour développer l'amitié entre la France et les Etats d'Afrique.

               Aussi je ne vois que des avantages à ce que des cours de droit public, de sociologie et d'histoire des idées politiques en Afrique, soient aménagés pour lui dans votre Université nationale.

               En attendant le plaisir de vous revoir, je vous prie d'agréer, Monsieur le Président, l'expression de ma très haute considération *et de ma réciproque de ma respectueuse et ta fidèle amitié.*

Son Excellence
Monsieur El Hadj Omar BONGO
Président de la République Gabonaise

Appendix 27: Robert Bourgi's request to Jacques Chirac to enroll Salim Farhat's daughter in a Paris university (October 4, 1984).

JHR/db

Le Maire de Paris

Paris le 4 Octobre 1984

Monsieur le Président et Cher Ami,

     Vous avez bien voulu appeler mon attention sur la situation de votre fille que vous souhaitiez voir admise dans une université parisienne.

     Il m'est agréable de vous faire savoir qu'à la suite de la pressante démarche que j'ai effectuée auprès du Professeur Michel GUILLOU, votre fille a été inscrite à l'Université de Paris XII.

     Je vous prie d'agréer, Monsieur le Président, l'expression de ma considération très distinguée.

Bien Cordialement

Jacques CHIRAC

Monsieur Salim FARHAT
Vice-Président de la section
e Côte d'Ivoire de l'Union
ibanaise Culturelle Mondiale

Appendix 28: A letter from Jacques Chirac to the Lebanese businessman Roger Abinader, to be published in the Ivorian press (October 23, 1984).

Jacques Chirac

Paris, le 23 octobre 1984

Cher Monsieur,

Notre ami, Robert Bourgi, m'a transmis les dossiers relatant les excellents résultats de vos diffirentes équipes sportives et je me permets de vous adresser mes très sincères félicitations pour une oeuvre aussi dynamique au profit de la jeunesse ivoirienne.

J'espère avoir bientôt le plaisir de vous rencontrer et je vous prie de bien vouloir accepter, Cher Monsieur, l'expression de mon très c lial souvenir.

Monsieur Roger ABINADER
B.P. 2149
ABIDJAN 01
COTE D'IVOIRE

Appendix n°29: Very annoyed reaction from Michel Bujon,
head of the RPR in Côte d'IVoire, who complains about the financing
of the RPR by the Lebanese, described as "swarthy" (October 29, 1984).

MICHEL BUJON

ᴅᴇʟᴇɢᴜᴇ ᴀᴜ ᴄᴏɴsᴇɪʟ sᴜᴘᴇʀɪᴇᴜʀ
ᴅᴇs ғʀᴀɴçᴀɪs ᴅᴇ ʟ'ᴇᴛʀᴀɴɢᴇʀ

01 B P 1769
ABIDJAN 01
32 98 93 ᴛᴇʟᴇx ; ᴜɴɪsᴛᴇᴍᴀ 23761

Abidjan, le 29 Octobre 1984

Madame Marie Antoinette ISNARD
Déléguée Nationale
Chargée des Relations Publiques
et des Français de l'Etranger

CONFIDENTIEL

Chère Amie,

Comme nous en avions parlé Vendredi matin lors de notre trop
brève communication téléphonique, je vous adresse ci-joint l'extrait
du journal FRATERNITE MATIN où est reproduite la lettre de Jacques
CHIRAC à Roger ABINADER, ou plutôt le montage partiel qui semble en
avoir été fait.

Il ne s'agit bien sur que d'une très banale lettre de félicitations, mais dans le contexte local, elle est unanimement perçue
comme une lettre de remerciement pure et simple, pour des services
qu'en filigrane, chacun trouve des plus transparents. Telle est en
tout cas l'opinion qui s'exprime narquoisement dans les dîners en
ville. Inutile de dire qu'en d'autres milieux, les commentaires sont
infiniment moins nuancés !

Je sais bien qu'il ne s'agit là que d'une simple opération
publicitaire de la part d'ABINADER, qui très fier d'entretenir des
relations qu'il considère comme privilégiées avec Jacques CHIRAC, n'a
pas résisté au plaisir de le faire savoir.
Mais l'effet produit n'en demeure pas moins désastreux envers nos
militants et la quasi totalité des membres du bureau, dont le premier
réflexe a été d'envisager de cesser toute activité, et même de
renvoyer leur carte.

Il est en effet particulièrement décourageant de voir ruiner
une somme d'efforts considérable accomplie depuis quelques temps pour
remonter un électorat désabusé, à cause d'une correspondance en
apparence anodine.

Je trouve assez ahurissant qu'aient été si mal pesées, les conséquences possibles de la publication d'une telle lettre sur nos compatriotes, dont certains sont directement touchés dans leurs intérêts économiques, par une concurrence libanaise omniprésente, parfois déloyale, et bien souvent arrogante.

On n'ose imaginer qu'il puisse s'agir d'une opération réflé chie destinée à mettre la Délégation en porte à faux. Toujours est-il que le résultat est rigoureusement le même que s'il s'était agi d'un torpillage en règle.

Il n'est maintenant plus possible de rattraper l'affaire. Nous devrons simplement essayer de réparer les dégats et Dieu sait s'ils ont été ravageurs.

Pour éviter la réédition de ce genre d'incidents à l'avenir Bernard SA.. et moi, avons donc immédiatement pris rendez-vous avec Roger ABIBADEN, que nous avons rencontré Samedi matin.

Il est en effet indispensable de définir le plus rapidement et le plus diplomatiquement possible, nos relations avec la communauté libanaise locale. A l'issue de cette entrevue, un modus vivendi serait possible, bien que délicat. Il aurait par exemple été plus que maladroit lors de cette entrevue, de faire savoir à Roger ABIBADEN qui a par ailleurs été relativement coopératif, que la parution de sa lettre était très mal perçue par nos compatriotes. Les enveloppes libanaises sont certes bienvenues, mais elles doivent demeurer discrè- tes, sinon elles finiront par nous couter plus cher en voix, qu'elles ne nous rapporteront en capitaux.

Mais ce genre de mise au point n'est pas de notre ressort et devrait avoir été fait avec les nuances d'usage. Et il faudrait pour cela que certains à la bai... de Paris cessent de jouer en sous- main, un jeu plus qu'équivoque.

Nous avons, en effet, ... par ... l'ABIBADEN lui-même, que RICHARD avait été contacté pour savoir s'il était d'accord de publier cette lettre. Il n'est bien évidemment ... au courant du danger le fau vert, sachant combien le destinataire ... il flatté de le faire. Je persist à penser qu'il se pouvait en ignorer les conséquences, où alors il fait preuve d'une ... le ... politique ... ... ou porte ... ... s'il ... .

-3-

Si demain LFS publie un article du style "CHIRAC et
l'argent des affairistes libanais" j'aimerais bien pouvoir entendre
les explications de ce triste sire . Vous savez que je suis calme,
et je pèse là mes qualificatifs.

La Délégation de Côte d'Ivoire représente ici l'appareil du
Rassemblement. Elle est chargée avant tout de mobiliser les électeurs en
faveur de Jacques CHIRAC.
Si d'autres considérations, au nom d'un intérêt supérieur, priment ses
activités, il serait préférable que nous en soyons informés. Cela
éviterait beaucoup de travail à tous ceux qui se mobilisent sans
compter depuis des années et ne manqueront pas d'avoir la désagréable impression d'être pris pour d'aimables joacrisses. Car le résultat d'une
démobilisation de la Délégation ne serait peut-être pas pire que les
conséquences que nous allons devoir être amenés à supporter, si
certains à la Mairie de Paris persistent à intervenir directement et
de manière brouillonne, dans les affaires de la Côte d'Ivoire.

A moins d'un an des élections au CNRI, tout ceci est
mal séduar, et risque de vous coûter au moins un siège au bénéfice
d'une éventuelle liste Le Pen. Alors que CHENAL était d'accord pour
pour prendre la tête d'une liste où nous aurions placé trois RPR sur
les quatre premiers, et plus important, était gonflé à bloc pour
tenir tête à l'UDF, dans les négociations difficiles qui ne manqueront pas de s'ensuivre. Car quelle image voulez vous que nous
donnions maintenant à un électorat hypersensible aux arguments racistes
les plus démagogiques : le RPR, un parti financé par des capitaux
"basanés" ? Certains ne l'ront, et se font déjà un plaisir de le dire.

De toute façon, je ne manquerai pas de vous tenir réguliè-
rement informés de l'évolution de la situation.
En attendant, que nous poursuivions notre action avec détermination :
c'faut d'enthousiasme.

Vous trouverez sous ci-joli livers documents, dont le
nouvel organigramme du bureau de la Délégation, et le numéro 1 de
" La Lettre de l'UDF ", qui vient d'être diffusé. Le numéro 2
est prêt et sera diffusé avec " LIBERTES " la semaine prochaine ;
Il présentera le programme de travail des commissions aux Assises,
et invitera nos correspondants à un effort de réflexion dans ces domaines.

360

-4-

J'espère que vous en trouverez la formule satisfaisante.
Elle est basée sur la nécéssité de rétablir la vérité des faits, tout
en manifestant une présence soutenue auprès des militants

Espérons que rien de nouveau ne viendra encore se mettre
en travers de notre action, car je ne vous cache pas qu'il serait
alors impossible d'éviter la débandade totale de nos troupes.
Et je ne peux m'empêcher d'éprouver un certain sentiment d'amertume
à cette perspective, après tous les efforts fournis.

Dans un tout autre ordre d'idées, pourriez vous nous
communiquer les coordonnées d'un mandataire à CHARTRES, pour une
personne qui désire se faire inscrire sur les listes électorales de
cette ville ?

Je vous en remercie par avance, et vous prie de croire,
Chère Amie à l'assurance de mes sentiments les meilleurs, et les
plus amicaux.

Michel BUJON

PS : Excusez la mauvaise qualité de cette lettre, mais compte tenu
du caractère confidentiel de sa teneur, je l'ai frappée moi-même, et
ai du faire des photocopies des pages les plus " rafistolées ".

Appendix 30: Letter from Michel Aurillac, President of Club 89, to Robert Bourgi, October 26, 1984.

Michel Aurillac

Le 26 octobre 1984

Mon Cher Robert,

        Nous nous sommes manqués au déjeuner Messmer. J'ai peur que vous ne soyez venu au Club trop tard et que personne n'ait pu vous indiquer l'adresse que, de mon côté, je n'avais pas notée.

        Si je suis la cause involontaire de votre absence, je vous prie de m'en excuser.

        Le Maire m'a redit combien il avait été heureux de votre visite et tout le bien qu'il pense de votre action.

        Le virement du Club 89 d'Abidjan est bien parvenu. Je tiens à vous en remercier. Il faut maintenant pour la régularité de nos écritures que vous m'adressiez, comme convenu, la liste des membres bienfaiteurs qui ont contribué à cette souscription.

Monsieur Robert BOURGI
01 BP 3811
ABIDJAN 01
Côte d'Ivoire

Appendix 31: Letter from Jacques Chirac to Robert Bourgi, January 4, 1985.

Jacques Chirac

Paris, le 4 janvier 1985

Cher Ami,

J'ai bien reçu votre dernière lettre et j'ai été très sensible au message de Madame TOMASINI à qui je viens d'ailleurs de répondre.

Je souhaiterais pouvoir vous rencontrer à l'occasion de votre prochain passage à Paris afin de déterminer avec vous les modalités d'une coopération que vous pourrez apporter utilement au RPR dans les domaines des relations entre notre Mouvement et les pays africains.

Je vous renouvelle mes voeux les meilleurs pour vous-même et les vôtres à l'occasion de cette nouvelle année et d'accepter, Cher Ami, l'expression de mon très amical souvenir.

Bien cordialement

Monsieur Robert BOURGI
Professeur Faculté de Droit
01 B.P. 3811 ABIDJAN 01

COTE D'IVOIRE

Appendix n°32: Letter from Jacques Chirac to Omar Bongo, February 23, 1985, informing him that he had entrusted Robert Bourgi with a mission on the problems of French-speaking Africa south of the Sahara. This mission was to be carried out in conjunction with Ambassador Jacques Kosciusko-Morizet.

Jacques Chirac

Paris, le 23 février 1985

Monsieur le Président, *et Très Cher Ami*

A la suite de notre dernier entretien, et compte tenu de vos amicales suggestions, j'ai décidé de confier à notre ami Robert Bourgi une mission, au titre du R.P.R., de contacts et d'information sur les problèmes de l'Afrique francophone au Sud du Sahara.

Robert Bourgi m'est apparu en effet, par sa connaissance des pays concernés, par sa formation et par ses qualités, tout désigné pour ces fonctions.

Il exercera sa mission auprès de Jacques Kosciusko-Morizet et auprès de moi.

J'ai tenu à ce que vous soyez le premier informé de cette décision qui, je l'espère, vous conviendra.

Avec Toute ma reconnaissance je vous prie de bien vouloir accepter, Monsieur le Président, et Très cher Ami, l'expression de mes très respectueux, fidèles et cordiaux amités ainsi que mes sentiments de très haut attachement.

Son Excellence Monsieur El Hadj Omar BONGO
Président de la République du GABON

"They Know I Know Everything"

Appendix n°33: Note from Jacques Foccart to Robert Bourgi following his appointment as Club 89 delegate for Africa south of the Sahara (May 27, 1985).

JACQUES FOCCART
95, Rue de Prony
75017 Paris
Tél. 227-11-27

Le 27 Mai 1985

260/85

Cher Ami,

Merci de votre gentille lettre du 14 Mai.

Je suis heureux que la décision ait été publiée dans la Lettre de la Nation.

Nous nous sommes manqués de peu hier puisque vous arriviez au début de l'après-midi alors que je prenais l'avion pour rentrer le matin.

J'avais oublié de parler de votre nomination au Président BONGO qui d'ailleurs devait être certainement au courant, mais j'avais demandé à son Directeur de Cabinet de le faire, en m'excusant de mon oubli.

Je vous verrai certainement avant que vous receviez cette lettre, c'est pourquoi je ne m'étends pas davantage et je vous dis donc à Samedi prochain.

Bien Amicalement

J. FOCCART

Monsieur Robert BOURGI
01 B.P. 3811
ABIDJAN 01

Côte d'Ivoire

Appendix 34: Robert Bourgi's personal notes on his "period" in Abidjan (1981-1986).

DOCUMENT 126

Période Abidjanaise

(1981-1986)

De 1978 à 1986: Comme coopérant français, je suis Chargé de Cours à la Faculté de Droit d'Abidjan.

En Février 1981 – Marie-Antoinette Isnard me transmet les félicitations de Jacques CHIRAC pour une action pour le triomphe des idées du RPR (lettre du 26.2.81).

— En Mars 1981 Je préside le Comité de soutien en Côte d'Ivoire pour la candidature de Jacques CHIRAC (lettre du 7 mars 1981 Je délégué du RPR en Côte d'Ivoire)

— En 1982 je fonde et préside le Club 89 en Côte d'Ivoire : je reçois Michel AURILLAC (Président national du Club 89) en 1982 et Alain JUPPÉ en 1984.

— Le 12 Mars 1981, lettre de Jacques CHIRAC : me désigne comme Délégué habilité à contrôler toutes les opérations de vote, de dépouillement et de décompte des voix. Confirmation par le Consul Général de France à Abidjan, lettre du 24 Avril 1981)

— Lettre de J. CHIRAC du 25 Juin 1981 : Il me félicite pour l'efficacité de notre action et veut me rencontrer à mon prochain passage à Paris.

— En 1985 : Jacques CHIRAC, Président du RPR, me nomme Chargé de mission du RPR pour les relations avec les Pays d'Afrique au Sud du Sahara.

② Financement de Jacques CHIRAC
fer dans ma période abidjanaise

Essentiellement libanais. Voir lettre de Jacques
CHIRAC à Roger ABINADER (23 Octobre 1984): dossiers
veut dire argent et de J. CHIRAC à M.
Salim Farhat (6 Novembre 1985); aussi qu'une
lettre de M. ABINADER à M. Jacques-Henri RICHARD.
(13 Juillet 1984)
        Une délégation de l'Union Libanaise Culturelle
Mondiale avait été reçue par J CHIRAC à la Mairie
de Paris en 1984 ou 1985. (Là aussi remise d'argent)
Une Audience de M. ABINADER et de l'Union Libanaise,
J'étais présent
        Tout cela est confirmé par la lettre de
M. BUJON (Membre du bureau du RPR en Côte d'Ivoire,
et délégué au Conseil Supérieur des Français de l'Étranger)
à Marie-Antoinette ISNARD (29-Octobre 1984)

        Voir page 3 de lettre "Capitaine basané "
   — Aussi lettres de M. ABINADER au Pdt Houphouët-Boigny
(13-7-1984) et de M ABINADER à Jacques CHIRAC (13-7-1984)

367

Appendix 35: Letter from Étienne Pinte, MP for Yvelines and deputy mayor of Versailles, to Michel Aurillac, president of Club 89, protesting against the blocking of Philippe Séguin's attempts to be appointed head of Club 89 (October 30, 1990).

ASSEMBLÉE NATIONALE

RÉPUBLIQUE FRANÇAISE

LIBERTÉ - ÉGALITÉ - FRATERNITÉ

COMMISSION
DES AFFAIRES ETRANGERES

PARIS, le 30 OCT 1990

Etienne PINTE
Député des Yvelines
Maire-Adjoint de Versailles

Monsieur Michel AURILLAC
Président du Club 89
45 avenue Montaigne
75008 PARIS

Monsieur le Président,

Il y a quelques mois, vous aviez exprimé le souhait de voir le Club 89 s'ouvrir et s'élargir à d'autres personnalités afin de lui donner un nouveau souffle.

C'est ainsi que vous aviez demandé à un certain nombre d'entre nous, déjà membres des Clubs, mais surtout à des personnalités encore non adhérentes de prendre des responsabilités au sein de ses structures de réflexion et de proposition. Vous aviez vous-même exprimé le désir de voir Philippe SEGUIN vous remplacer à la tête du Club, estimant qu'après dix années de présidence, le moment était venu de vous retirer.

Nous avions accepté votre offre pensant qu'il était de notre devoir d'apporter notre contribution à une démarche qui avait été intéressante entre 1981 et 1986 et que nous aurions pu revitaliser. Notre participation devait se traduire par notre entrée au Comité Directeur du Club ainsi que nous en étions convenus.

Quelle n'a donc pas été la stupéfaction de beaucoup d'adhérents présents à l'Assemblée Générale de samedi dernier de constater que non seulement vous n'avez pas exposé clairement les nouvelles orientations que devait prendre notre Association, mais que, de surcroît, vous n'avez rien fait pour rendre lisible le message qui aurait dû être le vôtre et qui aurait dû se traduire concrètement par l'élection d'une équipe conforme au projet d'ouverture tant espéré.

Votre maladresse a brutalement interrompu ce processus. Si vous souhaitiez sincèrement mener une démarche de renouveau, il fallait vous engager personnellement à la réussir. Vous avez échoué. En outre, nous avons eu le sentiment d'assister à des manoeuvres médiocres et méprisables de manipulations.

L'état d'esprit du Club que vous dirigez encore ne permettant ni l'ouverture à d'autres sensibilités ni la mise en oeuvre de procédures de choix clairs et démocratiques, je vous demande d'enregistrer ma démission de Président de la Fédération des Clubs des Yvelines et de celle de membre du Club 89.

Veuillez agréer, Monsieur le Président, l'expression de mes sentiments distingués.

Etienne PINTE

PALAIS BOURBON - 75355 PARIS - Tél. 40.63.69.27 - Fax : 40.63.52.42
HOTEL DE VILLE - 78011 VERSAILLES CEDEX - Tél. 30.21.20.20 - Fax : 39.02.07.86

Appendix 36: Proposed distribution of positions at the head of Club 89 by Omar Bongo on October 8, 1990.
PDT - MA (President: Michel Aurillac) - Vce-Pdt (Vice-Presidents: Philippe Séguin and Nicole Cathala) - SG: MR (General Secretary: Maurice Robert) - SGA: RAP (Deputy General Secretary: Roland d'Adhemar de Panat) - DN—RB (National Delegate for Developing Countries: Robert Bourgi)

EL HADJ OMAR BONGO
B. P. 546
LIBREVILLE

8 . 10 . 90

Répartition du Président Omar Bongo

1 Pdt ⟶ M.A
2 Vce-Pdt. ⟨ *1) P. Séguin*
  2) N. Cathala

SG . = M.R.
SGA . R.A-P.
DN = R.B

Vu
Omar Bongo

Jacques Chirac   Le 6 novembre 90

Cher Ami,

J'ai lu avec beaucoup d'intérêt, et de sympathie, votre lettre. Je comprends parfaitement votre position et j'en tiens compte.

J'ai vraiment regretté "l'affaire Séguin". J'ai toujours eu - même en période de difficultés, beaucoup d'estime et je dirai d'affection pour Philippe Séguin. De plus personne ne peut contester qu'il a quelque chose à dire! -

Il faut maintenant recoller les morceaux. Vous avez un rôle à jouer dans cet esprit.

Bien cordialement,

[signature]

Appendix n°38: Announcement of the death of Isabelle Foccart, wife of Jacques Foccart.

Appendix n°39: Letter from Laurent Gbagbo, founder of the Front populaire ivoirien (FPI) and opponent of Félix Houphouët-Boigny, sent by airmail to Robert Bourgi from Yopougon prison, his place of incarceration in Abidjan (March 29, 1992).

Laurent GBAGBO

Abidjan le 29 mars 1992

Mon cher Robert,

Imagine quels ne furent mon plaisir et ma joie de recevoir une lettre de toi alors que je suis enfoui dans cette prison de Yopougon ! C'est vraiment dans les moments les plus difficiles que se manifestent les vraies amitiés.

En ce qui concerne mes rapports avec le "Vieux", tu as raison de dire qu'il faut entre nous deux un "dialogue franc, loyal, sincère". Je souligne bien : FRANC, LOYAL, SINCÈRE. L'ai-je souhaité - il vraiment ? Je pense que non car il aurait pris l'initiative de me sourire. Je n'aurais pas refusé de répondre à une convocation (j'ose à peine dire : à une invitation) du chef de l'État.

Alors !? Les choses se dégradent ...

Je te remercie infiniment pour ton mot et espère que nous nous reverrons très bientôt.

Bien amicalement

Appendix 40: Letter from Omar Bongo, dated May 4, 1992, introducing Robert Bourgi as his personal advisor on a mission to the United States.

REPUBLIQUE GABONAISE   UNION - TRAVAIL - JUSTICE

**LE PRESIDENT
DE LA REPUBLIQUE**

                                        Libreville, le 04 Mai 1992

            Cher Monsieur,

            Je tiens à vous remercier d'avoir bien voulu recevoir à Washington la semaine dernière, Monsieur Robert BOURGI qui est mon Conseiller Personnel, chargé des problèmes juridiques.
            Je vous renouvelle l'invitation à vous rendre au Gabon que je l'avais chargé de vous transmettre verbalement.
            L'entretien qu'il a eu avec vous m'a été extrêmement profitable.
            Pour cette seconde rencontre, Monsieur Robert BOURGI sera accompagné de Monsieur l'Ambassadeur Michel Leslie TEALE qui est aussi mon Conseiller Spécial et que je considère en outre comme mon fils.
            Dans l'attente de vous accueillir dans mon pays, je vous assure, Cher Monsieur, de mes sentiments les meilleurs.

                        EL. HADJ OMAR BONGO

Monsieur William LEFHELT
1801 F Street N.W.
Washington D.C.
USA

Appendix n°41: Letter from Jacques Toubon, Minister of Culture and Francophony, to President Abdou Diouf, appointing Robert Bourgi (October 5, 1993).

République Française

Ministère de la Culture et de la Francophonie

3, rue de Valois, 75042 Paris Cedex 01 - Téléphone : (1) 40 15 80 00

Le Ministre

Monsieur le Président et très cher Ami,

Il m'est particulièrement agréable de dépêcher auprès de vous notre ami commun Robert Bourg qui exerce à mes côtés au Club 89 que je préside les fonctions de Délégué national pour les Pays en Développement.

J'ai chargé Robert Bourgi de vous entretenir d'un voyage que j'envisage d'effectuer dans votre Pays à la fin du mois de juillet 1993. J'apprécierais beaucoup que vous m'en indiquiez la date que vous aurez retenue et, pour ce qui est du programme, je me conformerai aux orientations que vous voudrez bien lui donner.

Je dois vous dire que c'est avec un réel plaisir que je vous rencontrerai afin de bénéficier de votre grande expérience acquise tant à la tête de l'Etat sénégalais que comme Président de la Conférence Islamique et comme secrétaire général de l'O.U.A.

Etant en charge de la Culture et de la Francophonie au sein du Gouvernement français, j'ai beaucoup à apprendre aussi de vous qui avez organisé et présidé à Dakar un Sommet de la Francophonie.

Dans l'attente de vous voir, je vous assure, Monsieur le Président et très cher Ami, de mes sentiments respectueusement et amicalement dévoués.

Jacques TOUBON

A son Excellence, Monsieur Abdou Diouf
Président de la République du Sénégal
DAKAR

Appendix n°42: Letter from Jacques Toubon, Minister of Culture and Francophony, to Congolese President Pascal Lissouba, commissioning Robert Bourgi (October 5, 1993).

République Française

Ministère de la Culture et de la Francophonie

3, rue de Valois, 75042 Paris Cedex 01 - Téléphone : (1) 40 15 80 00

Le Ministre

le 5 octobre 1993

Monsieur le Président et Cher Ami,

Je charge notre ami commun, Robert BOURGI, de vous remettre ce message par lequel je vous remercie du soutien que vous avez décidé d'apporter à mon projet politique de la Francophonie que j'exposerai lors du prochain Sommet à l'Ile Maurice.

C'est avec beaucoup de plaisir que je vous rencontrerai là-bas.

Je saisis l'occasion qui m'est offerte pour vous dire combien j'apprécie le courage dont vous faites preuve pour permettre à votre pays de sortir des épreuves difficiles qu'il traverse actuellement.

Soyez assuré, Monsieur le Président et Cher Ami, de ma fidèle et respectueuse amitié.

Jacques TOUBON

Monsieur Pascal LISSOUBA
Président de la République du Congo
BRAZZAVILLE

Appendix 43: Letter from Jacques Toubon, Minister of Culture and Francophony, to President Omar Bongo, commissioning Robert Bourgi (October 5, 1993).

République Française

Ministère de la Culture et de la Francophonie

3, rue de Valois, 75042 Paris Cedex 01 - Téléphone : (1) 40 15 80 00

Le Ministre   le 5 octobre 1993

Monsieur le Président et Cher Ami,

Je charge notre ami commun, Robert BOURGI, de vous remettre ce message par lequel je vous remercie du soutien que vous avez décidé d'apporter à mon projet politique de la Francophonie que j'exposerai lors du prochain Sommet à l'Ile Maurice.

Nous regretterons beaucoup votre absence à cette réunion où vos interventions ont toujours été remarquées pour leur bon sens et leur précision.

Soyez assuré, Monsieur le Président et Cher Ami, de ma fidèle et respectueuse amitié.

Jacques TOUBON

Son Excellence El Hadj Omar BONGO
Président de la République Gabonaise
LIBREVILLE

Appendix 44: Letter from Jacques Toubon, Minister of Culture and Francophony, mandating Robert Bourgi to attend the funeral of Félix Houphouët-Boigny, who died in December 1993 (February 4, 1994).

République Française

Ministère de la Culture et de la Francophonie

3, rue de Valois, 75042 Paris Cedex 01 - Téléphone : (1) 40 15 80 00

Le Ministre

le 4 février 1994

Monsieur le Président et Cher Ami,

J'ai demandé à notre ami commun Robert Bourgi de me représenter aux obsèques de notre regretté Président et Père Félix HOUPHOUËT-BOIGNY.

Le 7 février, vous aurez à vos cotés les représentants de presque tous les pays du monde. ce jour-là, je communierai avec vous par la pensée et par le coeur.

Vous savez quelle affection et quel estime j'avais pour le Président HOUPHOUËT-BOIGNY.

Il nous a tracé une route pour les relations franco-ivoiriennes et franco-africaines ; sur cette route-là, je serai et resterai votre ami, votre compagnon et votre partenaire.

J'ai chargé Robert Bourgi d'organiser avec vous et sous votre autorité la visite que je compte effectuer en Côte d'Ivoire le vendredi 25 février.

Je me réjouis de vous revoir à cette occasion et en attendant, je vous assure, Monsieur le Président et Cher Ami, de ma fidèle et respectueuse amitié.

Jacques TOUBON

Son Excellence Monsieur Henri KONAN BEDIE
Président de la République de Côte d'Ivoire
ABIDJAN

```
■ T E L E X ■            EXEMPLAIRE  1              ■ T E L E X ■
R494 : CULTCAB 215134F 364 1753 250500BA PARIS F ZCZC SBA851 C    1/2
```

```
■
CULTCAB 215134F
364 1753
250500BA PARIS F

ZCZC SBA851 CIF598 XIE898/009/SMH
FRXX BY CIAB 219
ABIDJANTELEX 219/198 30 1020
```

Jacques TOUBON

```
ETATPRIORITE
PRESIREPUBLIQUE ABIDJAN
A
MONSIEUR JACQUES TOUBON
MINISTRE DE LA CULTURE ET DE LA FRANCOPHONIE
3 RUEDEVALOIS
75042PARIS CIDEX 01


NO. 75419
MONSIEUR LE MINISTRE
VOTRE MESSAGE DE CONDOLEANCES A L'OCCASION DE LA SI DOULOUREUSE
DISPARITION DU PRESIDENT FELIX HOUPHOUET-BOIGNY M'A PROFONDEMENT
TOUCHE ET RECONFORTE. JE VOUS EN REMERCIE TRES SINCEREMENT.
AU DELA DES BIENFAITS DE SON ACTION POUR LA COTE D'IVOIRE, LE
PRESIDENT HOUPHOUET-BOIGNY DEMEURE L'INCARNATION MEME DE L'AMITIE ET
DE LA COOPERATION AVEC LA FRANCE. IL EN FIT DE LA LANGUE, LA LANGUE
OFFICIELLE DE LA COTE D'IVOIRE, AVEC TOUT CE QU'UN TEL CHOIX EMPORTE
D'HERITAGE CULTUREL  D'ADMIRATION ET MEME D'AMOUR POUR LE PAYS DU
GENERAL DE GAULLE  DONT IL FUT  VOUS LE SAVEZ  LE COLLABORATEUR
L'AMI LE FEAL.
A TOUS EGARDS, VOUS NE POUVIEZ AVOIR EN LUI QU'UN INTERLOCUTEUR
TRES ATTENTIF ET DEJA DEVOUE AUX OBJECTIFS DE VOTRE CHARGE ET DE VOS
CONVICTIONS
CROYEZ  MONSIEUR LE MINISTRE  QUE JE ME SOUHAITE DE TOUT COEUR
LES MEMES DISPOSITIONS POUR QUE DURE TOUJOURS SANS FAILLE LA SI
BELLE HISTOIRE D'ESTIME ET DE FIDELITE ENTRE LA FRANCE ET LA COTE
D'IVOIRE.
AVEC LES ASSURANCES DE MA HAUTE CONSIDERATION.


    HENRI KONAN BEDIE
 PRESIDENT DE LA REPUBLIOQUE DE COTE D'IVOIRE.



COL CKD
```

../..

Appendix 46: Correspondence between Jacques Foccart and Robert Bourgi, March 4, 1994).

Paris, le 4 Mars 1994

JACQUES FOCCART

95. Rue de Prony
75017 Paris
Tel 42 27 11 27
Fax 42 12 04 73

186/94

cher Henri,

Je vous remercie bien vivement de votre si gentille lettre du 2 Mars. Vos reproches amicaux m'ont touché. Il est certain que quelques que fois je me laisse aller à un certain pessimisme. Il est malheureusement souvent justifié, mais il ne faut pas se laisser gagner par ce sentiment et il faut lutter. Votre lettre m'amène à cette conclusion et c'est déjà un résultat.

Nous en reparlerons bientôt et en attendant je vous prie de croire à mes sentiments bien amicaux et fidèles.

Bien à vous

J.FOCCART

Monsieur Robert BOURGI
Avocat à la Cour
26, avenue Pierre 1er de Serbie
75116 PARIS

Appendix 47: Correspondence between Herman J. Cohen and Robert Bourgi, dated August 8, 1994.

Herman J. Cohen
3605 R Street, N.W.
Washington, DC   20007

Washington le 8 août 1994
via fax: 33-1-47-23-37-38

Cher ami:

Merci pour votre visite d'aujourd'hui. Votre famille est très sympathique.

Voici un papier à donner à notre ami Léon.

Bonne chance. Mon meilleur souvenir à Monsieur Afrique numéro UN, Jacques Foccart.

A bientôt,

Herman J. Cohen

Appendix 48: Message from Jacques Foccart to President Mobutu Sese Seko, following his visit to Gbadolite (September 9, 1994).

JACQUES FOCCART

95, Rue de Prony
75017 Paris
Tel. 42 27 11 27
Fax 42 12 04 73

Paris, le 9 Septembre 1994

574/94

*Monsieur C. Président de la République
et très cher Ami,*

Il m'est particulièrement agréable de vous faire parvenir ce message d'amitié et de confiance par notre ami commun, Robert BOURGI.

Je tiens à vous remercier encore de l'accueil particulièrement chaleureux et fraternel que vous avez bien voulu me réserver lors de mon trop bref séjour à GBADO-LITE le mois dernier.

Je vous remercie également bien vivement du message que vous m'avez fait parvenir par Robert BOURGI.

J'espère que ma visite aura servi à apaiser les esprits et à préparer le terrain pour une totale entente entre vous et votre Premier Ministre. Cette entente est absolument indispensable pour que votre pays retrouve sa prospérité et son dynamisme. Je sais que vous faites tous vos efforts pour atteindre ce but et je suis sûr du résultat.

En vous demandant de transmettre à votre épouse mes respectueux hommages, je vous assure Monsieur le Président de la République et très cher Ami, de ma très haute considération et de ma fidèle et affectueuse amitié.

Bien à vous

J. FOCCART

*Monsieur le Maréchal MOBUTU SESE SEKO
Président de la République du Zaïre
KINSHASA*

République du ZAIRE

Appendix n°49: Word of thanks from Alain Juppé to Robert Bourgi, June 1, 2003, for the latter's contribution to the success of his trip to Senegal and Gabon in May of the same year (June 1, 2003).

ALAIN JUPPÉ

Cher Robert,

Merci pour votre message de soutien, et pour ces magnifiques stylos qui me sont bien utiles dans ma tâche quotidienne ...

J'ai été heureux de vous revoir en Afrique et de vous savoir présent à notre Conseil National qui a été un beau succès

Bien cordialement

[signature]

Appendix 50: The Scac Delmas Vieljeux group approaches Jacques Foccart to defend its interests in Zaire, in particular the port of Matadi (January 24, 1995).

SCAC DELMAS VIELJEUX
-SDV-

DIVISION TERRESTRE INTERNATIONAL
☎ 46 96 42 74 - FAX 46 96 40 53

EV/OS   24 janvier 1995

Hervé JOBBE-DUVAL

ZAIRE - PORT DE MATADI

Au cours des années passées nous avons à plusieurs reprises mené des discussions avec les Autorités Zaïroises pour aborder l'ensemble du fonctionnement du Port de MATADI.

Les nombreux changements qui sont intervenus au niveau des Ministres de tutelle ne nous ont pas permis de faire progresser nos souhaits.

Nous avions élaboré l'idée de créer une société de gestion du Port de MATADI dans laquelle la Compagnie Maritime Zaïroise (CMZ), l'État zaïrois et SDV se partageraient les participations.

Notre idée était que notre Groupe puisse assurer l'organisation, le contrôle et la gestion de l'ensemble portuaire.

Le port de MATADI, compte tenu de la dégradation de ses installations est devenue pour l'ensemble des Armateurs un sujet de préoccupation et de désintérêt. Il est aussi le port le plus cher de la Côte Ouest Africaine.

Nous sommes persuadés que la gestion par une société privée amènerait rapidement une amélioration qui viserait à une augmentation des tonnages qui y sont traités et par voie de conséquence une diminution des coûts pour tous les utilisateurs (armateurs, transitaires, transporteurs routiers).

L'expérience de notre Groupe dans le domaine de l'organisation ou de la restructuration des ensembles portuaires nous incite à nouveau à souhaiter la reprise du dialogue avec les Autorités zaïroises.

Etienne VAILLANT.

CORRESPONDANCE A ADRESSER :
TOUR DELMAS-VIELJEUX - 31-32, QUAI DE DION BOUTON - 92811 PUTEAUX CEDEX FRANCE
TÉL. 33 (1) 46 96 44 33 - FAX 33 (1) 46 96 44 22 - TELEX 616 260 - TVA FR 64 512 110 481
SIÈGE SOCIAL CIDET - 29900 ERQUE GABERIC - SCAC DELMAS VIELJEUX - SDV - S A AU CAPITAL DE 564 186 620 FRANCS - RCS QUIMPER B 342 110 481

383

Appendix 51: Robert Bourgi's diary and personal notes (1996 to 2001).

"They Know I Know Everything"

Entretiens avec Monsieur Jacques CHIRAC à la Mairie de ①
PARIS avant son élection à la Présidence de la République
j'étais seul ou avec Monsieur Jacques ~~FOCCART~~ (1995)

Lundi 9 Janvier 1995 : chez Jacques CHIRAC avec
Monsieur FOCCART, rv à 11h30 = remise de 10.million
de NF (1 milliard d'anciens francs) – Un émissaire
gabonais (sécurité rapprochée) les avait portés dans
une mallette et les avait portés chez Monsieur FOCCART
au 95 rue de Prony 75~~017~~ Paris à 10 heures.
J'ai déjeuné avec Monsieur FOCCART ensuite chez Petrus.

Lundi 13 Mars à 11 heures arrivée du Président
MOBUTU au Bourget. Je dîne le soir même au
restaurant Lasserre avec le Maréchal MOBUTU et sa
famille. Je lui dis au Maréchal qu'il a rendez – vous
le lendemain à 12 heures chez Monsieur FOCCART
c'est à dire le mardi 14 Mars à 12 heures = le
Maréchal remet à M. FOCCART, 2 millions de dollars
destinés à Monsieur CHIRAC. M. FOCCART se chargera
de cette tâche.

Le Jeudi 16 Mars à 11h30, Monsieur FOCCART me
dit que M. CHIRAC était entré en possession de la
contribution du Maréchal MOBUTU. Le même jour
j'avais pris le petit déjeuner avec Nicolas BAZIRE
(D2 du Cabinet de Monsieur Edouard BALLADUR. Premier
Ministre) chez le Maréchal MOBUTU qui m'a dit, après le
départ de Nicolas BAZIRE, avoir reçu

② un coup de fil de " mon Ami Jacques CHIRAC..."

— Le Jeudi 20 Avril à 19h30, je pars pour Libreville par vol RK (Air Afrique)

— le Vendredi 21 Avril à 10 heures, je suis reçu par le Président BONGO qui m'annonce que le lendemain matin une voiture de l'Ambassade du Gabon viendra à mon domicile avec une personne de confiance me remettre une participation pour "Davin"— nom de code de M. CHIRAC (M. Davin, un Temps, fut Maire de Libreville). Je quitte le soir même Libreville pour Paris par Air Gabon.

— Le Samedi 22 Avril à 10 heures, l'émissaire du Président BONGO arrive à mon domicile Rue St Dominique (7e) à bord d'une voiture de l'Ambassade du Gabon (43 CD ou cd 43). Nous partons à l'Hôtel de Ville où j'avais rendez-vous à 11 heures avec M. CHIRAC. Remise rapide de 10 millions de francs. Je repars dans la même voiture de l'Ambassade du Gabon. Ce même jour, à 16 heures, je vais rendre compte à M. FOCCART à Luzarches— (Val d'Oise, villa Charlotte).

— CHIRAC est élu Président de la République et reçoit le Samedi 13 Mai à 15 heures : MM. FOCCART et Nibaux à l'Hôtel de ville et leur signifie qu'ils ne s'installeront pas au 2 rue de l'Elysée mais au 14

3) . Le coup est terrible pour M. FOCCART auquel
avait été promis le 2 ;

J. CHIRAC à l'Elysée

Entretiens de Me Robert BOURGI à l'Elysée (4)
soit seul (ou) accompagné (1995—2002)

Année 1995 : Mai 1995 : Election de M. Jacques CHIRAC
à la Présidence de la République.

Il m'est arrivé d'être signalé sous mon nom soit sous le nom
de CHAMBERTIN.

Rien à signaler, c'est Monsieur
J. FOCCART qui n'a jamais occupé le
14 de l'Elysée qui assure le relais
directement avec M. FOCCART.
que je voyais au moins 3 fois par
semaine à Paris, à Luzarches (Val d'Oise)
ou à Cavalaire (Var)

Année 1996
Visites régulières à M. FOCCART.
Le Mercredi 24 Avril 1996, je dîne avec la
famille MOBUTU et le couple CACOUB chez Taillevent
Le Maréchal MOBUTU, à part, me dit qu'il veut voir

dès le lendemain.

M. FOCCART reçoit le Maréchal MOBUTU le ~~Samedi 27~~ Avril à 9 h 30 et lui remet une contribution de 2 millions de dollars pour M. CHIRAC. A M. FOCCART de la remettre au Président de la République. M. FOCCART me dit le 7 Mai à 19 h 30 qu'il avait fait le nécessaire pour le Président de la République —

Mercredi 19 Mars 1997 ; décès de Jacques FOCCART

Lundi 24 Mars à 11 heures = obsèques de J. FOCCART

Lundi 24 Mars à 20 heures = avec J. CHIRAC et Villepin (bureau de Villepin)

J.C. " Maintenant que Jacques est mort,, vous travaillerez avec moi et Dominique

Lundi 28 Avril 1997 [PREMIER] rendez-vous
__19 h 30__ avec D de Villepin à l'Élysée
avec Claude Angeli (rédaction du Canard Enchaîné) dont je suis le témoin de mariage avec Stéphanie Mesnier. Étais-je Robert BOURGi ou Chambertin ?

__14 Mai 19 h 15__ RV avec D. de Villepin (Chambertin ou BOURGi, je l'ignore) Le 2 Juin 1997 avec Michel Rocard chez

(6) Dominique de Villepin. M. Rocard candidat au poste de M.A.E. du Gouvernement Jospin.
Vaste polémique ensuite, encore cette année.
Lundi 9 Juin 1997 à 18h45 = C/o Villepin avec le Préfet Marchiani.
Le 11 Juin à 19h C/o Villepin.

Le 15 Juin de 11h30 à 12 heures le Président de la République m'appelle dans ma voiture alors que je suis sur la route de Luzarches - Jour de la fête des Pères ; j'allais fleurir la tombe de M. Foccart et déjeuner avec Odette, gouvernante de M. Foccart, dans une auberge.
Jeudi 19 Juin à 18h   D. de Villepin.
Lundi 23 Juin   9h   D. de Villepin.
Samedi 28 Juin 19 heures = Suite du coup de fil de J. Chirac dans ma voiture = je (le) vois dans le bureau de Villepin. Artisan de la cohabitation suicidaire, Villepin est sur un poste éjectable. Isolé, voué aux gémonies du RPR et de Madame CHIRAC "Villepin, c'est Néron", je convaincs Chirac de le garder. (Oui), je sauve Villepin.
Lundi 1er Septembre à 18h45. D. de Villepin.
Vendredi 19 Septembre 19h30   Villepin.

F) Jeudi 20 Novembre 19h = Villepin

Mardi 20 Janvier 1998   19h30 = Villepin.

Mercredi 4 Février   19h30 = Villepin

Jeudi 12 Février 12h45 = Villepin

Vendredi 27 Février 19h = Villepin

Mardi 17 mars à 19h = Villepin.

Lundi 30 Mars à 19h15 = C/o Villepin avec D.

Amara ESSY (M.A.E de Côte d'Ivoire) = J. Chirac
assiste à l'entretien.

Jeudi 16 Avril 12h45 Villepin

Lundi 11 Mai 18h30 Villepin

Vendredi 22 Mai à 13h Déjeuner avec Villepin
à l'invitation de Georges Queguin au Bar au Sel
(Quai d'Orsay ; réservation M² Georges)

Jeudi 28 Mai 19h Villepin avec Claude

Angeli (Canard Enchaîné)

Lundi 15 Juin (1998) 19h = Villepin.

Vendredi 31 Juillet 17h Villepin avec le
juge Georges Fenech.

Jeudi 10 Septembre 18h30 Villepin avec David
Carton (journaliste)

Mercredi 23 Septembre 19h Villepin

⑧ Le Mercredi 14 Octobre 1998 à 18h30. Villepin

rereçu visite au Président BONGO à l'Hôtel Crillon –

J'assiste à l'entretien. Le Président BONGO

remet une contribution de 1 million d'euros

(valise commandant de bord) – Après l'entretien,

à bord d'une voiture ambassade Gabon, ac.... ....

du Colonel Kabori, nous partons à l'Élysée

et nous remettons la valise à Villepin dans son

bureau (entrée par l'avenue de Marigny)

Vendredi 23 Octobre à 17h50 Villepin.

Vendredi 6 Novembre à 18h Villepin

Vendredi 20 Novembre à 18h30 Villepin.

Vendredi 29 Janvier (1999) Villepin à 18h45

Lundi 15 Février 11h30 = Villepin.

Jeudi 15 Avril 1999 18h30 = Villepin

Lundi 17 Juin à 18h Villepin avec le général d'armée
Raymond Germanos

Lundi 17 Juin à 18h30 Villepin avec le général
Leroche (Inspecteur général d...
Service de Santé)

Lundi 28 Juin 18h Villepin.

Mardi 13 Juillet 18h30 Villepin

Mardi 20 Juillet 18h30 Villepin

(9)

Jeudi 23 Septembre 1999 18h = Villepin
Lundi 11 Octobre 18h = Villepin

Mardi 12 Octobre à 18h Villepin avec
Amara Essy (M.A.E. Côte d'Ivoire) = J.Chirac
assiste à l'entretien.

Vendredi 15 Octobre à 19h = Villepin
Vendredi 19 Novembre à 19h Villepin
Vendredi 26 Novembre à 19h30 Villepin

(2000) Mardi 4 Janvier 19h = Villepin
Mercredi 12 Janvier 2000 = Villepin avec
à 12h30 l'Ambassadeur

Éliséo Figueredo (Angola)

Lundi 24 Janvier à 18h30 = Villepin
avec l'Ambassadeur ivoirien Georges Ouegnin porteur
d'un message du Pdt ivoirien le Général Guei pour le
Président Jacques CHIRAC.

Mercredi 16 Février à 19h = Villepin avec

Laurent GBAGBO

Jeudi 23 Mars à 19h = Villepin

Lundi 10 Avril 18h30 Villepin

Mardi 25 Avril à 18h30 Villepin

Lundi 15 Mai 17h = Villepin

Mardi 23 Mai 19h = Villefin

Jeudi 25 Mai 12h30 Villefin

Lundi 3 Juillet 18h   Villefin

Mardi 18 Juillet 18h   Villefin.

Mardi 25 Juillet 8h30 Villefin (Bristol) ~~avec~~

Jeudi 7 Septembre 18h = D. Villefin.

Mardi 19 Septembre 18h30 Villefin

Lundi 25 Septembre à 18h45 Villefin.

Vendredi 29 Septembre = 17h30 = Villefin.

Lundi 9 Octobre à 18h = Villefin.

Vendredi 20 Octobre à 19h = Villefin

Mercredi 8 Novembre à 18h = Villefin

Mercredi 15 Novembre à 18h30 Villefin

Lundi 4 Décembre à 12h45 Villefin

Mardi 5 Décembre à 18h. Villefin

Mercredi 13 Décembre à 18h30 Villefin

Vendredi 22 Décembre = 19h = Villefin

(2001) pas retrouvé 1er et 2e trimestres 2001
Mardi 17 Juillet à 12h45 Villefin.
Samedi 21 Juillet à 19h Président. A. Wade
à l'Hôtel ~~Sofitel~~ Bristol = le frère de A. W. me dit qu'il

(11) Va aider J. CHIRAC :

Jeudi 26 Juillet 2001 19h = Villepin. Je
lui annonce que Pascaline BONGO va lui remettre
une contribution de son Père = 1 million d'euros
le lendemain Vendredi 27 Juillet à 11 heures -
Vendredi 27 Juillet à 10h30 = Pascaline BONGO
passe me récupérer à mon cabinet à bord de sa
voiture diplomatique. A ses pieds, 1 mallette de
commandant de bord qu'elle me donne. A l'Élysée,
je l'ai à la main à ses côtés - Dans
le bureau de Villepin et selon l'usage, je
mets la mallette derrière le bureau de Villepin.
et l'audience commence -

Lundi 30 Juillet à 12h30 Villepin à l'Élysée
Lundi 3 Septembre à 12h45 Villepin
Lundi 10 Septembre à 18h45 Villepin
Vendredi 14 Septembre à 18h30 Villepin

Le Vendredi 21 Septembre à 13h = le Président
A. Wade déjeune à l'Élysée ; et au cours du
déjeuner, il confirme au Pdt Chirac qu'il
va l'aider et que Karim sera chargé
de la contribution - X X X X

(12) Vendredi 28 Septembre 12h45 = Villepin

Lundi 1er Octobre à 12h30   Villepin.

Jeudi 11 Octobre 2001   le Président
COMPAORÉ arrive en visite officielle en
France (Hôtel Meurice)-
Vendredi 12 Octobre à 12h30   le Ministre
Salif DIALLO (Burkina Faso (agriculture)] est
reçu à l'Elysée par Villepin en ma présence.
Là, M. Salif Diallo dit à Villepin que le
Pdt COMPAORÉ va aider M. CHIRAC pour les
élections présidentielle de 2002. Mise au
point de cela à Ouaga. × × × ×

Mardi 23 Octobre à 12h30 = Villepin.

Mardi 30 Octobre à 12h~~h~~ Villepin.

Le Lundi 5 Novembre à 11 heures
Je prends le vol pour Ouagadougou, j'arrive
à Ouaga à 16 heures - Hôtel Silmande #523.
Je vois le Président COMPAORE le Mardi 6
Novembre à 16 heures à Ouaga 2000, en présence
de M. Salif Diallo -

(13) Je repars le soir même sur Paris -
Décollage 20h45 (siège 1F) - Arrivée
le 7 Novembre à 8 heures du matin (et)
le Mercredi 7 Novembre à 12h45, je vois
Villepin à l'Élysée - X X X
Mardi 13 Novembre à 19h30 - Villepin
Vendredi 15 Novembre à 19 heures = Villepin
Le même soir à 19h30 je vois M. Salif
Diallo à son hôtel (Sofitel Champs
Élysées 8 rue Jean
01 40 74 79 00 Goujon (8e)

X Là, M. Salif Diallo me dit
+ que la contribution revêt la
+ forme de 4 Djembés avec à l'intérieur de
+ ces djembés (3 millions de dollars) -

ET Le Dimanche 18 Novembre à 20 heures,
j'entre (avec) un émissaire burkinabé au
volant de ma voiture et dans la voiture
les 4 djembés que M. de Villepin, sa secrétaire,
l'émissaire et moi-même montons au bureau
de Villepin - Voiture garée dans la cour
d'honneur -

(iii) Mercredi 21 Novembre à 16h30   Villefin

Lundi 26 Novembre Villefin (12h55)-
Lundi 3 Décembre 13 heures = Villefin
Jeudi 6 Décembre = 12h30   Elysée
                           Villefin.

x++ Le même jour à 19 heures , Je rends
Visite au Président L. Gbagbo en visite
à Paris à son hôtel, Plaza Athénée -
Le lendemain à 9h , Laurent Gbagbo est reçu
à / l'Académie française - et à

[décembre] à 19 heures, L. Gbagbo est reçu au
Palais de Justice de Paris   X XX

Le Samedi 8 Décembre à 20 heures, dîner
Jacques Chirac . Laurent Gbagbo à l'Elysée.
Laurent Gbagbo confirme à J. CHIRAC
qu'il va l'aider pour 2002   X X X

ET le Jeudi 13 Décembre à
16 heures ; avec Eugène ALLOU
(Ambassadeur, D2 Protocole Ivoirien) nous
allons à l'Elysée dans ma Voiture avec

Appendix 52: Greetings from Jacques Foccart
to Robert and Catherine Bourgi (May 1, 1996).

Letter of thanks from Odette Leguerney, Jacques Foccart's historical
secretary, to the Bourgi couple for their best wishes.

*Beaucoup de bonheur pour
Tous –*

JACQUES FOCCART

Je vous embrasse bien affectueusement

1/5/96

Tél. 42 27 11 27

95, rue de Prony
75017 Paris

Odette Leguerney

*Merci pour toutes vos gentillesses
et mes meilleurs voeux de
bonheur et bonne santé pour
tous.
Je vous embrasse bien
affectueusement —*

Odette

JACQUES FOCCART

95. Rue de Prony
75017 Paris
Tel 42 27 11 27
Fax 42 12 04 73

Paris, le 31 Mai 1996

Confirmation

Chers Amis,

Depuis quelques années, l'habitude a été prise de nous retrouver tous, anciens du Secrétariat Général à la Communauté, le plus souvent à LUZARCHES et l'an dernier à l'Elysée.

Je serais heureux de poursuivre ce qui est presque devenu une tradition en vous recevant à LUZARCHES, le samedi 8 juin prochain, à 12 H, pour déjeuner.

J'espère qu'il vous sera possible de venir m'y retrouver avec la plupart des anciens de la rue de Grenelle ou de la rue de l'Elysée.

Pour une bonne organisation de ce déjeuner, je vous serais obligé de bien vouloir faire part de votre réponse à mon secrétariat, en téléphonant au 42.92.87.90, ou en m'adressant un petit mot à la Présidence de la République, 14, rue de l'Elysée, 75008 PARIS.

Bien amicalement à vous,

Bien Affectueusement

Jacques FOCCART.

Monsieur et Madame Robert BOURGI
96, rue Saint-Dominique
75007 PARIS

400

Appendix 54: Robert Bourgi's analysis of current events in Africa for Dominique de Villepin (October 10, 1996).

Robert Bourgi
Avocat à la Cour
Docteur en Droit

25, Avenue Pierre 1er de Serbie
75116 Paris

Tel 47 20 45 08
Fax 47 23 37 38
Palais C 1444

Jeudi 10 Octobre 1996

Monsieur le Secrétaire général,

J'ai pensé qu'il était bon que je revienne sur un certain nombre de réflexions que j'avais faites à Jacques Toubon verbalement et par écrit et ayant trait au paysage politique africain. Sauf erreur de ma part, J.T. devrait vous en parler parce qu'il partageait tout & fait mon analyse.

Zaïre: J'ai rendu visite à plusieurs reprises à Lausanne au Président MOBUTU; une fois, Fernand Wibaux et moi même avions fait le déplacement ensemble; lui était porteur d'un message du Président de la République et moi d'un message de J.T. J'avais trouvé le Maréchal un peu mieux que la fois précédente: mobilité plus grande, légèrement "replâtré", la voix plus claire sauf qu'au bout d'une vingtaine de minutes, la lassitude et la fatigue reprenaient le dessus.

J'ai revu depuis le Maréchal à 2 reprises et mon inquiétude ne fait que s'accentuer: amaigrissement, élocution lente, voix éraillée, et refus total de s'alimenter; pourtant, il m'avait emmené déjeuner à Annecy c/o Marc VEYRAT. Depuis 48 heures, je cherche en vain à le joindre au téléphone: Madame Présidente et son beau frère l'honorable Fangbi me répondent qu'il se repose et qu'il est fatigué.

Mardi à 12h30, KÉRÉKOU m'ayant à ses côtés avait lui aussi tenté en vain de lui parler; hier soir, dans l'avion

rance qui me ramenait de Kinshasa, même scénario. Alors
m'interroge. J'ai vu KENGO qui sera à Paris du 24 au 27/50.
Il m'a dit son inquiétude si le Maréchal venait à disparaître:
implosion du pays, fronde des généraux, menace aux portes sur ou
les marchés de l'est par Museveni et Kagame interposés..
Je sais notre Ambassadeur inquiet lui aussi. les Zaïrois veulent
revoir leur chef mais s'ils devaient revoir "le Léopard" tel
qu'il est aujourd'hui, ce serait une catastrophe sans nom.
        Je ne suis pas médecin mais je sais l'homme non seulement
atteint physiquement mais amoindri nettement sur le plan moral.
    J'ai en mémoire ce qu'il m'a dit la semaine dernière, quand
il me prit la main pour faire quelques pas avec moi: " c'est
dur, Robert, très dur mais j'y arriverai ". le choc émotionnel
fut terrible pour moi parce qu'il m'a fallu le conduire.

    Usez, je vous prie, de votre autorité et de votre audience pour
faire en sorte qu'il continue à se soigner en Europe et à se
reposer à Cap Martin. Je sais combien il sera attentif à ce
que lui diront "son ami Jacques" et Dominique, comme il
vous appelle l'un et l'autre.
        Mon K m'a dit qu'Alain JUPPE devrait le recevoir lors
de sa visite à Paris; je crois indispensable que le Président aussi
le reçoive en votre présence. LK ne tient que par la volonté du
Maréchal; et le sait comme il sait que les généraux mafieux
de la Garde Présidentielle et de la Garde Civile ne le louperont
pas si d'aventure ... Léon a besoin de se sentir soutenu et
conforté. Vous savez qu'en dehors de lui, il n'y a personne
au Zaïre ayant sa crédibilité et son sérieux.
        Le Président avait reçu LK fin 1996 à l'Hôtel de Ville
en présence de Dominique FOCCART.
        J'ai vraiment de la peine pour le Maréchal car il a
toujours été fidèle à notre Président et à notre combat
pour le triomphe de nos idées (à Lausanne 19.41.21.613.33.33)
    — CONGO Après une embellie lors de la visite   #407)
    du Président à Brazza, voilà que Pascal LISSOUBA retombe

dans sa paranoïa, ses divagations scientifico-intellectuelles totalement incohérentes et inintelligibles. soumis aussi à un entourage divisé, clanique, tribal' et ayant pour nerf moteur l'accumulation rapide d'argent et ce par tous les moyens.

Je crois qu'il va falloir peser lourdement sur Madame DUNARI, seule capable, à mon sens, d'agir positivement sur le Président et le comportement de tous les responsables, elle prise en compte aussi. Je pense qu'il ne serait pas inutile que vous la receviez lors de son prochain passage à Paris ; certaines vérités dites par vous, fermement, produiraient à coup sûr un effet salvateur pour ce pays.

— GABON : Les hommes" du Président Berbro se révèlent de plus en plus impuissants face à l'opposition et incapables de toute stratégie électorale. voici votre fidèle et bon Omar obligé de resserrer lui-même les boulons, de monter au créneau et de "dépreindre" l'opposition, individu par individu. Le score des municipales sera révélateur et fort important pour la suite : législatives et présidentielles.

— TOGO : vous connaissez depuis longtemps mon opinion ; PANOU, MAE, c'est le symbole même du nivellement par le bas. On croit rêver ou plutôt cauchemarder. Quel dommage que l'ami KODJO soit dénué de tout sens politique et qu'il soit irrémédiablement atteint d'égocentrisme accentué.

— <u>Côte d'Ivoire</u> : Des amis dirigent le pays mais je n'arrête pas de leur dire qu'ils ont tort d'ignorer Laurent GBAGBO ; il vaut mieux avoir cet homme "dedans" que "dehors". Là aussi, il y a confusion des genres ; mon Maître Georges BURDEAU m'avait enseigné que "jamais" l'intérêt général ne signifiait la somme des intérêts particuliers". Un homme se distingue par son honnêteté, sa discrétion et sa compétence. AMARA ESSY, M.A.E et qui fut, il y a 2 ans, Pdt de l'Assemblée générale de l'ONU, je comprends, à le fréquenter assidûment, pourquoi, dans ses dernières années, le "Vieux" HOUPHOUËT l'avait choisi comme confident et témoin ultime de ses réflexions...

— <u>SÉNÉGAL</u> mon pays natal et celui où reposent mes pauvres Parents et les miens disparus ne cesse de m'inquiéter. Les germes de l'explosion sont palpables : misère, famine, montée de l'intégrisme, division des hommes au sein du Pouvoir : Tanor DIENG / Moustapha NIASSE. Opposition de plus en plus structurée et consciente des carences du système et voyant le plus enfin en ses chances.

C'est en toute confiance et en amitié que je vous ai écrit.

Croyez moi votre bien dévoué

Robert BOURGI.

Robert Bourgi
Avocat a la Cour
Docteur en Droit

25 Avenue Pierre 1er de Serbie
75116 Paris

Tél. 01 47 20 45 08
Fax 01 47 23 37 38
Palais C 1444

URGENT

Jeudi 16 Janvier 1997

Monsieur le Secrétaire général,

Il serait bon que vous fassiez comprendre définitivement à Jacques GODFRAIN qu'il serait préjudiciable à nos intérêts et à notre politique africaine qu'il continue à penser qu'il doit obtenir du Maréchal MOBUTU le retour en France de l'Ambassadeur RAMAZANI.
Je vous en parle en toute confiance car Jacques G m'a appelé pour cela à plusieurs reprises et encore ce matin à mon domicile.
J'ai évoqué cela avec J. TOUBON ce matin à la Chancellerie et lui ai dit que j'vous en parlerai. J.T m'a encouragé à le faire et pense qu'il ne faut donner aucune publicité à cette affaire, qui en a déjà eu un peu trop.
J.G. est animé de bons sentiments mais ne semble pas comprendre qu'une nuée de journalistes attend à Cap-Martin le Maréchal pour ... pas en la matière. Je les sais planqués là-bas:
Je compte sur vous pour que l'ami J.G ne puisse pas faire le lien entre mon courrier et votre éventuelle intervention auprès de lui. Cette affaire doit être traitée à votre seul niveau en y associant vraisemblablement J.T.
Je crois qu'il était de mon devoir de vous prévenir.

Votre bien dévoué
Robert Bourgi

Monsieur Dominique de VILLEPIN
Secrétaire général de l'Elysée
Paris

MEMBRE D UNE ASSOCIATION AGREEE LE REGLEMENT DES HONORAIRES PAR CHEQUE EST ACCEPTE

Appendix 56: Thank-you card from Jacques Foccart's family following his death (March 20, 1997).

La famille et les proches de

JACQUES FOCCART

profondément touchés par les marques d'affection et de sympathie que vous leur avez témoignées vous remercient chaleureusement

Appendix 57: Letter from Alain Plantey, May 10, 1997, thanking Robert Bourgi for his contribution to Jacques Foccart's funeral.

INSTITUT DE FRANCE

ACADÉMIE DES SCIENCES MORALES
ET POLITIQUES

Paris, le 10 mai 1997

Cher Ami,

Ensemble, nous avons offert à notre Secrétaire Général de belles fleurs qui l'ont accompagné à Saint Louis des Invalides et à Luzarches.

Grâce à votre générosité, j'ai pu faire réaliser un portrait de lui qui me semble fidèle et expressif.

En remerciement de votre geste et en hommage à Jacques Foccart, je vous envoie ce souvenir,

avec l'expression de mon amitié très attristée.

cordialement

Alain PLANTEY

407

Appendix 58: Letter of comfort and friendship to Dominique de Villepin, considered at the time to be behind the dissolution of the National Assembly (June 19, 1997).

Robert Bourgi

50, BOULEVARD EMILE AUGIER
75116 PARIS
TÉL. 01 45 03 04 28

Jeudi 19 Juin 1997

Mon cher Dominique,

J'étais réellement chiffonné lorsque je vous ai quitté hier en fin d'après-midi.

Je comprends fort bien tout ce que vous pouvez ressentir après ce qui s'est passé le 1er Juin.

L'infortune née ce jour-là produit toujours les mêmes effets : elle permet aux médiocres écrasés jusque là par la dimension des projections et l'analyse visionnaire de reprendre "du poil de la bête" et de se croire désormais porteurs d'un projet de substitution.

Secouez-vous l'Ami et surtout ne <u>leur</u> laissez en aucune manière la possibilité de voir sur vous apparaître les stigmates d'un quelconque fléchissement ! C'est l'aîné de 8 ans qui vous parle parce qu'il vous estime beaucoup et sait que le proche avenir vous donnera raison ainsi qu'à ceux qui ont partagé votre défi. Être tenté d'enfermer notre Grand dans un cocon anesthésiant conduirait à lui rogner les ailes et diminuer son envergure qu'il a si grandes pourtant et si mystérieux pour l'autre.

Le Grand est fait pour l'Action et le Mouvement. Le forcer à ralentir la cadence le conduirait à sa perte car on négligerait et écraserait sa spécificité qui fait justement sa différence avec les autres.

Il ne faut pas qu'il oublie qu'il doit faire face à 2 ennemis — ceux de l'extérieur qui gouvernent — ceux de l'intérieur et ce sont ceux-là les plus dangereux pour l'avenir.

Je ne pense pas me tromper et je ne me ausnerai pas de le lui dire en votre présence. Lorsqu'il me recevra. A ce propos, j'ai appelé hier Marianne Hibon pour mon R.V. J'espère que vous avez pu de votre côté la sensibiliser

Redevenez vite le flamboyant Dominique car c'est celui-là qui a ouvert la route de l'Elysée à notre chef! . Dieu vous y aide! Votre fidèle

Robert Bourgi

Appendix n°59: Letter of encouragement, dated July 21, 1997, to Dominique de Villepin on current events in Gabon.

Robert Bourgi

50, BOULEVARD EMILE AUGIER
75116 PARIS
TÉL. 01 45 03 04 28

Lundi 21 Juillet 1997

Courrier devant demeurer confidentiel sauf à l'intention du Président.

Monsieur le Secrétaire général,

J'ai laissé passer 48 heures avant de vous parler de ce dîner chez moi où mes convives et moi vous avons tant regretté. Comme vous le savez ces convives pratiquent leur métier au niveau que vous connaissez et depuis tant d'années, mais ils sont aussi et avant tout de vieux amis et "complices" de tant de choses.

B.V. rentrait de Bxlles où il avait accompagné le Président ; C.A et S.M voient tout le monde et sont sollicités de mille et un cercles ... L'enseignement général est le suivant :

— Le Président, à Bxlles, a fait une impression énorme : retour de flamme ; énergie, disponibilité, combativité et surtout ce regard malicieux qui en disait long sur sa volonté de ne pas rester inerte dans cette cohabitation qui ira se durcissant. Le PM et tous ses ministres en sont conscients et se rendent compte finalement et discutent entre eux et autour d'eux que "le Père CHIRAC" n'est pas aussi simple qu'on le disait... Aujourd'hui il les surprend et les déroute.

— Son jeu actuel, son attitude de vigilance et de contrôle doivent être maintenus pour le plus grand bonheur des Français.

— Son intervention du 14 Juillet est "parfaite".

— Que le Président ne s'y trompe pas : la cohabitation avec Philippe SÉGUIN sera au moins aussi difficile ; P.S.

comité Directorial, a placé des hommes à lui et ceux que l'on a appelés les chiraquiens seront peu à peu "marginalisés puis désossés". Il a commencé à noyauter la machine, à la "nettoyer", et peu à peu, tant à l'intérieur de l'hexagone qu'à l'extérieur, il se rendra maître de la machine.

Dans ses propos discrets, il n'est guère tendre avec le Président. C'en est même "choquant" car, me disent-ils, il oublie que c'est J.C. qui l'a créé et fait. Mais, ajoutent-ils, "son caractère le perdra..."

— Quant à vous, mon cher Dominique, le traitement verbal qui vous est réservé par ceux qui, il y a peu, sollicitaient vos prébendes est inqualifiable. Seulement, me disent-ils, votre silence et votre discrétion, encore plus grands que de coutume, seront, à moyen terme, porteurs d'une régénérescence." Ils sont d'accord sur un point : très grand talent, très forte personnalité, grande ambition (une qualité!) et "vous jouerez un jour prochain dans la cour des très grands"...

— Ils pensent et disent que ce serait une erreur de faire de l'Élysée "l'auberge des recalés et des rejetés" à l'exception de Jacques TOUBON "tombé pour avoir voulu couvrir et protéger des amis politiques qui plombent et J.C. et le Mouvement..." Je suis obligé — par devoir amical — de ne rien altérer de leurs propos et une fraternelle amitié pour J.T. n'y est pour rien.

Je pars ce soir pour Libreville où le Président BONGO souhaiterait me parler "crûment" de la médiation sur le Congo et de ses coulisses. Je serai de retour jeudi matin à Paris et joignable, si besoin en était, à l'Hôtel Méridien de Libreville : 76 61 61 (indicatif 241). Autant vous dire que je refuserai Tout contact avec votre Ambassadeur sur place car, en retour, il ne "paie" jamais en loyauté. Ce monsieur ignore que j'ai sur place depuis toujours et pour longtemps des oreilles bienveillantes.

Croyez-moi, l'ancien le Secrétaire général et cher Dominique, votre fidèle ami. Mon indéfectible attachement au Président que je vous demanderai de féliciter pour sa réconfortante prestation. R.B.

Appendix 60: Personal note from Chirac and handwritten envelope thanking Robert for his notes (October 28, 1997).

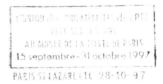 

Monsieur Robert BOURGI
50, Boulevard Emile Augier
75116   PARIS

28 octobre

Jacques Chirac

J'ai bien reçu votre mot du 27 octobre. Merci pour vos analyses & vos informations Toujours Très intéressantes.

Bien cordialement,

Appendix n°61: Letter from Pierre Salinger, dated November 6, 1998, "recruited" as a lobbyist for Gabon for the 1998 presidential elections.

PIERRE SALINGER
INDEPENDENT PUBLIC RELATIONS DIRECTOR
50, RUE DE BOURGOGNE, PARIS, 75007, FRANCE
TEL: 01-4705-3108   FAX: 01-4705-3109

November 6, 1998

Robert Bourgi
25 Avenue 1er de Serbie
75116, Paris

Fax to: 01-4723-3738

Dear Robert

I am sad not to have been sent to Gabon for the election. I would have worked out that election importantly and President Bongo would have won. One of the important things I would have done is work with the young children who represent 50 per cent of the population in Gabon 30 years old or younger. It is now possible that President Bongo will lose the election. It is also possible that it would not be a total democratic election and the United States would continue to look at President Bongo as a dictator.

There is also an important subject. When I was in Gabon in September of 1997, I received $500,000, of which I gave you $150,000 so I had $350,000. This money is now practically gone. Over the the last 12 months, I had to pay Shandwick Public Relations $204,000. I worked for Bongo $10,000 a month, total $120,000. There was also travel to Gabon with Richard Pollock which cost me $16,000 and I had to pay the hotel $2000. I also had to pay phone calls for President Bongo that cost $2300. So it cost $344,300 and I have only $5,700 left. To continue to work for President Bongo in the US and France, I probably need another $200,000.

I am now in Paris and still believe that it would be interesting to work on the election. You should convince President Bongo that if I do not show up, it could be a great mistake.

Best regards,

Pierre

Robert Bourgi
Avocat à la Cour
Docteur en Droit

Paris le 9 Novembre 1998

Mon cher Pierre,

J'ai bien reçu ton fax du 6.11. 1998.
Je suis vraiment peiné et surpris par son contenu.
J'ai cherché à te joindre au n° que tu as laissé
sur ton répondeur: 04 90 92 41 14 mais la
personne (un homme) qui m'a répondu ne te connaissait
pas. Je pars en Côte d'Ivoire demain et je
reviens le Samedi 14 Novembre au matin.
Je t'appellerai d'Abidjan où je résiderai à
l'Hôtel Ivoire (225) 44 10 45.
Pour le mandat en cours du Président BONGO et
jusqu'aux élections du 6.12.1998, le Président a jugé
qu'il n'était pas opportun que tu viennes
au Gabon sans rien ôter à tes éminentes qualités
tant personnelles que professionnelles.
Le billet Air France t'a été offert et seul
le Président BONGO, après les résultats des élections,
décidera s'il sera utile de poursuivre ton action.

25, avenue Pierre 1er de Serbie - 75116 Paris
Tél.: 47 20 45 08 - Fax: 47 23 37 38 Palais C 1444
MEMBRE D'UNE ASSOCIATION AGRÉÉE LE RÈGLEMENT DES HONORAIRES PAR CHÈQUE EST ACCEPTÉ

De ce côté-là, donc, mon cher Pierre, tu n'as pas d'inquiétude à avoir. Considère cette mission comme terminée.

Tu as accompli ta mission, loyalement et fidèlement, même si tu n'as pas pu obtenir une visite à la Maison-Blanche pour cette année —

Le Président BONGO ne t'en tient pas rigueur ; rassure-toi. Il t'apprécie beaucoup.

Mais il faut savoir rester discret et ne pas écrire ce que tu as défensé pour lui, et ce que tu as obtenu de lui. Jamais —

Le Président BONGO est vraiment un grand Monsieur et il ne s'occupe jamais de chiffres. Comme il ne demande jamais de comptes.

Il fait confiance. et tu as sa confiance —

Nous en reparlerons de vive voix.

Amitiés. Fidèlement

Robert

Appendix 63: Letter from Jacques Chirac congratulating Robert Bourgi on his promotion to Commander of the National Order of the Senegalese Lion (September 22, 2000).

LE PRÉSIDENT DE LA RÉPUBLIQUE

Paris, le   22 septembre 2000

Cher Ami,

Au moment où vous allez être élevé au grade de Commandeur dans l'Ordre National du Lion sénégalais, permettez-moi de vous adresser toutes mes félicitations.

Jacques Foccart aurait été très heureux de vous voir décerner cette distinction et je suis sûr que tous vos amis s'en réjouissent.

Bien cordialement,

Jacques CHIRAC

Maître Robert BOURGI
Avocat à la Cour
25 avenue Pierre Ier de Serbie
75116 PARIS

Appendix 64: Letter from Jacques Chirac, January 6, 2001.

Le Président
de la République

LETTRE

Monsieur Robert BOURGI
25. avenue Pierre 1ᵉʳ de Serbie
75116 PARIS

Jacques Chirac

Président de la République

vous adresse

ses remerciements et ses vœux les meilleurs

pour la nouvelle année

Merci, Cher Robert Bourgi,
pour votre amicale attention
à laquelle j'ai été sensible en
ce début d'année.
Je vous adresse également mes
meilleurs vœux pour 2001 et mes
cordiales amitiés,

417

Appendix 65: Letter from Bernard Guillet concerning the association France Orient, now France Orient-Maghreb, and thanking Robert Bourgi for his donation (February 21, 2001).

Association « France – Orient »

جمعية فرنسا الشرق

Paris, le 21 février 2001

Maître, *cher Robert*

Je me réfère à mon courrier du 18 mai 2000 ainsi qu'à notre récente conversation.

Je vous avais écrit dans ma lettre précitée combien nous étions heureux de vous accueillir au sein de notre Association France-Orient, devenue France-Orient-Maghreb.

Je tiens, aujourd'hui, à vous remercier pour votre généreuse contribution de 85.000 francs (quatre vingt cinq mille francs français) qui vous confère le titre de membre bienfaiteur (article 4 de nos statuts).

Je saisis enfin cette occasion pour vous inviter à participer à notre prochaine Assemblée Générale Ordinaire qui sera suivie par une réunion du Conseil de l'Association, le vendredi 2 mars 2001 à 17H30 dans les bureaux de l'Association.

Avec mon bon amical et fidèle souvenir –

Le Président
Bernard GUILLET

Maître Robert BOURGI
Avocat à la Cour
25 avenue Pierre 1er de Serbie
75116 PARIS

50, rue de Berri 75008 PARIS   Tél.: 01.58.50.30.30   Fax : 01.43.59.20.10   E-mail : info@franceorient.org.com
Association loi 1901

"They Know I Know Everything"

confidentiel

Très important

Le 13 Juin 2001

A l'Attention de Dominique de VILLEPIN

———

objet : Visites des Présidents Laurent GBAGBO et Abdoulaye WADE

Les Présidents L.G. et A.W. sont à la veille d'effectuer des visites en France : entre le 18 Juin et le 22 Juin.

La visite d'A.W. est une visite officielle.
La visite de L.G. est une visite privée, effectuée à l'invitation de son homologue français.

Jacques CHIRAC va s doit trouver là une occasion de confirmer et de préserver d'abord sa très grande connaissance de l'Afrique et des Africains et ensuite sa prééminence institutionnelle, parfois contestée, sur l'autre pôle de l'Exécutif.

La rencontre CHIRAC-GBAGBO ayant lieu le 18 Juin et celle du Président français avec A.WADE le 20 Juin, c'est par la première rencontre que j'aborderai ma réflexion.

(A) La rencontre CHIRAC-GBAGBO (18 Juin à 13 h)

J'accorderai, paradoxalement, un intérêt particulier & privilégié à la rencontre avec le Président L.G. D'abord, elle a été souhaitée par le Président ivoirien qui m'avait chargé de véhiculer ce souhait ; ensuite, parce que L.G, offrant historique du Président HOUPHOUËT-BOIGNY fait partie de l'Internationale Socialiste et apparaît, à ce titre, comme le compagnon de route des dirigeants socialistes français.

Je puis assurer qu'il en est tout à fait autrement

Je n'ai pas manqué de vous dire, à diverses reprises, combien L.G. avait été déçu par ses Amis de la gauche française auxquels il reproche de les avoir laissés, lui et son Gouvernement, "prisonniers" des Institutions internationales tant politiques que financières : Banque Mondiale, FMI, Commission de Bruxelles.

A l'appui de sa démonstration, à moi faite, il a relaté — afin de vous la relater — un entretien téléphonique assez tendu entre lui et Lionel JOSPIN il y a environ 5 semaines.

Au "Camarade Laurent" lancé par L.J. au début de l'entretien, L.G. a répondu : "... Je pense, cher Ami, que les socialistes français n'ont jamais compris le sens réel de ces termes camarade et socialisme; le socialisme français n'a rien à voir avec le socialisme à l'africaine; J'envoie à Paris une délégation conduite par mon premier Ministre et 3 ministres dont un Ministre d'État et vous ne trouvez rien de mieux que de la faire recevoir au niveau gouvernemental par un simple Secrétaire d'État au Commerce Extérieur. Alors que, dans le même temps, cette délégation était reçue à l'Elysée, avec des égards particuliers, et s'entretenait avec le Président de la République lui-même et le Secrétaire général de l'Elysée. En outre, je sais, que OUATTARA a des contacts et des soutiens au sein même de ton gouvernement : Fabius,..."

Oui, L.G. est un homme de gauche, un homme de progrès mais il a une fragilité; sans doute une relative faiblesse en politique, c'est que c'est un homme très sensible et très affectif. Les propos qu'il me tint ce jour-là à Abidjan, dans son salon particulier, à Cocody, lui venaient droit du cœur. C'est ce jour-là, qu'il me dit:

" Robert, je suis las et fatigué. J'ai besoin de réconfort et d'un soutien. Dis à CHIRAC et à Dominique de m'inviter sous quelque forme que ce soit mais de préférence à titre personnel et privé. Je veux faire une 1ère visite en France étant Président de la République de Côte d'Ivoire, sur invitation formelle de Jacques CHIRAC. Nous sommes, toi et moi, de vieux amis. En prison, quand HOUPHOUËT et OUATTARA m'y avaient jeté avec ma femme, mon fils et ma fille, tu as été parmi les rares à te manifester. Je souhaite que CHIRAC m'invite; qu'il ait pour moi des égards particuliers. J'en ai besoin ; la Côte d'Ivoire en a besoin ; elle traverse des moments difficiles, CHIRAC aime ce Pays et en souvenir d'HOUPHOUËT qu'il a aimé comme un Père, il se doit de le faire. Guy LABERTIT et ses amis passent leur temps à Abidjan; ils me saoûlent de paroles et de promesses; et je ne vois rien. Redis à Dominique et à CHIRAC mon admiration et pour le Général de GAULLE et pour CHIRAC lui-même. Ne l'ai-je pas dit à Dominique quand il a accepté de me rencontrer alors que je n'étais que Chef de Parti?... Cette faveur je ne l'oublierai jamais..."

421

L. G. est un Bété. C'est une ethnie de gens coriaces, au caractère difficile et entier. L.G. n'oublie pas; il n'oublie rien.

Son entourage et lui-même sont conscients de l'opportunité exceptionnelle qui s'offre à eux.

Il nous faut aussi marquer l'événement: à l'Élysée, le 18 Juin, faisons en sorte que L.G. constate qu'il a un Ami à l'Élysée et que ce dernier a pour lui des égards particuliers.

L.G. a une formation d'historien. Il connaît la symbolique historique. Il sait la dimension de la date du 18 Juin surtout quand le Président siégeant à l'Élysée est l'héritier naturel du Général de GAULLE.

L.G. aura avec lui pour relater et filmer l'événement beaucoup de journalistes et cameramen ivoiriens et africains. Mobilisez aussi ceux qui sont rattachés à la presse présidentielle française.

Jacques CHIRAC doit saisir l'occasion pour montrer que son amitié, son estime et son affection ne vont pas seulement aux dinosaures de la classe politique africaine.

Laurent G. est un homme chaleureux et plaisant malgré les marques indélébiles de l'exil et de la prison. Il appréciera fortement les effusions visibles, les mains posées sur l'épaule et les sourires éclatants; en somme, la "griffe CHIRAC". Tout sera expédié en France et en Afrique. Au moment où Lionel JOSPIN, à PRETORIA, affront pour nos amis francophones, affirme qu'il faut changer fondamentalement les données

- de la politique africaine, à Jacques CHIRAC de montrer que l'élargissement de la politique africaine n'exclue pas le maintien de liens historiques et traditionnels avec nos Amis francophones.

À certaines questions qui pourraient lui être posées sur le perron de l'Elysée, L.G. apportera certaines réponses qui conforteront la primauté de J. CHIRAC et son inégalable expérience en matière africaine.

Je me suis occupé de tout cela avec L.G.

L.G. m'a dit avoir besoin que J. CHIRAC

— lui offre des milliers de livres scolaires et littéraires destinés aux jeunes Ivoiriens dépourvus de ces outils de culture. Nous savons que tous les ans des milliers et des milliers de ces ouvrages vont au pilon. Sauvons les au profit d'enfants qui acquerront ainsi notre culture française.

— que Madame CHIRAC s'intéresse à des œuvres sociales en Côte d'Ivoire. Après Ouagadougou et LIBREVILLE, pourquoi ne pas offrir à Laurent G. l'occasion d'annoncer quelque chose dans ce domaine sur le perron de l'Elysée?

— que J.C. s'investisse personnellement dans les négociations difficiles de la Côte d'Ivoire avec les Institutions financières internationales.

— que J.C. lui ménage personnellement un entretien avec son Ami Georges W. BUSH. L.G. sait que le Président CHIRAC est lié à la famille BUSH.

Le 20 Juin, le Président J. CHIRAC reçoit le Président A. WADE

⒝ La rencontre avec A. WADE (20 Juin 13 heures).

Encore un Président, certes septuagénaire, mais "structurellement" partie intégrante de la nouvelle génération des dirigeants africains. Encore un Président qui a connu l'éloignement du Pays et la prison sans compter les brimades et les humiliations qu'on lui a fait connaître et subir. Qu'attend A. WADE du Président français ? Tout est dans ce qu'il m'a dit le Président WADE lors de notre dernier entretien à Dakar le 8 Mai au soir :

"..... Robert, c'est ton GORGUI qui te parle. (Gorgui = le Vieux). Il faut dire à CHIRAC et à Villepin que je suis un Ami ; que je veux être leur Ami ; que je suis un libéral, que j'admire de GAULLE et le Gaullisme ; que je ne veux pas être réduit à la simple amitié avec Madelin ; que je suis disposé, si on me le demande, à faire pression sur Madelin et BAYROU afin de donner toutes les chances à CHIRAC pour 2002 ; je peux le faire très discrètement à l'Élysée même. Il faut que CHIRAC repasse ; c'est dans notre intérêt à tous. Je veux que Dominique de Villepin rencontre mon collaborateur le plus direct, celui qui a toute ma confiance,

et qui représente le Sénégal de demain : Idrissa SECK.
(Ministre d'État, S.G. de la Présidence de la République).

Dis à CHIRAC et à VILLEPIN que je tiens, entre autres, à la réhabilitation du Pont FAIDHERBE à St Louis du Sénégal (coût 40 MF) ; qu'ils me trouvent un Don, une aide, ou des mécènes. C'est un ouvrage de la colonisation et le Pont FAIDHERBE est quelque chose de fort dans le cœur des Sénégalais et des Français.

"Je veux que CHIRAC défende un Plan OMEGA contre le Plan Thabo MBEKI… je ne suis pas un homme démonstratif, tu le sais, mais je suis sensible aux marques d'amitié que l'on peut avoir pour moi…"

Ai-je besoin de vous dire que cette conversation a eu pour langue, en très-grande partie, le Ouolof, que je parle, comme vous le savez, à la perfection.

Il y a là, pour notre Président, en ces deux occasions successives, une occasion de prouver, si besoin en était encore, que c'est à l'Élysée que se trouve le seul grand Africain français

ASSOCIATION FRANCE ORIENT - MAGHREB

جمعيـة فرنسـا المشـرق والمغرب العربي

Paris, le Jeudi 20 Décembre 2001

Monsieur et cher Robert,

Comme vous le savez, la dernière Assemblée Générale de notre Association s'est tenue, le 19 Mars 2001, dans nos locaux. Le Compte rendu de cette réunion vous a été adressé, en date du 23 Mars 2001. C'est ainsi que nous vous avons rendu compte des perquisitions dont nos locaux avaient fait l'objet et du harcèlement des juges Philippe COURROYE et Isabelle PREVOST-DEPREZ à l'égard de toutes les associations hébergées 50 rue de BERRI ainsi que de la permanence du député au Parlement européen, Monsieur Jean Charles MARCHIANI.

Hélas, la situation ne s'est pas améliorée au printemps de l'année qui s'achève puisque j'ai été mis en examen, le 12 Avril, puis soumis à un contrôle judiciaire très strict qui m'empêche notamment de me

./..

50, rue de Berri 75008 PARIS Tél. : 01.58.56.36.36 Fax : 01.43.59.26.16

٥٠، شارع دي بري ٧٥٠٠٨ باريس ـ فرنسا هاتف : ٣٦٣٦،٥٦،٥٨،٠١ ـ فاكس : ٢٦١٦،٥٩،٤٣،٠١

2/

rendre dans les locaux de la rue de Berri et de rencontrer un certain nombre de personnes (dont M. Jean Charles MARCHIANI, Vice Président, également mis en examen, Madame Saline MOUTIER, Trésorière qui a présenté sa démission et Madame Marie Danièle FAURE, elle même mise en examen et dans l'incapacité de rencontrer M. Jean Charles MARCHIANI).

Je suis persuadé que vous avez du penser que de tels problèmes allaient avoir raison de notre Association. S'il est exact que la gestion "à distance" de France Orient Maghreb a été particulièrement compliquée, nous sommes néanmoins parvenus à faire face à toutes les échéances, financières en tout premier lieu.

L'essentiel ayant été sauvegardé, il nous reste à redéfinir la stratégie de l'Association et de l'adapter aux circonstances du moment. C'est pourquoi j'ai l'honneur de vous convier à l'Assemblée Générale de notre Association qui se tiendra, le Jeudi 10 Janvier 2002 chez Monsieur Hervé BENAROUM, 96-98 rue de MONTREUIL, Paris 11ème, à 5 minutes de la place /..

427

⁵/ de la Nation.

L'ordre du jour de l'Assemblée Générale portera sur les points suivants:

1/ maintien de la domiciliation de l'Association France Orient Maghreb 50 rue de Bercy, Paris 8ème et sous location des locaux en partie ou en quasi totalité.

2/ fixation du montant de la cotisation 2002 soit 200 € ou 1312 FF.

3/ rapport du Président concernant le fonctionnement de l'Association (rapport moral et rapport financier)

4/ élections aux postes éventuellement vacants au sein du bureau de l'Association -

5/ calendrier des activités pour l'année 2002 et questions diverses.

Je rappelle que vous ne pourrez prendre part à l'Assemblée Générale (y compris aux votes) que dans la mesure où vous aurez réglé votre cotisation
./..

4

pour l'année 2001 soit 1000 FF ou 153 €.
Dans le cas où vous ne pourriez pas participer
à cette Assemblée Générale (absence ou impossibilité
du fait de l'instruction menée par le juge COURROYE)
je vous invite à me retourner votre procuration
par l'intermédiaire du bulletin ci-joint —

Enfin, dans l'hypothèse où vous ne souhaiteriez
plus faire partie de l'Association, je vous serais
reconnaissant de bien vouloir me retourner une
lettre dans ce sens —

Dans l'attente de vous revoir ou de vous lire,
Veuillez recevoir, Monsieur et cher Robert, l'assurance
de mon bien amical souvenir.

Bernard Guillet

BERNARD GUILLET

(15) à l'intérieur d'un sac énorme, 3 millions de Dollars (enveloppés dans une grande affiche Austin-Mini) - Entrée par l'avenue de Marigny.

2002

Vendredi 4 Janvier 19h = Villepin Elysée.
Jeudi 10 Janvier 18h45 = Elysée . Villepin.
Vendredi 11 Janvier 12h30 = avec Pascaline Bongo. Villepin. Chirac et
Jeudi 24 Janvier 19h = Elysée. Villepin. Paris
Jeudi 31 Janvier 12h30 = Villepin Elysée
Mercredi 6 Février = 20h . Elysée : Villepin.

Le Président BONGO arrive à Paris le 7 Février 2002 et doit diner à l'Elysée le Vendredi 8 Février 2002 avec les Présidents BIYA (Cameroun) et COMPAORÉ (Gabon)

C'est vraisemblablement ce jour-là à 14 heures 45 qui avec un émissaire gabonais (protection rapprochée) je porte 2 sacs (3 millions de dollars) dans le bureau de Villepin où se trouvent déjà Villepin, Pascaline BONGO, le Président CHIRAC et BONGO. Sacs posés derrière la canapé situé à côté du bureau de Villepin. Et moi

16) sortons ("j'ai eu honte réellement
pour mon pays")

Jeudi 7 Mars 18h30   Villefin.

Lundi 18 Mars 17h30   Villefin

Jeudi 4 Avril 12h30   Villefin
Mercredi 10 Avril 19h30   Villefin avec

Karim WADE qui remet à Villefin une
mallette contenant 1 million de dollars.
(Voiture diplomatique).

Vendredi 19 Avril 19h30 . Villefin (ou
17h30 (changement de dernière minute.

Mardi 23 Avril 17h30   Villefin.

Mercredi 24 Avril 18h45   c/o Villefin (avec

Denis Tillinac, F. Szpiner, Valérie Terranova -
Ils souhaitaient faire partie du gouvernement.
Échec des 3

Samedi 27 Avril 18h   Villefin.   (ou
                                      Jeudi 2 Mai
                                         18h30

Jeudi 2 Mai 18h30   Villefin

(17) Jeudi 9 Mai 19h45 = Villepin au

Quai D'ORSAY

Villepin, MAE, je ne remettrai plus les pieds à l'Élysée.

Vendredi 24 Mai 20h = Villepin au Quai d'O.

Samedi 1er Juin 15h45 c/o Villepin avec Pascaline BONGO et Paul TOUNGUI; les 2 Gabonais et Villepin partent ensuite à l'Élysée où ils sont reçus à 16h15

Vendredi 7 Juin 20h = Villepin

Dimanche 21 Juillet (12h) à Ouaga, j'assiste au tête à tête entre D. de V. et le Président COMPAORÉ

Mardi 1er Octobre 19h15 = D. de Villepin.

Mardi 5 Novembre 19h30 = D. de Villepin avec M. Salif DIALLO (Ministre agriculture du Burkina-Faso.

Mercredi 27 Novembre (ABIDJAN) Villepin à Abidjan 12h, j'assiste au tête à tête GBAGBO - Villepin

(18) Lundi 16 Décembre 10h30 = avec Pascaline
BONGO chez Villepin.

(2003)

le Mardi 7 Janvier à 19h30 = Salif
Diallo, Alassane Ouattara et moi chez Villepin
Lundi 13 Janvier à 19h30 Alassane Ouattara
et moi chez Villepin.

Mercredi 15 Janvier à 21 heures
moi c/o P. A. WILTZER : Ministre délégué à la Coopération

Mardi 21 Janvier 18h30 Salif et moi c/o D. de Villepin
Diallo

Mercredi 22 Janvier 19h15 = Salif et moi c/o Villepin
Diallo

Vendredi 24 Janvier 8 heures c/o Villepin, avec
Salif Diallo et les 3 mouvements rebelles ivoiriens
Vendredi 24 Janvier à 18 heures avec Blaise [Pdt]
COMPAORÉ chez Villepin.
Vendredi 24 Janvier 19 heures avec Gbagbo, [Pdt] BEDIE [Pdt],
Soro et Ouattara chez Villepin
Samedi 25 Janvier 20h30 = Villepin

(19) Samedi 1er Février 19h = Villepin

Samedi 8 Février 12h30   Villepin

Samedi 15 Février à 12h30   avec le Ministre

Salif Diallo chez Villepin.

Vendredi 28 Février 8h   petit déjeuner avec

Villepin.

Jeudi 13 Mars à 15h   avec P.A. WILTZER

Ministre délégué à la Coopération.

Le 4 Mai au soir à 23h25, je décolle pour Libreville où je retrouve Pascal DROUHAUD et Virginie Aubin pour préparer le séjour de JUPPÉ au GABON. Puis au Sénégal.

Le Mardi 6 Mai, avec JUPPÉ au déjeuner offert par le Président BONGO. Le Mercredi 7 Mai 9 heures, nous décollons tous de Libreville pour DAKAR à bord d'un avion affrété par Karim WADE présent à bord avec Juppé et toute sa délégation

434

"They Know I Know Everything"

(20) Le Mercredi 7 Mai à 18h, audience du Président A. Wade. et à 20 heures, dîner par le Président Wade en l'honneur de JUPPÉ.

Le Jeudi 8 Mai à 11heures au Camp Dial Diop, sur MON intervention auprès du Pdt WADE, Alain JUPPÉ préside une prise d'armes ; c'est la Victoire de 1945. Suis présent avec Karim Wade — Je repars le soir même à 23h sur Paris (AIR FRANCE).

Le Vendredi 16 Mai à 19heures chez Villepin avec le Ministre Salif Diallo

Le Mardi 27 Mai à 17h30 Villepin.

Dimanche 22 Juin 19h Villepin

Mardi 22 Juillet à 19h45 Villepin avec un émissaire burkinabé = énorme buste de l'Empereur (galerie de Souzy - Voir facture) (livré par son fils)

(21) Mercredi 10 Septembre 19h30   Villefin.

Lundi 6 Octobre 19h30 = Villefin

Vendredi 17 Octobre 19h = Villefin

Jeudi 13 Novembre 19h30   Villefin

Vendredi 21 Novembre 20h   avec
Villefin c/o le Président BONGO - Laurent
GBAGBO (Pdt RCI) est au dîner XXX

Lundi 8 Décembre 19h30   Villefin

Vendredi 19 Décembre 19h   Villefin

2004

Vendredi 21 Janvier 19h45 Villefin

Mercredi 28 Janvier 12h30   Villefin

Dimanche 1er Février à 19 h = avec Villefin
c/o le Président GBAGBO
Mercredi 3 Mars XXXX = 19h = Villefin avec J.D
                       OKEMBA (500.000 euros)
Vendredi 12 Mars 12h45 Villefin - XXX

(22) Jeudi 25 Mars 19h   Villepin

Samedi 10 Avril · 19h = |Beauvau|

VILLEPIN

Samedi 24 Avril à 19h~~RS~~   avec le

Président COMPAORÉ (descendu au Bristol) chez

Villepin

Samedi 5 Juin 19h   Villepin

Samedi 26 Juin 19h avec Pascaline BONGo

chez Villepin

Dimanche 4 Juillet 19h Villepin

Dimanche 19 Septembre 19h 30 = Villepin

Dimanche 10 Octobre 19h30 = Avec J.M.ARZE

(Ambassadeur du Gabon) chez Villepin =

Jeudi 21 Octobre à 20h   avec Manuel

Vicente (Angola. Sonangol) chez Villepin

Jeudi 28 Octobre 13h   O.BONGo déjeune

chez JCHIRAC

Vendredi 29 Octobre à 13h   Le Président BONGo X
et sa fille Pascaline X
et moi déjeunons C/o Villepin. Le Président BONGo X
laisse une mallette 1 million euros

(23) Mardi 2 Novembre 13h   D. Villepin déjeune
c/o le Président BONGO au Meurice - Suis présent.

X   Mercredi 17 Novembre 13h   X X X
X   les Présidents A. Wade et OBiang Nguema
X   déjeunent à Beauvau - Suis présent; Karim
X   aussi; après le déjeuner ds ls appartements du
    Ministre, ls Présidents rejoignent le Ministre dans
    son bureau : le Président OBiang. remet
    une mallette d'1 million d'euros à Villepin

    Dimanche 28 Novembre 19h30   Villepin

    Jeudi 30 Décembre 18h30   Villepin

    ┌─────────────────┐
    │   2005   │
    └─────────────────┘

    Mercredi 26 Janvier 19h45 c/o Villepin
    avec J Dominique OKEMBA (Congo)
    (500.000 Euros)

    Dimanche 6 Mars 19h45 = Villepin
    Jeudi 17 Mars 22h   avec Villepin c/o
    le Pdt BONGO (dîner à La Sablière)
    Jeudi 24 Mars 20 h   avec c/o Villepin avec
            l'Ambassadeur J.M. ADZE (1 million d'euros)

438

(24)

Vendredi 22 Avril 13h = le Président O. Bongo, sa fille Pascaline et moi déjeunons chez Villepin

Mardi 26 Avril 18h30 Villepin

Samedi 14 Mai 19h30 . Villepin

Jeudi 26 Mai 20h avec Pascaline Bongo chez Villepin.

Dimanche 12 Juin 18h30 Villepin

à MATIGNON (il prononce le Mercredi 8 Juin à 15h son discours de politique générale)

Mercredi 22 Juin à 20h15 Villepin c/o le Président Bongo au Meurice ; j'assiste à l'entretien

le Jeudi 23 Juin le Président Bongo et Madame Bongo, Pascaline Bongo, moi-même déjeunons à Matignon - Mme de Villepin est présent. Au café, le garde des Sceaux, Pascal Clément vient saluer le Pdt Bongo

(25) Lundi 27 Juin à 20h30, avec Desidério Costa
(Ministre angolais du Pétrole) c/o Villepin

Mardi 19 Juillet 20h Villepin

Lundi 5 Septembre 19h45 Villepin

Samedi 10 Septembre 16h, le Président
A. Wade et Karim, chez ~~le Président~~ Villepin.
J'assiste à l'entretien.
Samedi 10 Septembre à 19h30 avec
Pascaline BONGO à Matignon, c/o Villepin.
L'Ambassadeur J.M. ABBE nous rejoint
à 19h heures essoufflé et remet à
Villepin une mallette contenant 1,5
million de d'euros - (un million et demi
d'euros)
La remise de fonds s'est passée en fait
le Samedi 24 Septembre à 18 heures
(le scénario tel décrit ci-dessus)

2° Clash Villepin - BOURG

le Lundi 10 Octobre à 19 h 45 au
Pavillon de musique. Nadine IZARD
était venue me chercher à Monceau-fleurs
Bd des Invalides). (Finie la vache à lait
Villepin sera la diète)

Et le Vendredi 14 Octobre à 19 h
au Bristol je rejoins le 1er Cercle
le Nicolas Sarkozy (Ministre de l'Intérieur)

Mes relations avec Villepin
ne seront pas finies car

le Samedi 22 Octobre je vois
le Président BONGO à la Sablière
avant un grand diner à l'Hôtel Atlantique

27) Après mon clash avec Villepin au
Pavillon de Musique à Matignon,
le Président BONGO, informé par mes
soins, me demande de "descendre" le
voir — Je prends l'avion le vol A.F du
Vendredi 21 Octobre à 23h15. pour Libreville
(siège 2E).

Le Président BONGO veut convaincre
le Premier Ministre de renoncer à
ses ambitions présidentielles et de
se ranger derrière Nicolas SARKOZY
(déjeuner à Beautour le 29 Octobre à 13h)
(2004)

Il ne dit plus rien sur
Villepin mais garder le contact. Accepte
de le voir — Villepin n'arrêtait pas
de me relancer directement. ou via Nadine

28) Je vois longuement le Pdt BONGO le Dimanche 23 Octobre à 16 h à la Sphère. Je repars sur Paris le Lundi 24 Octobre à 9 h 15.

J'accepte de revoir Villepin le Vendredi 18 Novembre à 20 h 15

Le Président SASSOU Nguesso (Congo Brazza) veut lui aussi convaincre Villepin de se ranger derrière M. SARKOZY. Il me demande d'aller le voir. Je pars à Brazzaville le Mercredi 7 Décembre. Je vois le Pdt Sassou Nguesso le Jeudi 8 Décembre à 12 h et je déjeune avec lui en tête à tête. De Brazzaville, je pars le Vendredi 9 Décembre à 8 h pour Libreville par vol spécial. Ce jour là, je vois le Président BONGO à 11 heures, et le soir même (à 16 h) je le quitte pour Abidjan.

㉙ le Samedi 10 décembre au matin
(7h30) Je partais pour Paris –

Dimanche 18 Décembre 19h30   avec

Pascaline BONGO chez Villepin.

2006

Lundi 23 Janvier 19h= Voeux Premier Cercle à
Nicolas SARKOZY

Mardi 7 Février . 19h Villepin à Matignon
Jeudi 9 Février 13h . Villepin déjeune c/o le
Président BONGO au Meurice (j'suis présent)

Mercredi 1er Mars 13h45 Villepin reçoit le
Président Sassou NGUESSO (Congo Brazza) à déjeuner.
Je viens au Dessert. Convaincre Villepin
de se ranger derrière SARKOZY
Dimanche 5 Mars 20h = avec J. DOKEMBA
(Conseiller Spécial de Sassou Nguesso) à Matignon . Convaincre
Villepin de rejoindre
N. Sarkozy

"They Know I Know Everything"

(30) Vendredi 17 Mars 16h30 à Beauvau
avec Nicolas SARKOZY en présence de C.Guéant.
Jeudi 6 Avril 19h30 avec Villepin
à Matignon: "rejoignez N. SARKOZY".
Mercredi 19 Avril 18h45 — Nicolas SARKOZY
à Beauvau (C. Guéant présent)
Mardi 23 Mai 12h30 = Nicolas SARKOZY
à Beauvau (. C. Guéant, présent)
Mercredi 24 Mai 19h30 C/o le Président
Wade (Paris) avec N. Sarkozy et C. Guéant.
Mercredi 7 Juin 18h30 = C/o le Président
BONGO (3 rue Josue 16e) avec N. SARKOZY
Vendredi 21 Juillet 13h30 Déjeuner à
Matignon
du Président Sassou Nguesso et Ambassadeur H. LOPES
j'assiste : " Dominique, rejoignez Nicolas"
Vendredi 21 Juillet 10h : C.Guéant à
Beauvau.
Mardi 25 Juillet 16h30 N. Sarkozy et Claude
Guéant.

(31*) Vendredi 28 juillet 8h30. Nicolas SARKOZY

Lundi 21 Août 12h à Matignon avec l'Ambassadeur du Gabon; message du Pdt BONGO:" Dominique, rejoignez N.Sarkozy"

Jeudi 31 Août Villepin C/o BONGO (Paris) (10 heures) Même objectif suis présent.

31 Août 18h Nicolas Sarkozy C/o Pdt BONGO (suis présent) Même objectif.

Vendredi 22 Septembre 18h. Nicolas SARKOZ C/o Pdt BONGO (Paris); Tjs m objectif. Suis présent

Mercredi 11 Octobre 8h30 = le Président Sassou Nguesso prend son p'tit déjeuner à Matignon (suis présent; tjs m objectif)

Jeudi 9 Novembre N.Sarkozy c/o le Président BONGO (Paris). Suis présent. Même objectif.

Mardi 19 Décembre 18h30 = pot offert par Nicolas Sarkozy (Bristol)

2007

Lundi 22 Janvier 2007 18h15 = Villepin à Matignon

Lundi 29 Janvier 2007 . Claude GUÉANT . (rue d'Enghien 18)
(10h)

Mercredi 31 Janvier 18h30   Premier Cercle ; rue d'Enghien 18

Mardi 6 Février 19h30   Villepin (Matignon)

Vendredi 9 Février 10h = N. Sarkozy et Claude Guéant

Mercredi 14 Février 18h45   Nicolas Sarkozy

Vendredi 9 Mars 18h   Claude Guéant

Mercredi 14 Mars 13h30   Déjeuner à Matignon avec
le Président Gasson.

Même objectif

Vendredi 16 Mars   16h= Claude Guéant

Lundi 19 Mars 12h   Nicolas Sarkozy et Claude Guéant
c/o le Pdt Bongo ; Jean Frère
(Paris)

Vendredi 6 Avril 11h15   Nicolas Sarkozy avec J. M. Aze

Mercredi 16 Mai 11h
Nicolas SARKOZY prête serment

Je suis son invité. Carré de famille .

33 — Dimanche 20 Mai 19h = C. Guéant à l'Elysée

Samedi 9 Juin ; reporté au 13 à 14h30

R.V. avec le Président N. SARKOZY

Les amis de Jacques Foccart

Levallois, le 12 février 2002

Le Délégué Général

Monsieur BOURGI
Robert
50 Boulevard Emile Augier
75116 PARIS

Nos Réf : ITD/VP

Monsieur

Nous avions bien reçu, en son temps, votre adhésion et nous vous en remercions. J'ai le plaisir de vous adresser votre carte d'adhérent et le cas échéant vos cartes correspondant à vos années de renouvellement.

La volonté de tous ceux qui ont bien connu Jacques Foccart à divers moments de sa vie est de lui rendre hommage. C'est notre objectif.

Je vous encourage à faire connaître autour de vous notre association au service de la France.

Dans un premier temps, nous vous avions demandé de faire adhérer tous ceux qui ont connu et apprécié Jacques Foccart.

Maintenant nous ouvrons l'association à tous ceux qui se reconnaissent dans les principes défendus par Jacques Foccart.

Veuillez agréer l'expression de mes salutations distinguées.

Annexe n°70 : Note de sensibilisation sur la personnalité d'Alain Belais, secrétaire général de la mairie de Nice, en quête de sa nomination au cabinet de Pierre-André Wiltzer, ministre délégué à la Coopération et à la Francophonie (March 2002).

NOTE

Le mercredi 3 juin, M. Alain **BELAIS**, chef de cabinet du ministre de la coopération et de la francophonie M. Pierre-André **WILTZER**, a reçu au ministère pour un petit déjeuner M. Christian **ESTROSI**, député des Alpes-Maritimes. Loin de se borner à des « retrouvailles niçoises », M. **BELAIS** ayant occupé jusque-là les fonctions de secrétaire général de la mairie de Nice, cette rencontre pourrait avoir porté sur l'éventualité d'une nomination prochaine au cabinet de M. **WILTZER** de M. Christian **GAMBOTTI** qui est connu pour être très proche de M. **ESTROSI** au point d'être considéré couramment comme un de ses « hommes de main ».

Si tel devait être le cas, la nomination de M. **GAMBOTTI** n'irait pas sans soulever un problème délicat. En effet, pour n'être pas connu à ce jour des services des R.G, l'intéressé n'en est pas moins réputé pour son affairisme multiforme, non seulement dans la région niçoise au regard de ses connexions supposées avec le « milieu » mais également à Paris où certaines de ses activités commerciales (éditoriales notamment) semblent se développer en relation plus ou moins directe avec le R.P.R. Enfin, M. **GAMBOTTI** passe, selon certaines sources, pour être la « tête de pont » de certains intérêts locaux niçois qui envisageraient désormais de pousser leurs activités dans certains pays africains, à l'abri d'une protection officielle au sein même du cabinet de la coopération.

Ce type d'interférence n'est guère souhaitable et il est en conséquence nécessaire de le prévenir. Il ne saurait être admis qu'un dérapage éventuel en ce domaine, si faible soit-il, vienne contrarier la visibilité de la politique africaine mise en œuvre par le ministre des Affaires étrangères et soit susceptible de mettre en cause la probité des membres d'un cabinet sur lequel il exerce sa tutelle.

Appendix n°71: Mandate from the State of Côte d'Ivoire given to Robert Bourgi to defend himself in the Noël Dubus case (April 18, 2002).

AMBASSADE DE CÔTE D'IVOIRE
EN FRANCE
——
102, AVENUE RAYMOND POINCARE
75116 PARIS

PARIS, LE

18 avril 2002

A
Monsieur le Juge Jean-Paul ALBERT,
Vice-Doyen
Pôle Financier du Parquet de
Paris

Monsieur le Vice-Doyen,

J'ai l'honneur de vous informer que dans l'affaire Noël DUBUS, j'ai commis Me Robert BOURGI pour défendre les intérêts de l'Etat ivoirien.

Veuillez agréer, Monsieur le Vice-Doyen, l'expression de ma très haute considération.

KOUDOU Kessié Raymond
Ambassadeur

451

COMMMUNIQUÉ DE PRESSE

URGENT POUR DIFFUSION IMMÉDIATE

L'Ambassade de Côte d'Ivoire engage des poursuites contre un ressortissant français

Paris, le 18 avril 2002 – Le samedi 13 avril 2002, un certain Noël DUBUS, qui se prénommerait également Seeger SAINT-JOHN, a été interpellé par la section économique et financière de la police judiciaire de Paris, sur plainte de l'Ambassadeur de Côte d'Ivoire en France, M. KOUDOU Kessié Raymond.

L'individu, de nationalité française, âgé d'une trentaine d'années, affirmait détenir des informations sensibles touchant à la sécurité et à la sûreté de l'Etat de Côte d'Ivoire – renseignements qu'il a tenté de monnayer auprès des autorités ivoiriennes tant à Paris qu'à Abidjan.

Par ailleurs, muni de fausses garanties, M. Noël DUBUS s'est présenté à des entreprises françaises comme un mandant agissant au nom et pour le compte de la Présidence de la République de Côte d'Ivoire afin de superviser ou signer des contrats de prestation d'audit, de sécurité et de protection des officiels ivoiriens.

M. Noël DUBUS a été déféré le lundi 15 avril 2002 devant la juge d'instruction de la section financière du Parquet de Paris, Mme DELAMOTTE-COLIN. Il a été mis en examen pour les chefs d'accusation de « tentative d'extorsion de fonds, menaces, appels malveillants et vol », puis placé en détention par le juge des libertés et des détentions mardi soir. L'affaire est instruite par le juge Jean-Paul ALBERT, du Pôle financier du Parquet de Paris.

L'Ambassadeur de Côte d'Ivoire en France, M. KOUDOU Kessié Raymond, a désigné Maître Robert BOURGI, Avocat au Barreau de Paris, pour défendre les intérêts de l'État ivoirien. Il renouvelle ses sincères remerciements aux autorités, à la police et à la justise françaises pour leur bienveillante attention dans le traitement de ce dossier.

Les autorités nationales ivoiriennes et leur représentant légal en France tiennent à affirmer que leur vigilance continuera d'être exercée avec la plus grande acuité à l'égard des individus qui pourraient à l'avenir se réclamer d'un quelconque mandat à eux confié par l'État de Côte d'Ivoire.

Contact presse :

Monsieur Toussaint ALAIN
Conseiller chargé de la Communication,
Ambassade de Côte d'Ivoire en France
06 67 90 76 45 – Fax : 01 47 78 11 30
E-mail : altoussaint@hotmail.com

Appendix 73: Invoice from Galerie de Souzy to the Burkina Faso Presidency for the bust of Napoleon presented to Dominique de Villepin (May 29, 2002).

PARIS le 29/05/2002

FACTURE:

Vendu ce jour à: **Monsieur le Président de la République du Burkina-Faso**
OUAGADOUGOU
BURKINA-FASO

La pièce ci-dessous désignée:

Une sculpture napoléonienne d'époque XIX° Siècle.

Prix de vente: **75 000 Euro T.T.C.**

En votre règlement par virement bancaire.
R.I.B. joint.

Galerie de SOUZY
98 Faubourg Saint-Honoré - 75008 PARIS
Tél. : 01 42 65 90 96 / 27 33
Fax : 01 42 65 90 97
www.desouzy.com - info@desouzy.com
R.C.S. n° 438785453000012

CIC Banque SNVB   **Relevé d'Identité Bancaire**

CADRE RÉSERVÉ AU DESTINATAIRE DU RELEVÉ.

références	domiciliation		Titulaire du compte
	SNVB PARIS HAUSSMANN		

code banque	code guichet	n° de compte	clé	
30087	00081	0176998143M	01	DE SOUZY SARL

International Bank Account Number (IBAN)

FR81	3008	7000	8101	7499	8143	M01	98 RUE DU FG ST HONORE

Bank Identifier Code (BIC)

CMCIFR2Y   75008 PARIS

Pierre & Pierre-Edouard de SOUZY, Antiquaires Place Beauvau - 98, rue du Faubourg Saint-Honore - 75008 PARIS
Tél: + 33 1 42 65 27 33 / 90 96 - **Fax:** + 33 1 42 65 90 97 - **Site Internet:** www.desouzy.com - **Email:** info@desouzy.com
Sarl au capital de 7 625 euro - RCS Paris B 438785453 - TVA Intracommunautaire FR 23438785453

Appendix 74: Message from Alain Juppé, President of the UMP, May 17, 2003.

Le Président

Cher Robert

Votre message d'amitié m'a beaucoup touché.

Dans cette période difficile, je tenais à vous remercier de tout cœur pour votre soutien et vos encouragements qui m'aideront à aborder cette échéance avec détermination et sérénité.

Bien fidèlement

Alain Juppé

Union pour un Mouvement Populaire
55, rue La Boétie 75384 Paris Cedex 08 Téléphone : 01 40 76 60 00 Internet : www.u-m-p.org

Très important

Mon cher Dominique,

J'ai plaisir à rédiger ces lignes pour vous entretenir d'un certain nombre de sujets et vous donner mon avis là-dessus.

Avant d'aborder cela, je tenais à vous redire combien j'ai apprécié que vous me fassiez l'amitié de me lire certains passages de votre prochain ouvrage.

Sur l'exquise musique des mots et des phrases flottait voluptueusement le parfum de la nostalgie des temps heureux de l'enfance et de l'adolescence.

La bouleversante évocation de votre Frère, si tôt parti, renferme en elle-même une flambée de bonheur, d'espérance et de vie.

Ce Frère tant aimé, Dominique, vit aujourd'hui à travers vous : la tendre complicité qu'il y a eu et qui demeure entre vous deux par delà l'éternité nourrit ardemment ce feu sacré qui vous dévore et vous embrase en donnant naissance à votre éblouissant talent.

Vous regardant et vous écoutant, ce soir-là, je voyais se télescoper les trois dimensions du temps.

L'ascèse cosmique qui est souvent ma compagne ne faisait ressentir la présence dans votre bureau, pourtant si silencieux, d'autres personnes de ce monde et d'ailleurs: visages familiers et connus et d'autres, inconnus de moi; sans doute, votre Mère, Prêtresse du Foyer, dont je palpais, à travers vos paroles, le profond amour que vous lui portez et dont elle vous enveloppe aussi.

Ami, continuez à cheminer ainsi.

Il y a longtemps que je suis convaincu qu'un peu plus tôt, un peu plus tard, dans le domaine de l'histoire, l'horizon naturel de votre destinée rencontrera, pour fusionner avec lui, l'horizon du destin de notre Pays.

J'en viens maintenant à l'évocation de problèmes purement politiques.

La guerre d'Irak est maintenant achevée. Je vois, çà et là, les esprits chagrins s'agiter.

Voici que des voix s'élèvent pour vous reprocher votre attitude et celle du Président dans ce conflit.

Balivernes et médiocrité! Vous n'avez pas, Dominique, à "rougir" de votre position et de votre discours. L'avenir, tôt ou tard, vous donnera raison.

Pour l'instant, tout semble céder devant la puissance militaire et financière américaine. Ministre d'une puissance secondaire, vous avez pu, vous Dominique, pénétrer les esprits et les coeurs.

Je ne garde des régimes. J'en réfère toujours aux peuples et aux nations.

Il y a, assurément, Dominique, un Peuple arabe, une Nation arabe.

Il vit. Elle vit, ne vous fiez pas aux apparences. Elles sont trompeuses.

Votre détermination et votre courage, dans cette dure période, sont autant de messages et de signaux que les Arabes ont entendus et captés. C'est l'Arabe qui vous parle, Dominique.

C'est le Musulman qui se confie à vous.

Enfin, c'est le chiite qui vous livre son analyse.

Les Américains n'en ont pas fini avec cette branche de l'Islam, si dure et si rigoureuse. Compliquée certes, mais loyale assurément.

457

Ma route, enfin, a "croisé" celle d'Alain JUPPÉ en Afrique noire : Gabon et Sénégal.

Il me plaît, Dominique, de vous dire que j'ai été heureux de le retrouver.

Oh ! je sais combien il m'a combattu !

Mais, rien ne compte devant le choix que je vous ai exprimé le soir des obsèques de Monsieur FOCCART en Mars 1997 en présence du Président.

"Je ne servirai, vous ai-je dit, personne d'autre que Jacques CHIRAC, vous-même et Alain JUPPÉ."

Je vous l'ai aussi écrit. Je n'envisage pas la France d'aujourd'hui et de demain sans la Trinité : CHIRAC - JUPPÉ - VILLEPIN.

Nos Amis BONGO et WADE ont eu pour lui des égards exceptionnels et lui ont réaffirmé leur fidélité absolue à la Trinité.

Alain JUPPÉ a été, à votre endroit, d'une amitié sans faille et d'une loyauté totale.

Nous reparlerons de tout cela, Dominique, quand vous aurez un moment.

Fidèlement à vous.

R.

458

Appendix 76: Word from Virginie Aubin, assistant to Alain Juppé, President of the UMP, on his trip to Gabon and Senegal (June 6, 2003).

[Handwritten letter on UMP letterhead]

Collaboratrice d'Alain Juppé - Voyage Gabon-Sénégal

Cher Robert,

Ce petit mot simplement pour te [remercier] de toute l'aide que tu nous as apporté dans l'organisation de ce voyage.

J'ai vécu des moments inoubliables, riches d'émotions partagées avec des gens dont la gentillesse et la

on pour un Mouvement Populaire
rue La Boétie 75384 Paris Cedex 08 Téléphone : 01 40 76 60 00 Internet : www.u-m-p.org

curiosité n'ont d'égal que la profonde amitié que [leur] pays porte à l'Afrique.

Je sais maintenant que tu fais partie de ces quelques [un]es bonnes étoiles que j'ai pu rencontrer et compte sur toi pour aider notre Président dans [l'avenir].

Amitiés

Virginie

459

Appendix n°77: Letter from Robert Bourgi declining the offer to recruit him from Jean-François Hénin, head of the oil company Maurel & Prom (September 5, 2003).

Robert Bourgi
Avocat a la Cour
Docteur en Droit

14, Avenue Pierre 1er de Serbie
75116 Paris

Tél. 01 67 20 44 08
Fax 01 67 27 37 38
Palais C 1143

Paris le 05 Septembre 2003.

Monsieur le Président,

Je tenais tout d'abord à vous remercier pour le déjeuner auquel vous m'avez convié dans vos bureaux en présence de votre collaborateur Frederic Boulet et de Michel Scarbonchi. Député au Parlement Européen.

Cette réunion fort sympathique et conviviale faisait suite à un entretien que, sur leur demande respective, j'ai accordé à MM. Boulet Scarbonchi à mon Cabinet le Lundi 1 Septembre.

Ce jour là, votre collaborateur avait évoqué la situation de votre Entreprise en République du Congo-Brazzaville et avait sollicité mon concours pour favoriser l'extension des activités de Maurel Prom.

Il m'a dit alors, réservant ma réponse, que nous nous retrouverons autour de vous le Vendredi 05 Septembre 2003.

J'ai pu apprécier ainsi la clarté et la sincérité de vos propos allant jusqu'à me dire que Monsieur Hubert PAN DINO, mon Ami, et Ami précieux du Président Denis Sassou NGUESSO existait dans votre dispositif relationnel et qu'en plus il vous avez été désigné par le Président congolais lui-même.

A la réflexion et cela pesé à l'aune de l'éthique qui régit l'ensemble de mes activités, j'ai le regret de vous informer que je ne vous apporterais pas mon concours en l'état.

Ne doutant pas que vous comprendrez le sens de ma correspondance, je vous prie d'agréer, Monsieur le Président, l'expression de mes sentiments cordiaux.

Robert BOURGI

Monsieur Jean François HENIN
Président Directeur Général de
Maurel Prom
66, rue Monceau
75008 Paris

Appendix 78: Message from Jean-Marc Simon, then French ambassador to Libreville, concerning Renaud Dutreil's visit to Gabon and the Élysée's attempt to cancel his meeting with Omar Bongo (March 22, 2004).

2203.04

JEAN-MARC SIMON

Ambassadeur de France

Je ne comprends pas cet imbroglio crée autour de la visite de Renaud Dutreil.

Tu imagines bien que je ne suis absolument pour rien dans le report du rendez-vous du premier jour chez le Président. Après ce changement de programme, je

Libreville
République Gabonaise

me suis d'ailleurs assuré qu'il y aurait bien un tête-à-tête strict avant la rencontre de la délégation le lendemain. Je fais cela depuis vingt ans !

J'aimerais bien savoir ce qui a pu donner lieu à ces interprétations, fort déplaisantes tu en conviendras.

Au demeurant la visite s'est très bien passée.

Bien à toi.

Jean-Marc Simon

462

Appendix n°79: A word of friendship from Bernard Debré,
Minister for Cooperation.

BERNARD DEBRÉ

Ministre de la Coopération

Merci de ton mot un cher Robert

Amtg

20, rue Monsieur, 75007 Paris. 47 83 11 02

El Hadj Omar Bongo Ondimba

Nicolas SARKOZY = Premier Ministre

D. de VILLEPIN = Ministre d'Etat, Ministre de l'Intérieur

F. FILLON = Ministre de l'Éducation Nationale etc

F. BAYROU = Ministre des Affaires Etrangères

M. ALLIOT-MARIE = Ministre de la Défense Nationale

M. GAYMARD = Ministre des Finances ou Justice

M. DUTREIL = Ministre des Finances ou Justice

J.F. COPÉ = Ministre du BUDGET

M. BARNIER = Ministre du Commerce Extérieur

M. DARCOS = Ministre de l'Agriculture

M S. VINÇON = Ministre de la Coopération

M. MUSELIER = Ministre de la fin à la Sécurité

M. DEVEDJIAN = Ministre de l'Industrie

M. HORTEFEUX = Ministre de la Culture et de la Communication

M. Donnedieu de VABRES = / Ministre Délégué auprès
/ du PM, chargé des
/ Relations avec le Parlement,
/ Porte-Parole du Gouvernement

M. Roselyne BACHELOT = Ministre de l'Environnement
M. Philippe DOUSTE-BLAZE = Ministre de la Santé
M. BORLOO = Maintenu dans ses
fonctions actuelles
M. Gilles de ROBIEN = Maintenu dans ses
fonctions actuelles.

Cher Robb

VINCENT /BOLLORÉ

Président Directeur Général

De passage à mon bureau entre 2 voyages, je
découvre ta lettre ... Désolé de ne pas être plus
présent mais je ne peux rien y faire : cela
dure comme cela depuis des années . Désolé que
tu te sents "blessé" mais si tu me connaissais

01 46 96 43 20

Cour Bolloré
31-32, quai de Dion Bouton
92811 Puteaux Cedex

depuis plusieurs années tu saurais que ça n'est
pas de l'impolitesse ou du désintérêt mais simplement
un emploi du temps terrible !

Amicalt .

Appendix 82: Chevalier de la Légion d'honneur, awarded by Jacques Chirac to Robert Bourgi (April 6, 2007).

Très Urgent

Robert Bourgi
Avocat a la Cour
Docteur en Droit

Paris le 8.04.08

Très chère Pascaline

Je confirme mon arrivée Mercredi 9 Avril 2008
à 21 heures locales par Falcon 50; immatriculation: LX.THS
Je serai accompagné de ma femme et de mon fils Olivier.
Trois journalistes de Canal plus seront aussi dans l'avion.
Ils travaillent avec Laurence FERRARI pour l'émission du
Dimanche à 12h45. "Dimanche Plus" (Emission politique d'une heure.
Ils m'ont interviewé cet après-midi sur la Françafrique et
la chute de Bockel. Tu peux faire confiance à ce que j'ai dit.
Ce sera diffusé dimanche 13 Avril à 12h45 heure de Paris –
Les 3 journalistes qui m'accompagnent dans l'avion et repartent avec moi
    – Anthony ORLIANGE = Journaliste
    – Jean Michel GARCIA = Cameraman
    – Fabien BLANCHET = Ingénieur du son.
Quand j'ai parlé de la mission GUEANT- JOYANDET, ils ont
été estomaqués et du coup, Laurence FERRARI m'a demandé
s'ils pouvaient filmer cet événement qui sera aussi diffusé
Dimanche prochain. Ils n'ont pas de visa – Je compte sur
toi pour qu'ils ne soient pas ennuyés et pour qu'ils puissent
filmer tout l'événement comme la presse locale du début à la
fin. J'espère te retrouver jeudi à 9 heures 30 dans le bureau
de PAPA.

Affectueusement à toi
Robert

Madame Pascaline BONGO ONDIMBA

468

Appendix 84: Agenda for Claude Guéant and Alain Joyandet's trip to Libreville (April 9, 2008).

Urgent

Voyage M. GUÉANT à LIBREVILLE

Départ Jeudi 10/04

décollage à 5 heures du matin (5 heures à Libreville)
Arrivée à Libreville à 12 heures locales
Départ de l'aéroport après accueil officiel vers le Palais
12h30 ——> 13h : tête à tête BONGO - GUÉANT
13h ——> Joyandet rentre seul les rejoindre
13h 15 ——> JOUBERT et les collaborateurs du Président se joignent à eux
13h 30 ——> déjeuner offert par le Président pour la délégation
française
14h45 ——> point de presse M Guéant puis de M. Joyandet.
15h30 ——> décollage pour Paris.

N.B. Pascaline BONGO et moi-même assisterons au tête à tête
BONGO - GUÉANT. M. GUÉANT y est habitué.

Amitiés   Robert BOURGI

URGENT pour Nathalie

01 42 92 80 88

Appendix 85: Ministry of Justice authorization for Robert and Catherine Bourgi to visit Jean-Charles Marchiani in La Santé prison (June 5, 2008).

Liberté • Égalité • Fraternité
RÉPUBLIQUE FRANÇAISE

MINISTÈRE DE LA JUSTICE

Paris, le 5 juin 2008

DIRECTION
DE L'ADMINISTRATION PÉNITENTIAIRE

DIRECTION INTERRÉGIONALE
DES SERVICES PÉNITENTIAIRES DE PARIS

MAISON D'ARRÊT
DE PARIS LA SANTÉ

La Directrice de la maison d'Arrêt de
Paris la santé

A

Maître Catherine BOURGI
Avocat à la Cour
14, avenue Pierre 1er de Serbie
75116 PARIS

A PART / 131

N° _185_ SMB/MLC

Maître,

Comme suite à votre demande d'autorisation de communiquer avec

MARCHIANI Jean-Charles - écrou n° 289 643

en date du 2 juin 2008 et à la réception, ce jour, du courrier de désignation de Monsieur MARCHIANI, j'ai l'honneur de vous faire savoir qu'il vous est possible de vous présenter à l'établissement, ainsi que votre collaborateur Maître Robert BOURGI, afin d'y rencontrer cette personne.

Je vous prie de croire, Maître, à l'expression de mes salutations distinguées.

Sylvie MANAUD-BENAZBRAT

42 rue de la Santé, 75674 Paris Cedex 14 Téléphone 01 45 87 60 60 Télécopie : 01 45 87 60 66

470

CABINET DE M. PHILIPPE COURROYE
PREMIER JUGE D'INSTRUCTION

AVIS DE LIBRE COMMUNICATION AVEC L'AVOCAT
(Article 115 du Code de procédure pénale)

N° du Parquet : ..
N° Instruction : . 2076/03/14 .
2076/03/18 et 2076/02/16
PROCÉDURE CORRECTIONNELLE

283253
A PART 171
4 SEP. 2004

Le Directeur de la MAISON d'ARRET
42 Rue de la Santé
75674 LA SANTE

est informé que la nommée M. MARCHIANI Jean-Charles, mis en examen,

placé sous mandat de dépôt par : M. Philippe COURROYE, juge d'instruction,

a pour conseil :Me Robert BOURGI et Me Catherine BOURGI avocats au barreau de Paris

Fait à Paris, le 03 Septembre 2004
Le Premier Juge d'Instruction

M. Philippe COURROYE

Appendix 86: Signed book by Dominique de Villepin (March 2012).

Among the countless autographed books that journalists, politicians, businessmen, historians and researchers have sent me, Dominique de Villepin's book in 2012 is undoubtedly the one that touched me the most, given our long-standing quarrel.

Appendix 87: Letter to Robert Bourgi from the new Gabonese president, Brice Clotaire Oligui Nguema, who will oust Ali Bongo in August 2023 (October 12, 2023).

Libreville, le 1 2 OCT. 2023

Mon cher Robert,

J'ai reçu, en ce laps de temps, de nombreuses lettres manuscrites de tant d'amis (es), de frères, de compagnons, de parents, mais il est indéniable que la tienne est agréable et d'un profond réconfort.

Souvenir et loyauté sont les maîtres mots que je retiens de cette missive, avec beaucoup d'émotions sur chaque ligne qui me rappellent les épreuves que nous avons traversées depuis le départ de papa, paix à son âme. Sa mémoire et ses mots pour nous, ses attentions et surtout ses remontrances ont guidé notre action, celle du Comité et moi-même : la patrie et l'honneur.

Nous avons du travail Robert, pour relever ce pays, ton pays, car tu l'as très bien exprimé, tu connais le Gabon avec ses sensibilités, son caractère, son peuple, sa chaleur, mais aussi ses défis et ses attentes, qu'il nous impose désormais. La tâche est ardue et nous y mettons du cœur pour éviter d'être Sisyphe. Nous devons à ce pays de le restaurer, de le conduire avec la grâce du Créateur, de le reconstruire pour les générations futures, avec la lucidité et surtout un amour inconditionnel, loyal et fidèle.

La République et la Nation ont besoin de leurs fils, d'ici, de tous les continents, de toutes races, de tous les âges, de toutes les confessions religieuses et de tous les cultes.

Je remercie Monsieur Nicolas Sarkozy pour son soutien. Ses conseils nous seront très certainement utiles. Maintenez resserrés les liens avec nos amis. Nous conviendrons de nos retrouvailles, car comme le dit l'Ecclésiaste : « il y a un temps pour toute chose sous les cieux ».

Nous mettons tout en œuvre, rassure-toi et convaincs les autres de cela, pour préserver la santé, la dignité et la vie de chaque citoyen gabonais, même au péril de notre quiétude personnelle. Je m'y suis personnellement engagé, et je m'y tiendrai, « au commencement était la parole », je donne la mienne !

Tant de souvenirs évoqués, de résolutions prises sur la foi de la conviction, c'est enfin notre essor vers la félicité ! Honneur et fidélité à la patrie.

Merci et à un avenir très proche, mon cher Robert.
De moi, très sincèrement.

Le Général de Brigade
Brice Clotaire OLIGUI NGUEMA

473

Bibliography

BAT, Jean-Pierre, *Le syndrome Foccart. French policy in Africa from 1959 to the present day*, Folio Inédit Histoire, Paris, 2012, 848 p.

BAT, Jean-Pierre, FORCADE, Olivier and MARY, Sylvain (dir.), *Jacques Foccart: archives ouvertes (1958-1974). Politics, Africa and the World*, PUPS, Paris, 2017, 425 p.

BAT, Jean-Pierre, *La fabrique des "barbouzes". History of the Foccart networks in Africa*. Nouveau Monde Éditions, 2015, 509 p.

FOCCART, Jacques, *Foccart parle. Tome 1. Entretiens avec Philippe Gaillard*, Fayard/Jeune Afrique, Paris, 1995, 501 p.

FOCCART, Jacques, *Foccart parle. Tome 2. Entretiens avec Philippe Gaillard*, Fayard/Jeune Afrique, Paris, 1997, 525 p.

FOCCART, Jacques, *Journal de l'Élysée: la fin du Gaullisme, tome V, 1973-1974*, Fayard/Jeune Afrique, Paris, 2001, 654 p.

GBAGBO, Laurent with MATTEI, François, *Libre. Pour la vérité et la justice*, Max Milo, 2021, 297 p.

GLASER, Antoine and SMITH, Stephen, *Sarko en Afrique*, Plon, Paris, 2008, 213 p.

HAREL, Xavier and HOFNUNG, Thomas, *Le scandale des biens mal acquis. Enquête sur les milliards volés de la Françafrique*, Fayard, Paris, 2011, 336 p.

LEJEAL, Frédéric, *Le déclin franco-africain, l'impossible rupture avec le pacte colonial*, L'Harmattan, Paris, 2023, 453 p.

MESSMER, Pierre, *Les Blancs s'en vont. Récits de décolonisation*, Albin Michel, Paris, 1998, 302 p.

OLLIVIER, Jean-Yves. *Ni vu ni connu. Ma vie de négociant en politique, de Chirac et Foccart à Mandela*, Fayard, 2014, 326 p.

PÉAN, Pierre, *Affaires africaines*, Fayard, Paris, 1983, 350 p.

PÉAN, Pierre, *La menace*, Fayard, Paris, 1987, 306 p.

PÉAN, Pierre, *La République des mallettes*, Fayard, Paris, 2011, 481 p.

PÉAN, Pierre, *L'homme de l'ombre*, Fayard, Paris, 1990, 585 p.

PÉAN, Pierre, *Mémoires impubliables*, Albin Michel, Paris, 2020, 667 p.

PENNE, Guy, *Mémoires d'Afrique (1981-1998). Interviews with Claude Wauthier*, Fayard, Paris, 1999, 392 p.

PESNOT, Patrick, *Monsieur X. Les dessous de la Françafrique*, Nouveau Monde poche, Paris, 2010, 511 p.

REVEL, Renaud, *Les visiteurs du soir : ce qu'ils disent à l'oreille du président*, Plon, Paris, 2020, 350 p.

ROBERT, Maurice, *"Minister" of Africa. Interviews with André Renault*, Le Seuil, Paris, 2004.

SMITH, Stephen and GLASER, Antoine, *Comment la France a perdu l'Afrique*, Calmann-Lévy, Paris, 2005, 278 p.

SMITH, Stephen and GLASER, Antoine, *Ces Messieurs Afrique. Le Paris-Village du continent noir*, Calmann-Lévy, Paris, 1994, 235 p.

SMITH, Stephen and GLASER, Antoine, *Ces Messieurs Afrique 2. Des réseaux aux lobbies*, Calmann-Lévy, Paris, 1997, 285 p.

VERSCHAVE, François-Xavier, *La Françafrique, le plus long scandale de la République*, Stock, Paris, 1998, 379 p.

VERSCHAVE, François-Xavier, *Noir silence. Qui arrêtera la Françafrique*, Les Arènes, Paris, 2000, 597 p.

WAUTHIER, Claude, *Quatre présidents et l'Afrique : De Gaulle, Pompidou, Giscard d'Estaing, Mitterrand*, Le Seuil, Paris, 1995, 718 p.

Table of Contents

Milton Keynes UK
Ingram Content Group UK Ltd.
UKHW032041191024
449815UK00008B/49